Mark R Townsend

PRACTICAL AVIATION LAW

PRACTICAL

AVIATION

LAW

Fourth Edition

J. SCOTT HAMILTON

J. Scott Hamilton is a member of the faculty of Embry-Riddle Aeronautical University. He previously served as general counsel for the Civil Air Patrol, then as the national organization's chief operating officer. Prior to that, he served as senior assistant attorney general for the State of Wyoming. While practicing aviation law in Colorado, he also served as a member of the faculty of the University of Denver College of Law and Metropolitan State College of Denver. He earned a BA degree in economics and business from Hendrix College, JD from the University of Denver, and LLM in aerospace law from Southern Methodist University. He is also an experienced pilot and skydiver who served as a HALO instructor in the Green Berets. Hamilton has published widely on aviation law.

© 2005 Blackwell Publishing
All rights reserved

Blackwell Publishing Professional
2121 State Avenue, Ames, Iowa 50014, USA

Orders: 1-800-862-6657
Office: 1-515-292-0140
Fax: 1-515-292-3348
Web site: www.blackwellprofessional.com

Blackwell Publishing Ltd
9600 Garsington Road,
Oxford OX4 2DQ, UK
Tel.: +44 (0)1865 776868

Blackwell Publishing Asia
550 Swanston Street,
Carlton, Victoria 3053, Australia
Tel.: +61 (0)3 8359 1011

Authorization to photocopy items for internal or personal use, or the internal or personal use of specific clients, is granted by Blackwell Publishing, provided that the base fee of $.10 per copy is paid directly to the Copyright Clearance Center, 222 Rosewood Drive, Danvers, MA 01923. For those organizations that have been granted a photocopy license by CCC, a separate system of payments has been arranged. The fee code for users of the Transactional Reporting Service is 0-8138-0641-0/2005 $.10.

Printed on acid-free paper in the United States of America

First edition, 1991
Second edition, 1996
Third edition, 2001
Fourth edition, 2005

Library of Congress Cataloging-in-Publication Data

Hamilton, J. Scott.
   Practical aviation law / J. Scott Hamilton.—4th ed.
     p. cm.
   Includes bibliographical references and index.
   ISBN 0-8138-0641-0 (alk. paper)
   1. Aeronautics—Law and legislation—United States. I. Title.

KF2400.H36 2005
343.7309′7—dc22

2004019630

The last digit is the print number: 9 8 7 6 5 4 3 2 1

CONTENTS

Preface   vii

PART I   ADMINISTRATIVE LAW

     1   Regulatory Agencies and International Organizations   3

     2   FAA Enforcement   31

     3   Aviation Medical Cases   67

PART II   AIRCRAFT ACCIDENTS

     4   Basic Principles of Liability   83

     5   Organizing the Business to Limit Liability   103

     6   Aviation Insurance   117

     7   Exculpatory Contracts   141

     8   Airline Liability   147

     9   Government Liability   169

     10   Accident Notification, Reporting, and Investigation   179

PART III   AIRCRAFT TRANSACTIONS

     11   Buying and Selling Aircraft   193

     12   Aircraft Leasing and Co-Ownership   211

PART IV   AIRPORTS, AIRSPACE, AND AVIATION SECURITY

13   Airports and Terminal Airspace   227

14   En Route Airspace   257

15   Crimes and Aviation Security   269

PART V   LABOR AND EMPLOYMENT LAW

16   Labor and Employment Law, Generally   295

17   Airline Labor Law   309

Key Aviation Organizations   319

Bibliography   323

Index   329

PREFACE

*P**RACTICAL AVIATION LAW* is designed to be used in conjunction with the *Practical Aviation Law Workbook* as a university text for aviation law courses and, standing alone, as a reference guide for aviation business managers, pilots, mechanics, aircraft owners, and others involved in aviation by vocation or avocation.

Except for certain treaties having worldwide or at least international effect, the scope of the book is limited to the law of the United States and may have little relevance to the domestic laws of other nations. Neither does it attempt to explore the entire seamless web of the law—only those areas particularly applicable to aviation. I recommend that students considering a career in aviation business management also take a business law course. While there is some slight overlap between the courses, principally in the area of buying and selling aircraft, the business law course gives broader coverage of legal principles that are applicable to all businesses.

As the title suggests, this book takes a practical viewpoint. It aims to provide the reader with basic legal knowledge and perspectives along with an understanding of how the legal system works in relation to aviation activities. It aims to provide that in a form that can be applied to help you recognize and avoid common aviation legal pitfalls, and to recognize when the moment has come to stop what you are doing and call your lawyer. If this book had a subtitle, it would be *How to Avoid Aviation Lawyers and When to Break Down and Call One*.

No book can hope to advise you what to do in every conceivable situation. In advising our clients, lawyers must take into consideration not only the law but also the facts and circumstances. In over thirty years of practicing law, in private practice, as government and later corporate counsel, I represented clients in well over three thousand aviation matters, and never saw two identical cases. While similar cases give rise to similar considerations, slight differences in the facts and circumstances often lead to major differences in the best approach to solving the problem. Examples in this book and its accompanying workbook are drawn largely from cases I encountered in my practice.

The law itself is also in a constant state of change. Even as I write, the Congress of the United States, fifty state legislatures, and a vast number of administrative agencies are daily making changes to statutes and regulations, while hundreds of federal and state courts are writing and publishing decisions on the constitutionality of those laws and regulations and decisions that modify, clarify, or sometimes confuse the common law. Indeed, such changes as have occurred since the third edition of this book was published (many of those changes made in response to the unprecedented terrorist attacks on and in the United States on September 11, 2001) are the main reason for this expanded fourth edition.

While this process of continual change keeps the lawyer's work from becoming routine to the point of boredom, it also means that what was good advice yesterday (or the day this book went to press) may no longer be good advice today. While the fundamental legal principles discussed in this book are less susceptible to sudden obsolescence than, say, a text on the Internal Revenue Code and IRS Regulations, *you are cautioned not to attempt to solve actual individual legal problems on the basis of information contained in this book.* That is one of those times when you should break down and call your lawyer.

I would like to thank the following people for their encouragement, advice, and support, without which I would not have undertaken and persevered with the writing and updating of this text and the related workbook and teacher's manual. These acknowledgments should not be construed to imply an endorsement of this teaching system by any of the persons or organizations mentioned.

Dr. Stacy Weislogel, chair, Dept. of Aviation, Ohio State University.

Professor Gary Kitely of Auburn University, who recently retired as executive director of the University Aviation Association, an organization that provides a wonderful forum and source of information to those of us who teach aviation-related courses in the nation's colleges and universities. He was a source of encouragement not only in the drafting of the manuscript, but also in the expanded international law coverage of the subsequent editions.

Dr. Rex A. Hammarback, director, University of North Dakota Aerospace Foundation, formerly a professor in UND's renowned aviation program.

Hon. John E. Faulk, NTSB administrative law judge (retired), a practicing attorney with the Trachtmann law firm in Melbourne, Florida, and an adjunct professor in the School of Aeronautics at the Florida Institute of Technology. Many of his recommendations based on his classroom experience using this teaching system have been incorporated as improvements to each successive edition.

Professor Terri Haynes, Chadron State College, Chadron, Nebraska. She deserves particular credit for encouraging me to avoid "legalese" jargon and write plainly to make the book as clear and understandable as possible to students and readers having no previous training in the law.

Jonathan Stern, Esq., partner in the Washington, D.C., office of the world-renowned Schnader, Harrrison, Segal & Lewis law firm and editor of the American Bar Association's *Aviation Litigation Quarterly.* Jon was especially helpful in providing materials, insights, and updates on the continuing evolution of international law governing airline liability.

Bill Behan, president, AirSure Ltd., Golden, Colorado. He provided information and advice on developments in aviation insurance, particularly the effects of the General Aviation Revitalization Act and the terrorist attacks of 9/11/01 on that industry.

John and Kathleen Yodice, a father and daughter team in the Yodice & Associates law firm in Bethesda, Maryland, who do yeoman service for general aviation as counsel for the Aircraft Owners & Pilots Association and others and have proved a reliable source of insights into recent developments in FAA enforcement, aviation medical cases, and (especially in the wake of 9/11) airport and airspace access issues.

The Lawyer-Pilots Bar Association, Southern Methodist University's *Journal of Air Law and Commerce*, and the University of Denver's *Transportation Law Journal*, each of which consistently provides wonderful forums and opportunities for attorneys and others interested in aviation law to share knowledge and ideas in print and in person in an atmosphere of professional collegiality. They have contributed greatly to the advancement of our profession and the quality of our services to our clients, and continue to do so.

My students past and present at Embry-Riddle Aeronautical University, in the Aerospace Science Department at Metropolitan State College of Denver, and at the University of Denver College of Law, who continue to relentlessly question, challenge, and demand clear explanations and sound reasoning, rightly refusing to settle for less.

The editors at Blackwell Publishing, formerly Iowa State University Press, who recognized the need for this teaching system and for periodic updates, turning this vision into the solid reality you are now holding in your hand.

My family, who encouraged me in this project and more-or-less cheerfully tolerated the many hours I spent sequestered writing and updating this work (often after a full day of practicing law and then teaching a class), and especially my wife, Charlotte, who did most of the typing of the original and each subsequent manuscript.

The credit is theirs; the errors are mine. Unless otherwise noted, all opinions expressed herein are entirely my own, and do not necessarily reflect the views of my employers, past or present.

All photos and illustrations are by the author, unless otherwise credited.

PART I

Administrative Law

CHAPTER 1

Regulatory Agencies and International Organizations

SINCE THE 1920s, Congress has created a plethora of regulatory agencies to administer the many federal programs it has initiated. Indeed, federal regulatory agencies continue to multiply, under Republican and Democrat administrations alike. If you are embarking upon a career in the aviation industry, whether in the private sector or as a government employee, you will deal with administrative agency regulations far more frequently than any other area of the law. Indeed, you will probably be confronted with making decisions based upon the Federal Aviation Regulations (FARs) on a daily basis. These regulations also establish standards of legal behavior by which a judge or jury may later decide whether you or your business are liable for negligence in the event of an aircraft accident. Hardly any aspect of the aviation industry today is unaffected by these regulations. That is why we begin this study with an examination of administrative law, with particular attention to the role of the Federal Aviation Administration (FAA) in administering the federal program of air safety regulation.

We will start with an overview of the administrative agencies most directly involved in aviation, distinguishing them from each other according to the specific role played by each in regulating the aviation industry.

The ease with which civil aircraft cross national borders, air transportation's key role in the global economy, and the recent horrifically effective use of civil airliners as weapons of terror have made the regulation and development of civil aviation a continuing subject of not only national but also international concern.

This chapter also introduces the International Civil Aviation Organization (ICAO) and the International Air Transport Association (IATA), organizations that, although not technically regulatory agencies, play an important role in harmonizing technical standards for civil aviation worldwide.

FEDERAL ADMINISTRATIVE AGENCIES

The terrorist attacks of September 11, 2001, shook the United States to its core. Few industries—indeed, few aspects of American life—were untouched, though some were more deeply affected than others. Civil aviation, having been so infamously and effectively abused in these attacks as a weapon of terror, has borne the brunt of the changes.

One result of the attacks was the most sweeping reorganization of the federal government in over a half-century.

Transportation Security Administration (TSA) (*www.tsa.gov*)
Barely two months after the attacks and for the express purpose of improving security in all modes of transportation, including civil aviation, Congress enacted the *Aviation and Transportation Security Act of 2001*, creating the Transportation Security Administration (TSA). The TSA was originally established as an operating agency of the Department of Transportation (DOT), but was later moved into the Department of Homeland Security when that agency was created.

Previously, operators of airports served by commercial airlines had been responsible for airport security, relying primarily on contractors, with some FAA oversight. The new law brought the responsibility for day-to-day screening of airline passengers, baggage, and cargo into the federal arena, under the new TSA, which immediately set about hiring and training security personnel. Most of the new federal screeners were the same individuals previously employed by those contractors that had been performing the function prior to its federalization. With a change of uniform and some additional training, they returned to the same work.

The TSA also took over from the FAA the responsibility for inspecting and testing security measures at airports, with the added responsibility for the same at other transportation facilities, including foreign aircraft repair stations. Congress also empowered the TSA to receive, assess, and distribute intelligence information related to transportation security. The new agency was directed to develop plans, policies, and strategies for dealing with threats to transportation security and to coordinate countermeasures with other federal agencies. Congress also ordered that the federal Air Marshal program be beefed up and that steps be taken to increase the availability and use of explosive detection systems at air carrier airports.

Transportation Security Oversight Board (TSOB)

Congress' initial investigation into the terrorist attacks revealed that various federal law enforcement agencies had clues that, if assembled together and investigated coherently, might have revealed the plot and enabled prevention, but that these agencies had tended to hoard, rather than share, potentially crucial intelligence information. In an effort to address that shortcoming, the Act also created the Transportation Security Oversight Board (TSOB), an extremely high-level panel composed of the Secretaries of Homeland Security, Transportation, Defense, and Treasury; the Attorney General, the CIA Director (or designees of any of the foregoing), along with a Presidential appointee representing the National Security Council (NSC). The TSOB was made responsible for assuring the coordination and sharing of intelligence relating to threats against transportation.

Department of Homeland Security (DHS) (*www.dhs.gov*)

Next, Congress and President George W. Bush created the new Department of Homeland Security (DHS). Paralleling President Truman's epic 1947 merger of all branches of the U.S. armed forces into a new Department of Defense (DoD) to better coordinate the nation's defense against military threats, 24 federal agencies were brought under the new DHS to protect the nation against further terrorist attacks. These include (*italics* indicate the agency's former home in the federal bureaucracy)

Secret Service
Coast Guard (*Transportation*)
U.S. Customs Service (*Treasury*)
Immigration & Naturalization Service (INS) (part, from *Justice*)
Transportation Security Administration (TSA) (*Transportation*)
Federal Protective Service (*GSA*)
Federal Law Enforcement Training Center (*Treasury*)
Animal & Plant Health Inspection Service (part, from *Agriculture*)
Office for Domestic Preparedness (*Justice*)
Federal Emergency Management Agency (FEMA)
Strategic National Stockpile & National Disaster Medical System (*HHS*)
Nuclear Incident Response Team (*Energy*)
Domestic Emergency Response Teams (*Justice*)
National Domestic Preparedness Office (*FBI*)
CBN Countermeasures Program (*Energy*)
Environmental Measures Laboratory (*Energy*)

National Biological Warfare Defense Analysis Center (*Defense*)
Plum Island Animal Disease Center (*Agriculture*)
Critical Infrastructure Assurance Office (*Commerce*)
Federal Computer Incident Response Center (*GSA*)
National Communications System (*Defense*)
National Infrastructure Protection Center (*FBI*)
Energy Security and Assurance Program (*Energy*)

The Aviation and Transportation Security Act originally assigned responsibility for screening all aliens applying for training at U.S. flight schools for security risks to the Attorney General. Due to comparatively low fuel costs, prevalent VFR weather, and abundant suitable airspace, the U.S., and particularly Florida and the desert southwest, were popular destinations for foreigners wishing to learn to fly. This requirement hit U.S. flight schools—many of which were heavily reliant on foreign students—hard and hundreds closed their doors. This duty was later reassigned to the new DHS and limited to students desiring to learn to fly aircraft with a maximum certificated gross takeoff weight of more than 12,500 pounds. As required by Congress, DHS now gives quick service on these foreign students, acting on them within five days.

It is to be fervently hoped that the new DHS will have greater and more rapid success than the DoD in coordinating the activities and minimizing the long-running rivalries between its charges. DHS' first Secretary, former Pennsylvania governor Tom Ridge, certainly has his work cut out for him in this regard.

Aviation Security is discussed in greater detail in Chapter 15.

Department of Transportation (DOT) (*www.dot.gov*)

The U.S. Department of Transportation houses a variety of federal agencies dealing with policy and regulation of various means of transportation of people and goods. DOT agencies having jurisdiction over various aspects of transportation include the Federal Aviation Administration, Federal Highway Administration, National Highway Traffic Safety Administration, Urban Mass Transportation Association, Maritime Administration, and St. Lawrence Seaway Development Corporation. In the aviation arena, DOT's head, Secretary of Transportation Norman Mineta, speaking to the Aero Club of Washington, recently expressed concern that global progress in aviation and the aerospace industry challenge America's long-held dominance. To counter that competitive threat, he announced a government initiative to design the Next Generation Air Transportation System, "a cleaner, quieter system based on 21st Century technology that will offer seamless security and added capacity to relieve congestion and secure America's place as global leader in aviation's second century." One announced goal of the initiative is to triple the capacity of our aviation system over the next 15 to 20 years.

Federal Aviation Administration (FAA) *(www.faa.gov)*

Congress made the FAA the agency primarily responsible for the regulation of aviation safety in the United States, and the agency's influence on the entire aviation industry is pervasive.

The FAA Administrator is the head of this agency.

For many years the FAA and its predecessor, the Civil Aeronautics Authority (CAA), enjoyed independent agency status within the federal bureaucracy, an arrangement that gave the agency's head direct access to the president. Now, however, since the FAA is but one of several divisions of the Department of Transportation (DOT), the secretary of transportation is the sole voice for all of these agencies in the president's cabinet. Some aviation interests feel that the development of sound aviation policy has suffered as a result of this organizational structure. A parade of proposals to liberate the FAA from the DOT has come before Congress from time to time, but none has passed yet, and as the years go by it appears more and more unlikely that any will. That is probably just as well, since another change has provided a measure of continuity. For many years, the position of FAA Administrator was one of the plums of political patronage. The Administrator served at the pleasure of the president and turnover in the job was frequent (averaging about every two years—hardly sufficient time to accomplish anything in so ponderous a bureaucracy). Now, however, FAA Administrator Marion Blakey and those who will follow her in the job are assured a five-year term in office.

The FAA's activities cover a wide range, and include:

REGULATION

The FAA regulates aviation safety and, to a certain extent, aircraft noise. The primary laws promulgated by the FAA are the Federal Aviation Regulations (FARs), which appear in Title 14 of the Code of Federal Regulations. This pervasive body of regulations addresses every conceivable aspect of aviation safety. Additionally, through those regulations prescribing airworthiness standards for the certification of new aircraft designs, the FAA has established aircraft noise limits. These latter regulations, developed in consultation with the Environmental Protection Agency (EPA), deserve credit as the primary incentive for the development of the quieter high-bypass-ratio fanjet engines that came into use on the second generation of airline transport jets—the Boeing 747 and McDonnell Douglas DC-10. By comparison, the engines used on the first generation of airline transport jets, such as the Boeing 707, McDonnell Douglas DC-8, and Convair 880 were positively thunderous. Indeed, as will be seen in Chapter 13, the first generation of airline jets (whose noise was not regulated by the FAA) appear largely responsible for creating the widespread enmity that persists today between airports and their noise-sensitive neighbors. Although these noisy jets are now banned from flying in the United States unless retrofitted with the quieter new technology engines or "hush kits," the legacy of public hostility to airports created by their noise decades ago remains an effective obstacle to the development of new airports and the expansion of existing airports in this country. At this writing, the FAA is engaged in setting maximum noise limits for certification of new single-engine propeller-driven small airplanes, based on criteria developed by the ICAO. The effect of this new certification standard on U.S. manufacturers is expected to be insignificant, since most have already quieted their aircraft to meet stringent European standards.

Under the Commercial Space Launch Amendments Act of 2004, the FAA's Office of Commercial Space Transportation now has sole regulatory authority over suborbital spacecraft.

In addition to the FARs, the FAA from time to time issues other mandatory orders having the force and effect of law on the subject of aviation safety. The primary examples are Airworthiness Directives (ADs), which are FAA orders requiring some inspection or modification of previously certified aircraft. These are generally issued when operating experience reveals the need to change some element of design of a particular type of aircraft or component to improve its operating safety. Such an improvement may be suggested by an accident or series of accidents, or by reports of difficulties experienced or observed by aircraft operators, inspectors, and mechanics in the field.

CERTIFICATION

It is virtually impossible for an individual or a business to participate legally in any aspect of civil aviation in the United States without first obtaining one or more certificates from the FAA. The FAA certifies not only flight crew members, including pilots, flight engineers, and navigators, but also ground support personnel including air traffic controllers, aircraft dispatchers, aviation maintenance technicians and repair specialists, repair stations, inspectors, and parachute riggers. It also certifies domestic, flag, and supplemental air carriers, other commercial and noncommercial operators of large aircraft, air travel clubs, helicopter air carriers, foreign air carriers operating within the United States, air-taxi and commercial operators of small aircraft, operators of helicopters hoisting loads externally, agricultural aircraft operators, airports serving certificated air carriers, pilot training schools, aircraft repair stations, aviation maintenance schools, and ground and flight instructors. In addition to obtaining an operating certificate, each flight crewmember and air traffic controller must also obtain an aviation medical certificate from the FAA.

Additionally, each civil aircraft of U.S. manufacture is the product of three separate FAA inspection and certification processes. The aircraft manufacturer who intends to introduce a new design into the marketplace must first produce prototype aircraft that are subject to an intense program of both flight and static testing to prove the design's conformity to certification standards contained in the FARs. Once this test program is completed to the satisfaction of the FAA, an FAA *Type Certificate is* issued on the design. Next, the manufacturer's production facilities and quality assurance program are submitted to FAA scrutiny. The agency must be convinced that the manufacturer's production and inspection methods are adequate to ensure that each and every airplane produced will be a precise replica of the design for which the type certificate was issued. Once this is accomplished, the FAA issues a *Production Type Certificate* and manufacturing can begin. Then each airplane produced is inspected and tested for conformity with the original design and receives an FAA *Airworthiness Certificate* before being delivered to the customer. Subsequent modifications and improvements to the design require additional FAA certification, through amendments to the Type Certificate, by issuance of a *Supplemental Type Certificate,* or by a one-time field approval for modification of an individual aircraft under an FAA Form 337.

REGISTRATION

The FAA also operates a single centralized registry for all civil aircraft in the United States. At the FAA's Aircraft Registry in the FAA Aeronautical Center in Oklahoma City, the agency maintains files on every aircraft that has ever been issued an "N-number" signifying U.S. registry (Fig. 1.1). These files include the entire history of the aircraft's ownership and other legal interests in the aircraft, such as liens and encumbrances. The utility and importance of this registry is discussed in greater detail in Chapter 11.

SECURITY

The Aviation and Transportation Security Act transferred the FAA's air carrier airport security function to the TSA. But in that Act, Congress

Fig. 1.1. If it has an "N-number," a quick check of the FAA Aircraft Registry can reveal who owns it and who has recorded liens against it.

ordered the FAA to improve flight deck security by requiring airlines to strengthen flight deck doors and keep them locked except as necessary to permit authorized persons to enter or exit, and to develop guidance for training flight deck and cabin crews to deal with threats. Congress also ordered the FAA to explore the use of video monitors in the cabin, along with methods to prevent disabling of the aircraft's transponder in flight (as the 9/11 hijackers had done, to make tracking of the aircraft more difficult) and improved methods for cabin crews to alert the flight deck of security breaches and other emergencies.

CARTOGRAPHY

In a recent development, responsibility for production of government aeronautical charts was transferred from the Department of Commerce's National Ocean Service (NOS) to the FAA. Over 300 NOS employees were transferred to a new FAA office designated as the National Aeronautical Charting Office (NACO).

EDUCATION

The FAA educates members of the aviation community on new developments and matters pertaining to aviation safety through a system of publications, such as the Advisory Circulars (AC), and through safety seminars and recertification programs for flight instructors, pilot examiners, mechanics holding Inspection Authorization, and others. (The agency also trains its own employees at the FAA Academy in the Aeronautical Center in Oklahoma City and numerous programs at its various facilities.)

FUNDING

Under the Airport Improvement Program (AIP), the FAA distributes federal matching funds for the construction of new airports, the improvement of existing airports, and related airport planning. These funds are appropriated by Congress from the Aviation Trust Fund comprising the proceeds of aviation fuel taxes paid by general aviation and passenger ticket taxes paid by persons traveling on U.S. commercial airlines. This funding program, which currently administers a $14 billion trust fund, expended at a rate of over $3 billion per year under a five-year authorization established by the Aviation Investment and Reform Act for the 21st Century ("AIR 21"), is discussed in greater detail in Chapter 13.

INVESTIGATION

The FAA investigates virtually all civil aircraft accidents in the United States, as well as some accidents occurring outside the country involving U.S. built civil aircraft, in connection with the agency's air safety regulation and enforcement function. As more fully discussed in Chapter 10, the FAA also often performs the on-site investigation of general aviation aircraft accidents under delegated authority on behalf of the National Transportation Safety Board (NTSB). The NTSB, however, has exclusive authority to make the federal government's official finding of the "probable cause" of all civil aircraft accidents, regardless of whether the factual investigation was conducted by NTSB or FAA personnel.

The FAA also investigates incidents in which aviation safety may have been jeopardized but no accident occurred, as when two aircraft pass within such close proximity as to create a collision hazard. The FAA also investigates all reports of violations of the Federal Aviation Regulations. The process of investigation and enforcement of the FARs is described in detail in Chapter 2.

OPERATIONS

The FAA operates a great variety of aviation facilities and equipment, including:

The Air Traffic Control (ATC) System. This system includes airport control towers, en route Air Route Traffic Control Centers (ARTCC or Centers), and Flight Service Stations (FSS), with their vast network of communication and radar systems. Although there are now some control towers operated by private enterprise and local governments at airports that do not meet activity-level criteria to qualify for a federally operated control tower, most control towers and all Centers and Flight Service Stations are FAA owned and operated (Fig. 1.2).

At this writing, there are proposals under discussion in Congress to take air traffic control out of the FAA and transfer the function to a government corporation organized along the lines of the U.S. Postal Service and Amtrak. Proponents of this move argue that cumbersome federal procurement law (applicable to the FAA, but not to a government corpora-

Fig. 1.2. Most ATC facilities, like this control tower at Cheyenne, Wyoming, are operated by the FAA, although some towers are operated by private corporations under contract to local governments. More widespread privatization of the ATC function is possible, as lawmakers search for ways to reduce federal spending.

tion) has hamstrung the FAA's effort to update ATC computer equipment and that without state-of-the-art equipment, flight delays, which are quite costly to the airlines, will continue to be experienced. Opponents of such reorganization note that most flight delays (72%) are caused by weather, with airport and terminal airspace congestion the second largest cause (at 21%), leaving no more than 7% of the delays susceptible to avoidance through updated ATC computers. Opponents also argue that the experience with other government corporations has been less than satisfactory, with the Postal Service and Amtrak providing steadily deteriorating service at increasing cost to the consumer.

Under present proposals, such a government corporation's board of directors would be composed primarily of airline representatives. General aviation interests fear that their airspace and airport access needs would be sacrificed to airline demands under such a structure. There are also widespread concerns that such a reorganization would be the first step toward imposition of user fees for all services provided by such a corporation (weather briefings, flight plan filings, clearances, and other communications), resulting in increased costs to civil aviation and decreased safety as cost-conscious individuals and companies may decide to forego the use of these services, rather than pay the additional fees.

The FAA's recent success in circumventing the convoluted federal procurement law process by using leasing, instead of purchasing, to open its new Air Traffic Control System Command Center (formerly Central Flow Control) facility in Herndon, Virginia, suggests an existing and very workable alternative to transferring the ATC function to a government corporation. Indeed, it appears that the only benefit from such a reorganization would be to get the sizable cost of operating the ATC system off the federal budget, so as to give the illusion of budget reduction without accomplishing any real savings.

The functions performed by the Flight Service Stations are a particular target under consideration for privatization as lawmakers look for ways to trim government services and reduce the federal budget. The suggestion, while controversial, is less so than privatization of the entire ATC function. If successfully accomplished, it may, however, be the first step toward that larger goal.

Real savings are more likely to result from shifting more of the decision-making to the cockpit, reducing the role of voice communications and permitting more direct routing through promising new technologies that integrate the capabilities of GPS navigation equipment with digital VHF data links and the mode-S transponder. This trend toward what is being called "free flight" may eventually permit a substantial reduction in

ATC staff, equipment, and facilities. At this writing, demonstrations of prototype technology are imminent.

Radio Aids to Navigation. The FAA also operates a vast network of radio aids to navigation, including radio beacons guiding aircraft over long distances (such as VORs and VORTACs) and others that lead the aircraft precisely to the runway threshold in all weather, such as instrument landing systems (ILS) and microwave landing systems (MLS). Other radio aids to air navigation in the United States are operated by the Coast Guard (Loran C), the Department of Defense (Global Positioning System (GPS) navigation satellites). Local governments also operate some radio aids to air navigation (many NDBs are owned and operated by local airport authorities). Even private enterprise gets into the act (several airlines own and operate their own approach aids, such as an ILS or MLS for their exclusive use at some remote airports). Now that the Department of Defense has made the full accuracy and reliability of the system available to all users, the superiority of GPS for air navigation is almost universally acknowledged. The FAA has already announced that it will not install any new MLS equipment. It is reasonably to be anticipated that the VOR network, which is quite expensive to inspect and maintain (due to the antiquated technology and remote location of much of this equipment) will be taken out of operation after FAA-operated Wide Area Augmentation Systems (WAAS) to improve GPS accuracy and reliability come on line. The long-range future of Loran C has also been called into question by the success and continued improvement of GPS.

National Airports. The FAA was for many years the operator of the two major Washington, D.C., air carrier airports (Reagan—formerly known as Washington National—and Dulles) designated as the "National Airports." These airports have since been turned over to the Washington Metropolitan Airport Authority for operation (Fig. 1.3).

Aeronautical Center. The FAA Aeronautical Center in Oklahoma City is a major record-keeping and training facility. There, you will find the FAA Aircraft Registry (discussed more fully in Chapter 11), which maintains the records of ownership and other legal interests in every civil aircraft ever registered in the United States (refer to Fig. 1.1); the Airman Records Branch, which keeps a dossier on every person ever issued an FAA certificate; the FAA Academy, which trains air traffic controllers, air safety inspectors, and other FAA personnel; and the Civil Aviation Medical Institute, which reviews and develops medical certification stan-

1 : Regulatory Agencies and International Organizations   15

Fig. 1.3. Formerly operated by the FAA, Washington, DC-area "National Airports" Reagan and Dulles are now operated by the Washington Metropolitan Airport Authority.

dards and drug and alcohol testing policy for persons in the aviation industry.

Technical Center.   The FAA Technical Center, located in Atlantic City, New Jersey (formerly known as the National Aviation Facility Experimental Center or NAFEC), is the site of FAA research and development (R&D) activities on radio aids to air navigation. The ILS, MLS, and new GPS/WAAS all-weather approach systems were developed and standardized largely at this facility, along with airborne collision avoidance systems such as the TCAS. Although Congress has recently demonstrated some confusion on the point, FAA research and development activities are limited to technology that interfaces with the ATC system. The FAA does no basic research on aircraft and flight system technologies, these being within the purview of NASA research. Where FAA and NASA R&D responsibilities abut or overlap, the two agencies work closely together to coordinate their efforts to avoid duplication, conflict, and waste. In the federal government, there is a new emphasis on interagency cooperation. The FAA, for example, works with other agencies to research and develop technology intended to improve flight safety. One recent example is Safer Skies, a broad initiative developed by the FAA with a broad range of government and aviation industry organizations to improve the safety record of commercial and general aviation. The initiative is developing recommendations on changes in training, technology, and procedures with the goal of reducing general aviation accidents by 20% in 2007. Weather-related accidents and accidents caused by controlled flight into terrain are the first targets for reduction. As a result of the ongoing work of Safer Skies, FAA, NTSB, NASA, and industry associations have also formed the General Aviation Data Improvement Team (GADIT) to gather better data on general aviation accidents. This program was initiated to address long-standing complaints about a lack of sufficiently meaningful data on the causes of general aviation accidents, especially those involving human error. Another example is the Advanced General Aviation Transport Experiments (AGATE), a consortium of industry, higher education, and government entities (organized by NASA and including the FAA) that focuses on developing technologies for general aviation. AGATE is intended to help revitalize the general aviation industry by advancing the use of new technology in aircraft and developing new training methods for pilots. A related NASA program, the Small Aircraft Transportation System, is discussed later in this chapter, in the section describing that agency.

National Transportation Safety Board (NTSB) *(www.ntsb.gov)*

The National Transportation Safety Board is an independent federal agency whose primary responsibility is to investigate transportation accidents, determine the "probable cause" of the accident, and recommend to the appropriate regulatory agencies (in the case of aviation, the FAA) measures that might prevent similar accidents in the future. Like the Department of Transportation, the NTSB's duties cover a broad range of transportation modes, including aviation, highway, rail, pipeline, and marine accidents.

The NTSB is one of the smallest federal agencies, having only about 300 employees, only a fraction of whom are trained aircraft accident investigators. Therefore, the board must frequently delegate its on-site aircraft accident investigation duties to the FAA. This is done particularly in nonfatal general aviation accidents, to allow NTSB field investigators to concentrate on airline and other high-profile civil aviation accidents.

Regardless of which agency's employees conduct the on-site investigation, it is always the NTSB that must analyze the information and make the official finding of the probable cause of the accident. This process is discussed in greater detail in Chapter 10.

Congress also recently assigned the NTSB the additional responsibility for coordinating and integrating the resources of the federal government and other organizations (such as the American Red Cross) to support the efforts of state and local governments and the airline to meet the needs of airline disaster victims and their families.

A recent study by the RAND Corporation (*www.rand.org/centers/icj*) examined the NTSB's ability to carry out its mandate to investigate major commercial airline accidents. The study found the board's resources strained to the breaking point by the number and complexity of recent major accidents, urging additional resources and sweeping management and process reform.

In aviation, the NTSB also serves as the first level of appeal in cases where the FAA has taken enforcement action to suspend or revoke a certificate or, under certain circumstances, to impose a fine. This process is discussed in detail in Chapter 2.

National Aeronautics and Space Administration (NASA)
(www.nasa.gov)

Although NASA's name is most commonly thought of in connection with its activities in the exploration of space, bear in mind that the first A in NASA stands for Aeronautics. While the space shuttle transportation system is currently the most obvious example of NASA's efforts, the contributions of NASA to aviation continue to be of considerable importance.

In the area of aerodynamics, NASA R&D has found a practical application in the form of the super critical airfoil now in general use on high-performance aircraft (in both wing and propeller cross sections) and the "Whitcomb winglet," both of which increase aircraft efficiency and conserve aviation fuels. Much of the basic research that led to successive generations of increasingly quiet and fuel-efficient high-bypass-ratio fan-jet engines was done at NASA.

The agency has conducted research on the use of liquid hydrogen as an alternative aviation fuel of the future, the design and propulsion of a second-generation supersonic or hypersonic transcontinental transport (the National Aerospace Plane, often referred to as the "Orient Express"). NASA research and development efforts in aviation have also led to advanced flight-control and aircraft deicing systems, along with improvements in civil aircraft crashworthiness.

18 ——————————————————————— **I : Administrative Law**

NASA's revitalized general aviation program, aimed at improving the U.S. aviation industry's market share, focuses on (1) propulsion, noise and emissions work to enable U.S.-built aircraft to meet world environmental standards; (2) systems research to put new technology in the cockpit (especially the "Highway in the Sky" program) and increase safety; (3) structure and materials development to transfer data on advanced metals and composites to the general aviation industry; and (4) aerodynamics research to increase aircraft speed, capacity, and fuel efficiency. NASA is also in the final stage of the Small Aircraft Transportation System Program (SATS), a five-year, $69 million program designed to demonstrate the viability of new technologies for enabling small aircraft to affordably reduce many of the expected problems in the nation's transportation system, such as increasing congestion on highways and at the major airports serving commercial passenger airlines. For example, SATS envisions the development and use of easy-to-operate all-weather aircraft that can fly into the more than 5,000 existing public use general aviation airports with minor modifications to the airports' landing and navigational facilities (Fig. 1.4). NASA hopes that success of the program will enable a doubling of the number of communities with air transportation, alleviate the gap between

Fig. 1.4. The ergonomically designed high-tech "glass cockpit" in this new Cirrus SR-22 four-seat general aviation aircraft exemplifies the easy-to-operate goal of the AGATE and SATS Programs. *Photo courtesy Cirrus Design.*

transportation demand and supply, and create new economic growth for communities throughout the nation.

NASA has announced ambitious long-range goals for its aviation program overall. These include the following:

1. Reduce the aircraft accident rate by a factor of 5 within 10 years and by a factor of 10 within 25 years.
2. Reduce nitrogen oxide emissions of future aircraft by a factor of 3 within 10 years and by a factor of 5 within 25 years, and reduce carbon dioxide emissions of future aircraft by 25% within 10 years and by 50% within 25 years.
3. Reduce the perceived noise levels of future aircraft by a factor of 2 within 10 years and by a factor of 4 within 25 years.
4. Increase aviation system capacity to allow aviation system throughput to double in 10 years and triple in 25 years.
5. Reduce the cost of air travel by 25% within 10 years and by 50% within 25 years.
6. Reduce public travel times by half in 10 years and two-thirds in 25 years.
7. Provide next-generation design tools and experimental aircraft to increase design confidence and cut the design cycle time for aircraft in half.

NASA also administers the Aviation Safety Reporting Program, which is designed to identify safety problems in the National Air Transportation System (especially in air traffic control). This program is described in greater detail in Chapter 2.

Civil Aeronautics Board (CAB)

Formerly the powerful and pervasive regulator of airline economics, including rates charged and routes served by U.S. airlines and foreign airlines serving the United States, the CAB was gradually wound down as a result of Congress's passage of the Airline Deregulation Act of 1978. The CAB finally ceased to exist on January 1, 1985.

Until Congress passed the Airline Deregulation Act, most states' Public Utilities Commissions (PUCs) also exercised tight control over economic aspects of intrastate operations of air carriers. Before providing commercial air service between cities within the same state, airlines were typically required to obtain a certificate of public convenience and necessity from the state's PUC, and to obtain that agency's approval of every route to be served within that state and of each fare to be charged on each such route. Such regulations were specifically preempted by the Deregulation Act, which now prohibits all states except Alaska (which is uniquely reliant on commercial air transportation for intrastate travel) from regulating federally certificated airlines.

Federal preemption does not, however, extend into the area of registration and taxation of aircraft, so that state aircraft registration requirements and personal property or ownership taxes on aircraft are commonplace. Typical state aircraft registration and taxation programs are discussed in some detail in Chapter 11.

Air Transportation Stabilization Board (ATSB) (*www.atsb.gov*)

Only 11 days after the terrorist attacks of September 11, 2001, Congress passed the Air Transportation Safety and System Stabilization Act to compensate victims of the attacks for their losses and to aid U.S. airlines' recovery from the financial consequences of the attacks. Victim compensation provisions of the Act are discussed in detail in Chapters 8 and 9. The Act created the Air Transportation Stabilization Board, comprised of the Secretary of Transportation, the Chairman of the Board of Governors of the Federal Reserve System (designated as Chair of the ATSB), the Secretary of the Treasury, and the Comptroller General of the United States (as a nonvoting member of the ATSB), or the designee of any of these officeholders.

The ATSB was empowered to issue up to $10 billion in federal loan guarantees to the airlines and to compensate airlines up to $5 billion for direct losses resulting from federal action grounding the airlines in the wake of the attacks.

National Mediation Board (NMB) *(www.nmb.gov)*

Unlike most other industries, the airlines are not governed by the National Labor Relations Board (NLRB) under the National Labor Relations Act. Rather, airline labor law is governed by (of all things) the Railway Labor Act of 1926 (RLA), made applicable to the airlines in 1936. The National Mediation Board supervises union elections and compulsory mediation procedures for resolution of major labor disputes under the RLA in the airline industry. These procedures are discussed in detail in Chapter 14.

National Labor Relations Board (NLRB) (*www.nlrb.gov*)

The NLRB governs labor relations in all U.S. industries except the railroads and airlines. Thus, the airlines are regulated by the RLA, and aircraft and component manufacturers and other aviation businesses are regulated by the NLRB. The NLRB's regulations and procedures are discussed in some detail in Chapter 13.

Federal Trade Commission and Department of Justice

The Federal Trade Commission and Department of Justice police all industries for anticompetitive practices. In aviation, this mostly involves airline and manufacturer mergers and acquisitions and collusion in pricing. The Department of Justice is also responsible for prosecuting federal crimes relating to aviation, such as aviation security and fraud cases. Crimes relating to aviation are discussed in Chapters 2 and 15. In the Aviation and Transportation Security Act of 2001, Congress directed the Attorney General, who is the head of the Department of Justice, to screen all aliens applying for training at U.S. flight schools for security risks. This responsibility was later transferred to the Department of Homeland Security.

National Institute of Justice

In the Aviation and Transportation Security Act, Congress directed the National Institute of Justice to assess potential use of nonlethal weapons by flight deck crewmembers to temporarily incapacitate intruders.

U.S. Customs Service

The U.S. Customs Service was formerly under the Treasury Department, but recently moved into the Department of Homeland Security. The Aviation and Transportation Security Act ordered all airlines providing international air transportation to the United States to secure their computer reservation systems against unauthorized access and to electronically transmit passenger and crew manifests to U.S. Customs prior to departure. Implementation of this feature has recently resulted in the delay or cancellation of numerous international flights to the U.S., as names on these manifests were matched against similar names appearing on the "watch list" of terrorist suspects.

Customs has long operated a fleet of modern turbine-powered aircraft to support the agency's drug-interdiction mission. As a part of the post-9/11 reorganization, these were moved into a consolidated Immigration and Customs Enforcement (ICE) branch of DHS and gained an added mission: Its Cessna Citation jets and Sikorsky Blackhawk helicopters are serving as first-level interceptors of general aviation aircraft intruding into the Washington, D.C. Air Defense Identification Zone (ADIZ) and security-restricted airspace, calling in the Air Force fighters standing alert at nearby Andrews Air Force Base if needed. Security restrictions on airspace access are discussed in greater detail in Chapters 14 and 15.

The State Department, the President, the Senate, and the Department of Transportation

The State Department negotiates treaties between the United States and other nations, including air transport agreements providing for reciprocal international air service. Once the State Department has negotiated such a proposed treaty, it must be approved and executed by the president and ratified by the Senate.

Foreign air carriers designated by their country to provide service to the United States under such an agreement must first receive a foreign air carrier permit issued by the Department of Transportation in consultation with the State Department; this permit is also subject to presidential approval. The president may disapprove a specific designated foreign carrier only for foreign relations or national defense reasons. Such permits have occasionally been denied or withdrawn in the application of U.S. foreign policy, as when Aeroflot's permit was suspended following the invasion of Afghanistan by the Soviet Union.

STATE ADMINISTRATIVE AGENCIES

State governments are also free to regulate commerce, so long as state rules do not conflict with federal law or unduly burden interstate and foreign commerce (see Chapter 13 for detailed discussion on the application of this concept to regulation of airport and airspace use).

In one recent example of state regulation, the State of Florida's Department of Environmental Protection (DEP) initiated enforcement action against Embry-Riddle Aeronautical University (ERAU) for the age-old and industrywide practice of "sumping and dumping." It is a crucial step in the preflight inspection of any powered flying machine to drain fuel samples from the aircraft's various fuel sumps to check for water, debris, and other contaminants ("sumping"). For virtually the entire first century of powered flight, it was routine practice throughout the general aviation community to then discard the collected sample by pouring it out onto the ramp ("dumping"). The problem is that fuel is toxic, flammable, and corrosive, which qualifies it as *hazardous waste*. Although most of a small dumped avgas sample evaporates, some (including the tetraethyl lead additive) remains to run off into the soil and water, making the practice an unlawful disposal of hazardous waste, punishable by a fine of up to $50,000 per day under Florida law—enough to motivate anyone to make a focused effort to break an old bad habit. In consideration of the university partnering with DEP to develop an educational campaign aimed at helping pilots break this old bad habit, the state reduced ERAU's fine for the past illegal practice.

INTERNATIONAL REGULATION

International Civil Aviation Organization (ICAO) *(www.icao.org)*

Although not technically a regulatory agency, the International Civil Aviation Organization, an organ of the United Nations headquartered in Montreal, has certainly had a profound worldwide effect on aviation standards.

ICAO was organized in late 1944 at the Chicago Conference. There (with World War II still raging in Europe and the Pacific), representatives of 52 allied and neutral nations gathered to chart global civil aviation's postwar course.

The two specific goals of the gathering were:

1. *Establishment of international technical standards* for aircraft airworthiness certification, flight crew certification, communications, and radio aids to navigation, and
2. *Establishment of principles and procedures for the economic regulation* of international civil aviation's routes, fares, frequency, and capacity.

The delegates' philosophy was clearly expressed in the preamble to the resulting treaty, the Convention on International Civil Aviation:

> WHEREAS the development of international civil aviation can greatly help to create and preserve friendship and understanding among the nations and peoples of the world, yet its abuse can become a threat to the general security; and
> WHEREAS it is desirable to avoid friction and to promote that cooperation between nations and peoples upon which the peace of the world depends;
> THEREFORE, the undersigned governments having agreed on certain principles and arrangements in order that international civil aviation may be developed in a safe and orderly manner and that international air transport services may be established on the basis of equal opportunity and operated soundly and economically; Have accordingly concluded this Convention to that end.

Today, at least 185 nations have signed the Convention on International Civil Aviation and ICAO has succeeded famously in achieving the first goal. ICAO-adopted technical standards, known as international Standards and Recommended Practices (SARPs), are published in a series of documents known as *Annexes*. The smooth and efficient functioning of international civil aviation is largely attributable to ICAO's work. Wherever you fly on earth, you have ICAO to thank for communications and navigation systems that are compatible with the equipment in your aircraft (no matter where in the world the aircraft and its avionics were built) and for the ability to communicate with air traffic control facilities worldwide in the English language (an area ICAO has targeted for further improvement, because ATC English capabilities vary widely across the globe). In recent years, ICAO developed internationally accepted standards for the transport of hazardous materials (Haz Mat) by air.

Work continues in this area. The FAA has identified international harmonization of aircraft certification and operating rules as a goal to help airlines cut costs. The European Community, as a part of its effort to break down regional trade barriers, has formed a multinational Joint Aviation Authority (JAA), which has adopted Joint Airworthiness Resolutions (JAR) now accepted by at least 28 European nations. Differences between these airworthiness requirements and those of the United States and other non–European Community nations result in numerous design modifications and redundant testing and certification processes. U.S. manufacturers have urged the FAA to move as swiftly as possible to harmonize its airworthiness standards with the European JAR. ICAO is deeply involved in this effort, as well as efforts to achieve greater standardization among commercial and airline transport pilot certification requirements globally.

The organization's Technical Cooperation Programme provides technical expertise and consultation, training, and airport and airway equipment to developing countries.

Recently, increased international concern over global environmental problems, such as the greenhouse effect and ozone layer depletion, has led ICAO to cooperate with other international organizations. The objective is to determine the extent of aviation's contribution to these problems and propose appropriate corrective action.

Accomplishments in the area of the Chicago conferees' second goal have been less impressive, but by no means insignificant. At that 1944 conference, the United States proposed basically a global free market for the airlines, proposing that the nations of the world agree to recognize the Five Freedoms of the Air. (See Fig. 1.5)

Although much of the world might jump at such a generous offer today, to gain greater access to comparatively lucrative U.S. markets, in late 1944 the United States was on the verge of being in position to monopo-

1 : Regulatory Agencies and International Organizations   25

Fig 1.5. The Five Freedoms of the Air, illustrated for an airline of nation A.

lize the international airline industry at war's end. It would take little more than a change of paint and uniforms to transform the U.S. military airlift fleet into civil airlines having a greater capacity than all the other nations on earth could hope to muster for many years.

Thus, it is not surprising that national protectionism prevailed over free-market competition. In a treaty known as the *Chicago Convention on*

International Civil Aviation, the conferees all agreed only to the principle of national sovereignty in airspace, providing that no scheduled international air service may be operated over or into a nation or its airspace without its permission.

A separate agreement known as the *Transit Agreement* was also signed at that time in Chicago by fewer than all the conferees, agreeing to the first two Freedoms (overflights and nontraffic stops). Foremost among the nonsigners were the security-obsessed nations of the communist bloc. The other Freedoms were left to be negotiated between individual nations, although ICAO did develop a standard form of bilateral agreement for the exchange of air routes as a part of the Chicago Conference. The form has been widely used and is generally recognized to have contributed significantly to the high degree of consistency in global bilateral commercial air service agreements negotiated over the past 50 years.

Additional Freedoms discussed since the Chicago conference and included in some bilateral or multilateral air service agreements are:

- **Sixth Freedom:** The right to carry traffic from one nation through the homeland and on to a third nation.
- **Seventh Freedom:** The right to carry traffic between two foreign nations without going through the home country.
- **Eighth Freedom:** (Also called *cabotage*) the right to carry traffic between two points in a foreign country, such as if a European airline were authorized to operate commercial flights between New York and Los Angeles. If the origin and destination are located in geographically separated parts of that country, such as if the route was between Los Angeles and Anchorage, it is also called *grand cabotage.*

Meanwhile, back in the United States, the president's National Commission to Ensure a Strong Competitive Airline Industry, finding that this bilateral agreement system is no longer conceptually sound nor sufficiently growth-oriented in today's global trade environment, recommended that U.S. negotiating efforts should be focused on creating multinational agreements and that the stature of international air service negotiations should be elevated by appointment of an "Ambassador-at-Large" to lead these negotiations.

Open Skies Agreements are the latest fashion in treaties for international air service. Unlike the bilateral agreements typical for many decades after the Chicago Convention, Open Skies Agreements (which may be either bilateral of multilateral) do not limit the service to be provided by airlines of signatory nations to specific city pairs (i.e., New York City—Paris), but give the airlines of both countries the right to operate from any point in either country to any point in the other, as well as to and from third countries (Fifth Freedom "beyond rights"). Other features of Open Skies Agreements designed to encourage competition include:

- **Free Market Competition:** No restrictions on number of airlines the signatory nations may designate to provide service under the treaty, on capacity, frequency of service, or types of aircraft.
- **Pricing Determined by Market Forces:** A fare can be disallowed only if both governments concur—"double disapproval pricing"—only allowed for certain specified reasons intended to assure competition.
- **Fair and Equal Opportunity to Compete:** Carriers of both countries may establish sales offices in the other country, may convert earnings and remit them to the home country in hard currency and without restrictions, may provide their own ground handling services ("self handling") or choose among competing providers, may arrange ground transport of air cargo, and are guaranteed access to customs services.
- **Cooperative Marketing Arrangements:** Designated airlines may enter into code-sharing or leasing arrangements with airlines of either country, or with those of third countries and even with surface transportation companies.
- **Liberal Charter Arrangements:** Airlines may choose to operate under the charter regulations of either country.
- **"Seventh Freedom" Rights:** Some Open Skies Agreements include authority for an airline of one country to operate all-cargo services between the other country and a third country via flights not linked to the airline's homeland.
- **Safety and Security:** Each government agrees to observe high standards of aviation safety and security, and to render assistance to the other in certain circumstances.
- **Dispute Settlement and Consultation:** The model text agreement (available on the State Department website, *www.state.gov*) includes procedures for settling differences that arise under the agreement.

The increasing emphasis on opening air transportation to competition is also causing reexamination of legal restrictions on foreign ownership of U.S. airlines.

ICAO has adopted a new strategic action plan to adapt within the framework of the Chicago Convention to rapidly changing circumstances in the airline industry (see *www.icao.org/ecao/en/sap2000.htm*). A few scholars have even suggested that it would be timely for ICAO to convene a new conference to revisit its original second goal, in post–Cold War light.

Thawing of tensions between Cold War adversaries is evidenced by a program agreed to between Russia and Canada to facilitate regular commercial airline traffic between North America and Asia to fly over the North Pole. If this initiative leads to bilateral agreements to make the route widely available, the shortened routing will shave hours off many routes, saving the airlines millions of dollars each year in fuel, staff costs, and intermediate airport landing fees.

Perhaps the most intractable problem ICAO has dealt with is that of unlawful interference against civil aviation (hijacking and terrorism). The first reported episode occurred in 1784, when a young man forced his way into the basket of a Charliere (helium) balloon and demanded at swordpoint to be flown. ICAO statistics show that such incidents were extremely rare until 1968, when hijacking suddenly became a fad. Some 200 aircraft hijackings occurred worldwide from 1968 through 1970. The perpetrators were mostly criminals seeking to escape, mentally unstable persons, or political militants. Persons in the latter category have also been responsible for most of the recent hijackings and acts of sabotage against civil aviation, such as the blowing up of Pan Am flight 103 over Lockerbie, Scotland, and the hijacking of four U.S. airliners for use as weapons to perpetrate the most lethal terrorist attack in human history on the twin towers of the World Trade Center in New York City and the Pentagon in Washington, D.C. (A few acts of sabotage against airliners have simply been murders perpetrated in hope of collecting on the life insurance of a targeted passenger.) The problem is one of global dimensions, which no single country could effectively solve. Yet, the frequent presence of a political motive for such acts has greatly complicated efforts to achieve global consensus. In such situations, although the nation whose airliner is attacked and others unsympathetic to the particular political cause may view the attackers as terrorists or common criminals, other nations and factions sympathetic to the attackers' cause may view them as freedom fighters or even religious martyrs.

Given the level of factionalism and hatred in the world, it sometimes seems amazing that any agreements can be reached over such politically charged issues, but under ICAO's leadership, about 100 nations have signed treaties agreeing to promptly return hijacked aircraft to their countries of origin, to permit hijacked passengers to continue their journey as soon as possible, and to hold suspected hijackers for investigation and either prosecute them under their own law or extradite them to the country whose aircraft was hijacked for prosecution. The threat has by no means been eliminated; a substantial number of nations have not signed the treaties, and some continue to offer safe haven to hijackers and terrorists whose political agendas they support. Although significant progress has been made, there is still work to be done in dealing with this problem, and the threat is unlikely ever to be totally eliminated.

Meanwhile, as efforts continue to achieve world peace and to improve international civil aviation safety, the role of ICAO will continue to increase in importance. For example, the FAA delegated its international airline and airport safety oversight strategy to ICAO, which will take the lead in performing on-site safety visits. "ICAO will be the standard setter and safety monitor," said FAA director of flight standards Nick Lacey, "since the FAA is faced with budget realities that will not allow it to offer as many international programs as currently demanded." FAA aviation inspectors will be used primarily for domestic certification and oversight.

International Air Transport Association (IATA) *(www.iata.org)*

When the Chicago Conference failed to reach agreement on its second goal of regulating international civil aviation's routes, fares, frequency, and capacity, the international airlines formed their own trade association, the International Air Transport Association, to address these issues. IATA is also headquartered in Montreal. Operating initially as a cartel to divide up the markets for international air transportation and to fix prices on international air routes, IATA activities soon came into conflict with U.S. antitrust laws. As a result, IATA discontinued that function.

Today, IATA's most important function is its clearinghouse in London, which settles accounts amounting to over $30 billion annually for interline revenue transactions simultaneously between member airlines. The Air Transport Association (ATA) performs a similar clearinghouse function for U.S. domestic airlines. Without these clearinghouses, arranging travel requiring a change of airlines would be an unbelievably complicated nightmare, particularly in the international arena where currency differences and fluctuating exchange rates add to the intricacy of the task.

IATA also works closely with ICAO on technical issues involving airline operations, safety and security and has formed an alliance with the Flight Safety Foundation to exchange information and promote the best airline safety practices.

IATA's Aviation Training & Development Institute offers a wide variety of courses in airline and airport management, aviation law, aviation security, airline safety, pilot selection, crew resource management, and airport planning. These courses are taught in Miami, Montreal, Singapore, Amman, Mauritius, and Johannesburg, as well as by distance learning. (For more information, see *www.iata.org/atdi*.)

The association also publishes a number of useful reference works vital to the industry, including the best sellers *Dangerous Goods Regulations* and *World Air Transport Studies* and others on airport charges and worldwide taxes on aviation. (These publications are available at *www.iataonline.com*.)

CHAPTER 2

FAA Enforcement

AS WE SAW in the previous chapter, the Federal Aviation Regulations (FARs) have always been the "law." The FAA employs thousands of aviation safety inspectors and hundreds of attorneys to enforce this body of law. Aviation professionals and general aviation operators are probably now more likely to encounter an FAA inspector than any other law enforcement officer.

Because most FAA law enforcement activities are characterized as *administrative law* rather than *criminal law,* FAA inspectors are not required to advise suspects of their legal rights. In an effort to appear to be good cooperative citizens, aviators and aviation managers often make voluntary statements to FAA inspectors and air traffic controllers that can be subsequently used by the FAA to suspend or revoke their certificates or to punish them by imposing substantial fines.

The purpose of this chapter is to furnish a practical working knowledge of your legal rights in FAA investigation and enforcement situations. A separate course of study can and should be devoted to the organization and content of the FARs.

When the FAA has reason to suspect that an individual or company has violated one or more of the Federal Aviation Regulations, the FAA can choose from a variety of penalties to punish the violator:

1. *Administrative Dispositions.* When the FAA considers the violation to be minor, of little consequence but too serious to ignore altogether, it may dispose of the case administratively through the issuance of a warning notice or letter of correction.

a. *Warning Notice.* Being issued a Warning Notice by the FAA is very much like receiving a warning from a police officer in a traffic case. The notice outlines the facts about the incident and indicates that it may have been a violation of the FARs but that the FAA has decided not to file formal charges.
b. *Letter of Correction.* When a minor violation involves a condition that has since been corrected (for example, if the FAA inspector found an aircraft's ELT battery out-of-date and the owner immediately rectified the discrepancy), the FAA may issue a Letter of Correction outlining the facts of the incident or condition, stating that it may have been a violation of the FARs, but noting that in light of the corrective action taken, no enforcement action will be pursued.

The Letter of Correction is also used to provide for *remedial training* for some FAR violations, instead of punishment. This allows a pilot or mechanic suspected of a violation to submit to a course of remedial training (instead of having to face a certificate suspension or fine) if:

i. The violation did not occur in connection with an operation for compensation or hire in air transportation, *and*
ii. The FAA is satisfied that you have a constructive attitude so that remedial training will probably lead you to a life of future FAR compliance, *and*
iii. Your violation was not one that would indicate an underlying basic lack of qualification to hold your certificate, *and*
iv. You don't already have a bad record of noncompliance with the FARs, *and*
v. Your violation was not deliberate, grossly negligent, or a criminal offense.

Unlike reexamination (discussed later in this chapter), remedial training does not include a testing component, so as long as you take the agreed training with an instructor of your choice during a time period that you and the FAA agree to, you will be off the hook with a Letter of Correction.

In my experience, most FAR violations are unintentional errors made by people who are really trying to fly right but make a human error. A little refresher training with an instructor never hurt anybody, and every client I have been able to help get into this program has come away feeling like a better pilot for the experience. And, it doesn't result in an FAR violation going on your record. Presented with the option between remedial training and an enforcement action, I'd snap up the opportunity for remedial training every time.

If a Warning Notice or Letter of Correction is issued, this becomes a part of your airman record at the FAA Aeronautical Center in Oklahoma City. Warning Notices and Letters of Correction are automatically removed from your airman record two years after issuance. Meanwhile, this record is always consulted by FAA inspectors investigating alleged violations, and if it appears that the person or the company under investigation has a previous administrative disposition of record, a harsher penalty will be sought in the subsequent case, on the theory that "last time we were nice guys and gave him a break, and he obviously didn't learn his lesson from that, so this time we have to hit him harder to get his attention." Under current FAA policy, administrative dispositions are frequently used to provide remedial training to rusty individual certificate holders and under self-reporting programs for air carriers and manufacturers (discussed later in this chapter), but legal enforcement action in the nature of a certificate action or civil penalty is still taken frequently.

2. *Certificate Action.* Where the violation is one of an operational nature (rather than, for example, a mere delinquency in record keeping), the FAA prefers to suspend or revoke the FAA certificate(s) held by the violator. The election between revocation or suspension—and, if suspension is elected, the duration of the suspension imposed—is determined by the FAA attorney handling the case, with the advice of the inspector who conducted the investigation and by reference to a table of sanction guidelines issued by the FAA's Washington, D.C., headquarters. Factors considered by the attorney in reaching this decision include

   a. *Precedent.* Penalties previously imposed by the FAA and upheld by the NTSB on appeal in similar cases serve as a guideline for future penalties.
   b. *Current FAA Enforcement Priorities.* In the course of its safety-regulating duties, the FAA looks for patterns appearing in its investigations of accidents, incidents, and violations, and as a matter of policy focuses on certain types of misbehavior that may appear to be "getting out of hand" or causing particular concern. These receive increased emphasis in inspections and related enforcement actions. When an alleged violation falls within an area designated by FAA management for such special emphasis, penalties harsher than those previously applied for such a violation may

be sought on the theory that precedent punishment has proven insufficient to deter such violations.
   c. *Individual Considerations.* In selecting the sanction to impose on an individual violator, the FAA attorneys are also instructed to consider the following factors:
      i. The degree of hazard to the safety of other aircraft and persons or property in the aircraft or on the ground created by the alleged violation;
      ii. The nature of the violation (whether inadvertent or deliberate);
      iii. The violator's previous record (the FAA expects everyone to obey the law and have a violation-free record, so a previous violation is considered an aggravating circumstance that will lead to a harsher penalty in a later case, but a clean record is not considered a mitigating factor to reduce the penalty);
      iv. The alleged violator's level of experience (more-experienced pilots are expected to make fewer mistakes);
      v. The attitude of the alleged violator (a positive attitude toward FAR compliance may soften the penalty, while a bad attitude may lead to harsher treatment);
      vi. The nature of the activity involved (private, public, or commercial, the latter calling for a harsher penalty);
      vii. Any ability of the alleged violator to absorb the sanction without any real impact (such as by taking an earned vacation during the period of suspension or an employer's offer to pay any fine imposed); and
      viii. Whether the violation indicates an underlying lack of qualifications on the part of the violator to hold a certificate (either as the result of lack of skills or knowledge or an attitude of disrespect toward the FARs)
   d. *The Horror Factor.* The FAA attorney's subjective "gut" feeling about the seriousness of the violation also plays a role in the selection of a penalty. Few FAA attorneys are pilots or have any other practical background in aviation, so this evaluation is often affected by views expressed by the investigating inspector and any sensational publicity that may have appeared in the news media.

3. *Civil Penalties (fines).* The FAA attorney has the option of imposing a fine instead of taking certificate action in some cases. (Constitutional prohibitions against double jeopardy have generally been construed to allow the FAA to either impose a fine or to take certificate action, but not to do both for the same violation.) For operational violations, FAA enforce-

ment policy generally encourages the use of certificate action against individuals and civil penalties against companies. However, if the FAA feels that the management of a certificate-holding company (such as an air carrier or repair station) is not making a serious effort to obey the FARs it will not hesitate to suspend or revoke that company's operating certificate. A civil penalty may be the only punishment available against an FAR violator who is not required to hold an FAA certificate, such as an ultralight pilot or skydiver. If the FAA attorney elects to proceed with a civil penalty (fine), the agency may seek to collect a maximum of $1,000 per violation in most cases against individuals and some businesses, $10,000 per violation by air carriers and airport operators, or $250,000 for falsification of documents.

Most incidents give rise to more than one regulatory violation, if only because whenever an FAR is violated, the FAA almost always adds a residual charge of a violation of FAR 91.13 (careless or reckless operation) on the theory that it is careless or reckless to violate any FAR. For continuing operations, the FAA may count them on a per-flight or per-day basis. For example, if an airplane made a dozen flights after an AD was due but had not been performed, the operator could be fined $1,000 per flight for the overdue AD plus $1,000 per flight for a careless or reckless operation. In the alternative, if this situation was allowed to exist while the aircraft was operated over a period of 30 days, each day could count as a violation of each of these regulations. In either event the potential fine could quickly build to an astronomical number. If the violator is an air carrier or airport operator, multiply that result by 10.

4. *Summary Seizure of Aircraft.* If the FAA charges you or your company with a violation and is concerned about your ability to pay such a fine, the agency also has the power to seize the aircraft involved and hold it until the fine is paid or bond is posted to cover the fine.

5. *Reexamination.* If an accident, incident, or report of an FAR violation causes the FAA to be concerned about your competency, the FAA may require you to submit to reexamination in the area of concern. This may include a repetition of written, oral, flight, or other practical tests required for the certificate involved. The FAA must have some reasonable basis for requesting such reexamination, but if it does you have no right of appeal and *must* submit to reexamination, at your own expense. If you do not submit to reexamination within a reasonable period of time, that in itself is an FAR violation for which the FAA may suspend or revoke your certificates. For example, if during IFR operations, ATC observed you

having some difficulty executing a published instrument approach procedure, wandering all over the sky, it might then require you to submit to another instrument flight test with concentration on instrument approach procedures as a condition of keeping your instrument rating. Before any reexamination, it is wise to spend some time with an instructor polishing your skills and updating your knowledge in the area in question. Where an FAR violation caused the concern about your qualifications, the FAA can both require you to submit to reexamination and punish you for the violation by certificate action or fine. This is generally not considered to violate the constitutional prohibition against double jeopardy since the reexamination is not considered punishment.

Investigations

The FAA is required by Congress to investigate all reports of FAR violations, regardless of how farfetched the initial report may sound. Most reports of FAR violations are investigated by FAA inspectors, usually those assigned to a Flight Standards District Office (FSDO).

The majority of FAR violations come to the attention of these FAA inspectors during the regular conduct of their duties, including aircraft accident investigations; routine checks (such as base inspections of aviation businesses); airport surveillance (including ramp checks of aircraft operators and the hated "weekend duty" when the inspector on call for accident investigations may meanwhile roam around local general aviation airports, looking for problems like a cop on the beat).

The FAA's air traffic controllers are the second major source of reports of FAR violations. For example, if a flight operating under Instrument Flight Rules (IFR) deviates from an altitude assigned by the ATC, a report may be forwarded to the inspectors for investigation and prosecution as an FAR violation. In fact, the ATC computer program has a feature, officially named the Quality Assurance Program and generally called "the Snitch Patch," that *automatically* calls many deviations from clearances to the attention of FAA enforcement personnel. ATC has caught and reported thousands of airspace violations since the terrorist attacks of 9/11/01 caused a dramatic increase in the designation (often on extremely short notice) of temporary flight restrictions (TFRs). Some of these errant pilots have been intercepted by fighters and escorted to a nearby airport (not usually the airport of intended landing), where they were met and interrogated by Secret Service agents eager to assure that the pilot had no terrorist intent. FAA enforcement has sometimes followed. See Chapter 14 for more on airspace regulation.

The third largest source of reports of FAR violations is the general public. Reports from the general public arise largely out of "buzz jobs," when a citizen is frightened or annoyed by low-flying aircraft, or low-flying aircraft spook livestock in a rural area (Fig. 2.1). Since the terrorist attacks of 2001, the general public has been particularly jumpy about low-flying aircraft, fearing that the pilot intends to crash into them or spray them with some lethal substance.

The FAA has a toll-free telephone number (800-255-1111) at its Washington, D.C., office for the Safety Hotline anyone can call to report FAR violations. The FAA promises to keep the caller's identity confidential if requested and begins a preliminary investigation of each report within one day.

Although the circumstances leading up to an FAA enforcement action are sometimes downright laughable, finding yourself the focus of one is anything but amusing. For example, a DC-3 freighter had just landed at

Fig. 2.1. Caught up in the exuberance of spring break, this young collegiate pilot was caught on video buzzing a crowded South Padre Island, Texas, beach. The proliferation (in at least the tens of millions) of small portable imaging devices (including film, digital, and video cameras and even cell phones capable of recording and transmitting digital images and video clips) in the hands of ordinary citizens and law enforcement officers has greatly increased the likelihood that low-flying aircraft and their pilots will be identified and successfully prosecuted.

a Florida airport and as the crew was taxiing to park, they noticed a group of young Civil Air Patrol (CAP) cadets drilling on the ramp to the immediate left of the aircraft's course. As the cadets paused to watch the proud classic airliner taxi grandly by, the captain said to the first officer: "Your aircraft." The first officer took the controls, responding: "I have the aircraft." The captain then opened the cockpit window, released his seat belt, rose, lowered his trousers, and "mooned" the passing cadets, failing to first notice that the proud mother of one of the cadets was videotaping the drill and the taxiing DC-3. Mother was appalled. When she showed the videotape to the FAA, it was not amused either, and issued an Emergency Order of Revocation of the pilot's airline transport pilot (ATP) certificate, alleging that he lacked the "good moral character" required to hold such a certificate, along with careless or reckless operation. At the hearing (more on this process momentarily) before a female NTSB Administrative Law Judge (ALJ), the video tape was shown several times, to the pilot's increasing embarrassment. By the conclusion of the hearing, the pilot's attorney was able to beat the moral character charge, but the judge found in favor of the FAA on the charge of careless operation (based largely on the first officer's testimony that he was laughing so hard he could barely steer the aircraft). She reduced the penalty accordingly to a 10-day suspension of the captain's ATP certificate, with credit for time served. The moral of the story, in this era of proliferation of personal digital and video cameras (and even cell phones that can take and send digital photos and video clips), is that before doing something frisky with your flying machine, you should ask yourself: "How is this going to look to the FAA and the NTSB ALJ when (not *if*) they see it on video?"

The Crucial Moment (Ramp Checks, etc.)

Although you have the right to appeal the charges and have a hearing with your attorney present to represent you, as a practical matter the most crucial moment in the entire process is likely to be your first contact with an FAA representative. In my experience, the person under investigation will frequently make damaging admissions in early statements to the FAA, not even realizing that she is under investigation for a suspected violation. If you fall into this trap, such admissions may later make it impossible for your attorney effectively to defend the formal charges brought against you.

Although on appeal the FAA will have the burden of proving its charges, your early admissions may be all that it takes. For example, in a violation alleged to have been committed by a general aviation airplane operating noncommercially and under visual flight rules (VFR), one of the most difficult elements for the FAA to prove on appeal may be the identity of the pilot-in-command of the aircraft at the time of the alleged violation (for example, in a simple low-flying case). If you have already admitted to the FAA that you were flying the airplane (although you may vigorously dispute charges that you were flying too low), that admission can be used against you on appeal. The testimony at hearing might go something like this:

> FAA ATTORNEY: Inspector Hardnasty, did you contact the Respondent, Mr. Badguy in the course of your investigation?
> FAA INSPECTOR: Yes, sir, I telephoned his home that same afternoon, and a person who identified himself as Mr. Badguy answered. I told him that we had received a complaint from a citizen that his plane was flying low over the town of Brooklawn earlier that day. He told me that he had been flying over Brooklawn about that time, but stated that he had been at least 1,000 feet above ground level at all times.

Thus, the pilot has helped the FAA to identify him as the pilot-in-command, an element that might have been impossible to prove without his admission.

Part of the problem here is the nature of the FAA inspector's job, which requires him to be the kindly Dr. Jekyll when he's counseling aviators and aviation companies to help us get the certificates we need and to stay out of trouble, then to transmogrify into the vicious Mr. Hyde and prosecute us to the fullest extent of the law when we are suspected of violating an FAR. Another part of the problem is our attitude toward the FAA. From our earliest flight training, we are trained to think of the FAA as our friend. If we want to obtain a pilot certificate, add a rating to an existing certificate, or get authority to start an air-taxi business, we first go to see our friends at the FAA (the same inspectors who may later bring an enforcement case against us). If we find ourselves confused by an FAR and need guidance to interpret it, we go to see our friend FAA Inspector Hardnasty. If we find ourselves in a dilemma in flight, perhaps lost in clouds with failing navigational equipment, we radio for help to our friends in FAA ATC. And each of these contacts is to be commended; for it is only through such contacts that we can live through such in-flight emergencies and remain in compliance with the regulations.

But many of the FARs are quite vague and subject to differing interpretations. Despite your best efforts to comply you may someday find, much to your chagrin, that an FAA inspector's interpretation differs from yours. As a result of this difference of opinion you or your company may lose the FAA certificates necessary to conduct your business (or at least a prerequisite to your personal pleasure flying). For example, you may have undertaken a flight you believed proper under your authority as a commercial pilot only to find an FAA inspector later believes that you could not have legally performed the flight without also holding an air-taxi/commercial-operator certificate issued under FAR Part 135. Or, being human, you may simply make an inadvertent mistake that results in an FAR violation. In either event, the first contact you have with the FAA over this problem may be the most crucial moment in the entire experience. Yet unless you are in the habit of traveling around with your lawyer handcuffed to your wrist, which most of us are not, your first contact with the FAA—the most crucial moment in the entire case—will occur without your having the benefit of legal advice. In fact, it is very likely that you may not even realize until it's too late that your good old Dr. Jekyll buddy from the FAA is talking to you this time in his Mr. Hyde enforcement role. If you committed some crime, such as holding up a convenience store, the first law enforcement officer to contact you during the course of the investigation would have to advise you of your legal rights before anything you said could be used against you in court. We've all seen those cops-and-robbers TV shows where the suspect is given the *Miranda warning* advising him of his rights. Most FAR violations, however, are not crimes and the courts have held that the FAA does not have to advise you of your legal rights before taking statements from you with the intent of using them against you to take away your certificate. The courts consider such cases "merely administrative."

You have most of the same rights as a criminal suspect in that situation; it's just that the FAA doesn't have to advise you of those rights before interrogating you, so I will: *When questioned by the FAA, you have the right to remain silent. Anything you say can and will be used against you later to take away your certificate or fine you. You have the right to have your attorney present during any questioning.* (Unfortunately, you do not have the right to require the government to appoint an attorney to represent you if you can't afford one.)

Although in a formal "ramp check" the inspector will usually identify himself as such, FAA inspectors are not required to identify themselves before striking up a conversation with you. Because of this, and because they are not required first to advise you of your rights, many people have given FAA inspectors enough information to hang them without even realizing that the person they were talking to was an FAA inspector. Indeed, in my experience, it is quite common for some FAA inspectors to try to trick people into confessing their participation in violations in order to perfect an otherwise difficult enforcement case. The seemingly friendly person who strikes up a conversation with you on the ramp some sunny Sunday may well be an FAA inspector on airport surveillance duty hoping to get you to say something he can later use against you in an enforcement case. He doesn't have to identify himself unless you inquire whether he works for the FAA and request to see his FAA identification. After 9/11, in addition to their FAA ID, real FAA inspectors now carry badges. They frequently begin an investigation by subterfuge since the law permits them to, and it's certainly a lot easier than trying to get answers out of people who know what's going on, know their rights, and have an attorney at hand.

My favorite example of this occurred in a small rural community. The town was having its annual July 4th celebration at a lakefront park, and a local skydiving club was invited to participate. Because the town might have been construed by the FAA as a "congested area" under the FARs, an airshow waiver was obtained from the FAA to permit the jump under certain conditions, notwithstanding the general FAR prohibition against parachuting over and into congested areas. A condition of that waiver was that the parachute jumpers must land in the lake. During his descent, one of the jumpers decided that he didn't really want to get his parachutes wet and go to the trouble of drying them out before repacking them. So he turned his parachute and steered to a landing in a cul-de-sac on a dirt road on the very fringe of town, where he landed safely without any perceptible danger to the three shanties in the neighborhood and their associated chicken coops. As he was gathering up his parachute, a beat-up old green pickup truck came bouncing down the road and pulled up beside him.

"Kind of missed your spot, didn't you, sonny?" inquired the bib overall–clad driver.

"Nah, I just decided I didn't want to get my chutes wet," the jumper replied.

"Would you like a ride back over to where the other fellows landed?" offered the driver.

The jumper gladly accepted, and the friendly conversation continued during the ride, with the kindly old farmer asking things like: "What's your name? My, that's an unusual name, how do you spell that?" and "Where do you work, George?"

As they were nearing the place where the other jumpers had gathered, there was a lull in the conversation and the jumper took it to be his turn, asking: "What's your name?" followed by "Where do you work, Al?"

The answer to his final question was "I'm an FAA aviation safety inspector at the Denver Flight Standards District Office."

The truck stopped, the driver dropped the jumper off, then went on to his office to file a violation that would prove unbeatable, given the jumper's admissions.

This example is only the most vivid and amusing of the great many I've seen in which people had no idea they were under investigation for an FAA violation until they had already made damaging admissions. I've seen other cases in which inspectors (without having first identified themselves) struck up conversations with people on airport ramps, in Fixed Base Operator (FBO) offices, at social gatherings, or have telephoned and begun asking questions without revealing their purpose.

If, however, the person does claim to be an FAA representative, you should request to see his FAA ID to verify the claim. Be sure to compare the face to the photo on the ID. In one recent case, FAA inspectors performing a base inspection on a major airline switched ID cards before going through the airline's security, then hit the airline with a $20,000 fine for the security breach. If the person claiming to be from the FAA can't produce an FAA ID, or if the photo on the ID doesn't match the face of the person carrying it, call airport security or the police immediately.

Is there some way you can tell when your FAA inspector has made that switch from the kindly Dr. Jekyll who's your buddy to the vicious Mr. Hyde who is trying to take away your certificates? Is there some clue to alert you to the possibility that you are under investigation, that your certificate may be in jeopardy? Yes, there is, and it is this: Someone from the FAA wants to talk to you about *history* (and by *history* I mean anything that has already occurred, whether years, months, minutes, or even seconds ago). Whenever an FAA representative wants to discuss history with you, an annunciator light should start flashing and bells ringing in your mind to alert you that you are probably now a suspect in an FAA enforcement case.

Now, of course, there is always the possibility that this particular FAA representative is writing the definitive history of aviation in the United States in her spare time and is only checking to be sure she has the facts straight for the chapter devoted to your role. But the probability of that is remote. The only other reason that someone from the FAA ever wants to discuss history is that she has been assigned the duty of building an enforcement case against you or the company you work for (or both).

One lawyer-pilot friend of mine, who had successfully defended numerous pilots to the embarrassment of her local FSDO, encountered an FAA inspector on the ramp as she was heading toward the FBO office at the conclusion of a flight. He wanted to ask her some questions. Recognizing a ramp check when she saw one and knowing he was out to get her, she said she'd be glad to talk to him, but first she had to make a restroom stop (entirely plausible to any pilot). The inspector took a seat in the office outside the door when she entered the women's restroom, where she climbed out the window, got in her car and drove home. Whenever he finally realized he'd been tricked, he probably made a very nasty note in his file.

So there you are. The FAA inspector is in your face or on the other end of that telephone line and wants to talk about history with you. The annunciator light is flashing and the bells are ringing in your mind, and you have that tightness in your throat that comes with recognition that the FAA is out to get you. Congratulations! At least you know what's going on, unlike many of the previous victims of FAA investigation and enforcement actions. But what are you going to do about it? Well, a good opener is always: "Why do you ask?" You may as well see if you can find out what this is all about, first, if you aren't already certain.

Then, you are on the horns of a dilemma. You know that you have the right to remain silent, that anything you say will almost certainly come back to haunt you by helping the FAA take away your or the company's certificates (or both), and that you have the right to have your attorney present during any questioning. But your attorney isn't present, and the FAA wants to talk *now*. Additionally, you may suspect that if you exercise your rights and refuse to discuss the historical facts the inspector is looking for, she will make a little note in her file that "the suspect displayed a belligerent, uncooperative attitude," or something to that effect. You may fear that if the inspector decides you lack a constructive attitude, you may be denied the opportunity to participate in remedial training (instead of an enforcement action to suspend or revoke your certificates or fine you) and that you will be singled out for harsher treatment than normal. And that is exactly what may happen. You may have only two alternatives, both unpleasant (but not equally so): An angry inspector who may be unable to prove a case against you because you did not confess or a happy inspector who can prove a case against you because you did confess. Pushed to that choice, I will go with the first choice every time.

Never discuss historical facts with the FAA without first consulting your attorney. You must be firm on that point. It is also, however, important to not appear disrespectful of the inspector, the FAA, or the FARs. It is definitely in your interest to try to avoid the appearance of a bad attitude by maintaining a polite, soft-spoken presentation and professional demeanor toward the FAA inspector. You might try saying something like

> Gee, Inspector, I really would like to talk to you about this, but I think the professional thing for me to do in this situation is to talk to my attorney first.

May I have your business card, so that I can call you back after I consult with my attorney?

Many FAA inspectors are not beneath persisting in trying to cajole you into telling them what they want to know in the face of your resistance, and they have been known to say things like

Aw, shucks, I think you're blowing this way out of proportion. It's not that big a deal, and probably nothing will come of it. I've just had a file dumped in my lap, and I have to check it out. The sooner I get the answers to these questions so I can fill out this report, the sooner I can close the file.

So you relent and answer their questions. They write down the answers and close the file as promised. Then they put it in an envelope and send it to the FAA attorney who takes action to suspend or revoke your certificate. You appeal, and the FAA proves its case by using the answers you gave the FAA inspector. It happens every day. Don't be a chump. You must hold your ground and firmly but politely decline to discuss any historical facts with the FAA until you have consulted your attorney.

Another context in which that crucial moment of the first contact with an FAA representative may occur is by an invitation to telephone or visit the air traffic control tower or center. If you are personally invited (by the controller on the frequency or a line service person while you are securing the aircraft after a flight) to telephone or visit the ATC facility, that annunciator light should start flashing in your mind to alert you that you are probably suspected of an FAR violation. Controllers aren't inviting you up there because they want to show off their new radar screen to an appreciative taxpayer, and they don't want you to phone in so they can compliment you on the awesome skill you demonstrated in your crosswind landing. They want to talk to you because they think you have a made a mistake.

Once again, you are on the horns of a dilemma. If you do telephone or visit the tower in response to their request, you may help them prove a case against you by identifying yourself as the pilot-in-command and by making other damaging admissions. If you don't, they may decide you lack a constructive attitude and come down harder on you.

My favorite example of the former occurred at Harlingen, Texas, then home of the Confederate Air Force (CAF), since renamed the Commemorative Air Force, a charitable organization that led the movement to restore and preserve American and foreign military aircraft of World War II vintage. A middle-aged commercial pilot flew his personal Piper Commanche on a personal pleasure trip to Harlingen for the CAF's big annual air show. He arrived VFR in VMC at dusk on the evening before the show. The flight was uneventful and there was no other traffic in the pattern when he arrived. He had not filed a flight plan. As he was tying down the Commanche on the line, a line service attendant from the flying service tapped him on the shoulder and said something like: "Pardon me, sir, but when you get done tying the aircraft down, they'd like you to pay them a visit in the tower." The pilot replied (probably with an audible gulp): "Tower? What tower?"

It seems that the pilot did not have the latest sectional aeronautical chart and thus did not realize that the airport had acquired an FAA control tower in the interim since the chart he was using had expired, so he had landed without establishing radio contact. Being an otherwise good and responsible citizen, however, he dutifully reported to the tower where he straightforwardly admitted his mistake, expressed sincerest apologies, and made it quite clear that he was mortified and had learned a valuable lesson. All in all, he found it a very frank and gratifying professional exchange with the controllers. He left believing that the problem was solved and that nothing would come of it. A few weeks later, the FAA instituted proceedings to suspend his commercial pilot's certificate for six months for the violation.

Then he contacted me for the first time. We appealed the case to the NTSB (more on how this process works later) and as the hearing was approaching, I was trying to figure out some way to defend this case and drawing a blank. After all, the guy had confessed, hadn't he?

Going over in my mind each element of the case the FAA would have to prove at the hearing, I thought about how they would prove he was the pilot-in-command who had visited the tower and confessed. I expected that the FAA attorney would call as a witness one of the control tower operators who was present during this visit and would proceed to prove the identity of the pilot-in-command like this:

> FAA ATTORNEY: Did you request that the pilot of the Commanche visit the control tower?
> CONTROLLER: Yes, sir. I telephoned the flying service and asked them to send someone out and request that the pilot pay us a visit in the tower when he got done tying down his airplane.
> FAA ATTORNEY: Did the pilot visit the control tower in response to your request?
> CONTROLLER: Yes, sir, he did.
> FAA ATTORNEY: And do you see that person present here in the courtroom, today?

CONTROLLER: Yes, sir, that's him in the green shirt, sitting over there next to Mr. Hamilton.

So I didn't bring my client to the hearing.

Sure enough, the control tower chief appeared as a witness and the questions and answers proceeded along the expected lines until the crucial question about recognition. Although my client was not present in the courtroom, the gallery was packed with a number of my students who had come to observe the proceedings. The tower chief paused, took his eyeglasses out of his pocket and put them on, then studied each face carefully before he finally replied: "No, sir, I don't."

You could have heard a pin drop as the FAA attorney realized that he had walked into an ambush and was about to lose his case for inability to prove the identity of the pilot-in-command.

Then the darndest thing happened. The tower chief started rummaging around in his flight bag, pulling out unfilled approach-plate revisions, crackers, stale sandwiches, charts, tomorrow's fresh shirt—all the usual contents of the working aviator's flight bag. Suddenly realizing that everyone in the courtroom was staring at him as if he'd gone mad, he paused, turned to the judge and said: "But, Your Honor, while he was up there, he signed our guest book and I believe I have a copy of that with me." With some further rummaging in the bag, he found the copy of the relevant page from the "guest book," and the FAA introduced it as an exhibit. There, in the most legible handwriting you've ever seen, was my client's signature.

So we lost the case.

Current FAA enforcement policies require ATC personnel to report all observed FAR violations to the inspectors for investigation. Although once routine, controllers are no longer permitted to solve problems with pilots by friendly chats.

If I get that invitation to visit the tower, I'll strongly *Roger* it and tie down the airplane and if the situation permits, disappear as rapidly as possible, not waiting around to refuel or leave a trail of little exhibits-to-be like signed gas slips, car rental agreements, and so forth.

Another lawyer friend of mine who also does a lot of FAA enforcement defense work got a request to telephone the tower after landing at an unfamiliar airport. Trying to strike a careful balance between appearing to have a constructive attitude but not giving the FAA ammunition to use against him in an enforcement case, he made the call. When the approach controller answered, he said: "Yes sir, and I'll need your name for our log." My friend laughed and replied: "I know why you need my name and I'm sure not going to give it to you, but if you think I did something wrong I'd sure like to know what it is so I won't do it again." The controller then explained the problem to him, he responded positively and appreciatively, and nothing further came of it. Once the airplane is at the chocks, you are no longer "air traffic" and thus no longer required to obey the orders of air traffic controllers (like to present yourself somewhere or call anyone on the telephone). You have a great deal to lose by showing up or calling and identifying yourself without first talking to your attorney. Don't fall for it!

Displaying Documents

Although you are not required to discuss anything with the FAA without having your attorney present, you are required by FARs 61.3(1) and 61.51(i) to present your pilot certificate, medical certificate, and logbook to FAA or NTSB investigators or any federal, state, or local law enforcement officer for inspection upon reasonable request. Unless you are a student pilot on a cross-country, however, you are not required to have you pilot logbook with you and it is probably best that you don't (even if you do, if you catch my drift). FAR 21.181(b) also requires that you make the aircraft's airworthiness certificate available for inspection by the FAA. If you are operating under FAR Part 91, these are the only documents you are required to present, and you are only required to *present* these documents for inspection, not to *surrender* them (unless the person making the request presents you with a written Emergency Order of Suspension or Revocation signed by an FAA attorney, described later). It is important that you exercise your rights here, as well. If the inspector starts to pocket or otherwise depart with your certificate and logbooks in her possession, you must insist upon their immediate return. Otherwise, you may later be held to have surrendered them voluntarily and given up all your rights to appeal any suspension or revocation of these certificates. Again, it may be necessary for you to firmly but politely insist upon preserving your rights in this regard. Present, but do not surrender, these documents. Present, but do not discuss anything about these documents without first consulting your attorney. If the FAA inspector ignores your protests and begins to depart the area with your certificates or logbooks anyway, scream bloody murder and get witnesses who can later testify that you did not voluntarily surrender these documents to the inspector. But do not under any circumstances lay a hand on the FAA inspector. You don't want to add a criminal charge of assaulting a federal officer to your problems. If you are operating under FAR Parts 121 or 135, however, document production requirements are substantially greater.

Aircraft Inspection

During the course of ramp inspections, FAA inspectors routinely ask permission to board the aircraft. If you are operating under FAR Part 135 or 121, the inspector must be granted immediate flight deck access upon request. FAR Part 91 operators on the other hand are not required to grant FAA inspectors entry to the aircraft on an oral request and should not grant such a request. Even if you allow the inspector on board to get in out of the rain, as a gesture of kindness, the inspector is not going to come aboard with blinders on. If anything appears amiss, the inspector's observations will be used against you later in an enforcement case. Even without your permission, inspectors may examine the aircraft's exterior without removing any inspection covers or opening cowlings or hatches. They can even press their noses against the Plexiglas and peek in from the outside. Just don't allow entry unless required.

It is not unusual for a difference of opinion to arise between the pilot and an FAA inspector over an issue of airworthiness during the course of a ramp check. The safest way to handle this is to call over a qualified mechanic to resolve the disagreement, if one is available. If not, you are on the spot: If you go ahead and fly, you may find yourself the guest of honor in an enforcement case for operating an unairworthy aircraft. But if you cancel your trip and later verify that your airworthiness assessment was correct, you will have suffered the inconvenience and consequences unnecessarily. If you feel confident that the aircraft is airworthy and that proceeding with your trip is worth the risk of an enforcement action, you can turn around and put the inspector on the spot. State that in your opinion, the aircraft is airworthy and you intend to fly it unless the inspector is so certain of her position that she is willing to issue a written Aircraft Condition Notice (FAA Form 8620-1). State that if she does, then you will defer to her judgment and not operate the aircraft until a qualified mechanic can inspect it.

The Letter of Investigation

Sometimes, you have no indication that the FAA is after you until you receive a letter in the mail. The *Letter of Investigation* (LOI) comes from an inspector at the Flight Standards District Office (FSDO) investigating a complaint or report of violation. The letter indicates that the FAA has received a report that you were involved in an incident in violation of the FARs. The letter will describe, in short summary form, what they believe you did and when and where they believe you did it, and will invite you to respond in writing within 10 days with your side of the story. Aviation lawyers call the LOI the "invitation to hang yourself," because a surprising percentage of recipients immediately sit down and (without the benefit of counsel) draft a complete narrative response and send it off to the FAA in the naive expectation that once the FAA sees their side of the story, the problem will go away. Fat chance! What almost always happens, instead, is that the writer will give the FAA admissions against self interest that the FAA can then use to prove its enforcement case.

For example, the FAA LOI states that on May 31, 2005, the addressee was the pilot in command of Avitat Husky aircraft N2020BZ, and operated the aircraft over the Colorado River in the vicinity of Lake Havasu City, Arizona, at approximately 7:30 p.m. The letter goes on to state that the aircraft was observed flying at an altitude as low as 50 feet above swimmers and watercraft, contrary to Federal Aviation Regulations. The pilot's reply letter typically says something like: "When I flew my Husky over the river that evening, I never got below 500 feet AGL." Gotcha! The FAA may have had no proof of the identity of the pilot in command of the aircraft, so they sent an LOI to the owner hoping to draw him out. Sure enough, he fell for it and gave them a written confession that he was the pilot. That admission, of course, would constitute ample proof of the pilot's identity, sure to satisfy any ALJ.

Do not fall for the "invitation to hang yourself." Take it to your aviation lawyer for advice. After considering your explanation of events, your lawyer may choose to craft a carefully worded admission-free response for your signature, respond on your behalf revealing that you are represented by counsel, or recommend no reply be sent.

When to Talk to the FAA

Talking to the FAA in *advance*, as when you don't understand an FAR and need an interpretation or other professional guidance to enable you to avoid committing a violation, is highly recommended.

And while you really are "air traffic" (while the aircraft is actually in operation and in communication with ATC) cooperate fully and be absolutely truthful in all communications. This advice applies even if you've made a mistake and fear that ATC has caught it. This is simply because any failure to be truthful could have far worse consequences than the suspension or revocation of your certificate.

Imagine that ATC has cleared you to climb and maintain Flight Level 380. Because of some distraction, you climb through your assigned altitude without leveling off, and ATC, noticing your mode-C encoder return, asks you to "say altitude." Realizing that you have made a mistake and that your certificate may be in jeopardy for violating an FAR by deviating from the clearance, you may feel a strong temptation to report level at 380 to avoid such troubles. The problem is that if you do that and succeed in conning the controller into believing that you really did not bust your altitude, the controller may not issue a deviating vector to the MD-11 that is coming at you head-on at Mach .85 at your real altitude. The consequences of that could make an enforcement case look like pretty light stuff. So I urge that as a practical matter you cooperate fully and report truthfully to ATC during all aircraft movements (from chock to chock, you might say). But once the aircraft is stopped, ATC is on its own, and discussions of historical events should be limited to situations in which your attorney is present to advise you.

You should also be careful to avoid getting into arguments with controllers on the frequency. Nothing is more certain to result in an enforcement case being filed against you than you jamming the frequency with some ranting filibuster over a difference of opinion with the controller. Carry out your responsibilities as pilot-in-command and do not accept clearances that would, in your professional judgment, endanger the safety of the flight. But save the debate until you're safely back on the ground, you and the controller have both had time to cool off, and you've consulted your attorney. There is a better way to clear up past misunderstandings and prevent future conflicts with ATC. The radio frequency is not the appropriate forum for debate.

Additionally, it may benefit an air carrier or an aircraft and parts manufacturer to take the initiative to report violations to the FAA under certain circumstances. Under the Air Carrier Reporting and Correction Program, recently extended to cover manufacturers as well, the FAA will use a Letter of Correction instead of enforcement action if:

1. the carrier or manufacturer discovers that it has been operating in violation of the FARs in some respect,
2. the violations were not deliberate or intentional,
3. the violations do not indicate a basic underlying lack of qualification on the part of the company,
4. the company has already taken or agreed to take corrective action to prevent a recurrence of such violations, and
5. the company reports the violations to the FAA before the FAA learns about the violations from another source.

In such a case, it is to the company's distinct advantage to take the initiative to report its violations to the FAA before the FAA learns about them from another source, which is very likely. Competitors or disgruntled employees may tip off the FAA or the FAA may "hear it through the grapevine." The aviation community is close-knit, talkative, and has no secrets.

Even if the FAA does find out about the violation from another source before the company reports it, if the company takes immediate corrective action to prevent a recurrence of the violations, the FAA will consider this action favorably to reduce any penalty to be imposed.

Immunity from Sanction: The NASA Report

If any occurrence during your flight operations results in an unsafe situation or causes you concern that the FAA or anyone else might think that you did something wrong (unless an accident or crime was involved), it is advisable to file an Aviation Safety Reporting Program (ASRP) report with NASA. There are three reasons to file this report: (1) You may make an important personal contribution to improving aviation safety; (2) you may receive immunity from sanction for an FAR violation; and (3) you have nothing to lose by filing the report.

The purpose of the NASA Aviation Safety Reporting Program is to identify problems in the National Air Transportation System to provide a sound basis for improving the system. The reporting form is free at all FAA offices, including Flight Service Stations, or by writing to FAA Aeronautical Center, Distribution Section, AAC-45C, P.O. Box 25082, Oklahoma City, Oklahoma 73125. A copy of the form is reproduced here (Fig. 2.2), and NASA will accept a copy that you make out of this book. It is a good practice always to have at least one of these forms with you in your flight case.

Filing a report may accomplish several things.

First, you *may make an important personal contribution to improving aviation safety*. Here's an example from a CFII client I represented: The day was marginal VMC with haze, and the light twin was cleared for a practice ILS approach to runway 35R. The ATC clearance for the approach received from the airport control tower, stated: "Piper 43 Tango is cleared for the practice ILS approach, runway 35 right; report power lines."

The pilot in the left seat was under the hood for the practice approach, while the flight instructor in the right seat was keeping a careful lookout for other traffic. The flight instructor was being especially watchful this day because he was aware that in accordance with local noise-abatement procedures, VFR departures were taking off toward them on the same runway (17L for these departures). It had been agreed that the flight instructor would handle the required call at the power lines since only he could see out the window and know when the aircraft arrived at this visual reference point about two miles from the runway threshold.

IDENTIFICATION STRIP: *Please* fill in all blanks. NO RECORD WILL BE KEPT OF YOUR IDENTITY.
This section will be returned to you promptly.

TELEPHONE NUMBERS where we may reach you for further details of this occurrence:

(HOME) Area _____ No. _____ - _____ Hours _____
(WORK) Area _____ No. _____ - _____ Hours _____   (SPACE RESERVED FOR ASRS DATE/TIME STAMP)

NAME _____   TYPE OF EVENT/SITUATION _____
ADDRESS _____
_____   DATE OF OCCURRENCE _____
_____   LOCAL TIME (24 hr. clock) _____

Except for reports of aircraft accidents and criminal activities — which are not included in the ASRS and should not be submitted to NASA — all identities contained in this report will be removed to assure complete reporter anonymity.

PLEASE FILL IN APPROPRIATE SPACES AND CHECK ALL ITEMS WHICH APPLY TO THIS EVENT OR SITUATION.

REPORTER'S ROLE DURING OCCURRENCE
(pilot-flying, radar controller, cabin crew, maintenance, etc.) _____

REPORTER	FLYING TIME	CERTIFICATES/RATINGS		ATC EXPERIENCE	
○ captain/pilot	total _____ hrs.	○ student	○ private	○ FPL	○ developmental
○ first officer	last 90 days _____ hrs.	○ commercial	○ ATP	radar _____ yrs.	
○ other crewmember	in acft type _____ hrs.	○ instrument	○ CFI	non-radar _____ yrs.	
○ controller		○ multiengine	○ F/E	supervisory _____ yrs.	
○ _____		○		military _____ yrs.	

DESCRIBE ONE AIRCRAFT IN THIS SECTION (PILOTS DESCRIBE YOUR OWN) AND ADDITIONAL AIRCRAFT IN THE "DESCRIBE EVENT/SITUATION" SECTION:

AIRFRAME/ENGINES			OPERATOR		PURPOSE OF FLIGHT	FLIGHT PLAN	
○ low fixed wing	○ ultralight	○ reciprocating	○ scheduled carrier		○ passenger	○ VFR	○ IFR
○ high fixed wing	○ wide body	○ turboprop	○ supplemental carrier		○ cargo	○ SVFR	○ none
○ rotary wing	○ small complex	○ turbojet	○ FBO/flying school		○ business		
○ advanced/automated cockpit (e.g., CRT's, FMS, etc.)			○ commuter	○ air taxi	○ training	**NAVIGATION IN USE**	
○ _____			○ corporate	○ charter	○ pleasure		
crew size _____ pax seats _____			○ government	○ private	○ _____	_____	
gross weight _____ no. of engines _____			○ military (_____)		○ _____	_____	
			○ _____				

AIRSPACE/LOCALE			ATC/ADVISORY SERVICE		FLIGHT CONDITIONS		LIGHT AND VISIBILITY	
○ uncontrolled	○ ATA	○ PCA	○ ground	○ approach	○ VMC	○ IMC	○ daylight	○ dawn
○ control zone	○ TRSA	○ TCA	○ local	○ departure	○ mixed	○ marginal	○ dusk	○ night
○ special use airspace	○ ARSA	○ unknown	○ center	○ FSS	○ t'storm	○ rain	ceiling _____ feet	
○ airway/route	○ MTR	○ _____	○ UNICOM	○ CTAF	○ turbulence	○ fog	visibility _____ miles	
ALTITUDE _____ ○ MSL (or) ○ AGL			Name of ATC Facility _____		○ windshear	○ snow	RVR _____ feet	
NEAREST CITY _____ STATE _____					○ ice ○ _____			

SPECIFY LOCATION BY REFERENCE TO AN AIRPORT, NAVAID, OR OTHER FIX (distance, bearing, etc.): _____

AIRCRAFT FLIGHT PHASES AT TIME OF OCCURRENCE (preflight, takeoff, cruise, hover, etc.) _____
IF A CONFLICT: Evasive action? ○ yes ○ no ○ no time ○ unknown. Estimated miss in feet _____ vert'l _____ horiz'l.

DESCRIBE EVENT/SITUATION

Keeping in mind the topics shown below, discuss those which you feel are relevant and anything else you think is important. Include what you believe really caused the problem, and what can be done to prevent a recurrence, or correct the situation. (CONTINUE ON THE OTHER SIDE AND USE ADDITIONAL PAPER IF NEEDED.)

CHAIN OF EVENTS		HUMAN PERFORMANCE CONSIDERATIONS	
— How the problem arose	— How it was discovered	— Perceptions, judgements, decisions	— Actions or inactions
— Contributing factors	— Corrective actions	— Factors affecting the quality of human performance	

NASA ARC 277 (Rev. Oct 84) PREVIOUS EDITIONS ARE OBSOLETE

Fig. 2.2. NASA aviation safety report form.

National Aeronautics and
Space Administration

Ames Research Center
Moffett Field, California 94035

Official Business
Penalty for Private Use $300

| NO POSTAGE |
| NECESSARY |
| IF MAILED |
| IN THE |
| UNITED STATES |

BUSINESS REPLY MAIL
FIRST CLASS   PERMIT NO. 12028   WASHINGTON, D.C.

POSTAGE WILL BE PAID BY NASA

FIRST CLASS
AVIATION SAFETY DATA —
DO NOT DELAY

NASA Aviation Safety Reporting System
Post Office Box 189
Moffett Field, California 94035

NATIONAL AERONAUTICS AND SPACE ADMINISTRATION

NASA has established an Aviation Safety Reporting System to identify problems in the aviation system which require correction. The program of which this system is a part is described in detail in FAA Advisory Circular 00-46C. Your assistance in informing us about such problems is essential to the success of the program. Please fill out this postage free form as completely as possible, fold it and send it directly to us.

The information you provide on the identity strip will be used only if NASA determines that it is necessary to contact you for further information. THE IDENTITY STRIP WILL BE RETURNED DIRECTLY TO YOU. The return of the identity strip assures your anonymity.

AVIATION SAFETY REPORTING SYSTEM

Section 91.57 of the Federal Aviation Regulations (14 CFR 91.57) prohibits reports filed with NASA from being used for FAA enforcement purposes. This report will not be made available to the FAA for civil penalty or certificate actions for violations of the Federal Air Regulations. Your identity strip, stamped by NASA, is proof that you have submitted a report to the Aviation Safety Reporting System. We can only return the strip to you, however, if you have provided a mailing address. Equally important, we can often obtain additional useful information if our safety analysts can talk with you directly by telephone. For this reason, we have requested telephone numbers where we may reach you. Thank you for your assistance.

NOTE: AIRCRAFT ACCIDENTS SHOULD NOT BE REPORTED ON THIS FORM SUCH REPORTS SHOULD BE FILED WITH THE NATIONAL TRANSPORTATION SAFETY BOARD AS REQUIRED BY 49CFR830.

---

15. NARRATIVE DESCRIPTION (continued): *(Use additional sheets if necessary)*

Fold as indicated, fasten with staple or tape, and mail. Thank you for your cooperation.

Meanwhile, however, things had gotten very busy at the airport and the air traffic controller was broadcasting nonstop instructions to a variety of aircraft in the area, with no breaks to permit reply. As the flight continued down the ILS past the power lines, the flight instructor was still awaiting an opportunity to broadcast his position report when through the haze he thought he saw something moving toward them on the runway. He ordered his student to execute an immediate missed-approach procedure (a climbing right turn on this particular approach) and the opposing traffic, a fast-moving Learjet, passed about 50 feet below and behind them, much too close for comfort. If the flight instructor had hesitated another second in initiating a missed approach, a midair collision would almost certainly have resulted.

The flight instructor subsequently learned that this was not the first time something like this had happened at the airport. He immediately filed an Aviation Safety Report with NASA. As a result of his report, the standard clearance for practice ILS approaches to that runway when opposite-direction VFR departures were in progress was changed to add the phrase "if unable, execute immediate missed approach." As a result of this change, the margin of safety was dramatically improved during these operations. That pilot's report may have saved someone else from having a midair collision there.

Second, you *may receive immunity from sanction for an FAR violation.* The FAA considers the filing of an Aviation Safety Report with NASA to be indicative of a constructive attitude that will make future violations less likely. Therefore, the FAA's policy, as set forth in FAA Advisory Circular AC 00-46D, is that (with certain exceptions to be discussed momentarily) the FAA will not impose a fine or suspend or revoke a pilot's certificate for an FAR violation if such a report was timely filed. They may, however, issue an order to make your violation a part of your airman record. Such an order is appealable like any other if you believe you did not commit a violation.

In order to get the benefit of this possible immunity from sanction, you must mail the report within 10 days after the incident. Upon receipt, NASA places its receipt stamp on the identification strip at the top of the form (refer to Fig. 2.2), snips off that strip and mails it back to you as your receipt. Save this receipt; it is now one of your most valuable possessions. If the incident results in the FAA taking enforcement action against you, brandishing this receipt is much like showing the cross to a vampire. It virtually stops the FAA in its tracks (pretty strong magic).

Exceptions to this are that the violation must not have been deliberate (the Aviation Safety Report form is not a coupon good for one free buzz job) and must not have involved a crime or accident. Nor does it protect you where the incident indicates a lack of qualifications or competency, as discussed previously under FAA penalties (number 5, "Reexamination").

Third, you *have nothing to lose by filing the report*. Except for reports involving aircraft accidents or crimes, NASA keeps these reports confidential and ensures the anonymity of the reporter and all other parties involved in a reported incident. With those exceptions, the FAA cannot find out about an incident from your filing of an Aviation Safety Report and the FAA is prohibited by FAR 91.25 from using the report or any information derived from it in an enforcement action.

The form itself is free and easy to fill out (I can tell you from my own extensive personal use of the form that it takes only a few minutes) and NASA even pays the postage. So it can't hurt and may help you to file an Aviation Safety Report whenever you encounter a condition or procedure you consider unsafe or you have the slightest clue that someone may claim that you committed an FAR violation. When in doubt, fill it out. Don't wait to see whether the FAA is going to take action against you. It frequently takes longer than 10 days for the FAA to let you know that they believe you have done something wrong. In fact, some inspectors seem to deliberately wait until after the 10th day following the incident before attempting to make the first contact with the violator, in hope that the violator will not feel motivated to file an Aviation Safety Report and will lose this chance for immunity.

If there was more than one flight crewmember on the flight deck at the time of the incident, all should file their own reports. One report doesn't protect the whole crew, only the individual who filed it. The company operating the aircraft should also file a report since it can be charged with a violation as the aircraft's "operator," under the broad definition of "operate" in FAR 1.1.

FAA Aviation Safety Action Program (ASAP)

A new FAA program known as the Aviation Safety Action Program (ASAP) applicable to participating airlines holding FAR Part 121 operating certificates and repair stations holding certificates issued under FAR Part 145 also provides an opportunity for employees of those companies to avoid FAA prosecution for unintentional violations. The program, which is described in detail in FAA Advisory Circular AC 120-66B, is intended to increase the flow of safety information to both management and the FAA. It provides incentives to encourage employees of participating air carriers and repair stations to promptly disclose safety information that may include possible FAR violations without fear of punitive FAA sanctions or company disciplinary action. Participation in the program is voluntary. In order to participate, the airline or repair station and its labor organizations (see Chapter 17) must enter into a Memorandum of Understanding (MOU) with the FAA. In order to seek immunity, the employee must report the event that may constitute an FAR violation to company management within 24 hours after the end of the duty day. Immunity from sanction under this program is neither absolute nor automatic. The circumstances of each case are reviewed by an Event Review Committee (ERC), usually composed of a management representation, a representative of the employee's union, and an FAA inspector from the Flight Standards District Office holding the company's certificate (Certificate Holding District Office, or CHDO). If the ERC determines that the event was inadvertent, did not involve an intentional disregard for safety, was not an intentional falsification (such as a record of repair to an aircraft) or a crime, and did not involve substance abuse, the matter will be disposed of administratively, by a letter of correction or warning letter.

If the ERC does not reach consensus (unanimous agreement), the CHDO Inspector's opinion will be determinative.

Initial reports from companies and employee unions participating in the program have been somewhat mixed, but generally more favorable than unfavorable (particularly from company management).

Even if you are an employee of a participating company and choose to take advantage of the program, it is wise to also file a timely report with the NASA Aviation Safety Reporting Program described above.

Prosecution and Appeal

Under present FAA enforcement policies, violations by individuals not resolved by remedial training or a letter of correction almost always result in certificate action (suspension or revocation), and violations by companies that are not so egregious as to indicate that the company's management is not dedicated to FAR compliance usually lead to civil penalties (fines). We will now examine what happens once the case reaches the FAA's lawyers.

Certificate Actions

Notice of Proposed Certificate Action. If the FAA attorney decides that your violation calls for suspension or revocation of your certificate, you will receive a Notice of Proposed Certificate Action. This is a letter describing exactly what FARs you are believed to have violated and stating exactly what the FAA proposes to do about it (for example, a 180-

day suspension of your airline transport pilot certificate). You will be offered the opportunity for an *informal conference* with an FAA attorney.

Informal Conference. This is a settlement conference. It is a chance to sit down with the FAA attorney and an inspector, let them get a feel for your attitudes and professionalism and be sure they understand what really happened and why you did what you did. With one exception, the FAA cannot use anything you say at the informal conference to prove its case against you if a settlement is not reached and you end up in a hearing before the NTSB on appeal. The only time any statement you make at the informal conference could come back to haunt you later would be if you tell a different story when you testify under oath at the NTSB hearing than you told the FAA in your informal conference. In that case, the FAA can use your prior inconsistent statement to impeach your credibility.

You should already have a lawyer by now, but if not, be sure to hire one to go with you to the informal conference. Remember: The FAA's lawyer is your adversary and cannot advise or help you. As a result of the informal conference, the FAA attorney may offer to reduce the period of suspension or to allow you to pay a fine instead of having your certificate suspended. Remedial training may still be an option. On rare occasions, where you can demonstrate at the informal conference that you did not commit the violation, the FAA attorney may agree to drop the case.

Order of Suspension or Revocation. If your attorney is unable to negotiate a settlement that you are willing to accept at the informal conference, the FAA attorney will soon issue an Order of Suspension or Revocation against your certificate. Unless the order is captioned as an *Emergency* Order of Suspension or Revocation (more about these later), it does not take effect immediately. You can defer the effective date of the order by filing an appeal with the NTSB within 20 days from the date the order was served on you. These orders are usually sent by certified mail to the address you have on file with the FAA at Oklahoma City and service is complete if anyone at that address signs for it. Your appeal must be filed within those 20 days; if it is, the effective date of the FAA's order will be postponed until your NTSB appeal is finally decided so long as your attorney carefully follows the board's Rules of Practice in Air Safety Proceedings. If you fail to get your appeal filed with the NTSB within 20 days after someone signed for the order at the last address you have on file with the FAA in Oklahoma City, the order becomes final and you can't appeal it. Therefore, it is very important that you make it a habit to comply with FAR 61.60, which requires you to give written notice of each change in your permanent address to the FAA Airman Certification Branch, Box 25082, Oklahoma City, Oklahoma 73125. If you overlook that, the FAA sends you an order at the last address it has on file for you and whoever is living there now signs for it but doesn't get it to you within those 20 days, the order becomes final and you lose your appeal rights.

Many young people attending college or working at jobs that require frequent moves use their parents' addresses for their permanent mailing address with the FAA. This is fine, so long as your parents promptly forward your mail to wherever you are. But if you just let it pile up at their house and stop by and pick it up every few weeks or months, you may one day find that your certificate has been suspended or revoked and the deadline to appeal the order has passed.

NTSB Appeal. As soon as you receive the Order of Suspension or Revocation, take it to your lawyer to file the appeal with the NTSB. The FAA will file its order with the board as its Complaint, and your attorney will have to promptly file an Answer with the board, stating which of the FAA's allegations you admit (if any) and which you deny. The board will assign your case to one of its administrative law judges to hold a hearing.

Discovery. Upon request from your attorney, the FAA will provide a list of witnesses and exhibits it intends to use at the hearing and copies of all previous statements it has received from those witnesses, along with copies of proposed exhibits, so that you will know what evidence you can expect to defend against at the hearing. You should expect to reciprocate and provide the same information regarding your intended defense.

Hearing. Eventually your case will be set for a trial-type hearing before an NTSB administrative law judge (ALJ) in a major city near you or near the place of the alleged violation (usually where the majority of the witnesses are located). All of these judges are lawyers and some of them are experienced pilots. They are based in Washington, D.C., Denver, Fort Worth, and Los Angeles, traveling over large territories called circuits hearing FAA enforcement and aviation medical appeals.

The hearing is show time, the *only* opportunity you (and the FAA) will ever get to prove your case. These are formal hearings, very much like civil trials. You are not entitled to a trial by jury in these cases. The NTSB administrative law judge alone will decide your fate. The FAA is required to put on its witnesses and exhibits first, having the burden to prove the violations charged. The FAA does not have to prove its case "beyond a reasonable doubt" as though it were a criminal case, only by a "preponderance of the evidence" (theoretically 50.1%) as in a civil trial.

Your attorney will have the opportunity to cross-examine the FAA's witnesses in an attempt to discredit their testimony. Once the FAA has presented evidence of each of its charges against you, the burden shifts to you to go forward with your defense, also through the sworn in-person testimony of witnesses and the presentation of exhibits. The FAA attorney now has the right to cross-examine you and your witnesses to discredit your testimony.

In an extremely controversial recent development, the NTSB has taken the position that the board and its administrative law judges are bound by the FAA's own interpretation of the applicable FAR, even if that interpretation is announced for the first time during the course of the case under consideration. This is called *"due deference."* Aviation defense counsel are understandably outraged that the board would make a mockery of the most fundamental concepts of due process of law by taking the position that the law is whatever the FAA says it is, even if the agency never announced the interpretation before punishing someone under it.

Once all testimony and exhibits have been presented, the judge will decide the case, usually giving you an oral decision then and there at the end of the hearing. The judge has several options. He may (1) find that the FAA has proved all of its charges and affirm the Order of Suspension or Revocation, (2) decide that the FAA has proved some but not all of its charges and reduce the term of suspension, (3) reduce a revocation to a suspension, (4) change the penalty from certificate action to a monetary fine, or (5) find that the FAA failed to prove its case and dismiss the Order of Suspension or Revocation. The ALJ cannot impose a harsher penalty than the FAA ordered. If either side is displeased with the judge's initial decision (and sometimes both are), it may appeal that decision to the full board (the five political appointees in Washington, D.C.).

Appeal to Full Board. This is a paper appeal. Both sides must file written legal briefs with the board, arguing their positions and setting out their views of the governing law. As long as your appeal and brief are timely filed, your certificate remains in effect until the board decides the appeal. The only basic issues the full board will consider are (1) Did the judge afford both sides a fair hearing? (2) Did the judge apply the correct law to the facts that were proved at trial?

Where witnesses at the hearing have testified to differing versions of events so that the judge had to decide which witness to believe, the board on its review will not reconsider that credibility choice. The board recognizes that the judge, who is able to look the witnesses in the eye and observe their gestures, mannerisms, and testimony, is in a better position to decide who to believe than the board, which has nothing more to go on than the written transcript of the testimony and the exhibits.

You will not get a hearing before the full board, nor is there any opportunity to present additional evidence not presented to the ALJ. The attorneys just mail legal briefs to Washington and eventually (at this writing about a year after the appeal to the full board was filed) the board's decision will arrive in the mail, unannounced. Either party may appeal the full board's decision to the U.S. Court of Appeals. (Note that you never get the opportunity for a trial to a court or a jury.)

Appeal to U.S. Court of Appeals. This is another paper appeal based largely upon written briefs filed by the attorneys for both sides, although the court of appeals will usually permit the lawyers to argue the case orally to the three-judge panel that will decide it. Again, there is no opportunity for either side to present evidence that was not considered by the administrative law judge.

This appeal does not automatically prevent the FAA's order from taking effect, but unless the NTSB found that you lacked the qualifications to hold the certificate, the board will grant your attorney's motion to stay the effectiveness of the order until the court of appeals decides the case. The court of appeals will eventually issue its decision by a written order. At this writing, most courts of appeals seem to be averaging about two years from appeal to decision. This decision is the end of the road for your appeal rights.

"Taking It All the Way to the Supreme Court." Unlike lesser courts, the Supreme Court of the United States may pick and choose the cases it considers. The only way to get them to consider your case is through an arcane procedure known as a Petition for Writ of Certiorari (pronounced "sur-shur-err-eye"). This is really a paperback book your attorney must have printed to convince the Supreme Court that your case presents fascinating legal issues of nationwide import that cry out for the Court's attention. The Court receives many thousands of such petitions each year, most from indigent and incarcerated prisoners who are relieved of the expense of a formal printing and may have nothing better to do with their time than sit in a prison's law library and generate petitions. In a typical year, the Supreme Court will choose to consider about 80 cases. Although it has been presented many opportunities to do so, the Supreme Court has never selected an FAA enforcement case for review. Face it: The odds are that the Supreme Court is not going to select your case for consideration, either.

Surrendering Your Certificate. If you don't appeal or you finally lose your appeal, you must physically surrender your certificate to the FAA for the suspension or revocation. It is not enough just to stop flying, and you will not begin to receive credit for the period of suspension until you have surrendered your certificate to the FAA. If you refuse to surrender your certificate at this point, the FAA will have the U.S. Attorney obtain an order from a U.S. District Judge for you to appear in court and explain why you have not surrendered your certificate. If you still refuse to surrender it, you may then be jailed for contempt of court until you surrender your certificate.

Emergency Cases. If the FAA decides that permitting you to continue to operate during the appeal process would unreasonably endanger aviation safety, it can issue an Emergency Order of Suspension or Revocation. An emergency order is effective to suspend or revoke the certificate at the moment it is delivered to the certificate holder. The certificate must be physically surrendered then and there, and continues to be invalid during the appeal process. Because this procedure effectively denies you the benefits of due process of law, the FAA typically uses emergency orders only in the most extreme cases of danger, as when an air carrier persists in operating unairworthy aircraft or an unqualified person continues to fly. For the same reason, the NTSB rules provide for extremely accelerated hearing and decision on emergency cases. In a nonemergency case, it typically takes about two years to go through the process of hearing and initial decision by the administrative law judge followed by briefing and a decision on appeal by the full board. In emergency cases, this entire process is required to be completed within 60 days. The recently enacted "Hoover Bill" (so-called because it resulted from an epic FAA abuse of its emergency authority in a case against legendary airshow performer Bob Hoover, which provoked a great uproar in the aviation community) was intended by Congress to provide some protection against FAA abuse of the emergency authority. Under this change in the law, a certificate holder who believes the use of the emergency authority is not justified has 48 hours from receipt of the emergency order to request the NTSB review the administrator's determination that an emergency exists. The board must decide that issue within five days. In practice, the Hoover Bill appears to have had little effect. In the first 200 cases in which the FAA's use of the emergency authority was challenged, the NTSB converted only 3 into nonemergency cases, thus allowing the certificate holder to continue to exercise the privileges of the certificate pending the outcome of the appeal.

Getting Your Certificate Back

If your certificate is suspended, it will be automatically returned to you by mail at the end of the period of suspension. *Revocation* may sound as though your certificate is gone forever, but that is not necessarily so. If the revocation resulted from a drug-related conviction involving the use of an aircraft, revocation is permanent. The only and rarely used exception is if the FAA is convinced that allowing you to be recertified will facilitate law enforcement efforts (perhaps as an incentive to persuade you to testify against higher-ups in a smuggling operation or to enable you to work undercover as a government informant).

Revocation for an FAR violation not having a drug crime connection, however, means that (unless the FAA otherwise agrees) you will usually be prohibited from applying for recertification for one year. After that year, to regain certification you will have to take and pass each of the written, oral, and practical (flight or other) tests for each certificate revoked (but you still get credit for your previous flight time or other applicable experience).

However, if it was an airline transport pilot (ATP) certificate that was revoked and if the basis for revocation was a falsification, recertification may be difficult. The FARs require that an ATP be of "good moral character." Although probably no vaguer regulation was ever written, it is safe to say that the FAA usually views a person who previously obtained or attempted to obtain a certificate or rating under false pretenses as lacking in good moral character.

Civil Penalties (Fines)

As previously noted, the FAA may choose to punish FAR violations by fines rather than by suspension or revocation of certificates. Individuals may be fined up to $1,000 pear violation, businesses and airport operators up to $10,000 per violation, and anyone (whether an individual or a business) up to $250,000 for falsification of documents. Against individuals who do not qualify for an administrative disposition, the FAA prefers to use certificate actions for operational violations and will usually allow the violator to pay a fine instead only for paperwork violations, such as failing to properly record maintenance actually performed. For violations committed by air carriers, air carrier airport operators, repair stations, and other aviation businesses who did not take advantage of self-reporting to obtain immunity, the FAA's policy prefers the use of fines. If, however, the violator's actions appear indicative of a management disposition not to obey the law, the FAA will instead act to suspend or revoke the company or airport operator's certificate. Where the violator does not hold an FAA-issued certificate (such as a person flying or maintaining an aircraft without the requisite certificate, or a parachute jumper, who is not required to hold an FAA certificate), a fine is the only punishment the FAA can impose.

The procedure in these cases is labyrinthine and depends upon whether at the time of the violation you were acting in the capacity of an airman or aircraft mechanic and how much money the FAA is trying to collect.

In any civil penalty case, you will receive some sort of letter notifying you what the FAA believes you did, what FARs they believe you violated, the maximum amount of the fine allowed by law, and usually an offer to compromise the case for some specified lesser amount. Although in these cases, the FAA attorney is not required to offer you the opportunity for an informal conference, she will usually afford you such a conference if you request it. Just as in a certificate action case, the informal conference can be a good opportunity for you and your attorney to sit down with the FAA attorney and inspector and discuss the situation frankly but off the record in an effort to negotiate a settlement of the case.

If settlement efforts fail and the FAA is seeking to impose a fine of no more than $50,000, it will issue an Order Assessing Civil Penalty under FAR 13.16. If the violator was acting in the capacity of an airman or aircraft mechanic in commission of the violation, the appeal goes to the NTSB and follows the identical appeal procedure described earlier for certificate actions.

A different procedure applies if the accused was not acting as an airman or aircraft mechanic in committing the violation. Most of these cases are airport security violations committed by the rather astonishing number of passengers who, even in the face of the well-advertised post-9/11 heightened airport security, present themselves for preboarding screening with a prohibited weapon on their person or in their baggage. In these cases, the appeal is first to a Department of Transportation (DOT) administrative law judge who holds a trial-type hearing, with the FAA having the burden of proof by a preponderance of the evidence. Appeal from the initial decision of the DOT ALJ in these cases goes to an FAA "decisionmaker" (an attorney in the FAA's Chief Counsel Office in Washington, D.C.) on appeal by either party. The decisionmaker's order is then appealable to the U.S. Court of Appeals, followed by a petition for certiorari to the Supreme Court of the United States, just like in a certificate action case.

If, however, the FAA is seeking to impose a fine of more than $50,000, it must turn the case over to the U.S. Attorney's office with a request that they file a civil lawsuit to collect the proposed fine. These cases are filed in the U.S. District Court (the federal trial court) and are heard by a U.S. District Judge under the Federal Rules of Civil Procedure and Federal Rules of Evidence. The accused can even demand a jury trial. Again, appeal is to the U.S. Court of Appeals followed by a petition for certiorari to the Supreme Court of the United States, under the same procedures described earlier for certificate actions.

Falsification

It is both an FAR violation and a federal felony (major crime) to make a false statement on any federal form or in your pilot logbooks or other documents you maintain or present to the FAA to show FAR compliance, qualification for a certificate or rating, or to prove currency. If you succumb to the temptation to exaggerate your experience or qualifications in your logbook or on an application for a certificate or rating, or falsify aircraft maintenance records, crew duty time, or training records, that folly may bring your aviation career to an abrupt halt, and you may find yourself spending years in jail.

For the FAR violation, the FAA will revoke every certificate and rating you hold (whether the particular certificate or rating was obtained by fraud or not) probably by an emergency order taking effect immediately. For the federal felony the U.S. Attorney will file criminal charges against you, punishable by up to five years in a federal prison and/or a $250,000 fine. Nothing infuriates the government in general and FAA in particular more than being lied to. This is understandable because our aviation certification programs are in large measure an honor system, and the integrity of that system depends on each of us being absolutely truthful with the FAA. For that reason, the FAA and the Justice Department (of which the U.S. Attorney's office is a part) prosecute falsification cases with a special vengeance.

Other crimes involving aviation are discussed in Chapter 15.

Clearing Your Record

Having an FAR violation on your record will put you at a competitive disadvantage for advancement in your aviation career. It may also increase the cost of your aircraft insurance, or even make you uninsurable.

Administrative dispositions, such as Warning Letters and Letters of Correction, are automatically deleted from your FAA airman record after two years.

2 : FAA Enforcement — 65

Until recently, all other records and enforcement actions remained on your record forever. Now under the FAA's new expunction policy, cases closed with no enforcement action taken are cleared off your record within 90 days and enforcement actions resulting in suspension of your certificate are cleared off your record after five years. Only records of enforcement action resulting in revocation of your certificate stay on your record for the rest of your life.

It should be apparent from this chapter that everyone involved in aviation, whether as a manager, flight crewmember, mechanic, or dispatcher, has a strong personal incentive to understand, keep abreast of changes to, and meticulously comply with the FARs. This is both to prevent aircraft accidents and to avoid fines or a suspension or revocation of your valuable FAA-issued certificates. It should also be apparent that whenever your efforts to comply fall short of perfection, everyone involved should promptly file an Aviation Safety Report with NASA and consult an attorney.

CHAPTER 3
Aviation Medical Cases

YOU MUST HOLD a current FAA medical certificate in order to serve as a pilot or air traffic control tower operator (except that glider and balloon pilots may self-certify that they have no known medical defects that would make them unable to pilot one of these aircraft).

The FAA's scrutiny of applications for medical certification is heightening with increasing accumulation of medical and related data on citizens in computer data banks of various government agencies and increasing cross-matching of this data between agencies. For example, in order to obtain an FAA medical certificate, you are now required to give the FAA written permission to access your driving record file in the National Driver Registry (NDR) database of traffic violations. This data is routinely crossmatched with information you provide for an FAA medical certificate. Aviators who are unaware of this process and the potential consequences frequently succumb to the temptation to be less than candid on applications for medical certification, with immediate and catastrophic results to their aviation careers. Personal, financial, or employer-imposed pressures may also lead a person who is not fully cognizant of the possible consequences to act as a pilot or required crewmember at a time when he is medically disqualified. The purpose of this chapter is to ensure that you have a practical working knowledge of how to analyze various aeromedical problems and dilemmas and arrive at the best solution or response.

I often see a classified ad listing an aircraft for sale telling a tale of tragedy of Shakespearean sadness encapsulated in the succinct phrase *Must sell, lost medical.*

It's not often that I'm moved almost to tears by *Trade-A-Plane* but that one gets me every time. I always want to call them up and say, "Wait! Before you sell your aircraft, are you sure you've done everything possible to get your medical certificate back?" You see, you don't always have to take no for a final decision.

Sometimes the FAA can be persuaded to change its mind and reinstate your medical and in some circumstances, the NTSB can order the FAA to issue or reinstate your medical certificate. We will now examine how the medical certification process and appeal procedure works. The procedure is very different from that of enforcement cases.

FAA Health Standards

Doctors and lawyers tend to communicate with their colleagues in their own professional languages, which are often largely unintelligible to outsiders. FAR Part 67, which describes the medical standards and certification procedures for aviators, was written by doctors and lawyers in a not particularly readable mixture of the languages of both professions. To make sense of the specific FAA medical standards, it is helpful to bear in mind that each of these standards was designed to enable the FAA to answer the following basic questions about your health:

1. Can you see well enough to control the aircraft, see and avoid other aircraft, distinguish runways from taxiways at night, and recognize light gun signals in the event of radio failure?
2. Can you speak and hear well enough to effectively converse with other crewmembers on a noisy flight deck and with air traffic controllers?
3. Are you likely to suffer disorienting vertigo or loss of equilibrium in flight?
4. Are you likely to suffer a suddenly incapacitating medical event in flight?
5. Are you likely to operate an aircraft irresponsibly so as to endanger other people?

The specific medical standards in Part 67 are designed so that if you have any medical condition that would result in an unfavorable answer to any of these basic questions, you are not qualified for an FAA medical certificate. Therefore, your Aviation Medical Examiner (AME) should not issue you a medical certificate if you fail to pass the hearing and vision requirements of Part 67 or if you have a history or diagnosis of any of the following "specific disqualifying conditions":

1. Diabetes requiring insulin or other hypoglycemic medication for control. (If your diabetes can be controlled by careful attention to diet, you are not disqualified.)

2. Heart attack (myocardial infarction).
3. Angina pectoris (the crushing chest pain that is your clue that you are having a heart attack).
4. Other evidence of coronary artery disease (such as an irregular electrocardiogram [EKG]).
5. Heart valve replacement.
6. Permanent cardiac pacemaker implantation.
7. Heart replacement (transplant).
8. A psychosis.
9. A personality disorder that has repeatedly manifested itself by overt acts.
10. A bipolar disorder (formerly known as manic depressive disorder).
11. Epilepsy.
12. A disturbance of consciousness without a satisfactory medical explanation of the cause.
13. A transient loss of control of nervous system function(s) without a satisfactory medical explanation of the cause (such as a so-called transient ischemic attack).
14. Substance dependence, abuse or misuse (including alcohol and a wide variety of drugs and controlled substances) within the previous 2 years.

Compare these "specific disqualifying conditions" to the previous basic questions the FAA is trying to answer about your health. The vision standards are designed to be sure that you can see well enough to control the aircraft, see and avoid other aircraft, distinguish runways from taxiways at night, and recognize light gun signals in the event of radio failure. Hearing and speech standards are to ensure you can communicate with other flight crewmembers on a noisy flight deck and with air traffic controllers.

Concern for risk of sudden and unpredictable in-flight incapacitation compels your AME to disqualify you if you are a diabetic requiring insulin (who may be incapacitated by insulin shock), have suffered a heart attack or have coronary artery disease (which can lead to an incapacitating heart attack). The same concern requires your AME to disqualify you if are epileptic, or have experienced a loss of consciousness without a satisfactory medical explanation (so that your next seizure might happen while you're at the controls of an aircraft in flight).

Concern over potential irresponsible operation of aircraft endangering others disqualifies people having a psychosis or other psychiatric problems that have led to irrational behavior, as well as substance abusers.

A "history or diagnosis" of any one of the specific disqualifying conditions prevents your AME from issuing you an FAA medical certificate regardless of how good your health may otherwise appear during the examination.

There are also catchall subparagraphs that disqualify you for any other physical condition that in the opinion of the Federal Air Surgeon could make it unsafe for you to exercise airman certificate privileges or if you are taking any medication or undergoing any course of treatment that would adversely affect your performance.

Some examples of physical conditions the Federal Air Surgeon has found disqualifying under this "other physical condition" catchall, depending on severity and treatment, include arthritis, asthma, chronic lymphocytic leukemia, colitis, colon cancer, glaucoma and ocular hypertension, hepatitis C, hyperthyroidism, hypothyroidism, lymphoma and Hodgkin's disease, migraine syndrome, prostate cancer, sleep apnea, and urolithiasis (kidney stones).

Some examples of medications the Federal Air Surgeon presently considers disqualifying include antidepressant or seratonin blocker drugs (SSRIs) such as Prozac, Paxil, and Zoloft.

Getting Certified When You Don't Meet the Standards

You may have a "history or diagnosis" of one of those specific disqualifying conditions or otherwise fail to meet Part 67 standards but now present no special risk. Perhaps you had a heart attack but then underwent heart surgery, quit smoking, went on a low-cholesterol diet, and are following a good exercise regimen so that you are now no more likely to have another heart attack than anyone else of your age. Maybe you were able to beat an alcohol or drug habit. Maybe the history or diagnosis was erroneous (doctors are human and sometimes make mistakes too). Or perhaps the Federal Air Surgeon has disqualified you because in his opinion your condition, medication, or current course of treatment is incompatible with safe flying. Your treating physicians may strongly disagree with the Federal Air Surgeon's opinion. Shouldn't you be free to fly? Yes, and if you can convince the FAA that despite your medical history you are now fit to fly, you can.

STATEMENT OF DEMONSTRATED ABILITY (SODA)

Pilots who have a static disability that is not expected to worsen may be certified through a process referred to a Statement of Demonstrated Ability (SODA).

Let's start with the easiest ones: vision and hearing problems. If your vision doesn't meet FAA standards without eyeglasses or contact lenses but does with these lenses, all that may be required is for your AME to add this limitation to your medical certificate: *"Holder shall wear correcting lenses while exercising the privileges of his/her airman certificate."*

If you failed the color-vision test, you may be able to get your medical certificate by arranging a test to determine whether you are able to distinguish between the red, green, and white of the control tower light gun that would give you directions in the event of a radio failure. If you can, you get your medical certificate even if your color vision isn't perfect. If your hearing is below standards but you can demonstrate that you can still hear and understand ATC instructions and flight deck conversation, you should be able to get your medical certificate, although it may have a limitation on it requiring you to use a noise-canceling headset while flying.

If you have a below-the-knee amputation of a leg from an accident, but have a prosthetic limb that generally enables you to function normally, and your AME is of the opinion that this would present no problem with operating the aircraft's controls, she has authority to issue you a student pilot certificate with the limitation "For Student Pilot Purposes Only" to enable you to take a check-ride with an FAA examiner. If you pass the check-ride by demonstrating that you are in fact able to operate all of the aircraft's controls despite your disability, you will be issued a SODA.

SPECIAL ISSUANCE

If your problem is a history or diagnosis of one of the specific disqualifying conditions, but you can prove that in spite of that history you are unlikely to become suddenly incapacitated while flying (or to fly irresponsibly), you may obtain an FAA medical certificate by "special issuance." The burden will be on you and your doctors to convince the Federal Air Surgeon that you are now an acceptable risk to flight safety. If you can, the Federal Air Surgeon has the discretionary authority to issue you any class of medical certificate by special issuance, even though you don't meet the letter of the law.

The one exception to this is the diabetic who requires insulin injections to control the disease. Until recently, the FAA considered insulin-treated diabetes mellitus (ITDM) absolutely disqualifying for any class of medical certificate. No special issuance medical certificates of any class were granted to individuals with ITDM. In response to a petition from the American Diabetes Association, the FAA has now opened third-class aviation medical certification by special issuance to individuals with ITDM who haven't experienced any further complications, such as heart or kidney disease, neurological abnormalities, or vision problems. The conditions for special issuance to individuals with ITDM, which include stringent monitoring requirements, are available on the FAA's website. This change has opened up the joy and freedom of personal flying (under a student, recreational, or private pilot certificate) to over 210 such individuals, at this writing. Flight operations by these individuals are, however, limited to the United States, as ICAO has yet to adopt comparable rules. It continues to be the FAA's position that individuals with ITDM still pose too great a risk of sudden incapacitation to allow first- or second-class medical certification, which would allow them to carry passengers for hire.

Periodic renewal of medical certificates issued under this special issuance process, once as slow and cumbersome as getting the first special issuance, is now being expedited under the FAA's new "Quick-Cert" program. This program is part of Federal Air Surgeon Dr. Jon Jordan's stated goal to provide "same-day medical certification" to qualified applicants.

The safety record of pilots operating under specially issued medical certificates has proven every bit as good as that of the general pilot population over the years, so this enlightened and humane process of personalized evaluation is likely to remain a feature of aviation medical certification.

RECONSIDERATION

Upon review of your application and completion of your examination, your AME has three alternative courses of action available: (1) if you appear qualified, issue the medical certificate, (2) if your qualifications are in question, defer the certification decision to FAA superiors, who review the question and decide whether to issue or deny your certificate, or (3) if you appear disqualified, deny your application.

If your AME defers issuance, the review process begins automatically without further action on your part, but if your AME denies you a medical certificate, you must request that he issue you a denial slip and forward your application to the FAA Aeromedical Certification Branch in Oklahoma City for reconsideration *of* the denial. If this step is not taken, you are considered to have withdrawn your application for a medical certificate.

If the Oklahoma City office also denies your application, it may be necessary for you to request further reconsideration by the Federal Air Surgeon in Washington, D.C., in order to preserve your appeal rights.

SUSPENSION OR REVOCATION

If while you hold a current medical certificate, the FAA learns that you are not medically qualified to hold that certificate, it may issue an or-

3 : Aviation Medical Cases   73

der of suspension or revocation of your medical certificate. Such orders are usually issued on an emergency basis, since your qualifications are in question.

APPEAL

If you receive a final denial of your application for a medical certificate from the FAA or the FAA issues an order of suspension or revocation of your existing medical certificate, you can appeal the decision to the NTSB. Your appeal will be heard by one of the board's administrative law judges, like the hearing you would receive on appeal of an enforcement case, as discussed in Chapter 2.

If the appeal is from an FAA order suspending or revoking your medical certificate, the FAA has the burden of proving by a preponderance of the evidence that you are not medically qualified. In the case of an FAA denial of your application for medical certificate, however, you have the burden of proving (again, by a preponderance of the evidence), through the sworn in-person testimony of qualified physicians supported by copies of your medical records, that you are qualified. In either case, if you convince the ALJ, the NTSB can order the FAA to issue you a medical certificate or set aside the FAA's order suspending or revoking your current medical certificate. From the ALJ, the route of appeal goes to the full board, court of appeals, and Supreme Court under the same procedures described for enforcement cases in Chapter 2.

Not all cases of denial, suspension, or revocation of a medical certificate are appropriate for appeal. If you have a history or diagnosis of one of the specific disqualifying conditions, and there is no real question that the history or diagnosis is accurate, appeal to the NTSB is futile. In that situation, the petition for special issuance is the only process by which you can have any hope of obtaining your medical certificate. If, however, the FAA position is based upon an erroneous or a subjective application of the catchall conditions, an appeal to the NTSB may succeed. If your physicians testify convincingly that your physical condition does not make you an especially risky pilot or that the medication or treatment you are taking is unlikely to interfere with your safe performance in flight, the NTSB may overrule the FAA.

TRUTH OR CONSEQUENCES

If you love flying, your periodic FAA medical exam is always a time for concern, because without a medical certificate, you can't fly powered aircraft as pilot-in-command. So when you sit down in your AME's office to fill out the application form to obtain or renew your medical certificate, you may be tempted to omit some details of your medical history or otherwise fail to tell the whole truth on that form (Fig. 3.1).

Although this temptation is understandable, it is a temptation you must resist. FAA medical certification is in large measure an honor system, the integrity of the entire process depending upon your truthfulness. If you succumb to temptation and obtain a medical certificate by false representations and are found out, the consequences will be horrendous.

As we saw in Chapter 2, it is both an FAR violation (FAR 61.59) and a federal felony (major crime) to make a false statement on any FAA form. For the FAR violation, the FAA will revoke not only your medical certificate but also all pilot and other FAA-issued certificates you hold, probably by an emergency order taking effect immediately. For the criminal violation, the U.S. Attorney will file charges against you punishable by up to five years in a federal prison and/or a $250,000 fine. Nothing infuriates the FAA more than being lied to, and it and the Justice Department (of

Fig. 3.1. No one looks forward to taking an exam, and the periodic medical examination required to exercise the privileges of your certificate is no exception. The temptation to cheat is always present, but the potential consequences of giving false or incomplete information can be career ending.

3 : Aviation Medical Cases   75

which the U.S. Attorney's office is a part) prosecute falsification cases with a special vengeance.

This extends not only to medical information called for on the application form but also to all questions on the form. For example, questions 18.v. and w. on the application form (Fig. 3.2) ask whether you have a history of certain alcohol- or drug-related traffic convictions or a history of other misdemeanor or felony convictions. The answers you give on this application will be automatically compared to information already entered in the National Driver Registry (NDR) database, which includes reports of traffic convictions from all 50 states. The National Crime Information Center (NCIC) computer database contains records of other convictions from all states as well as federal criminal convictions. If you have a record of an applicable traffic or other conviction but deny this on your application for an FAA medical certificate, these computers will compare notes and catch you and you will be prosecuted. You must answer all questions on the application form truthfully.

Having a record of such a conviction doesn't necessarily disqualify you from receiving a medical certificate. Those questions are on the form because the FAA is looking for clues that you may have (1) an alcohol or drug problem (as might be suggested by convictions for driving under the influence) or (2) a psychiatric disorder (such as a sociopathic personality, which might be suggested by a criminal record) that might cause you to fly irresponsibly.

If you truthfully reveal a single conviction, it probably won't even slow down the issuance of your medical certificate.

Changes in Your Health

What if your health changes for the worse while you hold an unexpired FAA medical certificate? Are you required to report the change to the FAA? Not until you next apply for a medical certificate and then only if one or more of the questions on the application form covers it. Are you required to stop flying? It depends. If what has happened to you since your medical certificate was issued is one of the specific disqualifying conditions; a deterioration of your vision or hearing that puts you below FAA certification standards; or a condition, medication, or course of treatment that unquestionably makes it unsafe for you to serve as a pilot, FAR 61.53 mandates that you refrain from exercising pilot privileges. You don't have to tell anybody and you don't have to surrender your medical certificate, but you do have to stop acting as a pilot or other required flight crewmember (such as a flight engineer on some airline aircraft). If you continue to exercise pilot privileges, you risk FAA enforcement ac-

Fig. 3.2. FAA application for aviation medical certificate.

tion (which would almost certainly take the form of an emergency revocation of your pilot certificate), and your aviation insurance company would be in a position to deny coverage for any accident occurring during such operations.

If on the other hand the medical event does not fit within one of these categories, you have to use your own best judgment. If the medical problem is something that can lead to an unpredictable and suddenly incapacitating event in flight, you should stop flying. If your medical condition, medication, or course of treatment may impair your judgment or ability to control the aircraft precisely, to see and avoid other aircraft, to understand and follow the instructions of air traffic controllers, or otherwise perform competently as a pilot, you should stop flying. One of the responsibilities we have as members of the aviation community is to use good judgment and not fly when we don't feel up to it. Even if it may be technically legal, it just isn't prudent and as we will see in greater detail in Chapter 4, it may be negligence to do something that is not prudent.

If you are taking medication (whether by prescription or off-the-shelf) ask yourself: "Can this drug affect my vision, alertness, judgment, or sense of balance?" If it's a prescription medicine, ask your doctor. If it's an off-the-shelf medicine (such as a cold remedy), consult the label or package insert. The Physicians Desk Reference (PDR), available from most booksellers, is also a good reference to check. If the answer is yes, FAR 91.17(a)(3) requires that you refrain from acting as a pilot or other required flight crewmember while you are taking the medication and until it is effectively out of your system. In order to predict when the medication will be effectively out of your system, the FAA and medical profession agree that the best rule of thumb is to wait twice the recommended dosage period after the last dose was taken. For example, if the instructions call for taking a dose every 4 hours, you could expect to be free of the medication's side effects 8 hours after taking the last dose. If the instructions call for a dosage range, such as every 4–6 hours, then you should use the longer period in making this computation and wait 2 x 6 = 12 hours. Then you are legal to resume flying *unless* the symptoms have returned. While you are reading the label or package insert watch for hidden alcohol, especially in cough syrups and liquid decongestants such as NyQuil, which could also bring into play the 8-hour and other criteria of FAR 91.17.

Do not fly if you have a cold or sinus infection. Changing atmospheric pressure encountered with climbing and descending can cause serious sinus and ear problems, including the risk of major permanent damage, and the pain caused by a sinus block may be so excruciating as to incapacitate you as a pilot. Use your best judgment, watching out for wishful thinking and rationalization, and don't fly if it wouldn't be wise.

Required Reports

You are not required to report a change in your health to the FAA before your next application for a medical certificate. You must, however, report any conviction for a drug- or alcohol-related traffic offense or the denial, cancellation, suspension, or revocation of your driver's license related to such an offense. Under FAR 61.15, this report must be filed with the FAA Civil Aviation Security Division (AAC-700), PO. Box 25810, Oklahoma City, OK 73125, not later than 60 days after the conviction or motor vehicle action. The interagency computer interface described earlier is keeping such a close watch in this area that the FAA sometimes issues an order of suspension or revocation for failure to make the report by the 61st or 62nd day! The FAA and NTSB agree that you are required to make this report even if you aren't doing any flying, and even if you don't have a current medical certificate, for as long as you hold a pilot certificate. Don't forget!

Requests for Additional Medical Information

Whenever the FAA has some reasonable basis to suspect that you may not be qualified to hold a medical certificate, it can request that you furnish additional medical information or submit to further medical testing in the area in question. If you receive such a request, you are required to comply promptly and at your own expense. Failure to furnish the additional information requested is sound legal ground for the FAA to suspend or revoke your medical certificate under FAR 67.31 until you provide the information.

Drug and Alcohol Testing

Mandatory drug and alcohol testing has become a routine requirement throughout the aviation industry. The Supreme Court has found drug and alcohol testing (both in prehire screening and random sampling of employees) in transportation-related jobs to be constitutional.

Refusal to submit to a mandatory drug or alcohol test is grounds for suspension or revocation of your pilot certificate under FARs 61.14(b) and 91.17(c).

Accident statistics show a significant correlation between alcohol use and aircraft accidents, so the FAA has given very high priority to identifying pilots who abuse or are dependent upon alcohol or drugs and grounding them until they have recovered.

Get Help

The FAA's medical bureaucracy can be extremely frustrating to deal with, and it's easy to miss a crucial procedural step or have your application get lost in the bureaucratic maze and seem to go around in circles for years awaiting a decision. An attorney who is knowledgeable in FAA medical certification procedures can be a tremendous help in evaluating your situation, choosing the best approach to the problem, and organizing and presenting the medical information to the FAA or NTSB in the most cogent and persuasive form.

Members of the Aircraft Owners & Pilots Association (AOPA) and the Experimental Aircraft Association (EAA) can get help with medical certification problems through these organizations, as well. The "Members Only" sections of both organizations' websites are a good place to start.

To read more about FAA aviation medical certification standards and some valuable tips on how to stay in shape to pass your aviation medical exams, see Dr. Richard O. Reinhart's book, *FAA Medical Certification: Guidelines for Pilots (3d ed),* also published by the Iowa State University Press.

PART II

Aircraft Accidents

CHAPTER 4

Basic Principles of Liability

THE LAW IS generally subdivided into administrative, civil, and criminal law. In the preceding part, we examined the workings of administrative law, law made and enforced by administrative agencies in the aviation industry. We also touched on the criminal law implications of falsifying applications for FAA certificates and other records required by the federal government and for security violations. Criminal law aspects of aviation security, an area undergoing rapid change in the wake of the terrorist attacks of 9/11/01, will be further explored in greater detail in Chapter 15. For now, we will turn our attention to the civil law, which may be further subdivided into *tort* law and *contract* law. In this part on aircraft accidents, we will examine the workings of tort law and techniques available to reduce the risk of liability for the consequences of aircraft accidents. In the following part on aircraft transactions, we will examine contract law in the context of buying, selling, leasing, time-sharing and managing aircraft.

This chapter introduces the basic principles of liability and procedures for civil litigation arising out of aircraft accidents, building the foundation for the rest of this part, which focuses on risk management techniques useful to avoid such liability. The purpose of this chapter is to ensure that you have a working knowledge of the kinds of behavior you must refrain from to avoid such liability.

What Is a Tort?

A tort is not what the Queen of Hearts served for dessert. A tort is an act or omission that causes injury to another person by breach of a legal duty not arising out of a contract and subjects the actor to liability for damages in a civil lawsuit.

Whenever you read a headline like this one from a recent *USA Today*: "Jury awards $480 million to 3 hurt in plane crash," you are almost certainly reading about a tort case. Chapters 5 through 10 will cover risk management techniques to reduce the impact of tort liability for aviation accidents, including selection of an appropriate form of organization for the aviation business, insurance, exculpatory contracts, and statutes and international agreements that limit the tort liability of airlines and governments. This chapter focuses on basic principles of tort liability.

Torts may be further subdivided into two kinds: *intentional torts* and *negligence.*

Intentional Torts

Intentional torts are all "acts" while negligence may consist of either an act or an omission. Some intentional torts are also crimes under federal, state, or local law, and may also be FAR violations. In such a case, the wrongdoer may be not only subject to a fine or imprisonment in a criminal action, but also ordered to pay compensation to the victim in a civil tort action and fined or subjected to certificate suspension or revocation by the FAA or other federal or state regulatory agencies—all for the same misbehavior. The courts have generally held that this is not *double jeopardy,* which is prohibited by the Constitution of the United States, interpreting that provision only to prohibit the government from *criminally* penalizing a person twice for the same misdeed.

For example, state criminal charges including 110 counts of murder and 110 counts of manslaughter (one of each for each person killed in the crash) were filed against SabreTech, Inc., an airline maintenance contractor, and several of its employees in connection with the 1996 ValuJet DC-9 crash in the Florida Everglades, a crash that also gave rise to extensive civil litigation and FAA enforcement action. The state criminal action was ultimately settled for a $500,000 fine.

Meanwhile, a federal grand jury indictment charged SabreTech with several criminal violations of the Hazardous Materials Transportation Act in connection with the crash. In that case, the trial judge sentenced SabreTech to pay $2 million in criminal penalties and $9 million in restitution to victim's families (over and above the civil settlements already reached). This was the first time an aviation business was convicted of criminal charges arising out of a commercial jet airliner crash in the U.S., and some legal analysts suspect that the fine would have been much larger if the company had not already been in bankruptcy at the time. On appeal, the U.S. Court of Appeals overturned the $9 million portion of the sentence for restitution.

4 : Basic Principles of Liability

In the civil (tort) action, SabreTech and its insurers paid out some $262 million in settlements to the families of the victims.

In addition, the FAA initiated a $2.23 million civil penalty action against SabreTech for related FAR violations. The company settled that case by a compromise agreement to pay the FAA $1.75 million.

Now, let's look at some intentional torts that may arise in an aviation context, exposing a person and his or her employer to civil liability.

BATTERY

Battery is a harmful or offensive contact with another person with intent to cause the contact or apprehension of contact and without the consent of the other person (or where consent is obtained by fraud or duress). This could range from punching a person in the nose to uninvited sexually oriented contact.

ASSAULT

An *assault is* simply an attempted battery that missed. If you tried to punch someone in the nose but he ducked and you missed, you have committed the intentional tort of assault.

INTENTIONAL INFLICTION OF MENTAL DISTRESS

The name of this intentional tort is an accurate description of what you are prohibited from doing. Here is an example: A flight instructor is aloft in a trainer with a student. The student pilot keeps repeating the same mistake. The flight instructor, in a fit of temper, reaches over and releases the student's seat belt while rolling the airplane into a very steep bank toward the student's side, grasps the handle of the cabin door beside the student, and threatens to expel the student. That is *intentional infliction of mental distress.*

FALSE IMPRISONMENT

Anyone can commit the intentional tort of false imprisonment; you don't have to be a law enforcement officer. *False imprisonment* consists of intentionally confining, restraining, or detaining another person against her will. This occurs most often in the aviation industry in the debt-collection context when people or businesses resort to some use of force instead of litigation to collect a debt. Here's an example: An FBO's manager notices on the ramp an aircraft belonging to a person who owes the FBO some money. The manager sends a line service attendant out to block the aircraft's departure with a gas truck and to physically drag the owner into the office. That's false imprisonment.

FALSE ARREST

False arrest and false imprisonment sound so similar that fiendish professors are especially fond of asking you to distinguish between them on examinations. *A false arrest is* a false imprisonment carried out by a false or erroneous assertion of legal authority to detain the other person. An example of a false arrest would occur if the line service attendant in the previous example went out to restrain the debtor aircraft owner and found a very large, ill-tempered, and capable adversary. Deciding to outwit rather than attempt to overpower the owner, the quick-thinking attendant approaches the owner from the rear, pokes a finger in his ribs and shouts: "Freeze! FBI! Lock your hands behind your head and come with me. Don't make any fast moves." This false assertion of legal authority ("FBI!") escalates this false imprisonment into a false arrest. The same might be true if you tried to make a "citizen's arrest" of someone you observed violating an FAR. The legal authority to perform a citizen's arrest is generally limited to felonies (major crimes like murder, robbery, or burglary) and does not extend to misdemeanors, violations of administrative regulations, or civil matters such as debt collection.

TRESPASS

Trespass is an intentional invasion of someone else's land. This intentional tort comes into play most frequently in aviation in the context of off-airport landings or landings on airports that are not open to the public, without prior permission of the owner.

Your intent can be determinative of whether you committed a trespass. If you are flying along and suddenly experience a catastrophic engine failure, pick the most suitable open area within gliding distance, and land there without permission, most courts would hold that you did not commit a trespass. That is because you did not intend to invade the landowner's property, but did so only in response to the emergency. At the other extreme, if you are out flying around and decide to land without prior permission in someone's field or on an airport not open to the public to practice your short or soft-field landing technique or have a picnic, any court would agree that you were trespassing.

Something of a legal gray area exists in flight operations that are routinely expected to terminate in off-airport landings, such as free flight in hot-air balloons and cross-country glider flying. In the absence of a real and credible in-flight emergency, most courts would probably find these landings to constitute trespassing. Thus, in these operations, pilots and ground crews should take special care to obtain the landowner's permission before landing (for example, by orally hailing the landowner from the low-flying balloon or radioing the ground crew to go ahead to the farmhouse to request permission to land and before driving recovery vehicles into the landing area). All possible care should be taken to avoid damaging standing crops and fences or frightening livestock in the landing and recovery efforts. A humble, respectful, and apologetic attitude, coupled with an immediate and sincere offer to pay for any damage caused by the landing and recovery crews, may appease the landowner and prevent a legal or physical confrontation.

CONVERSION

In legal language, this is not what a modifier does to your airplane to make it go faster. Think of conversion as being to personal property (such as someone else's airplane) as trespass is to someone else's land. *Conversion* is defined as the act of assuming rights to personal property that are inconsistent with the rights of the owner or person entitled to possession. As an example, if you somehow obtained a key and took someone's airplane joyriding without his permission, you would commit the intentional tort of conversion.

Conversion also sometimes occurs during improper debt-collection methods. For example, an FBO manager spots an airplane belonging to a person who owes the FBO money on a competitor's ramp. The manager sends an employee down the line with a tug to pull the airplane back to the FBO's hangar and locks it up to hold it until the debt is paid. This may constitute a conversion. (Circumstances under which liens against aircraft for services, fuel, parts, etc., provided to the aircraft may be exceptions to the law of conversion are examined later in Chapter 11.)

An interesting feature of the law of conversion is that it gives the aircraft owner the option to sue for either (1) money damages (for the consequences of being deprived of the use of the aircraft while it was in the converter's possession) or (2) a court order that the converter has bought the aircraft, compelling payment of its fair market value. (You took it; you bought it. Pay for it.)

The general theme you may have noticed running through these intentional torts is that the law encourages respect for the personal and property rights of others. The law frowns on resort to force or threat of force to resolve controversies instead of reason, persuasion, and (if all else fails) court procedures. When asked what he thought of Western civilization, Gandhi is reported to have replied: "I think it would be a good idea." The law of intentional torts is an effort in that direction, preferring the use of civilized means to dissolve disputes and seeking to avoid situations that may provoke violence.

Negligence and Liability

Negligence is the most common form of tort involved in aircraft accident litigation. If there is a common theme running through all facets of American law—administrative, civil, and criminal—it is this: You *are responsible for the consequences of your actions.*

Negligence means failing to do an act that a reasonably careful person would do to protect others from harm or doing an act that a reasonably careful person would not do under the same or similar circumstances.

The four elements of a negligence case are (1) a *duty* to be reasonably careful, (2) *a failure* to be reasonably careful, (3) which is the *proximate cause* of (4) *injury* to another person or her property.

If you are not reasonably careful and injure someone or damage his property you will be found negligent and will have to pay the other person (or his survivors) for the damage you caused.

Let's examine each of these elements in greater detail in the context of aviation accidents.

DUTY

Your *duty* to be reasonably careful to avoid harming others extends to anyone who might foreseeably be injured by your neglect. Whether you are a flight crewmember, an aircraft owner/operator, a manufacturer of aircraft or components, an airport owner/operator, an aircraft mechanic or inspector, an air traffic controller, or other person involved in aviation, you have a duty to be reasonably careful. That duty extends to everyone who could foreseeably suffer harm if you are not careful. This could include, for example, other flight crewmembers, passengers, people on the ground and their property, the owner of the aircraft and the owners of any personal property carried aboard the aircraft.

FAILURE TO USE CARE

Who decides whether you were "reasonably careful" under the circumstances, and how? The jury or (if you do not request a jury) the trial judge decides whether you were reasonably careful. It is unlikely that either the judge or the jurors will have any aviation background. Instead, they will rely upon the testimony of aviation expert witnesses, the FARs, and other written guidance introduced as exhibits at trial.

If mandatory government standards such as an FAR or Airworthiness Directive (AD) state what you must do, then that is what is reasonable. Otherwise, the question the judge or jury must decide is what "a reasonably prudent person" in your position would have done under the circumstances.

4 : Basic Principles of Liability   89

Nonmandatory guidance such as the *Aeronautical Information Manual* (AIM) and Advisory Circulars (AC), along with the opinions of aviation expert witnesses who testify at trial, may be considered.

INJURY
Ordinarily, this must be real physical *injury* or property damage, not just frightening someone. If, however, you've inflicted mental distress that resulted in an emotional breakdown requiring hospitalization, it would be considered real physical injury.

Even if you were not reasonably careful, if your carelessness did not actually cause such harm to someone, you cannot be successfully sued for negligence. For example: You failed to perform an adequate preflight inspection, attempted to take off on almost empty fuel tanks, and the engine quit on takeoff. But when it did, you were able to abort the takeoff without damaging the aircraft or harming its occupants or anyone else. In that situation, you could not successfully be sued for negligence since there was no injury. (But that will not stop the FAA from suspending or revoking your pilot certificate for careless operation under FAR 91.13, inadequate preflight action under FAR 91.103, or for your lack of the care, judgment, and responsibility required of the holder of a pilot certificate.)

PROXIMATE CAUSE
Your neglect must have actually caused the injury, at least by setting in motion a sequence of events that would not otherwise have occurred. Indeed, most aviation accidents result not from a single mistake but from a series of errors that snowball and cause the accident. The legal concept of *proximate cause* is not the same thing as the NTSB's finding of probable cause. Nor will the NTSB's opinion of probable cause be admissible as evidence at trial. However, facts found by NTSB investigators during their investigation of the accident will be admissible at trial.

For example: A single-engine general aviation aircraft flying from San Francisco to Denver reports an engine stoppage to ATC over the Colorado Rockies. The aircraft is substantially damaged attempting a forced landing, and its occupants are seriously injured. The NTSB is notified, and an investigator heads for the scene. Having first determined the time the aircraft took off from San Francisco and the time the engine stoppage was reported to ATC, and knowing the standard fuel capacity and burn rate for the type of aircraft involved, the investigator suspects fuel exhaustion. Arriving at the scene of the accident, the investigator sniffs around, but smells no avgas. He removes the overturned aircraft's fuel caps. No fuel runs out, nor can he find any trace of leaked fuel on the ground. Then, the investigator probes the fuel tanks with a dipstick, but still finds no fuel. A salvage crew dispatched by the owner's insurance company arrives on the scene to dismantle the aircraft and haul it out. The NTSB investigator watches as the aircraft's wings are disconnected from the fuselage and asks the salvage crew to stand each wing on end, root downward. No fuel runs out. Based upon these facts observed by the investigator, the NTSB later determines the probable cause of the accident to have been the pilot's inadequate preflight planning and failure to properly monitor his fuel supply, resulting in in-flight fuel exhaustion.

When the injured passengers sue the pilot for negligence, the NTSB investigator's testimony as to what he did and what he saw would be admitted into evidence. Then, instead of being able to use the NTSB's finding of probable cause as evidence, the plaintiffs would have to hire their own expert witness to analyze the facts found by the investigator and testify to an opinion of the proximate cause of the accident, based upon those facts. That opinion may, of course, well be the same one the NTSB expressed in its finding of probable cause.

There may be more than one proximate cause of an accident, and more than one person's negligence may be proximate causes of the accident. Consider this example: A student pilot is flying solo, shooting touch-and-go landings at a tower-controlled airport in a rented light trainer. The controller observes the student pilot turning onto a close-in base leg that will bring the trainer into a position on final approach close behind a landing heavy jet. The controller, however, fails to instruct the student to extend downwind or to warn the student of the possibility of wake turbulence from the heavy jet. The student encounters the wake turbulence on short final, loses control of the airplane and crashes, destroying the rented trainer. Under these circumstances, a judge or jury might find that the student pilot, the student's instructor, and the air traffic controller each owed a duty to the aircraft owner not to allow the aircraft to encounter wake turbulence, to avoid risk of damage to the trainer. In this case, the judge or jury might find that the student pilot, the student's instructor, and the controller had each failed to exercise reasonable care to avoid this accident. The judge or jury might find that each of them proximately caused the accident: the student (by failing to recognize and avoid the potential wake turbulence encounter), the instructor (by failing to teach the student wake turbulence recognition and avoidance techniques), and the controller (by failing to warn and guide the student away from the observed danger).

Where multiple defendants are found negligent, some states allow judges and juries to apportion the percentage of negligence among them

4 : Basic Principles of Liability

(as fractions of 100%) and to apportion the resulting damage accordingly. In these states, if the trainer that was destroyed was worth $150,000 and the judge or jury apportioned the negligence equally among the student, instructor, and ATC, then each would be liable to the aircraft owner for $50,000. Some states provide for *joint and several liability* in such cases, with no apportionment by the court. In these states, even if more than one defendant is found negligent, the victorious plaintiff can collect the entire judgment ($150,000 in this example) from any defendant found negligent. In these states, plaintiffs' attorneys tend to follow the path of least resistance by enforcing their judgment against the defendant having the "deepest pockets" (the one most able to pay).

Proof of Negligence

The procedure at trial is that the plaintiff (the person who claims to be injured) must first present evidence to prove each of the four elements of negligence to satisfy the *burden of proof*. Here, too, the proof must be by a *preponderance of the evidence* (51%), not beyond a reasonable doubt. There are, however, a few legal exceptions to this procedure that may lighten the plaintiff's burden of proof under some circumstances.

NEGLIGENCE PER SE

Where the plaintiff can prove that the accident resulted from violation of an FAR intended to prevent such accidents, the FAR violation also constitutes civil negligence as a matter of law. If an FAA finding of such a violation has already become final (either because the aviator or company failed to appeal or defend an enforcement action, or because all appeals have been exhausted and the FAA's finding has been affirmed), that finding may be used in a subsequent civil trial to prove negligence. This is known as the doctrine of *res judicata* (the thing is decided). If not, the judge or jury may take the FAR into account and make a finding in the civil trial of whether the regulation was violated. In either case, such a finding of negligence as a matter of law based upon an FAR violation is called *negligence per se* (as such). Therefore, complying with the FARs and defending against charges of FAR violations takes on special importance in civil litigation. Losing (or failing to defend) an FAA enforcement case arising out of an accident may also cause you to lose the civil suit!

RES IPSA LOQUITUR

The legal doctrine of *res ipsa loquitur* (the facts speak for themselves) can be relied upon by a plaintiff to prove negligence, even if no one knows what really happened to the aircraft, if the accident is not the sort of thing that normally occurs unless someone was negligent;

the aircraft involved in the accident was within the exclusive control of the defendant (person or business being sued); and

whatever happened, the accident was not caused by any fault of the plaintiff.

This doctrine effectively relieves the plaintiff of the burden of proving some specific act of carelessness proximately caused the accident. It has been used successfully by survivors of passengers where an airliner has crashed and the cause of the crash could not be determined, as when the aircraft was lost at sea.

STRICT LIABILITY FOR DEFECTIVE PRODUCT

A person (or business) selling any product (including an aircraft or aircraft component) delivered in a defective condition unreasonably dangerous to the purchaser, an anticipated user, or other persons in the area of anticipated use is *strictly liable* even if the seller was careful if

the seller is in the business of selling such a product; and

the product is expected to be used without substantial change in the condition in which it is sold.

In such a case, negligence need not be proved and the seller is liable for resulting injury to users and others even if the seller exercised all possible care in the manufacture, inspection, and sale of the product and even if the seller had no contract with the injured person.

This is *common law* (law made by judges deciding cases over the years, as distinguished from *statutory law* made by legislatures and *regulations* adopted by administrative agencies). The courts have always given high priority to protecting people's health and safety as a matter of public policy. In the area of product liability, the courts have reasoned that manufacturers of products and others in the stream of commerce (such as distributors and dealers) are in the best position to ensure that products delivered to customers are safe. The courts believe that the best way to make those businesses exercise every possible effort to ensure safe products is to make them pay every time someone is injured by an unsafe product.

Note that this applies only to injuries and damage to persons and property, *other than the product itself*, caused by the defect. Damage to the product itself (such as a defective aircraft) is covered by warranty law, which we will discuss later in Chapter 11. Bear in mind that strict liability for defective products applies only where the seller is in the business of selling such products and not to a private sale by a private owner. Even an airline that routinely sells many of its aircraft each year as it upgrades or "right-sizes" its fleet is not exposed to this strict liability if it sells a dangerously defective airplane, because the airline is in the business of carrying passengers and freight, not selling airplanes.

STRICT LIABILITY FOR ULTRAHAZARDOUS ACTIVITIES

The courts may also impose strict liability without regard for negligence where a nonparticipant is injured as a result of the defendant's conducting what the court considers to be an *ultrahazardous activity*. For example, if farm workers or nearby residents were poisoned by an aerial application of restricted-use pesticides, a court may deem that application to be an ultrahazardous activity and hold the aerial applicator strictly liable for the consequences, even if the defendant had used reasonable care in the application.

Defenses

Once the plaintiff has carried the burden of proving negligence at trial, either by proof of the four basic elements or by proving negligence per se, *res ipsa loquitur,* or strict liability for a defective product or ultrahazardous activity, the burden then shifts to the defendant. To prevail, the defendant must then present evidence to rebut the plaintiff's proof and support any legal defenses asserted. Such defenses may include:

SUDDEN EMERGENCY

Under the *sudden emergency doctrine,* the law recognizes that the stresses imposed by the sudden onset of an in-flight emergency situation may interfere with human decision-making. Imagine that you take off in a fully loaded multiengine aircraft on a high-density altitude day and an engine quits 50 feet over the lake at the end of the runway. Imagine, instead that you have the luxury of a night to study the *Pilot's Operating Handbook* in the comfort of your library and draft an essay on emergency procedures in the event of engine failure on takeoff. In which of these imaginary situations are you most likely to arrive at the right answer in time?

By applying the sudden emergency doctrine, the judge or jury weighing the reasonableness of your behavior may take into account the sudden emergency. Thus, an imperfect performance that might otherwise have been considered not reasonably careful could still be found not to constitute negligence in the face of a sudden emergency.

You do not, however, get the benefit of this reduced standard of care if your own prior negligence caused the emergency. For example: If the engine failure in our example resulted from fuel starvation caused by either your attempt to take off on almost empty fuel tanks following an inadequate preflight inspection, or your failure to select the proper fuel tank for takeoff because you did not follow the pre-takeoff checklist in the airplane flight manual, the sudden emergency doctrine would not relieve you of responsibility for the consequences of the resulting crash.

ASSUMPTION OF RISK

If the injured person can be proved to have known and understood the scope, nature, and extent of the risk involved in the flight and to have voluntarily and freely chosen to incur that risk, the *assumption of risk doctrine* may serve to relieve others of legal responsibility for harm befalling that person.

Consider the following scenario: An aeronautical engineer who is a professional experimental test pilot and also holds an airline transport pilot certificate with flight instructor rating goes flying with a friend in the friend's aircraft, which is placarded against intentional spins. In the air, the engineer-pilot says, "I've heard that these babies really go flat in a spin and can't be recovered." The owner-friend replies, "Aw, that's an old wives' tale, and nothing could be further from the truth. It's very docile and easy to recover. Would you like me to show you?" The engineer-pilot enthusiastically replies, "I sure would!" The owner deliberately spins the aircraft and the spin goes flat. The owner is unable to affect a recovery and crashes, injuring the engineer-pilot. Under these facts, a judge or jury might find that, given his background, the engineer-pilot knew and understood the scope, nature, and extent of the risk involved and voluntarily and freely chose to incur that risk. The engineer-pilot having assumed the risk, his former friend (the owner of the aircraft) should not be held liable to pay for the engineer-pilot's injuries.

Contrast this scenario: The same owner has taken a friend with no aviation background flying in the same airplane. After takeoff, the passenger inquires about the placard: "What does this mean, 'intentional spins prohibited'?" The owner replies: "Oh, that's a bunch of FAA bull. This baby spins and recovers like a dream. Here, I'll show you." The owner deliberately spins the aircraft, the spin goes flat, the owner is unable to recover, the airplane crashes, and the passenger is injured. Under these facts, a judge or jury would almost certainly find that the injured passenger, having no aviation background or knowledge, was unlikely to have known or understood the scope, nature, and extent of the risk of spinning that airplane and did not voluntarily and freely choose to incur that risk. Thus, the doctrine of assumption of risk would not apply to relieve the owner of legal liability to pay for this passenger's injuries.

CONTRIBUTORY NEGLIGENCE

If the plaintiff's negligence was also a proximate cause of the accident, this fact may reduce the extent of the defendant's liability or relieve the defendant of all liability. Most states have now adopted a *comparative negligence* approach. This allows the judge or jury to decide what percentage of the proximate cause of the accident was attributable to the defendant and what percentage resulted from the plaintiff's own (contributory) negligence, then apportion liability for the plaintiff's injuries accordingly. A few states, however, still follow the harsh and old-fashioned contributory negligence approach, which holds that if the accident was even slightly the fault of the person injured, that person is not entitled to any compensation from anyone else, no matter how negligent that someone else may have been.

Among states having the more modern comparative negligence laws, two different general approaches to the apportionment of liability are found. In some states, the jury simply makes a finding of percentages and then apportions liability for the plaintiff's injuries accordingly. In states following this approach, the result is pretty simple. Say a jury in one of these states found that an accident was caused 60% by the plaintiff's carelessness and only 40% by the defendant's carelessness. If the jury further found that the plaintiff had suffered $1 million in injuries (medical expenses, lost income, etc.), then by applying the 60–40 split, the defendant would be liable to pay the plaintiff $400,000 and the plaintiff would have to bear the other $600,000 of loss. Other states draw a line, usually at 50%. In these states, if the jury finds the plaintiff's contributory negligence accounted for 50% or less of the cause, the apportionment process described above applies, but if the jury finds the plaintiff's contributory negligence to have been more than 50% of the cause, the defendant has no liability. If more than one defendant is found negligent, some states provide for further apportionment among them, while others impose joint and several liability among all negligent defendants, as discussed earlier.

Under the humanitarian doctrine of *last clear chance,* a defendant cannot rely upon the plaintiff's contributory negligence to escape liability if the facts show that even though the plaintiff was negligent, the defendant had the last clear chance to extricate the plaintiff from a position of peril. This is another example of the courts striving to protect people's health and safety. Thus, if a pedestrian carelessly steps out in front of your car as you are approaching a green light, you must still step on your brakes and try to avoid running over the person. Likewise, an air traffic controller observing on radar an aircraft receiving ATC services descending below a minimum safe altitude in a mountainous area is encouraged to alert the flight crew of their error before an impact with the ground results.

GOVERNMENT CONTRACTORS

The government contractor defense shields manufacturers from liability for injuries and death to both military and civilian personnel caused by the manufacturer's products that are ordered by the government for military use (Fig. 4.1). The defense protects the manufacturer only from design defects, and not manufacturing defects. Liability for design defects cannot be imposed upon a civilian manufacturer of military equipment if

> The United States approved reasonably precise specifications;
> The equipment conformed to those specifications; and
> The manufacturer warned the United States about any dangers in the use of the equipment that were known to the supplier but not to the United States.

The defense continues to protect the manufacturer even after the equipment passes into civilian hands.

Fig. 4.1. Manufacturers of aircraft designed to government specifications for military use may be shielded from suit by the government contractor defense.

STATUTES OF LIMITATION

All states have *statutes of limitation* that impose time limits on how long a person has after an injury to file suit or be forever barred. These vary from state to state and according to the nature of the case.

STATUTES OF REPOSE

Statutes of repose impose time limits on how long after a product is manufactured the manufacturer may be held liable for injuries caused by defects in the product (whether in design or fabrication and whether brought under a strict liability or a negligence theory).

Under the provisions of the *General Aviation Revitalization Act (GARA)* passed by Congress in late 1994, there is now a federal 18-year statute of repose for FAA-certified general aviation aircraft having less than 20 seats (Fig. 4.2). This means that the original manufacturer cannot be held legally liable for injuries caused by one of these aircraft that is more than 18 years old. GARA does not apply if the manufacturer deliberately concealed the defect, nor does it apply to claims by passengers receiving emergency medical transportation or persons on the ground who

Fig. 4.2. When this new Maule is delivered to its first buyer, GARA's 18-year statute of repose begins to run. Manufacturers of parts and equipment added later in the aircraft's life are protected by GARA, beginning 18 years after each such item is installed.

were injured by an aircraft accident. As new parts and equipment are added to the aircraft as replacements or upgrades, a new 18-year period begins to run *for that part or equipment, only.* Before GARA's enactment, about $40,000 of the cost of a new general aviation aircraft was attributable to the "tail" of potential liability for aircraft produced long ago. (In the U.S., today's fleet of single-engine aircraft has an average life of 28 years, so GARA eliminated the manufacturer's exposure to liability for more than a third of the average life of one of these aircraft.) Before GARA, that cost made it so difficult for U.S. manufacturers to compete against their foreign competitors that Cessna suspended production of its piston aircraft line until Congress enacted GARA.

According to the General Aviation Manufacturers Association (GAMA), the number of product liability lawsuits brought against general aviation aircraft and component manufacturers has decreased since the enactment of GARA. One major general aviation aircraft manufacturer told the General Accounting Office (GAO, the investigative arm of Congress) that the number of open lawsuits the company was defending fell from a high of around 900 in the early 1980s to a total of about 80 in early 2001. Meanwhile, general aviation manufacturing rebounded, with shipments of piston aircraft, for example, increasing nearly fourfold between 1994 and 2000.

Although GARA has accomplished its intended purpose of revitalizing the production of general aviation aircraft in the U.S., it has had unintended (though foreseen) adverse side effects on other segments of the general aviation industry. These will be discussed in Chapter 6, Aviation Insurance. GARA has not had any beneficial effect on the average price of new single-engine piston aircraft (the largest segment of the new fixed-wing aircraft market), which has continued to increase, even when the price is adjusted for inflation.

Some states also have statutes of repose that may apply to aircraft larger than those protected by GARA. The state of Indiana, for example, has a seven-year statute of repose on all products. An accident that occurred there provides a good example of the working of a statute of repose. A DC-3 was taking off from an Indiana airport on a skydiving flight when, just after liftoff and as the landing gear was retracting, an elevator control cable jumped off a pulley under the flight deck floor and jammed. The flight crew kept the aircraft's wings level, reduced power, and successfully bellied the airplane into a cornfield. Unfortunately, on impact one of the propellers separated from the engine, penetrated the aircraft's fuselage and injured one of the jumpers. The jumper's attorney then sued everyone in sight, including McDonnell-Douglas (the Douglas Commercial Airplane

Company had delivered the airplane to the U.S. Army Air Corps about 40 years earlier, as a C-47). McDonnell-Douglas's attorneys moved for an order to dismiss the manufacturer as a defendant, based upon Indiana's statute of repose. The trial court agreed that the Indiana statute governed the case, and dismissed the claims against the manufacturer under the statute of repose because the product had been first sold more than seven years previously.

EXCULPATORY CONTRACTS
In some comparatively rare circumstances, individuals and aviation businesses can protect themselves from potential liability for aviation accidents beforehand through contracts with voluntary participants. These contracts are discussed in Chapter 7.

INTERNATIONAL LAW
International treaties govern the tort liability of airlines in international flight operations. These are covered in detail in Chapter 8, along with special legislation enacted to protect the airlines and others from litigation arising out of the terrorist attacks of 9/11/01.

Employers' Liability

An employer is said to be *vicariously liable* for torts committed by its employees within the scope of their employment. As an example: An airline flight crew descends below decision height (DH) on an ILS approach in bad weather without having the runway in sight. They allow the aircraft to descend into a stand of trees short of the runway, causing a crash. Because the crew's negligent approach was conducted within the scope of their employment by the airline, the airline is also liable for the consequences and must pay for the passenger injuries and deaths that result. The crewmembers also remain personally responsible for the results of their negligence, and they (or their estates if they are killed in the crash) can be sued along with their employer. Vicarious liability adds the employer as a responsible party but never relieves the individual employees of personal liability for their negligence.

If the employee is not doing the employer's work, but is "off on a frolic of his own," then the employer is not vicariously liable for the employee's negligence.

Damages and Attorney Fees

A defendant's potential liability in tort cases is generally limited to *compensatory damages,* the sum that will compensate the injured persons or their survivors for the consequences of the accident. This may include resulting medical expenses (both past and future), lost earnings, and pain and suffering. Reading a headline like "Jury Awards Smith $10 Million Verdict in Plane Crash," many people reflexively equate Smith's victory to winning the lottery. Close examination of the facts, however, will usually show that Smith suffered horrible and lasting injuries that have left her confined to a wheelchair or bed, unable to earn a living or enjoy most of the activities she had before the accident. She is in constant pain and faced with incredible expenses for medical care, past and future. You can be pretty certain that if someone from the Eyewitless News Team were to shove a microphone into Smith's face and say, "Can you tell our viewers whether you would rather have this $10 million or be medically restored to the health you enjoyed before the crash?" Ms. Smith would much prefer to be her old self. But unfortunately the capability of the medical profession to restore broken bodies is still far short of omnipotence, so an award of money is the best a court can do to compensate the victim.

In fact, the judgment rarely accomplishes even that. The plaintiff's lawyer will usually have undertaken the case on the basis of a contingent fee, whereby the lawyer is paid only in the event of victory and then a percentage of the amount collected. This is not necessarily a bad thing, since these cases demand a tremendous amount of work and investment of expense by the plaintiff's lawyers and most injured people could not afford to hire attorneys to represent them in these cases if they had to pay the attorney's usual hourly rates. But the practice does result in plaintiffs actually receiving something less than full compensation for their injuries because of the so-called *American Rule,* which says that under most circumstances, win or lose, each party to a lawsuit is responsible for paying her own attorneys' fees. Personal injury litigation is not a get-rich-quick scheme. In most cases, the most the injured person can hope for is to receive compensation for her injuries, less her attorney's fee.

An exception (and it is a very rare exception) to this is in cases where the jury is allowed to award *exemplary or punitive damages.* In most states, juries are allowed to impose these damages over and above the compensatory damages only where the defendant's negligence was so extreme as to indicate a wanton and reckless disregard of the possible consequences of his actions. Thus they are called "exemplary" damages (to hold the wrongdoer up as an example to others that society will not tolerate that kind of behavior) or "punitive" damages (to punish the wrongdoer). Exemplary and punitive damages are the same thing; some states use one phrase and some use the other. In order to get an award of exemplary or punitive damages, the plaintiff's attorney must convince the jury that the wrongdoer just didn't give a damn whether anybody got hurt or killed. It isn't enough that the defendant was simply negligent.

For example: An airliner crashes due to a defect in its design. The manufacturer's business records reveal that it knew about the problem and the potential for catastrophe long before the accident, but rather than acting to correct the defect, the manufacturer chose to cover up the problem. A jury might well find that kind of behavior indicative of a wanton and reckless disregard for the possible consequences of its failure to remedy the problem, that the manufacturer just didn't care whether anyone got hurt or killed, and might award exemplary or punitive damages. It really takes something that outrages the jury to get punitive damages, and juries are not easily outraged.

Litigation Procedures

The first notice that you get that you've been sued should come in the form of a *Summons and Complaint*. When that is received, it is time to stop what you are doing and contact your lawyer immediately. Lawsuits are like ball games: If you don't show up on time to play, you lose by default. Your lawyer typically has only 20 days to file a well-considered *Answer* with the court. If you blow that deadline, the plaintiff may get a judgment against you by default, depriving you of your opportunity to defend yourself against the charges.

Before trial, your lawyer will have the opportunity to find out what the other side's case is all about through *discovery*, including written *interrogatories* (questions to be answered in writing), *depositions* (sworn testimony by prospective witnesses), and the examination of documents and other physical evidence (by a *motion to produce*). Indeed, until discovery has been conducted, it is usually extremely difficult for your attorney to advise you realistically of the strengths and weaknesses of your and your opponent's positions and thus whether a settlement offer should be made (and if so, in what amount). Discovery can be very expensive and time consuming, but it is a crucial part of the litigation process.

Indeed, litigation is a very expensive and often-inefficient way to resolve disputes, so that many people and businesses are now turning to alternative methods of dispute resolution including arbitration, mediation, and hybrid approaches, with some success.

While such creative new approaches present attractive alternatives to the costs inherent in litigation, probably the most cost-effective approach is to prevent the accident through strict adherence to the FARs, rigorous training programs, meticulous inspection and maintenance, and habits of uncompromising care. Prudence pays. After all, if the accident doesn't happen, you don't get sued. Another beauty of accident prevention is that you don't need to hire a lawyer. You already know how to do it. In the next three chapters, we will examine other techniques you can use to control the risk of liability for aviation accidents. This field is generally referred to as *risk management.*

CHAPTER 5

Organizing the Business to Limit Liability

IN MY OBSERVATION, far more aviation businesses have failed as a result of poor business practices than from poor aviating. This chapter examines the selection of a form of business organization to protect owners from personal vicarious liability for torts committed by other employees of the business in the scope of their employment. It also examines attitudes, approaches, and practices that I have often seen bring aviation businesses to grief.

The purpose of this chapter is to provide you with an appreciation of the value of selecting and maintaining the appropriate form of business to protect the owners of the business from such liability, and to provide you with a practical working knowledge of how to manage a business to avoid the most common and dangerous legal pitfalls.

Forms of Business

The form in which your aviation business is organized is one factor that can be used to control the potential consequences of legal risks inherent in doing business. The primary forms of business organization are sole proprietorship, general partnership, limited partnership, limited liability company (LLC), limited liability partnership (LLP), and corporation.

Although the form of your business cannot protect you personally from liability for your own negligence or intentional torts, it may protect you from vicarious personal liability for torts committed by employees of the business in the scope of their employment and from debts of the business.

In a *sole proprietorship*, the business is owned by a single individual who is personally responsible for debts of the business and (under the principle of vicarious liability discussed in the preceding chapter) for torts committed by employees of the business while acting within the scope of their employment. Thus, people who choose to do business as sole proprietors continually risk not only what they have invested in the business but all of their personal assets (including homes, airplanes, cars, and everything else they may own) in the event of an accident or difficulty in paying business debts. While the freedom to "be your own boss" afforded by the sole proprietorship is greater than that in any other form of business organization, it comes with a very high risk attached.

The same personal exposure to liability applies to each of the partners in a *general partnership*, and even *limited partnerships* are required to have at least one general partner whose personal assets are at risk for business liabilities (although the limited partners enjoy protection from personal liability similar to that afforded shareholders of a corporation).

Until recently, the *corporation* was the only form of business in which no owner (shareholder) of the business took on the added risk of vicarious personal liability for torts committed by employees of the business or debts of the business. Most states, however, have recently adopted laws permitting businesses to be organized as *limited liability companies (LLCs)*, or *limited liability partnerships (LLPs)* all of whose owners enjoy the same protection against personal liability as the shareholders of a corporation. It is likely that the LLC and LLP will soon be an option in all states. (Although relatively new to the U.S., the LLC is hardly a bold experiment, having existed in Europe and South America since the 19th century.) Tax considerations of the particular enterprise drive the choice between a corporation, LLC, or LLP as the more appropriate form of business (a properly formed LLC or LLP can possess both the limited liability of a corporation and the pass-through tax treatment of a partnership). However, not even a corporation, LLC, or LLP will protect you from personal liability for the consequences of your own negligence.

Consider this scenario: One of your company's charter pilots is flying the president of your local bank, the most prosperous physician in the county, and a high-rolling investor to the Big City for a meeting. Severe icing is encountered on the approach and the pilot loses control of the aircraft, crashing into a schoolyard full of children playing at recess. There are no survivors aboard the aircraft and many of the children are killed or injured. Assume further that for some reason the accident is either not covered by your aircraft liability insurance policy (more on this in the next chapter) or that the losses are in excess of the amount of that policy. If the business is a sole proprietorship or a general partnership, the sole proprietor or general partners can be held personally liable for the pilot's negligence that caused the accident and could lose everything he/they have. If the business is a limited partnership, only the general partner risks being held vicariously liable for the pilot's negligence and losing everything with the limited partners' maximum risk being that their investment (their share of the business) will become worthless. But if the business is a corporation, LLC, or LLP, its owners (the corporation's shareholders) have no exposure to personal vicarious liability for the pilot's negligence that caused the accident. The worst that can happen to them is that the accident will bankrupt the business so that their investment (stock) becomes worthless.

Obviously, the corporate form, LLC, and LLP afford the best protection against personal liability arising out of vicarious liability for torts committed by a business's employees and for debts of the business. While such protection is a very important consideration in choosing the form of your aviation business, it is by no means the only consideration. Other considerations that also bear upon selecting the appropriate form for your business include capitalization requirements and tax considerations.

Choosing the optimum form for your business before you begin operations is an important risk-management step. You should consult both your accountant and your lawyer to help you reach an informed decision on the choice. The professions of law and accountancy are very similar to the practice of medicine in that prevention can be far more cost-effective than subsequent attempts to cure a situation that has been allowed to get out of hand. The initial organization of your aviation business is a prudent occasion to invest in preventive lawyering and accountancy.

Forming and Operating a Corporation

If you choose to incorporate the business, inquire whether your lawyer would be willing to serve as the corporation's *agent for service of process*. If the corporation is sued, this is the person upon whom the process server must serve the Summons and Complaint, the first representative of the corporation to find out about the lawsuit. As mentioned in the previous chapter, your attorney may have only 20 days (and even less under some circumstances) to file an Answer or other pleading with the court. Having your attorney as the corporation's agent for service of process can eliminate the possibility of someone getting a default judgment against the corporation because the Summons and Complaint were not delivered to the corporation's attorney in time.

The *articles of incorporation* are to a corporation what a constitution is to a nation. They are the most basic document expressing what has been created. Although most states allow you to create a corporation by filling in a very simple form and paying a small filing fee, you will probably find that the cost of having your attorney draft original customized articles of incorporation is well worth the modest additional cost. When the state accepts your articles of incorporation and issues a *certificate of incorporation,* the legal equivalent of a birth in the family occurs. The law recognizes the corporation as a "person" having rights and an existence separate from and independent of its owners (unlike any other form of business organization). Sole proprietorships and partnerships are considered to be identical to their owners.

This birth alone, however, may not be sufficient to protect you from personal liability for the torts of the corporation's employees or for corporate debts. That is because of the *alter ego doctrine.* Under that doctrine if, notwithstanding the fact of incorporation, you continue to *operate* the business as though it were a sole proprietorship or partnership, a plaintiff's attorney may later be able to "pierce the corporate veil" to reach your personal assets to satisfy liabilities or debts of the business. The key to avoiding such a revolting turn of events is to take great pains to make it obvious to the public, including customers and suppliers of the business, that they are dealing with a corporation. (The same is true of an LLC or LLP.) This is done by carefully following the "duck rule."

It is said that if you come upon a creature in the wild and it looks like a duck, quacks like a duck, waddles like a duck, and leaves a slippery trail of spoor like that of duck, you may safely assume that the creature is a duck. This is the duck rule. To ensure that people know that they are dealing with a corporation, you must be sure that the business looks like a corporation, quacks like a corporation, waddles like a corporation, and leaves the trail of spoor left by a corporation.

No single factor discussed here automatically determines whether a plaintiff can pierce your corporate veil. The issue of whether the business was really being operated like a corporation rather than a sole proprietorship or partnership is a complex question of fact that the judge or jury will ultimately decide, based on many factors. But ignoring any of these factors increases the risk that a plaintiff's attorney will succeed in piercing the corporate veil to reach your personal assets.

LOOKING LIKE A CORPORATION

Showing the Corporate Name. A corporation's "last name" must always be *Incorporated* (or the abbreviation *Inc.*), *Corporation* (or the abbreviation *Corp.*), or *Limited* (or the abbreviation *Ltd.*). The latter is not the same thing as an LLC or a limited partnership, but is one acceptable way of denominating a corporation. One of these becomes the legal last name of this new person, the corporation. Unless your name is Cher, you always use both your first name and your last name in business dealings. Corporations must do the same thing. Remember: You're trying to be sure

5 : Organizing the Business to Limit Liability 107

that all those you're doing business with know they are dealing with a corporation. Every piece of paper that has the business's name on it must include that official last name because that is what puts people on notice that they are dealing with a corporation. The same is true of signs around your facility, on the aircraft, and on other equipment (Fig. 5.1). Wherever the corporate name appears, the entire correct legal name should appear.

One single piece of paper not conforming to this rule can put your corporate protection in jeopardy. The plaintiff can present that piece of paper as an exhibit at trial and testify: *"You can see from this that I had no reason to know that I was dealing with a corporation."* This problem most often comes up when a business that began as a sole proprietorship or partnership later incorporates, simply adding Inc., Corp., or Ltd. to the previously used trade name. Frugal managers may decide to use up all the old stationery, invoices, checks, and other printed forms before having the corporate last name added at the next printing. Others have been known to deliberately

Fig. 5.1. Although the "Inc." on this FBO's sign looks like an afterthought, it should suffice to put the public on notice that they're dealing with a corporation.

omit the corporate last name for aesthetic reasons. Such an approach may defeat the liability-limiting purpose of incorporating the business.

Once the corporation is formed, every last blank piece of letterhead, form, check, and other office and shop supplies having the old name (which does not reflect the corporate status) should be shredded, then burned. If even one escapes, Murphy's Law ("if anything can go wrong, it will") dictates that you will see that piece of paper later, at trial, as Exhibit A in the plaintiff's attempt to pierce the corporate veil to reach your personal assets.

Adequate Capitalization. There is no hard-and-fast rule on how much capitalization (money and assets) is required for a corporation. But the more you strive to keep it an empty shell having no assets exposed to potential claimants, the more likely it is that a judge or jury will pierce that corporate veil to reach your personal assets. Your attorney and accountant can help you decide what assets should be held in the corporation's name, given the nature and circumstances of your particular business.

Multiple Shareholders. Although a single shareholder may legally own a corporation, this is another factor the judge or jury could consider as one brushstroke in the big picture of whether it was really being operated as a corporation. Having more than one shareholder makes the business look more like a real corporation to most people.

QUACKING LIKE A CORPORATION

If your nickname is "Buzz" and you start your business as a sole proprietorship under the trade name Buzz's Flying Service, and then later incorporate the business, you need to change your way of talking and writing to people. You must carefully avoid giving them the impression that they're really still doing business with good old Buzz and not with this new faceless corporate person, Buzz's Flying Service, Inc. For starters, make it an office policy that anyone who answers the telephone now answers it with, "Buzz's Flying Service, *Inc.* How may we help you?"

In your business conversations and correspondence, you must change your old style, now taking care to avoid personalization. Back when the business was a sole proprietorship, it was okay to say things like, "My company can install that new color radar set in your airplane" or, "I can't imagine why you haven't received payment for that last parts invoice but *I'll* take care of that today." If the business is really organized as a partnership, then its entirely appropriate for you to say things like, "*My partner,* Ace, can do an annual inspection for you." But if the business is a corporation, this kind of talk can be the undoing of your protection because

5 : Organizing the Business to Limit Liability

it sounds to the listener as though she is dealing with only you or your partners, not with a corporation.

Remember: A corporation is a separate legal entity, a "person" in the eyes of the law, and its customers and suppliers must be put on notice that it is the corporation, not an individual or group of partners, they are dealing with. Thus, it would be more appropriate to say, "Yes, *the corporation* can install that color radar set in your airplane" or, "I'll check on why you haven't received payment for that last parts invoice and see if *the corporation* can send you a check for that today." The word *partner* must be banished from your language. You may say, "Our shop foreman, Ace, can do an annual inspection for you." Even if you and Ace are each the holder of 50% of the shares of stock in the corporation, you are not "partners." It may be a hard habit to break, especially if you have grown up in the rural West where *partner* often serves as a generic term of friendship or esteem (as in, "Howdy, partner") rather than an expression of a form of business relationship. But if you want to get the most liability protection out of your corporation, you'll eliminate that kind of language.

THE CORPORATE WADDLE AND THE CORPORATE SPOOR

This is a matter of acting like a corporation and leaving a trail of paperwork that shows it. Although a corporation is a person in the eyes of the law, only human persons can do the corporation's work.

How to Sign for a Corporation. Although a corporation can legally enter into a contract, it takes a human person acting on behalf of the corporation to sign the contract and write the check. If you are that person, you want to be sure that it is apparent to the world that you are signing that contract or writing that check only on behalf of the corporation, as its agent and not personally. There is only one proper format in which to sign anything if you are signing it for the corporation and not individually. This signature block must include three elements: the corporation's full legal name, your signature, and your corporate title (Fig. 5.2). If you omit the

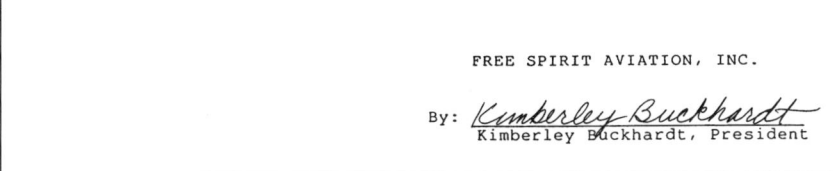

Fig. 5.2. Proper form of corporate signature.

first or third of these elements, you risk personal liability. On corporate correspondence, if the letterhead shows the corporation's full legal name, that need not be repeated in the signature block.

Keeping Personal and Corporate Assets Separate. If you want the world to recognize the corporation as a separate person, then you must do so too. Don't put that person's money in your pocket. Care must be taken never to commingle personal and corporate funds or other assets, and corporate debts should never be paid directly from personal funds. Corporate debts should be paid only from corporate funds. If you pay them from your personal funds, that is not acting like a corporation but like a sole proprietorship. This is not to say that you can't find a way to get the money into the corporation to enable the corporation to pay its debts. The corporation can acquire funds in the following ways:

- Sale of shares of stock (capital investment)
- Income from operations
- Debt (loans)
- Sale or leasing out of assets

For example, imagine that the corporation's hangar rent and payroll are coming due and the corporation is short of cash to make these payments (perhaps because especially horrible winter weather has severely cut back on income for the month's flight operation revenues). If you are a shareholder in the corporation and are in a financial position to help out, there are several ways you can do so without opening up the possibility of someone being able to pierce the corporate veil to reach your personal assets as a consequence. You could loan money to the corporation to cover its needs; you could buy some more stock in the corporation; or you could purchase assets from the corporation (and lease them back to the corporation if they are needed to continue operations).

Any of these transactions is proper since each respects the corporation as the separate legal person it is. Care must be taken, however, to document the transaction properly, leaving the all-important paper trail. If you choose to make a loan, then a *promissory note,* which includes a commercially reasonable rate of interest, should be filled out. If you choose to purchase corporate stock, the corporate minute book and stock certificate book should reflect that this transaction was handled in the manner prescribed in the corporation's articles of incorporation or bylaws. A properly signed and sealed *stock certificate* should be issued to you in exchange for the funds and the transaction recorded in the corporation's *stock cer-*

tificate register. If you purchase assets from the corporation, a *bill of sale* should be issued and the transaction reflected on the corporation's financial records. If you lease the purchased equipment back to the corporation, that should also be done by written *lease.*

Although all this is somewhat time-consuming, it is the proper way of doing business and absolutely necessary to preserve the maximum personal protection from doing business in the corporate form. You can bet that if there's an accident that is not completely covered by the corporation's liability insurance, the plaintiff's attorney is going to examine your corporate books and records during the discovery process. He'll search in hope of being able to pierce the corporate veil to reach the personal assets of the owners (shareholders). If you have been careful to document each such transaction, that effort will be frustrated. Your corporate lawyer and accountant should be called upon to assure that these transactions are properly documented in the corporation's financial records, minute book, and stock certificate book.

Making and Documenting Corporate Decisions. Part of the process of acting like a corporation is making corporate decisions at the appropriate level and keeping the paper trail that proves that you have done so. Corporate decisions may be made at several levels: the shareholders, the board of directors, an executive committee of the board of directors, officers, or employees.

The powers, duties, responsibilities, and procedures for corporate decision-making should be spelled out as clearly as possible in the articles of incorporation or bylaws. In normal corporate operations, the only decision the shareholders have the right to make is to elect a board of directors to govern the corporation. The board of directors elects officers. Typically, the board of directors makes decisions affecting corporate policy and major business decisions, while officers (such as a chief executive officer or CEO) execute that policy and make the day-to-day business decisions.

When in doubt whether a particular decision can be made by a corporate officer or should be referred to the board of directors, a good rule of thumb is to ask yourself: "Is this what the corporation is in business to do?" If the answer is "yes," then the officer can probably make the decision. If the answer is "no," then the matter should probably be taken up with the board of directors.

Take, for example, a full-service FBO. A customer calls to rent an airplane. If the corporation is in the business of renting airplanes, one would expect that the decision of whether to rent the individual an airplane could be made by an employee, following written corporate policy.

Suppose instead that the airport manager calls to inform the FBO that another enterprise on the airport is going out of business and the airport authority wants to know whether the FBO would like to take over and operate that facility under lease, in addition to or instead of the FBO's present facility. Although physical facilities are necessary to the corporation in operating its business, renting space from the airport authority is not what the corporation is in business to do. Moving or expanding is a big decision, a matter of policy. Therefore, this is a decision that is probably going to have to be made by the board of directors.

Whenever a meeting of the shareholders or the board of directors takes place, a written record (referred to as *minutes*) must be prepared. The minutes detail when and where the meeting occurred, who was present, and what was decided (it is generally not required to reflect everything that was discussed, only decisions that were reached). These minutes should be kept in the corporate minute book, the primary paper trail that serves as evidence that the corporation was operated as a corporation, with decisions being made in the proper manner at the proper level of authority. An empty or long-neglected corporate minute book turned up in the inquisitive process of discovery can be a powerful weapon to a plaintiff's attorney who is trying to pierce the corporate veil to reach your personal assets.

Duties to Employees

Regardless of the form of your business (whether a corporation, limited liability company, partnership, or sole proprietorship), the business has certain legal obligations toward each of its employees. These include a duty to provide *workers compensation insurance* and *unemployment compensation insurance, to pay agreed wages and withhold payroll taxes,* and to *provide a safe place to work.* Attempts by management to avoid carrying out these duties have brought many businesses to grief. Particularly in the small business just starting out, management may be reluctant to incur the expense and keep the records required to withhold payroll taxes and provide mandatory insurance. In such a situation, management may succumb to the temptation to call the people who work for the business *independent contractors* rather than employees, in an attempt to avoid the responsibility to provide the mandatory insurance and withhold payroll taxes. Such a decision may have catastrophic consequences.

WORKERS COMPENSATION INSURANCE

In the popular mythology of American social welfare, state statutes compelling employers to provide workers compensation insurance coverage to compensate their employees for on-the-job injury are celebrated as a great victory of the working class over exploitative employers. Actually, however, workers compensation insurance is far more advantageous to the employer than to the employee.

Because of the large number of businesses purchasing the insurance, it tends to be relatively inexpensive, although rates have risen substantially in the last few years, particularly since the terrorist attacks of 9/11/01 caused so many deaths of employees of businesses located in the World Trade Center.

The law of most states provides that if the business has covered its employees with workers compensation insurance, an employee who is injured on the job is prohibited from suing the employer for such injuries. If one of your mechanics or pilots backs into a spinning prop or is otherwise killed or injured on the job, you'll be instantly convinced of the value of workers compensation insurance in protecting the business from liability. This protection is well worth the expense and paperwork involved and in most states is mandatory for businesses having *any* employees.

WITHHOLDING PAYROLL TAXES

The Internal Revenue Service (IRS), like dynamite, is stronger than you are and has no friends. Revenue-collecting authorities have extraordinary powers not enjoyed by other administrative and law enforcement agencies. A friend of mine who practices tax law extensively sometimes makes the pseudo-Freudian slip of referring to the IRS as the KGB. The analogy is entirely appropriate, given the extraordinary powers afforded revenue agents. For example, the IRS has the benefit of *hindsight review*. This means that even though a business considered certain workers independent contractors (and may even have obtained workers' signatures on contracts stating that they were independent contractors), the IRS may later decide that the person was really an employee for the purpose of the business's duties to withhold payroll taxes.

In making that determination, the IRS applies a *right to control and direct* test, examining a number of factors to determine whether a person is an independent contractor or must be considered an employee. Factors the IRS considers to favor a determination that a person is (or was) an employee (rather than an independent contractor) include whether the person:

1. Is required to comply with company instructions about when, where, and how work is done;
2. Has been trained by the company;
3. Is integrated into the company's general business operations;
4. Must render services personally;

5. Uses assistance provided by the company;
6. Has a continuing relationship with the company;
7. Is required to work a set number of hours;
8. Must devote substantially full-time work to the company;
9. Works on the company's premises;
10. Must perform work in a preset sequence;
11. Must submit regular progress reports;
12. Is paid by the hour, week, or month;
13. Is reimbursed for all business and travel expenses;
14. Uses company tools and materials;
15. Has no significant investment in the facilities that are used;
16. Has no risk of loss;
17. Works for only one company;
18. Does not offer services to the public;
19. Can be discharged by the company; or
20. Can terminate the relationship (quit) without incurring liability.

Here is an all-too-frequent scenario: An FBO wishing to avoid the expense and paperwork inherent in insuring and withholding payroll taxes for its flight instructors elects to treat them as independent contractors. One day, IRS agents show up at the business and inquire into the whereabouts of one of these instructors, mentioning that the instructor didn't file federal income tax returns during the time he was instructing for the business. "Gee," the manager replies, "he left here a couple of years ago and I haven't seen him since, although I did hear a rumor that he was killed in the crash of a drug-smuggling plane in Columbia, so you guys are probably out of luck." Undeterred, the agents explain that their investigation has further revealed that the business does not seem to have withheld payroll taxes for this individual or paid those taxes to the government, as required. "Oh, no, he wasn't an employee. He was just an independent contractor," the FBO manager explains. "We even require our flight instructors to sign a contract showing that. Here is a copy of the one he signed."

Unfazed, the agents persist in their interrogation, gaining the manager's admissions that the flight instructor did give ground instruction in the FBO's classroom, had the use of a desk at the FBO, and used the FBO's FAA-approved syllabus to teach. The instruction was given in aircraft provided by the FBO, according to a schedule determined by the FBO's dispatcher. The instructor had to give the instruction himself; he couldn't send a buddy in to substitute for him if he had something else he'd rather be doing.

Applying 20/20 hindsight, the revenue agents may decide that under these facts the FBO had the "right to control and direct" this flight instructor's work. If so, the delinquent taxpayer was really an employee and the FBO, having failed to withhold and pay payroll taxes for this employee, must now pay those taxes to the IRS, with interest and penalties. If the business does not cooperate in promptly taking care of that obligation, IRS agents may freeze the business's bank accounts and seize its assets until the matter is resolved. It is not unusual in such a case for IRS agents in full SWAT team attire to show up at the business unannounced, armed with automatic weapons, to take over the property and lock up the hangars, offices, and aircraft.

And that's not all. If the business doesn't have the funds to pay this tax liability, the assets can be sold to satisfy it. If the sale of assets still doesn't satisfy the entire tax liability, then if the business is a sole proprietorship or partnership, the proprietor or partners are personally liable for the balance due the IRS. If the business is a corporation, its directors can be held personally liable for unpaid tax liabilities of the corporation. The business and its owners (or in the case of a corporation, directors) can't even escape that tax liability by filing bankruptcy. Tax liabilities are, by statute, not dischargeable in bankruptcy.

It is therefore tremendously important for businesses (whatever their form) to resist the temptation to evade the duties owed to their employees and the government through the subterfuge of trying to call such workers independent contractors. This is not to say that a business can never have independent contractors. For example, if you take one of your business's airplanes to Frida's Paint Shop to be painted, specifying the type of paint and design required and receiving a price quote for the job and an expected completion date, the paint shop would be a legitimate independent contractor. The work is being done at the independent contractor's facility, not your place of business, and the independent contractor is providing the paint, equipment, and labor. If Frida chooses to do the painting between midnight and 4:00 a.m., or to remove the paint by bead blasting instead of hand stripping, she may do so without consulting you. That is a legitimate independent contractor. If on the other hand you hire Georgia to paint the aircraft in your business's hangar, using your equipment, reporting for work at a specified time and working until an agreed quitting time, and doing the work under your supervision, that person is an employee. That cannot be changed even if you and she agree that she's an independent contractor and she signs a written agreement to that effect.

Lines of Defense in Risk Management

If you decide, with the advice of your lawyer and accountant, to form your business as a corporation, LLC, or LLP (to protect you from potential personal vicarious liability for torts committed by other workers), this should not constitute the entire risk-management plan for the business. The problem of risk management is very similar to the problem of national security. France's experience with the Maginot Line showed that, to be effective, a defense must be in-depth and diversified. The same is true of business risk-management strategies. While organizing the business as a corporation, LLC, or LLP is an important element in the risk-management plan you develop for your business, it should not be the only one.

As we have already seen, your accident prevention program should be a primary facet of your risk-management plan, since accidents prevented are lawsuits prevented. Liability insurance should also be a major element in your risk-management strategy. We will examine aviation liability insurance in the next chapter. If you cannot purchase sufficient liability insurance coverage for a particular operation, exculpatory contracts (discussed in Chapter 7) may also enter into your risk-management strategy.

CHAPTER 6

Aviation Insurance

ADEQUATE INSURANCE must be a key feature of your risk-management plan. To most of us, the language of insurance is a foreign language. Buying aviation insurance is like ordering in a French restaurant: If you can't read and speak the language, you can't be certain that you are ordering what you really want or that you've received what you ordered. Think of this chapter as a short but essential foreign language course.

The purpose of this chapter is to equip you with a working knowledge of aviation insurance sufficient to enable you to

1. Determine the insurance needs of an aviation business or general aviation aircraft owner-operator and order the correct coverage.
2. Analyze the policy received to ensure that it actually includes all of the features that you ordered, adequately covers your needs, and contains no unanticipated pitfalls or other unpleasant surprises.
3. Recognize when changing circumstances make changes in insurance advisable.

Insurance Fundamentals

Let's first examine the cast of characters in the aviation insurance industry and see who plays what roles.

SALES

Aviation insurance is sold by agents, by brokers, and directly by some insurance companies.

An insurance *agent* represents one or more insurance companies as a salesperson and is usually compensated on a commission basis by a percentage of premiums collected on policies sold. While also engaged in selling insurance, the *broker* differs from the agent in that the broker is not contractually bound to represent a specific insurance company but is free to represent you, the buyer, in shopping around to find the best available deal. The broker's compensation is also by commission. Some insurance companies, like Avemco, sell insurance directly to the customer over the telephone from national offices having 800 numbers instead of through sales networks of agents or brokers.

INSURING AND UNDERWRITING THE RISK

Insurance Companies. In general aviation, most policies are issued by a single insurance company. That company carries the entire risk (responsibility to pay for insured losses) under the policy.

Underwriters. Most airline insurance policies spread the risk over several insurance companies through the process of *underwriting*. This is generally done through a *clearinghouse* such as The Underwriters at Lloyds (Lloyds of London). There, many insurance companies are represented. When a request is received to quote a rate to provide a particular insurance coverage for an airline, the clearinghouse affords the participating companies representatives the opportunity to "subscribe" to cover a portion of the risk for a stated price. Once the various subscribed insurance companies' portions total 100%, the clearinghouse quotes the price and if the buyer accepts, issues the policy or a certificate of insurance.

Aviation Managers. Some insurance companies that write aviation insurance employ their own personnel to review applications received from prospective customers, decide whether the customer is an insurable risk, and determine an appropriate price for providing the requested coverage. Other insurance companies, however, contract that function to outside companies called aviation managers.

CLAIMS

If you have an accident, you are required by the policy to immediately report it to your insurance company. The policy itself should state to whom the report is to be made. When in doubt, call the agent or broker who sold you the policy first. Claims on the policy will be investigated and settlement offers extended by an *insurance adjuster*. The adjuster represents the insurance company in determining whether the loss is covered by the policy and, if so, the monetary value of the damages and extent of the insurance company's obligation to pay.

INSURANCE PRINCIPLES

There are two basic principles underlying all insurance: *spreading the risk* and *minimizing the risk*.

Spreading the Risk. There is an element of risk involved in all aviation operations. Aircraft accidents are statistically improbable events, but the financial consequences can be disastrous to an operator. Insurance serves to spread the risk of that unlikely but potentially catastrophic event over many similar operators, much as though all had contributed their premiums to a common contingency fund to cover such eventualities. By spreading the risk in this fashion, we enjoy a situation in which an adequately insured operator does not face the risk of financial ruin in the event of a single accident.

Underwriting accomplishes the same thing for the insurance companies, spreading the risk among the several insurance companies in the pool that underwrote the policy. It works. Even in the worst disastrous aviation accident in history (the runway collision between two fully loaded airline 747s on a foggy day at the Tenerife Airport in the Canary Islands), not one of the insurance companies that had underwritten a portion of the insurance for the airlines involved suffered financial ruin. Neither did either of the airlines.

Insurance companies insuring airports, airlines, and other high-dollar-value risks often reinsure a portion of their potential liability under the policy with another insurance company. This may be done either on a pro-rata basis (with a result similar to the sharing of risks underwritten through a clearinghouse) or on an *excess* basis with the first insurance company required to pay, for example, all losses under a $20 million aircraft liability policy up to the first $10 million, with the reinsurer responsible for paying losses falling within the next $10 million of the coverage.

Minimizing the Risk. Insurance companies have long recognized the value of accident prevention in avoiding claims against their policies. If the insurance company views the aircraft operator as "an accident looking for a place to happen," the operator may find it impossible to purchase insurance at any price. Among operators considered insurable risks, one factor used to compute the price (premium) of the coverage is the insurance company's best estimate of how likely this operator is to have an accident. Operators perceived as being the safest are able to purchase insurance less expensively than average operators, and below-average operators may not be able to purchase insurance at any price.

Insurance companies expect the persons and businesses they insure ("*insureds*") to demonstrate an attitude of "*protecting the policy,*" taking care to avoid accidents. If after issuing a policy the insurance company learns that the operator has reduced its pilot training program, is deferring maintenance, or otherwise reducing safety margins, the insurance company may become concerned that an accident is more likely than originally estimated. In that case, the company may cancel the insured's coverage, often on as little as 10 days' written notice (although if it does, the company must refund any unearned portion of the premium). If you ever have insurance canceled, you will find it much more difficult to buy insurance in the future. If one insurance company has decided you're a bad risk, others will be wary.

If you're going to be in the aviation business, then in addition to your accountant and lawyer, you need to develop a good working relationship with an insurance agent or broker who specializes in aviation insurance. Just as insurance is a foreign language to most of us, aviation insurance is a unique dialect within that language, not generally understood by people who don't live with it daily. An agent or broker who doesn't speak the dialect can get you in a lot of trouble, whereas one who does can keep you out of trouble. You'll still need to understand the rudiments of the language and the dialect yourself, so that you can communicate effectively with your broker or agent (or a direct writer) to order the insurance coverage you need and to confirm that you got what you ordered.

Aviation Insurance Coverages

All prudent aircraft owners (whether in the aviation business, using aircraft in support of other business enterprises, or recreational flyers) should have *aircraft insurance,* including both *liability* and *hull* coverages. In addition to the workers compensation insurance and unemployment compensation insurance discussed in the last chapter, aviation businesses may also need *airport liability insurance,* including *premises liability* and *hangarkeeper's liability,* as well as *products liability.* Prepaid legal services or *loss of license insurance* may also be desirable to defend your personal pilot or mechanic certificate or protect your income during suspension or revocation. *Excess liability* coverage may also be prudent. We will now examine features of each type of insurance, with a particular focus on what you need to know in order to select and order appropriate coverages and ascertain that you have received what you ordered when the policy arrives.

Aircraft Insurance

The aircraft insurance policy consists of two distinct types of coverage: *liability* and *hull*.

LIABILITY COVERAGE

This covers your liability for injuries to others including passengers in the aircraft, persons and property on the ground, and other aircraft and their occupants. It generally does not cover flight crewmembers (who are expected to be covered by workers compensation insurance for professional pilots, and health and life insurance).

HULL COVERAGE

This covers damage to or destruction of the insured aircraft resulting from an accident. It generally does not cover damage to the aircraft's engines in connection with an engine failure. However, if the engine failure leads to other damage to the aircraft, as in an ensuing off-airport landing, that damage is not excluded merely by virtue of an engine failure having set the sequence of events in motion. Hull coverage may be purchased to cover *all risks, all risks while not in flight,* or *all risks while not in motion.* For helicopters, coverage may be further broken down to include *all risks while rotors are in motion* or *all risks while rotors are not in motion* (Fig. 6.1). For operable aircraft intended to be operated, only *all risks* hull insurance will cover virtually anything that might happen to the aircraft. The lesser coverages, though a great deal less expensive, are suitable only for aircraft that are not operable and are not intended to be operated, such as aircraft undergoing long-term restoration, rebuilding, or modification that will preclude flight in the near future.

The buyer may have a choice between methods of valuing the aircraft for purposes of determining the amount to be paid by the insurance company in the event of an accident resulting in a total loss of the aircraft. (An aircraft is considered a "total loss" when it is more economical to pay the entire value of the hull insurance and then sell the wreckage for salvage than to pay the cost to repair the aircraft.) The most common valuation method is *stated value*. In a stated value policy, the insurance policy specifies the exact dollar amount the insurance company will pay to the aircraft owner in the event of a total loss. Rare (and possibly extinct) is the *current market value* policy. In contrast to stated value, a current market value policy permits the adjuster to take into account the current bluebook value of the aircraft at the time of the accident, along with factors peculiar to the aircraft (such as its general pre-accident condition, including paint, interior, engine times, and avionics installed or removed). The adjuster may re-

Fig. 6.1. For helicopters, hull insurance risks may be purchased to cover all risks, all risks while rotors are in motion, or all risks while rotors are not in motion. As with fixed-wing airplanes, only all-risk coverage protects the owner/operator in any conceivable event causing damage to an operable aircraft.

ly on these factors to reduce the current market value below average bluebook values, lowering the settlement offer to the owner.

Given a choice, thoughtful aircraft owners prefer stated value hull coverage because it leaves no uncertainty as to how much the insurance company must pay in the event of an accident resulting in a total loss. Current market value policies have historically led to controversy between the insurance company and the aircraft owner after a total loss, since the insurance adjuster's subjective assessment of the current market value of the aircraft immediately pre-accident may differ from that of the owner. This in turn frequently leads to a vexing, time-consuming, and expensive arbitration or litigation process to resolve the controversy. The use of stated value hull insurance avoids this uncertainty and potential for controversy.

The value you choose to state for the hull insurance merits careful consideration, both beforehand and for as long as you own the aircraft. The insurors will not allow you to overstate the value since that may motivate you to not protect the policy. On windy nights they would lie awake worrying that you might be out there helping your tie-down chains slip in order to turn a profit on the transaction. You should be careful not to understate the value, but state it at a figure that would purchase a comparable aircraft similarly equipped. Then reconsider whether that is still an adequate figure each year as you renew or replace your aircraft insurance. For many years, now, the prices of used general aviation aircraft have been steadily climbing. This trend, along with improvements made to the aircraft in the interim (such as added or updated avionics equipment, an overhauled or remanufactured engine, or a new paint job and interior) may have substantially increased the value of the aircraft (and the cost to replace it with a comparable aircraft). The value stated in your hull coverage should be increased to reflect that increase in value.

If you have financed the purchase of the aircraft and not yet paid off the loan, the lender will insist you carry hull coverage. A savvy lender will also require that it be named as the *loss payee* (to whom the insurance company makes the check payable in the event of a hull damage claim). In the event of a total loss, upon receipt of the check, the lender will retain the balance owed on the loan, then pay any remainder to the aircraft owner. On receipt of payment for repairable damage, the lender simply pays the proceeds directly to the mechanic or repair station upon completion of the repairs. In either event, the lender's security (the aircraft or insurance proceeds) is effectively in the lender's control, which makes it feel more secure (more to come on this point in Chapter 11 on buying and selling aircraft).

Regardless of the method of valuation employed in the hull coverage, once the owner accepts payment for a total loss under the hull coverage, the insurance company becomes the owner of the aircraft's remains *(salvage)* if any.

Purpose of Use

Another fundamental choice you will have to make when ordering aircraft insurance coverage is the *purpose of use* of the aircraft. In order of increasing premiums, typical purposes of use include *pleasure and business, industrial aid, limited commercial, commercial except instruction or rental, commercial,* and *special uses* (Fig. 6.2). Some insurance companies also rate *flying clubs* separately, at a rate somewhere between pleasure/business and limited commercial.

It is extremely important that you purchase coverage that will cover all purposes you may use the aircraft for, because if you have an accident during an operation conducted for a purpose other than one covered by the

Fig. 6.2. For some of the owners of these hot air balloons lifting off on an early morning launch, pleasure and business coverage may suffice; others may need limited commercial, commercial, or even special uses coverage.

policy, it will not be insured. If after you have purchased your aircraft insurance there arises any change in the purposes for which the aircraft is to be used, this should alert you to reconsider whether the new purposes are covered by your existing insurance or you need to purchase additional coverage to encompass the change. Let's examine what specific types of operations are typically covered by the various purpose of use options. The exact definitions employed by your insurance company should appear in the policy itself, but the following are fairly typical industrywide:

1. Pleasure and Business
2. Industrial Aid
3. Commercial Except Instruction or Rental
4. Limited Commercial
5. Commercial
6. Special Uses

Let's take a look at what activities each of these purposes of use is intended to cover.

PLEASURE AND BUSINESS

Sounds all-encompassing, doesn't it? You'll either be using the aircraft to have fun or to make money, right? Well, it isn't as simple as it might look at first glance (Fig. 6.3). Pleasure and business is generally defined to cover pleasure flying and personal flying incidental to or in direct connection with the insured's business, *excluding any operation for which a charge is made.*

In other words, this does not cover any type of commercial operation. The "business" in "pleasure and business" is a situation in which you might be using an airplane much as you would a company car. Imagine, as an example, that your business is selling computer software and you have developed a software program for FBO management. Since all of your prospective customers (FBOs) are located on airports, you use an airplane to make your sales calls. But if you make a sale, you don't charge the cus-

Fig. 6.3. The "pleasure" in pleasure and business coverage: the author's granddaughter enjoys a flight over the Rockies with grandpa in a Super Cub.

tomer extra for aerial delivery. That's the only kind of business use this covers.

INDUSTRIAL AID

Coverage includes everything covered by pleasure and business as well as the transportation of your business's executives, employees, guests, and customers—again *excluding any operation for which a charge is made.* This is the appropriate coverage for most corporate aircraft, assuming that the aircraft is dedicated solely to corporate use and never rented or chartered to others.

The next two are really opposite sides of the same coin and easily confused.

COMMERCIAL EXCEPT INSTRUCTION OR RENTAL

This covers all uses covered by pleasure and business plus industrial aid plus the transportation of passengers or cargo for hire, but *excludes commercial flight instruction* or *rental of the aircraft to other pilots.* If the business does only charters, cargo or mail hauling, and/or scheduled passenger carrying but never does commercial flight instruction or rents its aircraft to others, this coverage is adequate (Fig. 6.4).

LIMITED COMMERCIAL

This is the flip side of the coin, the opposite of "commercial except instruction or rental." Limited commercial also includes all of the operations covered by pleasure and business plus industrial aid plus commercial flight instruction and aircraft rental to other pilots, but *excludes carrying passengers or cargo for hire.* If you're a freelance flight instructor working with your own or a customer's airplane or an FBO not holding an FAR Part 135 air carrier operating certificate, so that your aircraft are used only for commercial flight instruction and rental, this may be adequate coverage.

COMMERCIAL

Generally referred to *as full commercial,* this covers every kind of operation we have discussed: pleasure and business, industrial aid, carrying passengers and cargo for hire, commercial flight instruction, and rental to other pilots. This is the coverage needed by a full-service FBO, but even this may not cover some of the more risky operations considered *special uses.*

SPECIAL USES

Flight operations that the insurance company believes involve a higher level of risk than those just described are rated as special uses and must

6 : Aviation Insurance 127

Fig. 6.4. This "freight dog" Grumman Goose amphibian is probably insured for commercial except instruction or rental purposes of use.

pay a higher insurance premium. This might include agricultural aviation operations, operations requiring an FAR waiver, aerial fire fighting, helicopter external-load operations, helicopter flight training, banner and glider towing, fish spotting, power line or pipeline patrol, and emergency medical service helicopter operations (Fig. 6.5).

Pilot Qualifications

Another decision you will have to make when ordering the aircraft insurance (and should keep in mind for the future, to be sure that all flight operations continue to be covered by your aircraft insurance) is *pilot qualification requirements.*

Generally speaking, the premium you pay for your aircraft insurance policy varies inversely with the minimum qualifications of the pilots who will be permitted to operate the aircraft. The more qualified and experienced the pilots, the cheaper the coverage. For the same airplane, a commercial instrument-rated pilot with over 1,000 flight hours, most of which were in the same make and model of the aircraft to be insured, would pay a much lower premium than a newly certified private pilot. If the aircraft

Fig. 6.5. Emergency medical service helicopter operations frequently require landings at unprepared accident scenes such as this city street, often at night and in challenging weather. The higher level of risk these essential operations involve compels insurance companies to rate them as a special use and charge a higher premium.

has tail wheel landing gear, then previous and recent tail wheel experience will be an especially important consideration.

Care must be taken to *never allow a pilot who does not meet the pilot qualification requirements of your insurance policy to operate the aircraft.* This has been known to trap not only private flyers who in gestures of generosity have allowed friends to fly their aircraft but commercial operators as well.

A typical scenario in which the commercial operator gets into trouble goes something like this: An air cargo business operating under FAR Part 135 has very strict qualifications for hiring pilots, and these are reflected in the company's aircraft insurance pilot requirements. These have helped the company obtain a relatively favorable price for this insurance. During the pre-Christmas rush, a major air express company calls seeking extra aircraft capacity. The big company offers a very attractive rate to the operator to help out, but the operator's present pilot complement is already flying up to the limits of duty time permitted by the FARs. Rather than pass up what appears to be a golden opportunity, the operator hires additional pilots to handle this extra work and lowers its standards by hiring pilots who fall short of the pilot requirements of the insurance policy in order to meet this need. Operations flown by those pilots will be uninsured.

This is not to suggest that the company should necessarily have passed up the opportunity. Only that whenever something changes in the way the company is doing business, management must consider whether the change will be covered by existing insurance or if expanded coverage must be purchased to encompass whatever is new. In this example, it might have been economical for the operator to pay an additional premium to lower the pilot qualification requirements of its aircraft insurance policy to take advantage of this business opportunity. Murphy's Law as applied to aviation insurance says that if you have an accident, it will happen (1) before your insurance policy becomes effective, (2) after it has expired, (3) within a policy exclusion, (4) during an operation for a purpose not covered by the policy, or (5) while the aircraft is under the command of an unqualified pilot.

Some pilots fall into lax habits of not logging all of their flight time (the FARs require only that you log flight time required to demonstrate currency). But as far as the insurance companies are concerned, if the time isn't in your logbook, you don't get credit for it for insurance purposes. So, if you got a price break on your insurance because you reported, for example, a thousand hours in type, but although you actually flew that time in type, you didn't log it all, you may actually be uninsured.

Other Considerations, Aircraft Insurance

Speaking of exclusions, watch out for policies that contain an *FAR violation exclusion clause*. This has become quite rare, but still turns up occasionally. This clause says that if the operation was in violation of an FAR, it is excluded from coverage by the insurance policy. The FARs are so sweeping in scope and in many instances so vaguely worded that it would be the very rare accident in which an industrious insurance adjuster could not find something about the operation arguably in violation of an FAR (if only FAR 91.13, careless operation). When you order the policy, be specific with your agent or broker that you will not accept a policy containing an FAR violation exclusion.

If you have financed the purchase of an insured aircraft and have not yet paid that loan in full, your lender (the *lienholder*) will require that it be named as the *loss payee* (to whom the insurance company writes the check in the event of a hull loss). The lender will also require that you purchase (at some additional premium) a *lienholder's interest endorsement* (sometimes referred to as a *breach of warranty endorsement)* in favor of the lender. Adding this endorsement to the policy assures the lienholder that even if the circumstances of an accident are such that the insurance company would not have to pay the owner-operator, the insurance company will pay the lienholder the balance due. Thus, even if you have a loss while the aircraft is being flown by an unqualified pilot or otherwise outside the policy, the lender gets paid.

But there's a catch. Such endorsements usually provide that if the insurance company has to pay a lienholder under this endorsement, the insurance company gets all of the lienholder's rights in return. Thus, if the lienholder is a bank that loaned you the money to finance a portion of the purchase price of the airplane, the insurer pays off the balance due to the bank. The insurance company then takes the bank's position on the promissory note you signed to borrow the money, and instructs you to keep those airplane payments (for your destroyed aircraft) coming (now to the insurance company, rather than the bank). Operate outside the policy at your own risk: That is always a losing proposition.

When you order the policy, if you intend to operate the aircraft in the near future, you should assure that the agent or broker with whom you are dealing has the insurance company's *authority to bind coverage.* (Not all do.) If this is an agency or brokerage with whom the insurance company has had a good working relationship of some duration, the insurance company will show its trust and confidence by authorizing it to issue a *binder,* locking in the insurance coverage. Otherwise, the application and premium must be received and reviewed by the insurance company before coverage will take effect. See the opportunity for a Murphy's Law uninsured accident in the latter situation?

A checklist for use in ordering aircraft insurance appears in Figure 6.6. You should fill this out before you call your agent or broker, to be prepared to accurately describe what it is you want to buy. Once the policy arrives, you should make it a part of your discipline to immediately sit down and read it—under conditions that ensure you will not be distracted. Read it carefully and thoroughly, using the same checklist you used to order it, double-checking to assure that you really got what you ordered. Although there is a refreshing trend toward "plain language" aircraft insurance policies, many are still written in convoluted insurance lawyer language difficult to decipher (and even what is "plain" to an attorney may not be plain to you). You should, however, do your best to understand what the policy says. Make up a hypothetical accident. Go through the policy and figure out whether it will pay off for the accident and, if so, what will be covered and how much will be paid. Try several of these exercises until you feel comfortable that you understand how the policy works.

AIRCRAFT INSURANCE CHECKLIST

General
    Purpose of use (check one)
        ____ Pleasure & business
        ____ Industrial aid
        ____ Limited commercial
        ____ Commercial except instruction or rental
        ____ Commercial ("full commercial")
        ____ Special use (describe):_____

    Pilot qualifications
    Pilot certificate & ratings required: _____
    Minimum total flight hours required: _____
    Minimum time in make & model required: _____
    Other requirements (total tail wheel, etc.): _____

    Does agent/broker have authority to bind coverage?
        ____ Yes
        ____ No

Liability coverage
    $ limits: _____

Hull coverage
    Risks covered (check one)
        ____ All risks
        ____ All risks not in flight
        ____ All risks not in motion
        ____ All risks, rotors in motion
        ____ All risks, rotors not in motion
        ____ Other: _____

    Method of valuation for total loss (check one)
        ____ Current market value ("blue book")
        ____ Stated value: $_____

    Loss payee (check one)
        ____ Registered owner
        ____ Lienholder (name): _____

    Breach of warranty (lienholder's interest) endorsement required? (check one)
        ____ Yes, in favor of (name): _____
        ____ No

Exclusions
    FAR violation exclusion (check one)
        ____ Yes
        ____ No
    Other exclusions:
    _____
    _____
    _____

Fig. 6.6. Aircraft insurance checklist.

You may even find some surprises you can correct before Murphy's Law gets you. For example, my first airplane (a Cessna 175) was initially tied down outside while I was wait-listed for hangar space to become available at our busy airport. One year, I changed insurance companies because my broker negotiated a better deal with a different company. He bound the coverage, and when the policy arrived I sat down that evening in my favorite easy chair and made myself read it. (Even though interpreting aviation insurance policies was part of what I did for a living, it was not a task I looked forward to, for duller prose was never written.) I was well into my reading when I came across a page captioned *Hail Endorsement.* I had never come across one of these before, and my attention perked up. It seemed to say that if the aircraft was caught in a hailstorm but the damage did not affect airworthiness, the insurance would not have to pay more than 10% of the stated value of the hull for those damages. An airplane whose surfaces look like a golf ball may still be deemed airworthy, but its resale value will be drastically reduced. Murphy must have slept better than I did that night because no hailstorm materialized before I could call my aviation insurance broker first thing the next morning. I instructed him to contact the insurance company and either have the hail endorsement removed from my policy or cancel the policy and find insurance with another company not requiring such an endorsement. He called me back shortly to advise me that the insurance company had agreed to delete the offensive endorsement from the policy and faxed me written confirmation the same day. I was very glad I had read the policy. Although the aircraft never did suffer hail damage, if I had overlooked that endorsement, it probably would have.

Another thing you should do to Murphy-proof yourself or your business is to maintain some kind of "tickler system" to alert you when your aircraft insurance policy expires. Mark it on calendars; have it coincide with your annual inspection; do whatever works to be sure that you are reminded. We are accustomed to our insurance agents bombarding us with reminders in the mail, by telephone and e-mail when our insurance policies are expiring. After all, they do want to sell us another one and earn another commission. But they are not required by law to do that, and human beings (and our computers) sometimes make mistakes. If the policy expires without renewal, you know when the accident will happen.

If your aircraft ever requires a *special flight permit ("ferry permit")* to be moved, think about your insurance coverage. Most aircraft insurance policies provide coverage only when the aircraft is being operated under a standard category airworthiness certificate. Therefore, operations under a special flight permit are not insured. You can probably purchase additional coverage for the ferry flight, but be certain that coverage has been bound before commencing operation under the permit.

If the aircraft is to be operated outside the contiguous (lower 48) United States, check the geographical extent of your coverage as described in your aircraft insurance policy. Chances are you'll need to buy additional coverage to cover the proposed area of operation.

Once you are comfortably satisfied that you have insurance that will adequately cover any conceivable situation, remain on guard to never let that fact enter into your safety decision-making. Remember: The insurance company expects you to *protect the policy*. If it suspects that you are thinking along the lines of, "So what if it doesn't make it; that's what we bought insurance for," your policy will be promptly canceled. Prevent accidents!

War Risk Insurance

In the past, most U.S. aircraft operators considered purchasing *war risk insurance* only when contemplating flight operation into areas of armed conflict in foreign countries, such as parts of South America, Africa, and the Middle East, since standard aircraft insurance policies exclude losses resulting from acts of war or rebellion, or a variety of other hostile acts.

The terrorist attacks on the U.S. homeland on September 11, 2001, abruptly changed that thinking.

The typical exclusion is Lloyd's form AVN 48B, captioned the "War, Hi-Jacking, and Other Perils Exclusion Clause." Although the exclusion has been included in most aircraft insurance policies since the reinsurers first required it in 1968, it has merited little concern on the part of domestic operators until recently. The new reality of terrorist activity within the United States using commandeered civil aircraft suddenly focused attention on the true breadth of this exclusion and brought home a realization of the exposure U.S. operators face for uninsured loss even in domestic operations.

This is one very broad exclusion, relieving the insurance company from responsibility to pay for losses resulting from a wide variety of mischief. Here's what it says:

> This policy does not cover claims caused by:
>
> War, invasion, acts of foreign enemies, hostilities (whether war be declared or not) civil war, rebellion, revolution, insurrection, martial law, military or usurped power or attempts at usurpation of power;

Any hostile detonation of any weapon of war employing atomic or nuclear fission and/or fusion or other like reaction or radioactive force or matter;

Strikes, riots, civil commotions or labor disturbances;

Any act of one or more persons, whether or not agents of a sovereign power, for political or terrorist purposes and whether the loss or damage resulting therefrom is accidental or intentional;

Any malicious act or act of sabotage;

Confiscation, nationalization, seizure, restraint, detention, appropriation, requisition for title or use by or under the authority of any Government, (whether civil, military or de facto) or by public authority;

Hi-jacking or any unlawful seizure or wrongful exercise of control of the aircraft or crew in flight (including any attempt at such seizure or control) made by any person or persons on board the aircraft acting without the consent of the Insured.

Furthermore, this policy does not cover claims arising whilst the aircraft is outside the control of the Insured by reason of any of the above perils.

The aircraft shall be deemed to have been restored to the control of the Insured on the safe return of the aircraft to the Insured at an airfield not excluded by the geographical limits of this policy, and entirely suitable for the operation of the aircraft (such safe return shall require that the aircraft be parked with engines shut down and under no duress).

If, as seems generally expected, acts of terrorism involving civil aircraft continue in the U.S., then it is prudent for aircraft owners to consider the potential this exclusion creates for an uninsured loss of their aircraft. The solution is to add war risk insurance to the aircraft insurance policy (and even that does not cover the atomic or nuclear weapon scenario).

The *Terrorism Risk Insurance Act (TRIA)*, enacted by Congress in 2002, affords aircraft owners the opportunity to purchase this insurance with the federal government essentially underwriting a portion of the risk.

Airport Liability Insurance

If your business is located on an airport, you will also need airport liability insurance. This may include *premises liability* and *hangarkeeper's liability* coverages.

PREMISES LIABILITY

Premises liability covers injury to nonemployees occurring at your place of business. For example: If your business is an aircraft repair station and a customer slips on an oily spot in your hangar and falls, suffering injuries, this is the insurance that will pay for those injuries. Any business, no matter where it is located, should have premises liability coverage. It's just that if your business is on an airport, this coverage becomes a part of your airport liability policy.

HANGARKEEPER'S LIABILITY

This insurance covers your liability for damage to other people's airplanes while they are in your care, custody, or control. This coverage pays off, for example, if a customer's airplane that is in your shop for work is damaged—by an employee misjudging and backing another airplane into it with your tug, damaging one or both, or the hangar collapses under a heavy snow load, crushing the customers' airplanes inside. If you are inspecting or repairing others' aircraft and sometimes need to perform a maintenance flight check on those aircraft before approving them for return to service, *in-flight hangarkeeper's* covers any damage the customer's aircraft may suffer during such operations by your employees. You need hangarkeeper's insurance only if other people's airplanes are being stored or worked on in your facility. The hull insurance coverage of your aircraft insurance covers such potential damages to your own aircraft.

Products Liability Insurance

Although you'd normally think of products liability insurance in connection with manufacturers of aircraft and aircraft components, this coverage is also needed by all businesses that perform aircraft inspection, maintenance, or modification, or supply aircraft parts, fuel, and lubricants. This insurance is needed to cover claims arising out of faulty workmanship, oversights in inspection, or errors and defects in design or manufacture of goods sold that might lead to tort claims for negligence or strict liability. For mechanics and repair stations, shops or modification centers, the coverage is sometimes referred to as *products and completed operations* coverage. To fully appreciate the importance of this insurance, take a moment to review a discussion of strict liability for suppliers of defective products in Chapter 4.

While the General Aviation Revitalization Act (GARA) discussed in Chapter 4 has succeeded in holding down the escalation in premiums for products liability insurance for manufacturers, overhaul facilities and maintenance shops and aircraft rental operations (not protected by GARA) have been particularly hard hit. Attorneys representing plaintiffs in cases arising out of accidents involving older aircraft, precluded by GARA from suing the manufacturer, have turned for recompense to those who overhaul, maintain, and rent them to others. This has resulted in

Fig. 6.7. General aviation aircraft overhaul facilities and maintenance shops have suffered from the effects of GARA, which has driven up their product liability insurance costs. Some smaller shops and shops with poor loss histories have found it no longer economical to remain in business in the face of these increased costs.

tripling and even quadrupling of premiums for these operators, a cost that has already driven many small aviation businesses to close their doors (Fig. 6.7).

Prepaid Legal Services and Loss of License Insurance

Several aviation organizations, including the Air Line Pilots Association (ALPA) and Aircraft Owners and Pilots Association (AOPA), offer a prepaid legal service program, either as a benefit of membership or an additional optional service available to members for an additional fee. These plans will pay the cost of an attorney to defend you in the event the FAA acts to suspend or revoke your pilot or mechanic certificate. Some of these plans cover aviation-related consultation in other areas as well (such as an initial consultation in the event of an aircraft accident). Loss of license insurance may provide you an income and the cost of learning another trade or profession in the event that the pilot, mechanic, or aviation medical certificate necessary to your work is suspended or revoked.

Excess Liability Coverage

In each of the various liability coverages we have already discussed, your objective should be to purchase enough insurance to cover the worst-case scenario in your business. (For aircraft liability, an aircraft full of your wealthiest customers crashing into the Anaheim Convention Center during a convention of the International College of Neurosurgeons; for hangarkeeper's liability, your hangar being full of the most expensive of your customers' aircraft when it burned down). Although it is rare today in the United States, you may find it impossible or prohibitively expensive to obtain that amount of coverage in these policies. If, however, you find yourself in that situation, you should explore the cost and availability of an *excess liability* policy (also referred to as an *umbrella* policy).

This insurance becomes available to pay liability claims only after all other applicable policies (such as your aircraft liability insurance or hangarkeeper's liability insurance) have paid to their policy limits. For example, let's say you have a million dollars of hangarkeeper's liability coverage. One of your employees fails to set the parking brake on the gas truck, which rolls into the hangar, collides with a customer's $20 million business jet and explodes. Your hangarkeeper's liability insurance company is responsible to pay for only the first million dollars of the loss. Unless you also have an excess liability policy in the additional amount of at least $19 million in this case, the remaining $19 million of the loss is uninsured, and your company is plainly vicariously liable to pay for these consequences of the employee's negligence.

For each of the liability coverages, the insurance company owes the insured the duty either to (1) *defend* claims against the insured that are covered by the policy *or* (2) *pay* (by settlement or judgment) the claim up *to the policy limit.*

Claims

The insurance adjuster who investigates the accident will carefully scrutinize the policy. This scrutiny will include (in the case of aircraft liability insurance) the insured purposes of use, pilot qualifications, exclusions, other conditions appearing in the policy, and the facts and circumstances of the accident to determine whether the accident is covered by the policy. If not, the insurance company has no obligation to defend or pay. If, however, the accident is covered by the policy, then the insurance company has the discretion to either

> defend the claim in court (if it believes that the plaintiff cannot prove you negligent or strictly liable) or

settle the claim out of court for any amount up to the policy limit, *usually without the consent of the insured.*

The insured's duties to the insurance company include the duty to

pay premiums as they become due,
be *truthful in all disclosures* made to the insurance company, and
cooperate with the insurance company during the investigation of a filed claim.

If an insured makes false statements on the insurance application (such as failing to report a previous aircraft accident or exaggerating the aircraft owner's pilot qualifications, however slightly), the insurance company may be legally able to avoid paying claims under the policy. The law in some states is that any false statement on an insurance application relieves the insurance company of the duty to pay for claims under the policy. In other states, the insurance company may escape liability only if there is some connection between the matter falsified and the cause of the accident. The only way to avoid such problems is to be extremely meticulous and tell the complete truth on insurance applications.

Subrogation

Most liability insurance policies provide that if the insurance company pays a claim under the policy, it has the right to pursue any claims the insured might have against someone else who caused or contributed to the cause of the accident. This right is called *subrogation.* In aviation, subrogation comes into play most frequently in the case of rented aircraft. Under ordinary negligence law, if a pilot operates a rented aircraft negligently, causing an accident that damages the aircraft, that pilot is liable to the owner for the cost of repair and lost rental income. If the owner's hull insurance pays the owner for the damage in that situation, that insurance company is said to be "subrogated to" the rights of the owner. The insurance company can sue that pilot for negligence (the policy may even permit the insurance company to bring that suit in the aircraft owner's name) to recover the money the insurance company paid the owner.

Businesses that rent airplanes to others and wish to protect their customers from subrogation may do so by purchasing a *waiver of subrogation endorsement* to their aircraft insurance policy. Another technique is to have the insurance company generically name renter pilots (who must also meet the pilot qualification requirements of the policy) as *additional insureds* on the policy. A few states require businesses renting aircraft to others to post conspicuous signs notifying renter pilots whether they are insured by or subject to subrogation under the business's aircraft insurance. Most states have no such requirement, however. If you are a renter pilot, you should personally examine the FBO or flying club's insurance policy to assure that you are personally protected from subrogation, either by being named as an additional insured on the policy or by a waiver of subrogation endorsement attached to the policy. If the business does not protect its rental customers in this fashion, you should purchase *aviation nonownership liability insurance*. This insurance would pay any such subrogation claim as well as claims made by passengers or persons on the ground suffering injuries or property damage if you have an accident while operating a rented aircraft.

Uninsured Matters

There are some aviation activities for which you cannot purchase liability insurance. At this writing liability insurance is not available for bodily injury to skydivers or hot-air balloon bungee jumping operations, at any price. In such a situation, the operator who chooses to engage in such operations without liability insurance may obtain a measure of protection through exculpatory contracts, discussed in the following chapter.

It is also noteworthy that in some states, liability insurance companies are prohibited from paying punitive damages assessed against their insureds because that would interfere with the intended "punishment" effect of such damages actually being suffered by the insured. This is yet another reason to always err on the side of caution in your training, inspection, maintenance, and operating practices.

CHAPTER 7

Exculpatory Contracts

ALTHOUGH EXCULPATORY contracts are a rarely used risk-management tool, inappropriate in most aviation operations, they can be extremely important for those that involve such a high level of risk as to be uninsurable. You should be aware of the availability of this risk-management tool and know when its use is appropriate. The purposes of this chapter are (1) to ensure that you recognize those unique circumstances where an exculpatory contract might be appropriate to limit potential liability and (2) to assure that you appreciate the value of utilizing the services of legal counsel in a "preventive lawyering" role in drafting these and other legal documents.

An *exculpatory contract* is an agreement between the aircraft or airport operator and a participant in an aviation operation by which the participant agrees not to sue the operator of the aircraft or airport if the participant is killed or injured during the operation. These contracts can range in complexity from multipage contracts typically signed today by sport skydivers (often after having viewed a video briefing by the skydiving center's lawyer on the serious legal import of the document) to the "fine print" on the back of a spectator's air show admission ticket.

Exculpatory contracts are among aviation's earliest risk-management tools. In her book *Tailspins: A Story of Early Aviation Days,* Edith Dodd Culver describes her first flight in 1916 at one of Glenn Curtiss's flying schools near Newport News, Virginia (known as the Atlantic Coast Aeronautical Station), in a Curtiss flying boat:

> I must confess that I did feel some qualms when I was asked, before climbing into the F-boat, to sign my life away as it were—that is to sign a paper absolving the Atlantic Coast Aeronautical Station of any claim in case the

F-boat crashed. But I learned that this was only routine practice for all passengers.

Today, an exculpatory contract is generally an appropriate risk-management tool only where

1. The operation is *not a common carrier* operation (such as carrying passengers for hire under the authority of an FAR Part 135 or 121 air carrier operating certificate);
2. The activity or relationship is *not* one in which the *law requires the operator to carry liability insurance* (the Federal Aviation Act of 1958 requires air carriers to maintain certain levels of liability insurance, and state laws require employers to provide workers compensation insurance for their employees); and
3. *Insurance,* although not required by law, is *not available* to the operator.

Exculpatory contracts are generally used in operations that are perceived by conservative insurance companies as being "out on the ragged edge," involving high risk or risks for which no actuarial statistics are available to the insurance company, constituting "unknown" risks. This might include airlifting skydivers (Figs. 7.1, 7.2) or bungee jumpers, or motion picture "stunt" flying (as in one of the James Bond movies, where a stunt pilot doubling for Agent 007 flies a tiny experimental BD-5J Microjet through a hangar while the hangar doors are closing, barely squeaking through at a 90° bank angle).

If the potential income from such an operation is sufficient to entice you to engage in it without liability insurance, then you should consult your attorney to explore the possibility of protecting you from claims by other risk takers involved by having everyone sign exculpatory contracts beforehand. Such contracts, which serve to relieve the operator of legal responsibility for the consequences of her own or her employee's negligence, have been held void as a matter of public policy in the state of New York. In most other states the courts very closely scrutinize such contracts but enforce them if (1) there is some *equality in bargaining power* between the parties, and (2) the subject matter is *not an essential of life* (such as food, medicine, medical care, shelter, public utilities, public transportation, or communications).

Some courts have upheld the fine print on the back of such things as admission tickets to races, air shows, and ski lifts as constituting valid exculpatory contracts, even where they have not been read or signed by the

7 : Exculpatory Contracts ─────────────── 143

Fig. 7.1. The author's daughter Stephanie studies an exculpatory contract immediately prior to making her first tandem skydive.

Fig. 7.2. She signed and found the thrill well worth the risk.

purchaser. Much greater legal protection is afforded, however, by a full-size legible contract signed by the person giving up the right to sue. That contract should include a statement fitting into the doctrine of *assumption of risk,* previously discussed in Chapter 4.

It should recite that the person who is signing the agreement *knows and understands the scope, nature, and extent of the risk* involved in the operation (which may include personal injury or even death) and that the person *freely and voluntarily chooses to incur that risk* (for thrills or remuneration, as the case may be). The contract is even more compelling if it provides the person the choice between (1) relieving the operator from legal and financial responsibility for accidents that may injure that person (including those resulting from the ordinary negligence of the operator and his employees and others whom the operator may wish to protect by the contract, such as an airport authority) or (2) paying the operator some additional price to be allowed to participate in the activity without waiving responsibility for negligence (but still assuming the risk).

The most effective format for this document requires the person giving up the right to sue to read it carefully and leave a trail of cross-outs and initials throughout the document to indicate having read and understood the agreement and made conscious choices before reaching the signature line.

A word of caution: If the person signing the agreement is a minor, however, you get no protection since a minor can later legally disavow any contract signed while a minor.

Each such contract should be handcrafted by your lawyer for your specific operation. This is another one of those preventive lawyering situations where it is very cost-effective to use your lawyer's skills and foresight to head off potential litigation. Frugal aviation business managers may be tempted to obtain copies of similar agreements relied upon by others who are or have been engaged in similar operations, then just change the name of the business or paste together a composite containing the favorite paragraphs from several such forms. This often results in documents that do not provide you the maximum available protection, at best, and may be the legal equivalent of what psychiatrists call "word salad" (nonsensical gibberish) affording no legal protection, at worst. Gathering other examples is fine, but take them to your attorney; don't try to play lawyer yourself.

Some years ago, I drafted an exculpatory contract for a skydiving operation that was later upheld as valid by the Colorado Supreme Court to bar a suit brought by a jumper injured during the company's air operations. Some of the rip-offs of that contract I've seen perpetuated by skydiving drop zone operators who obviously didn't have the assistance of legal counsel would be laughable if they were so not so legally pathetic. That's a lot like doing your own surgery: If everything goes perfectly, you may save yourself some money. But the odds do not favor everything going perfectly, and you may create far more expensive problems than you started with. Of course this applies to all legal documents, not only exculpatory contracts.

Bear in mind, too, that while some exculpatory contracts are better than others, the best exculpatory contract still does not provide you protection as good as adequate liability insurance. But if you are going to engage in operations that are uninsurable, the exculpatory contract is vastly superior to nothing and, coupled with organization of the enterprise as a corporation or LLC and a tight accident-prevention program, provides a risk-management plan having some depth and diversity.

It is also a good practice for an aviation business to have its legal counsel and insurance representative (broker or agent) review the company's risk-management program at least annually. The focus of this review is to assure that your risk-management program still adequately takes into account any changes in the company's operations, along with recent developments in the law and the insurance industry.

CHAPTER 8

Airline Liability

WHILE THE GENERAL principles of liability and risk management previously studied apply to U.S. airlines in their legal relationship with domestic passengers, a higher duty of care (the *highest degree of care*) is imposed upon them in those operations. The legal relationship between airlines and international passengers (at least from the time the passengers begin the process of boarding the aircraft until they reach a safe place within the terminal at their destination) is governed by a different and unique body of law. This law includes a new international treaty known as the Montreal Convention that is rapidly updating the old Warsaw Convention, which had been modified by a contract known as the Montreal Agreement for flights touching the U.S.

The purposes of this chapter are (1) to acquaint you with the heightened legal responsibility of airlines and the use of airline tariffs as a risk management tool vis-à-vis domestic passengers, (2) to enable you to recognize and avoid common mistakes that can deprive an airline of the protection afforded by international law, vis-a-vis international passengers. The law that governs an airline's liability for injuries to passengers varies, depending upon whether the passenger is traveling on a purely domestic or an international (or partly international) ticket. In both cases, special legal obligations and protections apply to airline operations that do not apply to other flights.

Airline Liability to Domestic Passengers

For the purposes of this discussion, we will define *domestic passenger* as an airline passenger whose ticket shows an origin and destination within the United States and whose *planned* routing does not include any stops outside the United States (Fig. 8.1).

Fig. 8.1. An airline flight may include a mixture of domestic and international passengers and carry a mixture of domestic and international cargo. The airline's legal responsibility for passenger injury or cargo damage can vary radically, depending on whether the injured passenger or damaged cargo is deemed domestic or international.

When a domestic passenger is injured, the first question that must be addressed is whether the airline was acting as a *common carrier.* An operator is considered a common carrier if it represents to the public, either in writing (such as by advertising) or by its course of conduct, that it will (1) *carry for hire* (2) at a *uniform tariff* (price) (3) *all persons* applying (or cargo presented), as long as there remains unused capacity in the aircraft.

These characteristics distinguish common carrier operations from private or contract flying. A tariff in airline terminology encompasses the total agreement between the airline and the passenger or shipper, although the price is the predominant factor in most tariff discussions.

For the purposes of distinguishing between common carriage and contract carriage, the principal controlling question is whether the price paid for the trip is a standard price then in effect for the class of service on the flight or is a negotiated (haggled) price. If the passenger paid an airline's listed fare (for example, a $400 round-trip coach class from Los Angeles to Washington, D.C.), that looks like a common carrier transaction. Contrast a member of a sports team traveling with the team that had negotiated a special price to charter either the entire aircraft or a block of seats. The latter appears more like contract carriage than common carriage. The reason this may be an important distinction is that under the common law, common carriers have been held to have the legal duty to exercise "the highest degree of care" to avoid injuring a passenger instead of the ordinary degree of care to be exercised by the hypothetical "reasonably prudent person" in our exploration of general principles of negligence in Chapter 4. Private and contract carriage is governed by that ordinary degree of care. The highest-degree-of-care standard applicable to common carriage is a tougher test. The courts have generally held the highest-degree-of-care standard to require that the airline and its employees exercise *the greatest degree of human care and foresight possible* to ensure the passengers' safe conveyance.

Although this is a much tougher standard than ordinary care, it is not as tough as strict liability. The courts have shown a practical streak in applying the highest-degree-of-care standard to particular situations, limiting it to a degree of care consistent with the practical operation and conduct of the airline's business. Thus, although a lawyer representing the family of a person killed in an accident resulting from structural failure of an airliner caused by an undetected flaw might argue that the highest-degree-of-care standard required the airline to disassemble every aircraft and scientifically test every component of the aircraft between each flight, a court would recognize the impracticality of that. So the court would refuse to hold that the airline had breached its duty to exercise the highest degree of care by not implementing such a procedure.

At trial, the jury will listen to all of the (often conflicting) testimony of the witnesses (both eyewitnesses expert witnesses) and will reach its own decision as to what really happened and why. Once all of the evidence (testimony, documents, and other physical exhibits) has been received, but before the jury withdraws to the secrecy of the jury room to deliberate, the judge will instruct them on the legal principles they must apply to the facts in order to reach a decision.

These *jury instructions* of the law can be crucial to the outcome. For example, the jury instruction given by the judge in a common carrier case is very different from that given in a contract carrier case. Consider the following scenario: Two jetliners take off from Dallas, Texas, bound for a college basketball tournament in Boise, Idaho. The first aircraft is an airliner operated by a commercial airline and the college basketball team and coaches are traveling on regular-fare tickets purchased for them by the college's alumni association. A few miles behind is an identical airplane owned and operated by a wealthy Texas oilman who is a dedicated alumnus of the school and great fan of its sports teams. The oilman has donated the use of his aircraft to transport his alma mater's basketball team and coaching team. The winds over the Rocky Mountains are westerly and in excess of 30 knots, with wind velocity increasing with altitude. As the two aircraft approach the Rockies, both flight crews observe lens-shaped clouds over the mountains. Both aircraft are experiencing a smooth ride and neither flight crew has illuminated the *fasten seat belts* sign. Suddenly, the first aircraft encounters severe clear-air turbulence that throws unrestrained passengers about the interior of the aircraft, injuring some. A moment later, the same thing happens to the second aircraft.

Injured passengers on both aircraft subsequently sue the aircraft operators for negligence. In the separate trials of the two accidents, expert aviation meteorologists testify that these wind conditions would indicate the probability of development of a standing "mountain wave" along the eastern side of the Rockies. They would further testify that the fact that such a wave had already developed was confirmed by the crews' observation of altocumulus standing lenticular (ACSL) clouds. This mountain wave generated the severe clear-air turbulence encountered by both aircraft. Pilot expert opinion testimony for opposing sides in both cases might then differ on whether a flight crew based in the Great Plains should have known how to recognize these indicia of mountain wave phenomenon, anticipated an encounter with clear-air turbulence, and illuminated the *fasten seat belts* sign to preclude passenger injury.

In the case of the airline, the judge would instruct the jury that as a common carrier it had the duty to exercise the highest degree of human care and foresight consistent with the practical operation and conduct of its business to safeguard its passengers from injury. In that case, the jury would almost certainly find that included a duty to ensure that the flight crews were familiar with all meteorological phenomena they might encounter anywhere on the company's routes, and might well further find the airline negligent for not having done so with this particular crew.

In contrast, in the private-carriage case of the second aircraft, a jury applying the lesser ordinary degree of care of a "reasonably prudent person" *might* find that reasonably prudent pilots based in the flatlands could be unaware of this mountain weather phenomenon without such ignorance constituting negligence. Admittedly, the latter case could go either way, but no one is ever certain what a jury is going to do in any particular case until it has done it. This example serves to illustrate the practical effect of whether the injured passenger was being transported by a common carrier or not.

This elevated standard of care does not apply to every conceivable situation in which a passenger might suffer injury as a result of airline negligence. Rather, the courts have generally limited application of this higher standard to the period between the times passengers depart a safe place within the terminal to board the aircraft until they reach a safe place within the terminal at the conclusion of the flight. Negligence of the airline and its employees could also conceivably cause injury to passengers at many locations within the passenger terminal, including the check-in area, concourses, boarding gates, and baggage claim area. The courts have generally held that the airline owes the passenger only reasonably prudent care within the terminal.

The defense of assumption of risk (see Chapter 4) is not available to airlines as a defense against suits brought by injured passengers (or survivors of passengers killed in an airline crash). This is because, recognizing the statistical evidence that commercial airline travel is the safest means of travel, the courts have held that the airline traveler cannot be considered to have chosen to incur some additional "known risk" by flying on an airline.

Air Carrier Risk-Management Tools in Domestic Operations

An airline can limit its liability for damage to or destruction of domestic passengers' baggage and shipped cargo, and may impose reasonable procedural prerequisites and timetables affecting litigation by passengers through its tariffs. Remember, the airline's tariffs (generally included in a *tariff book* that is available for review by passengers or shippers on request) contain all of the terms and conditions of the contract to transport the person or cargo, including (but by no means limited to) the price charged for the transportation. Although, as we have seen, the law as a matter of public policy goes to great lengths to protect human health and safety, it is somewhat less stringent regarding personal property. There are two areas in which the airline can use tariff provisions as risk-management tools against domestic passengers.

LIMITATIONS ON LIABILITY

The airline may in its tariff set a dollar limit (typically on a per-bag or per-pound basis) on its liability for the loss or destruction of passenger baggage or shipped cargo. Because of the public policy that highly favors the protection of human health and safety, however, airlines are prohibited from placing dollar limits on the amount of their liability for passenger injury or death.

PRIVATE STATUTES OF LIMITATION

Laws that impose time limits on how long after an event a person may file a suit, or be forever barred from filing suit, are called *statutes of limitations.* Airlines are permitted to impose *private statutes of limitation* through tariffs. Most airline tariffs set deadlines for the passenger (or his survivors) or shipper having a claim against the airline (for either personal injury or loss or destruction of baggage or cargo) to notify the airline in writing of the claim and to file suit. The deadline for suit in the tariff may be less than that provided in the applicable public statutes of limitation. At least where the period contained in the private statute of limitations is not so short as to appear unreasonable, the courts enforce these tariff provisions and dismiss lawsuits that, although filed within public statutory periods, are filed after the deadline set forth in the tariff.

Liability for International Passengers

A passenger is considered an *international passenger* if that passenger's ticket shows either (1) an origin in one country and a destination in another country or (2) an origin and destination in one country but a planned intermediate stop in a different country.

Note again that it is generally the passenger's *planned* route as printed on the passenger's ticket that determines whether the passenger is a domestic or an international passenger. Thus, a passenger holding a ticket for a nonstop flight from San Diego to Anchorage is legally a domestic passenger. Overflight of a foreign country (Canada, in this case) en route between two points in the country of origin does not make the flight international, nor would an unscheduled stop in another country, such as an emergency landing. But a passenger on a flight from San Diego to Anchorage with a planned stop in Vancouver, British Columbia, Canada, would be an international passenger. A passenger ticketed from San Diego to Vancouver or from Vancouver to Anchorage would be an international passenger.

THE WARSAW CONVENTION—A PIONEER SLIPPING INTO HISTORY

The legal relationship between airlines and international passengers began with an international treaty generally known as the *Warsaw Convention* and formally titled *The Convention for the Unification of Certain Rules Relating to International Transportation by Air,* a treaty now being rapidly overhauled worldwide by the new Montreal Convention discussed later in the chapter.

Application of the Warsaw Convention in recent decades often had bizarre, sometimes shocking and often baffling consequences. Indeed, if any sense can be made of this treaty, it is only by putting it into historical context. The final version of the treaty was written and agreed to by the

United States and many other nations in 1929. At that time, the international airline business was an infant industry. Visionaries saw that it held great promise to afford a better, safer, faster, and more comfortable way to travel, and thus to become a thriving industry if properly fostered and protected. But at that time, it was neither acceptably safe nor comfortable, nor were participant companies thriving.

The airline industry had experienced a fatality rate of 45 passenger fatalities per 100 million passenger miles flown (compared to modern rates of consistently less than a minor fraction of one passenger fatality over the same distance). Perhaps the safest new transport on the line was the all-metal Ford Trimotor, which is not remembered for the creature comforts its passengers enjoyed; the aircraft was incredibly noisy and neither adequately heated in winter nor cooled in summer. It was also slower and had less range than most of today's light private aircraft.

But while the state of the art was then crude, it was also widely perceived as having great potential for improvement, a perception that has been borne out by history. In drafting this treaty, the various nations' representatives who participated in the process set for themselves the objectives of protecting and promoting the infant international airline industry. They agreed that this would best be accomplished by adopting an international treaty that would

1. Protect international airlines from catastrophic loss in the event of a crash,
2. Promote airline safety,
3. Promote the availability of liability insurance to international airlines,
4. Provide uniformity of terms and conditions of transportation by air with those of other modes of transportation (ship, rail, bus, etc.); and
5. Provide a framework of internationally uniform law to govern international airline crashes.

A threshold problem faced by the delegates who drafted the treaty was that while all of these objectives were laudable, some of them tended to work against one another. For example, the same theory used to justify the imposition of strict liability against manufacturers of defective products (previously discussed in Chapter 4) would argue that safety is best promoted by making the airline strictly liable if a passenger is injured. But that approach would conflict with the objective of protecting international airlines from potentially catastrophic losses and promoting the availability of liability insurance. Thus, as in most legislation and treaties, compromises were reached between competing interests. In its final form, the treaty accomplished the following:

1. *A framework of internationally uniform law* was established. Treaty provisions standardized claims procedures in the event of international airline crashes. These procedures provide internationally uniform answers to these questions:

> a. In what nation's courts may a lawsuit arising out of the crash be brought?
> b. What nation's law governs the crash?
> c. When must the lawsuit be filed or forever barred?

The treaty provided that an international passenger can choose between four possible nations in which to bring a lawsuit for injury: (1) the nation of domicile of the airline, (2) the nation in which the airline has its principal place of business, (3) the nation in which the ticket was bought from the airline or from a travel agent, or (4) the nation that is the passenger's destination.

The treaty contains a globally applicable statute of limitations, providing that suit must be brought, if at all, within two years from the date of the conclusion of the passenger's trip, or its intended conclusion. Except where specific provisions of the treaty apply, the forum court (the court of the nation where the case is being tried) applies its own choice-of-laws rules in deciding what law governs the litigation.

2. *Uniformity of terms and conditions* was achieved not only within the airline industry, but also among all transportation modes. Treaty provisions standardized the documents of transport (the passenger's ticket and, for cargo, the *air waybill*) in formats and contents similar to those already in widespread use for transportation by ship, truck and rail. This assured that travel agents and shipping clerks accustomed to doing business with other transportation modes would quickly feel at home booking passage for customers or shipping goods on the airlines. (Neither the standardization of procedures nor the standardization of documents was particularly controversial. The rest of what the treaty did, however, was extremely controversial then, and that controversy did not abate during the 75 years between the treaty's ratification by the Congress of the United States and the recent ratification of the new Montreal Convention to replace Warsaw.)

3. In an effort *to promote safety,* the treaty imposes *strict liability* on international airlines for *passenger injury or death* and substantially limits defenses that would otherwise be available to international airlines under the common law against claims for the loss or destruction of cargo.

4. Here is the most controversial provision of all: To counterbalance strict liability and protect international airlines from catastrophic loss in the event of a crash—and in connection with that, to promote the availability of liability insurance to international airlines—the treaty limited the dollar amount of the airline's liability for the injury or death of a passenger to the sum of $8,300 (U.S.) and (less controversially) $16.50 (U.S.) per kilogram for the loss or destruction of cargo.

The Association of Trial Lawyers of America (ATLA), an association of plaintiffs' attorneys, strongly opposed ratification of the treaty and continued relentlessly after to lobby to persuade the U.S. government to withdraw from the treaty. ATLA's position was that even in 1929, this was a shockingly cheap price to pay for killing a U.S. citizen, and thus really operated to deny valuable legal rights to U.S. citizens who chose to travel internationally by air.

After 1929, there were a number of other international conferences resulting in several treaties that changed some aspects of the Warsaw Convention between those nations, including from time to time raising the onerous limit of recovery for personal injury or death. But opposition in the United States, spearheaded by ATLA, long prevented the United States from signing any of these subsequent treaties. By 1965, that opposition had reached such proportions the United States declared its intent to withdraw from the Warsaw Convention and to reconsider its prior grant of landing rights in the United States to the airlines of other nations unless those international airlines serving the United States would sign a contract with the U.S. government raising the limits of those airlines' liability for passenger injury or death.

The airlines met with representatives of the U.S. government on neutral territory in Montreal (home of ICAO) where they entered into the *Montreal Agreement,* a contract between the airlines and the U.S. government. The airlines agreed to increase the ceiling on their liability for injury or death of a passenger to $75,000 (U.S.) for those international flights "touching" the United States (originating in, terminating in, or having an agreed stopping place in the United States), regardless of the nationality of the passenger. International airlines wishing to subsequently enter the U.S. market were required to sign the Montreal Agreement as a condition precedent to such service.

Under the Warsaw Convention as modified by the Montreal Agreement, for international flights "touching" the United States, the airline was strictly liable for passenger injury or death, up to a maximum of $75,000 per passenger. Even that was not much money in the modern world.

Liability for International Cargo

The airline was also generally liable under the Warsaw Convention for the loss or destruction of air cargo to a maximum amount of $16.50 (U.S.) per kilogram. There were, however, five *defenses to cargo claims* that the airlines were permitted to use to defeat even that liability (the Montreal Agreement did not change any of the Warsaw provisions regarding cargo liability). These five defenses to international air cargo claims were

1. The airline took *all possible measures* to prevent the cargo loss,
2. *Pilot or navigational error* caused the cargo damage,
3. The shipper's *contributory negligence* caused the damage to the cargo,
4. The loss, damage, or destruction of the cargo was caused by an *act of God, war, or state* or
5. The *nature of the goods* caused the damage.

DEFENSES

All Possible Measures. This defense might apply if, for example, the crash that destroyed the air cargo was caused by a terrorist bomb so sophisticated as to be undetectable by state-of-the-art baggage screening equipment properly employed by the airline.

Pilot or Navigational Error. This is bizarre. Remember: This is a *defense.* If the court found that pilot or navigational error caused the cargo damage, the airline didn't have to pay the shipper even $16.50 per kilogram! For example: An international airline flight was transporting a cargo of gold bars from a bank in the United States to a correspondent bank in Asia. The flight crew wandered off the published instrument approach to the destination airport and collided with a hill enveloped in clouds. A crowd of ordinary citizens reached the crash scene before the authorities, and by the time order was established, the cargo of gold was nowhere to be found. The cause of the accident having been pilot or navigational error, the airline had no liability to the shipper for the loss of this cargo. The only logical explanation for such a result is that pilots seeking airline employment in the late 1920s (when the treaty was drafted) tended to be men who had learned to fly in World War I and had maintained flight proficiency through barnstorming and other feats of aeronautical derring-do. Altogether, a rather wild-eyed bunch of desperados in the eyes of conservative Wall Street investment-banker types whose financial support was needed to promote the growth of the airline industry.

At least where only personal property (cargo) was involved, it appears that the drafters of the treaty intended to give an added measure of security or incentive to such investors. Knowing that the airline would not be held responsible for the consequences (at least to cargo) of whatever foolishness those daring young men in their silk scarves and flying leathers might commit with company "aeroplanes" might make the risk acceptable. (Remember: This defense applied only to cargo and had no bearing on the airlines' strict liability for passenger injury or death.)

Shipper's Contributory Negligence. This defense would apply if the shipper was shipping, for example, a rare and precious vase from the Ming Dynasty and merely shipped it in a crate without sufficient internal energy-absorbing materials to prevent breakage.

Act of God, War, or State. This defense would apply if the cause of the loss, damage, or destruction of the cargo were a major force of nature. For example: The aircraft was picked up from the ramp by a tornado, scattering the cargo to the winds, was shot down or blown up in the course of warfare, or was seized by government agents.

Nature of the Goods. This defense was most often applied in the case of shipments of perishable goods where the shipper did not take any special precautions to purchase refrigerated shipment and the goods spoiled in transit. The cargo simply spoiled because it was perishable; that was its nature.

Warsaw Convention Notice

The Warsaw Convention required the airline to deliver to the passenger a ticket (or to the shipper of air cargo, an air waybill) placing that customer on *notice* that the provisions of that treaty (as amended by the Montreal Agreement) applied to the flight. The airline was required to give this notice in a timely manner, allowing customers the opportunity to take other measures to protect themselves from loss (as by purchasing additional insurance). Attacking the inadequacy of the actual notice given to a passenger prior to a particular accident flight became a favorite technique used by plaintiffs' lawyers to attempt to break the meager limit of liability. A long line of cases interprets the question of what constitutes adequate notice under Warsaw in a great variety of factual scenarios.

NOTICE MUST BE READABLE

Under Warsaw, the notice was required to be printed in 10-point type on a good-quality paper with good-quality ink, using an excellent printing press. Smaller type, cheaper paper and ink, and inferior printing machinery would diminish the readability. If the warnings on the airline ticket (Fig. 8.2) were not clearly readable without the use of a magnifying glass, courts could and often did hold that the airline failed to give the passenger adequate notice.

DELIVERY IN A TIMELY AND PROPER MANNER

Under Warsaw, for notice to be legally adequate, the ticket containing that readable notice was required to be delivered to passengers in a time and manner that permitted them the opportunity to read and understand the warnings contained on the ticket and to take other measures to protect themselves, as by purchasing insurance. In some cases, passengers received their tickets only at the last possible moment during the process of boarding, so that they had no opportunity to read the warnings on the ticket before the door closed and the aircraft was on its way. By then, there was no opportunity for passengers, had they then read and understood the warnings contained in their tickets, to have purchased additional insurance to protect themselves. In such a case, the courts held that the airline failed to give adequate notice.

CONSEQUENCES OF INADEQUATE NOTICE

If a court applying Warsaw found that the airline failed to give adequate notice to an international passenger who was subsequently injured or killed on the trip, the result could have serious financial repercussions for the airline and/or its insurers. In that situation, the airline was still strictly liable for the passenger's injury or death, but the airline was prohibited from availing itself of the dollar limitation on that liability it would otherwise have under the Warsaw Convention as modified by the Montreal Agreement.

If the court found that the airline failed to provide an international cargo shipper an air waybill adequately putting the shipper on notice, the airline could not avail itself of either the dollar limit or any of the five defenses that would otherwise apply.

ADVICE TO INTERNATIONAL PASSENGERS ON LIMITATION OF LIABILITY

Passengers on a journey involving an ultimate destination or a stop in a country other than the country of origin are advised that the provisions of a treaty known as the Warsaw Convention may be applicable to the entire journey, including any portion entirely within the country of origin or destination. For such passengers on a journey to, from, or with an agreed stopping place in the United States of America, the Convention and special contracts of carriage embodied in applicable tariffs provide that the liability of certain carriers, parties to such special contracts, for death of or personal injury to passengers is limited in most cases to proven damages not to exceed U.S. $75,000 per passenger, and that this liability up to such limit shall not depend on negligence on the part of the carrier. The limit of liability of U.S. $75,000 above is inclusive of legal fees and costs except that in case of a claim brought in a state where provision is made for separate award of legal fees and costs, the limit shall be the sum of U.S. $58,000 exclusive of legal fees and costs. For such passengers traveling by a carrier not a party to such special contracts or on a journey not to, from, or having an agreed stopping place in the United States of America, liability of the carrier for death or personal injury to passengers is limited in most cases to approximately U.S. $10,000 or U.S. $20,000.

The names of carriers, parties to such special contracts, are available at all ticket offices of such carriers and may be examined on request. Additional protection can usually be obtained by purchasing insurance from a private company. Such insurance is not affected by any limitation of the carrier's liability under the Warsaw Convention or such special contracts of carriage. For further information please consult your airline or insurance company representative.

NOTICE OF BAGGAGE LIABILITY LIMITATIONS

Liability for loss, delay, or damage to baggage is limited unless a higher value is declared in advance and additional charges are paid. For most international travel (including domestic portions of international journeys) the liability limit is approximately $9.07 per pound for checked baggage and $400 per passenger for unchecked baggage. For travel wholly between U.S. points federal rules require any limit on an airline's baggage liability to be at least $1250 per passenger. Excess valuation may be declared on certain types of articles. Some carriers assume no liability for fragile, valuable or perishable articles. Further information may be obtained from the carrier.

Fig. 8.2. Airline ticket warnings. At this writing, revisions are being drafted to include new Montreal Convention provisions.

1298 ATB (REV. 4-25-89A)

NOTICE

If the passenger's journey involves an ultimate destination or stop in a country other than the country of departure the Warsaw Convention may be applicable and the Convention governs and in most cases limits the liability of carriers for death or personal injury and in respect of loss of or damage to baggage. See also notice headed "Advice to International Passengers on Limitation of Liability."

CONDITIONS OF CONTRACT

1. As used in this contract "ticket" means this passenger ticket and baggage check, of which these conditions and the notices form part, "carriage" is equivalent to "transportation", "carrier" means all air carriers that carry or undertake to carry the passenger or his baggage hereunder or perform any other service incidental to such air carriage, "WARSAW CONVENTION" means the Convention for the Unification of Certain Rules Relating to International Carriage by Air signed at Warsaw, 12th October 1929, or that Convention as amended at The Hague, 28th September 1955, whichever may be applicable.

2. Carriage hereunder is subject to the rules and limitations relating to liability established by the Warsaw Convention unless such carriage is not "international carriage" as defined by that Convention.

3. To the extent not in conflict with the foregoing carriage and other services performed by each carrier are subject to: (I) provisions contained in this ticket, (II) applicable tariffs, (III) carrier's conditions of carriage and related regulations which are made part hereof (and are available on application at the offices of carrier), except in transportation between a place in the United States or Canada and any place outside thereof to which tariffs in force in those countries apply.

4. Carrier's name may be abbreviated in the ticket, the full name and its abbreviation being set forth in carrier's tariffs, conditions of carriage, regulations or timetables; carrier's address shall be the airport of departure shown opposite the first abbreviation of carrier's name in the ticket; the agreed stopping places are those places set forth in this ticket or as shown in carrier's timetables as scheduled stopping places on the passenger's route; carriage to be performed hereunder by several successive carriers is regarded as a single operation.

5. An air carrier issuing a ticket for carriage over the lines of another air carrier does so only as its agent.

6. Any exclusion or limitation of liability of carrier shall apply to and be for the benefit of agents, servants and representatives of carrier and any person whose aircraft is used by carrier for carriage and its agents, servants and representatives.

7. Checked baggage will be delivered to bearer of the baggage check. In case of damage to baggage moving in international transportation complaint must be made in writing to carrier forthwith after discovery of damage and, at the latest, within 7 days from receipt; in case of delay, complaint must be made within 21 days from date the baggage was delivered. See tariffs or conditions of carriage regarding non-international transportation.

8. This ticket is good for carriage for one year from date of issue, except as otherwise provided in this ticket, in carrier's tariffs, conditions of carriage, or related regulations. The fare for carriage hereunder is subject to change prior to commencement of carriage. Carrier may refuse transportation if the applicable fare has not been paid.

9. Carrier undertakes to use its best efforts to carry the passenger and baggage with reasonable dispatch. Times shown in timetable or elsewhere are not guaranteed and form no part of this contract. Carrier may without notice substitute alternate carriers or aircraft, and may alter or omit stopping places shown on the ticket in case of necessity. Schedules are subject to change without notice. Carrier assumes no responsibility for making connections.

10. Passenger shall comply with Government travel requirements, present exit, entry and other required documents and arrive at airport by time fixed by carrier or, if no time is fixed, early enough to complete departure procedures.

11. No agent, servant or representative of carrier has authority to alter, modify or waive any provision of this contract.

CARRIER RESERVES THE RIGHT TO REFUSE CARRIAGE TO ANY PERSON WHO HAS ACQUIRED A TICKET IN VIOLATION OF APPLICABLE LAW OR CARRIER'S TARIFFS, RULES OR REGULATIONS

Issued by the Carrier whose name is in the "Issued By" section on the face of the Passenger Ticket and Baggage Check. SUBJECT TO TARIFF REGULATIONS

Fig. 8.2. (continued)

Interpreting the language of the Warsaw Convention, the courts held that once an airline "accepts" passengers by allowing them to board the aircraft, a later opportunity to read the ticket and buy insurance at an intermediate stop did not cure the lack of notice.

Remember: A person can be an international passenger if he or she buys a ticket for a flight between two cities in the same country but with a planned stop in another country, as in the earlier example of a flight from San Diego to Anchorage with a planned stop in Vancouver, British Columbia, Canada. What if the Canadian stop was inadvertently omitted from the passenger's ticket, even though the airline did plan for the flight to stop there? The courts held that since that omission deprived the passenger of notice that the flight was international in nature and that the limits of Warsaw applied, the passenger was an *international passenger without notice*. Therefore, if the passenger was injured or killed on the trip, the airline would be strictly liable for the accident, but with no artificial limit on the dollar amount of that liability!

Punitive Damages Under Warsaw Convention

There was a difference of opinion between U.S. courts on the question of whether international passengers are permitted to recover punitive or exemplary damages from the airline. There is a provision in the Warsaw Convention that followed the basic rationale used to allow the award of such damages in certain cases (see the earlier discussion of exemplary or punitive damages in Chapter 4). The Warsaw Convention provided that if the accident was caused by *willful misconduct* of the airline (or its employees acting within the scope of their employment), the airline remained strictly liable for the passenger's injury or death but without the artificial dollar limit). In the case of an air cargo claim, in a willful misconduct case the airline could not avail itself of the benefit of the $16.50/kg limit or any of the five defenses to cargo.

The standards for application of this willful misconduct exception closely followed the standards permitting an award of exemplary or punitive damages in domestic negligence cases. Generally, our courts allowed the willful misconduct exception to be applied where the airline or its employees committed an act or omission that they should have known would cause an accident or implied that they had a reckless disregard for whether the act or omission might cause an accident.

Consider the following scenario: An airline's flight crew experienced mechanical difficulty relating to the aircraft's airworthiness in a foreign country and called airline management to request authorization to have the repairs performed there before departure. Airline management denied permission and ordered the crew to proceed on schedule with the passengers aboard and with the aircraft in its present condition, so that the airline's employees can perform the necessary repairs at the company's maintenance facility in the United States. When the crew expressed reluctance to do so, management threatened them with firing on the spot unless they followed orders.

If the uncorrected defect caused an accident on the flight, resulting in passenger injuries, deaths, and/or damage or destruction to air cargo, a jury might well have found that the airline's actions were so outrageous as to constitute willful misconduct. In that case, the artificial dollar limits on passenger injury and cargo damage would not apply, nor could the airline rely upon any of the five defenses to cargo. The result would be that the airline would be strictly liable for the actual dollar value of the losses suffered by the passengers and shippers.

One U.S. court of appeals held that the airline would still be liable for nothing more than that, since in its view international passengers may not recover punitive damages, but another has held punitive damages available in that context. In such a situation, the U.S. Supreme Court is usually called upon to decide which interpretation is correct, but ratification of the new Montreal Convention, barring punitive damages, has made the issue moot for future accidents.

The courts further interpreted the Warsaw Convention, as amended by the Montreal Agreement, to include airline liability for passenger injuries and death resulting from hijackings and terrorist attacks.

Other Liabilities Under Warsaw Convention

By its terms, the Warsaw Convention applies only from the time the passenger begins *"the process of embarking"* until the passenger has completed *"the process of disembarking."* Judicial interpretations paralleled similar decisions on the question of when airlines are responsible for exercising the highest degree of care for domestic passengers. The courts determined that an international passenger has commenced the "process of embarking" once that passenger has left *a safe place within the terminal* for the purpose of boarding the aircraft and has completed the "process of disembarking" upon reaching a safe place within the terminal on arrival (Fig. 8.3).

Bear in mind that the Warsaw Convention as modified by the Montreal Agreement, as well as the new Montreal Convention (discussed in detail later in this chapter, and not to be confused with the Montreal *Agreement*) govern only the legal relationship between the airline and the international passenger or shipper of international air cargo. They have no

8 : Airline Liability 163

Fig. 8.3. During the process of embarking or disembarking, treaties govern an airline's liability to international passengers, and the airline owes the highest degree of care to domestic passengers.

bearing on the passenger's right to sue others who may have caused the accident, such as the manufacturer of a defective aircraft or the federal government for negligence of air traffic controllers.

Since the ticket the passenger is traveling under generally determines whether the passenger is a domestic or an international passenger, it is not unusual to have both domestic and international passengers aboard the same flight. For example, on a flight from Chicago to Mexico City with a planned stop in Dallas, leaving Chicago there might be some domestic passengers traveling on Chicago-Dallas tickets and some international passengers traveling on Chicago-Mexico City tickets. If an accident occurred on the Chicago-Dallas leg, the legal rights of the domestic passengers against the airline would vary radically from the rights of the international passengers. Imagine that the aircraft encountered an unforeseeable microburst moments after takeoff from Chicago and crashed, killing everyone on board.

Claims representatives for the airline's insurance company would almost immediately offer the heirs of each international passenger the full $75,000 limit of liability under the Warsaw Convention as amended by the Montreal Agreement. After all, there could be no doubt that the carrier was strictly liable for these international passengers' deaths, *regardless of the cause,* and the survivors of these passengers (assuming adequate notice and no provable willful misconduct on the part of the airline) had no incentive to file suit since $75,000 is the most they could recover under these circumstances. Such claims tended to be settled very quickly by full payment.

In contrast, although the heirs of the domestic passengers did not face any artificial dollar limits on the amount they could recover from the airline, they must first prove that the accident was caused by some negligence of the airline or its employees (under the highest-degree-of-care standard). Unless they can prove that airline negligence caused the crash, they are entitled to receive nothing from the airline.

The Montreal Convention of 1999—Modernizing Warsaw

The Warsaw Convention accomplished its objectives (admittedly sometimes at considerable cost to injured international airline travelers or their survivors). Liability insurance is now readily available to international airlines, protecting them from catastrophic loss. Travel agents and shipping clerks now routinely and easily book air transportation for passengers and freight, more so now than for any other mode of transportation. A basic framework of internationally uniform law governing international airline passengers has avoided international legal chaos, and at least partly because of all of this, international airlines have made great progress in the more than 75 years since the Warsaw Convention was agreed to. The international airline industry is no longer an infant.

In recognition of this accomplishment and today's realities, representatives of 118 nations and 11 international organizations gathered in Montreal in May of 1999 for the International Conference on Air Law on the Modernization of the "Warsaw System," hosted by ICAO. The delegates found it timely to reconsider whether all of the convention's provisions are still justifiable or if some had served their purpose and merited retirement. By the end of three weeks of discussion, debate, drafting, and redrafting, a new treaty emerged. Formally titled *A Convention for the Unification of Certain Rules for International Carriage by Air*, it is generally referred to as the *Montreal Convention of 1999.*

By its provisions, the treaty would not take effect until 30 nations ratified it. This finally occurred in September of 2003, with the United States being the 30th ratifying nation. As in the past, many nations awaited ratification by the United States before making a ratification decision, since the U.S. refusal to agree to earlier efforts to amend Warsaw had rendered those international efforts largely wasted. Now that the U.S. has ratified the treaty, ratifications are flowing quickly from other nations.

Meanwhile, Warsaw and the Montreal *Agreement* continue to govern international air transport between the U.S. and those nations that have not yet ratified the Montreal Convention.

Many writers credit initiatives by the Japanese airlines, which in 1992 waived the protection of the Warsaw Convention's liability limits, for creating a climate for change that finally enabled this new treaty. In the Japanese compensation culture, where a business causes harm to members of the public it is traditional for executives to promptly make public apologies and for the business to compensate the injured promptly and without resort to litigation. Yet levels of compensation received by Japanese airline accident victims are second only to the United States, and a close second at that.

The Montreal Convention of 1999 should be recognized as a tweaking, a fine-tuning of the Warsaw Convention, rather than a rejection and replacement of that system. The principal changes include

1. Warsaw's strict liability approach survives, with changed limits. The airline is strictly liable for passenger bodily injury or death resulting from an accident occurring on board the aircraft or in the course of embarking or disembarking, for *the first 100,000 SDRs* (all monetary references are to Special Drawing Rights—SDRs—for ease of international currency conversion, with 100,000 SDR equaling about $140,000 U.S., at this writing) of provable compensatory damages. This value will be adjusted for inflation. SDRs are valued by the International Monetary Fund (IMF) by reference to the ever-changing values of a "basket" of the world's most stable currencies, presently the U.S. dollar, euro, British pound sterling, and Japanese yen. The U.S. dollar value of the SDR is posted daily on the IMF's website, and the currencies included in the "basket" are reviewed every five years to assure that it reflects the present relative importance of the various currencies in the world's trading and financial systems. SDRs are used as a point of common reference for valuation in many international treaties.
2. There is no artificial limit on the amount of recoverable compensatory damages *in excess of 100,000 SDRs* unless the airline proves itself free from any fault causing the accident. Warsaw's willful misconduct exception disappears.
3. Punitive damages are specifically precluded by Montreal.
4. New documentation provisions allow the use of electronic ticketing and electronic air waybills. Warsaw's notice requirements disappear.

5. Cargo liability limitations are set at an *unbreakable* 17 SDRs per Kg.
6. Warsaw's five defenses to cargo claims are replaced by these four. The airline is not liable if the destruction or loss of or damage to the cargo was caused by
   a. inherent defect, quality or vice of the cargo (similar to Warsaw's "nature of the goods" defense),
   b. defective packing of the cargo performed by someone other than the carrier, its agents or servants (similar to the "shipper's contributory negligence" defense in Warsaw),
   c. act of war or armed conflict (similar to the familiar "act of god, war or state" defense from Warsaw), and/or
   d. act of public authority carried out in connection with entry, exit or transit of the cargo (seizure or damage by U.S. Customs in the course of inspection being an example).
7. Airlines are liable for delaying passengers and their baggage, to limits of 4150 SDRs per passenger for passenger delay and 1000 SDRs per passenger for baggage delay. These limits are breakable if the passenger proves the delay was the airline's fault.
8. For code-sharing flights, the passenger may recover from either the airline operating the flight or the airline whose code appears on the passenger ticket.
9. The passenger's principal and permanent nation of residence at the time of the accident is added to Warsaw's list as a fifth place where suit may be brought (providing that the airline has a place of business there).
10. Where required by national law, the airline is obliged to make advance payments to meet the immediate economic needs of victims and their families (a routine practice in the industry today, even in the absence of any legal mandate).
11. Airlines are free to agree to higher limits or to waive the limits.

Attorneys practicing in this area of the law predict that as more nations ratify the Montreal Convention, aviation litigation will diminish. Specifically, they forecast that under Montreal, there will soon be

1. No litigation over the loss, damage or destruction of cargo,
2. Little or no litigation by passengers and their families to recover full compensatory damages for injury or death,

3. Few, if any, attempts by airlines to avoid paying compensatory damages above 100,000 SDRs unless the airline clearly did not proximately cause the accident, and
4. An end to the (sometimes extreme) efforts by foreign passengers and their families to bring suit in the United States instead of their home country.

All treaties must be regarded as works in progress (though the progress on updating Warsaw seemed measurable in geologic time), and the Montreal Convention of 1999 is no exception. Like Warsaw, over the years Montreal is likely to become encrusted with judicial interpretations like the hull of a ship with barnacles. The trend of these decisions may reveal flaws in the treaty that will merit amendment, as may developments in the airline industry.

Most criticism to date has not been that the new treaty goes too far, but that it does not go far enough. Someday, no doubt, another will go farther, but will still fall short of perfection in the eyes of some critics, still be overtaken by events.

September 11th Victim Compensation Fund of 2001

Included in the Air Transportation Safety and System Stabilization Act of 2001, enacted by Congress shortly after the terrorist attacks, is a $10 billion fund for compensation of victims physically injured or killed as a result of the terrorist-related aircraft crashes and another $5 billion for compensation of air carriers for losses incurred as a result of the attacks. In order to receive compensation from the fund, victims (including families of those killed in the attacks) are required to waive their right to file or be a party to a civil lawsuit seeking damages for such injuries.

The fund has been profoundly successful in preventing a litigation explosion from resulting from these horrific tragedies, as all but a few victims and their families elected to accept compensation from the fund in lieu of litigation.

CHAPTER 9

Government Liability

THERE ARE MANY opportunities for employment by the federal government in aviation, both in the military and in the civil and career services. As in private industry, the most successful government employees will be those whose education and training have equipped them not only to avoid creating legal problems for their employer but also to assist coworkers in avoiding the kinds of mistakes that could bring adverse legal consequences upon the employer.

The purpose of this chapter is to give you an understanding of the workings of the Federal Tort Claims Act in the aviation industry, to equip you to be a potentially valuable government employee, and to aid in your advancement to a civil service management or military leadership role within the federal government.

The common law, that body of law created by judges through hundreds of years of accumulated judicial pronouncements of what the law is, is a major source of the law in the United States and other *common-law* countries. This is a part of our legal heritage from England, which spread its common law over much of the world through colonization. In much (perhaps most) of the world, however, the decisions of judges are not recognized as an original source of law. In these countries *(civil-law* countries), only the law codified by the legislature or the executive branch is considered the law. Also, in civil-law countries, judges usually hear cases and find the facts without a jury. When the United States declared its independence from Britain in 1776, rather than risk the social and business chaos that might result from starting with a fresh slate, the new nation adopted the British common law of the time (with which it was comfortable and had no quarrel) as the common law of the United States.

This turned out to be a remarkably successful and practical approach to the problem, but with one peculiar twist: England was still a monarchy, so its common law included an artifact common to monarchies, the doctrine of *sovereign immunity*. This doctrine derived from less enlightened times when kings were considered appointed by deities. Deities, the line of reasoning went, were perfect. If a king did wrong, the appointing deity would be imperfect for having made the wrong appointment. Thus the king, having been appointed by a deity, could do no wrong. Since the king (sovereign) could do no wrong, he could not be sued by citizens claiming injury from an alleged intentional tort or negligence committed by the king (or by anyone in the government who was presumed to be doing the king's bidding). Under the doctrine of sovereign immunity, citizens could not sue their government.

The Federal Tort Claims Act

Remarkably, not only did this piece of legal baggage slip into the common law of the United States through that early wholesale adoption, but with respect to the federal government it remained the law until after World War II. When in 1946 Congress passed the Federal Tort Claims Act (FTCA, pronounced "fitca"), 170 years after the Declaration of Independence, Americans were finally permitted to sue our federal government. FTCA allows suit "for injury or loss of property or personal injury or death caused by the negligence or wrongful act or omission of any employee of the government acting within the scope of his office or employment, under circumstances where the United States, if a private person, would be liable to the claimant in accordance with the law of the place where the act or omission occurred."

LIABILITY

Under the FTCA, the federal government, like employers in the private sector, faces vicarious liability for the consequences of intentional torts or negligence committed by its employees acting within the scope of their employment. With a few exceptions to be discussed momentarily, the federal government is liable for the consequences of

(1) negligence or wrongful conduct (as previously analyzed in Chapter 4) of government employees who are
(2) acting within the scope of their employment with the federal government
(3) if a private employer would be liable for that employee's torts under the same circumstances.

EXCEPTIONS

There are several exceptions that distinguish the government's liability from that faced by employers in the private sector.

Geographic Limitation. The FTCA specifically excludes claims arising in a foreign country. This limitation has served to prevent the federal government from being sued, for example, for an accident that occurred at a U.S. Air Force base in Newfoundland that the United States operated under a long-term lease from Great Britain, since the lease did not transfer sovereignty over the area from Great Britain. Issues of liability for injuries arising out of U.S. military activities in the host nation are addressed on a nation-by-nation basis through separate *status of forces agreements (SOFA)* between the nations.

Combatant Activity. The FTCA does not apply to "any claim arising out of the combatant activities of the military or naval forces, or the Coast Guard, during time of war." Under this exception, a suit against the United States brought by the survivors of passengers and crew of an Iranian airliner shot down by a guided missile launched from a U.S. Navy cruiser, which misidentified the plane as a threatening military aircraft during the 1988 "tanker war" in the Persian Gulf, was dismissed by the court, which held that because of this exception such claims remain barred by the doctrine of sovereign immunity.

Activities Incident to Military Service. Congress also provided in the FTCA that the federal government is not liable for the negligent conduct of government employees if the person killed or injured was engaged in an *"activity incident to* [that person's] *military service."* This exception applies even during peacetime operations and has protected the federal government against suits in cases where, for example, a military air traffic controller negligently vectored a military aircraft into rising terrain at night, causing a fatal accident (Fig. 9.1).

Discretionary Function. Finally, Congress has specifically provided in the FTCA that the government would not be liable for the consequences of negligent or wrongful conduct by government employees performing a *discretionary function.* The courts have interpreted this proviso to draw a distinction between planning or policy-making activities of government employees and their operational decision-making. Planning and policy-making do not subject the federal government to liability under the FTCA, even if the plan or policy subsequently causes an accident. Only

Fig. 9.1. Military personnel and their survivors are not allowed to sue the federal government for death or injury occurring while on duty.

operational decision-making, if negligently done, may expose the federal government to liability for a resulting accident.

With these exceptions, the federal government is vicariously liable like any other employer for consequences of the negligence of its employees occurring within the scope of employment. The act applies only to "employees of the government," which it defines to include "persons acting on behalf of a federal agency in an official capacity." FTCA liability does not extend to acts by independent contractors of the government. Although the cases are by no means unanimous, most courts have held that the federal government is not liable for the negligence of nonemployee designees who may be seen as doing the government's work. Thus, the government has usually not been held liable for the acts of Aviation Medical Examiners (AMEs), Designated Airworthiness Representatives (DARs), Designated Engineering Representatives (DERs), Designated Manufacturing Representatives (DMRs), or aircraft mechanics holding Inspection Authorization (IAs). As the FAA begins to certify individual U.S. civil aircraft manufacturers as Certified Design Organizations (CDOs), allowing them to type-certify new aircraft designs as airworthy in accordance with FAA standards but with minimal FAA oversight (similar to the type-certification process already in place in Europe that gives European manufacturers a competitive edge in the speed of certification and production of new designs), we can expect to eventually see litigation to test whether the federal government is liable under FTCA for any negligence of a CDO in the design and certification process.

Most FTCA aviation cases have arisen out of allegations of negligence by federal air traffic controllers.

Intentional Torts. The government is not liable under FTCA for the intentional torts (see Chapter 4) of its employees, nor are those employees immunized by FTCA against personal liability for their intentional torts.

Punitive or Exemplary Damages. Under FTCA, the federal government (unlike a business in the private sector) is not exposed to the risk of punitive or exemplary damages.

Liability for Negligent Air Traffic Control

In early FTCA cases claiming ATC negligence, government attorneys argued that the government should not be liable because the air traffic controller's work is one continuous "discretionary function." The controller must continuously use judgment to issue heading vectors, altitudes, speed restrictions, and clearance limits to individual aircraft often having radically different performance capabilities, to avoid collisions and to make the entire mix of traffic being handled by that controller and receiving controllers downstream flow as smoothly as possible. The courts, however, rejected that argument, holding that what Congress intended by the discretionary function exception was to protect government and its *planners and policy makers* from being sued for the results of plans and policies that might later prove to have been unwise. The courts distinguished this from the admittedly high level of continuous judgment exercised by air traffic controllers, characterized by the courts as "mere operational details" not covered by the discretionary function exception. Thus, if the negligence of an air traffic controller employed by the federal government (there are some air traffic controllers at commercially operated air traffic control towers who are not federal employees) causes or contributes to an aircraft accident, the federal government may be held liable under the FTCA (Fig. 9.2).

The "activities incident to military service" exception may also come into play in air traffic control cases if the person killed or injured was at the time engaged in an activity incident to military service. For example,

Fig. 9.2. Most FTCA cases involve claims of negligence on the part of air traffic controllers.

imagine a military aircraft operating at night in cloud, receiving radar vectors from ATC. An ATC controller negligently vectors the aircraft into a mountain. The survivors of military personnel killed in the crash could not sue the federal government under the FTCA since they were aboard this flight incident to their military service. (They would not have been aboard the aircraft but for their military service.) If a similar accident occurred to a commercial airliner, passengers traveling under military orders would face the same bar. (But remember: This affects only the federal government's liability and has no bearing upon the liability of others whose negligence may have contributed to the crash such as the airline or aircraft manufacturer.)

In cases under the FTCA, government employees are held responsible for exercising the ordinary degree of care of the reasonably prudent person. In many ATC cases, the question of whether the controllers carried out their duty may be resolved by reference to the *Air Traffic Controller's Handbook,* an FAA publication often referred to as the "controller's bible." The handbook instructs controllers how to handle most air traffic situations, even prescribing the exact phraseology to be used in most circumstances. For example, where a controller concluded a takeoff clearance with the phrase "watch the propwash" instead of giving the wake turbulence advisory specified in the handbook, and the departing aircraft encountered wake turbulence, lost control, and crashed, the federal government was held liable under FTCA.

For situations not addressed by the *Handbook,* the controller's actions would be subject to the ordinary negligence test: What would a reasonably prudent air traffic controller have done under the same circumstances? In that situation, the plaintiff's and the government's attorneys would offer the testimony of expert witnesses.

As in other negligence cases, the controller's negligence must have been a proximate cause of the accident for the government to be held liable. It is not enough that the crash occurred while the aircraft was under some measure of ATC control or even that a controller's performance was imperfect. Some negligence of controllers must have caused or contributed to cause the crash.

Liability for Weather-Related Accidents

Primarily through Flight Service Stations (FSS) but also through air traffic control facilities, federal employees monitor the weather, advise pilots and dispatchers of current and forecast weather, and often suggest alternate routing around severe weather. Where the government has undertaken to provide such services, its employees must do so in a reasonably careful manner.

Where such federal employees significantly understated weather along a pilot's route, the federal government has been held liable. Examples include failing to report forecast icing conditions or understating their severity, reporting an incorrect altimeter setting, failing to report deteriorating runway visibility or braking action, or understating the severity of storms, as by reporting a known squall line as a "line of cells."

The FARs establish minimum visibility requirements for takeoff in commercial operations. No such takeoff minima are prescribed, however, for aircraft operating noncommercially under the general operating and flight rules of FAR Part 91. Thus, if an aircraft requests takeoff clearance when visibility is below commercial minima, the handbook requires the air traffic controller to inquire: "Are you carrying passengers or cargo for compensation or hire?" If an affirmative answer is received, the handbook requires the controller to refuse the aircraft takeoff clearance. If the controller issues a takeoff clearance in those circumstances to an aircraft admittedly carrying passengers or cargo for compensation or hire and an accident results, the government may be held liable (along with the aircraft operator). If, however, the flight crew answers in the negative, the controller may issue the aircraft clearance to take off without fear that the controller or the controller's employer will be held liable for any resulting accident.

Although it is legal for controllers to issue clearances and for pilots to attempt to take off in noncommercial operations when visibility is below commercial minima, a takeoff attempt may still be imprudent. Despite the pervasiveness of the FARs, flying still requires pilots continuously to exercise our own judgment. Not every inadvisable action is specifically prohibited by an FAR (though in hindsight an act not specifically prohibited by an FAR may be deemed to have constituted careless or even reckless operation in violation of FAR 91.13).

Pilots should always bear in mind that if a certain action is not specifically prohibited by the FARs, that does not necessarily mean that it's a good idea or would not be considered careless or reckless by the FAA or negligent by a jury. Crew fatigue, rusty instrument skills, questionable reliability of navigational avionics, or other variables may render imprudent an operation that would otherwise be considered routine. The pilot-in-command, bearing the ultimate responsibility for safety of the flight, constantly exercises judgment in the face of changing conditions. While the crew may never choose to ignore an FAR without fear of consequences both to their certificates and being found to be negligent per se, the fact that no FAR was violated is not proof that the crew was not negligent.

To the extent possible, the flight crew is responsible for considering not only the weather conditions reported to them but also their own observations. If the thunderstorm ahead is clearly visible to the crew by looking out the window or at the aircraft's on-board radar or lightning detector, the crew is obviously not justified in relying upon anyone else's assurance that the path ahead is clear. In such a situation, if the crew chooses to continue on that heading with catastrophic results, it is unlikely that the federal government's erroneous reporting of weather conditions ahead will be found a proximate cause of the accident since the true conditions were known to the crew. This is sometimes referred to as a *superseding* or *supervening cause.*

Liability for Negligent Airworthiness Certification

Each civil aircraft manufactured in the United States is the product of three separate FAA inspection and certification processes. First, the design must be proved to conform to aircraft certification standards contained in the FAR. At that point, the FAA will issue a Type Certificate approving the design. Second, the manufacturer must satisfy the FAA that its production and inspection methodology assures precise replication of the design for which the Type Certificate was issued, with each aircraft manufactured to acceptable standards of quality. The FAA issues the manufacturer a Production Type Certificate for the design once it is satisfied with the manufacturer's production facilities and quality-assurance program, and manufacture can proceed. As each individual airplane is completed, it is inspected and tested for conformity with the approved type design and issued its own FAA Airworthiness Certificate before being delivered to the customer. Subsequent modifications and improvements to the design each require additional FAA certification, usually under a Supplemental Type Certificate or FAA Form 337 field approval. Negligence in any of these phases of certification may lead to liability of the federal government.

The FAA will soon begin shifting some of its present workload in this process to the manufacturers as they become certified as CDOs. It remains to be seen whether that shift will also relieve the federal government of FTCA liability for negligence by those CDOs in that process.

Where FAA written standards (such as those included in the FARs and internal agency orders and handbooks) exist, the courts have held that FAA employees engaged in the certification process are not performing a "discretionary function," because they do not have discretion to deviate from these written standards. Therefore, the federal government can be sued for negligence in certification of the aircraft under the FTCA. If, however, the government employee assured exact compliance with those written standards, it is unlikely that the government would be found negligent in certification of the aircraft because the rulemaking process by which those standards were developed would be considered a discretionary function.

In aircraft design and manufacture, much as in-flight operations, FAA regulatory standards provide minima. On one hand, it is clearly both an FAR violation and negligence per se to certify as airworthy an aircraft that does not meet the FAA's standards. On the other hand, the fact that an aircraft design and a particular aircraft meet these published FAA technical standards does not bar a finding of negligence in design or manufacture or a finding that the aircraft was delivered in a dangerously defective condition. The manufacturer may still be found negligent or strictly liable for the consequences of an accident resulting from a design or manufacturing defect even if FAR standards were met.

Administrative Claim Prerequisite to Suit

Under FTCA, a person is required to file an administrative claim for compensation with the federal government and await a decision on that claim before filing suit. If suit is filed before the claim is decided, the court will dismiss it.

9/11 Claims

The Victims Compensation Fund discussed in Chapters 1 and 8 has served to protect the United States from litigation by victims of the terrorist attacks of September 11, 2001.

Personal Liability of Federal Employees

Unlike employees of private enterprise, individual federal employees enjoy protection from personal liability for the consequences of their on-the-job negligence. Federal law now provides that whenever a federal employee is sued personally for negligence in the performance of a federal job, the U.S. Attorney (the federal government's trial lawyer) will substitute the United States for the named employee as defendant, and defend the case in its own name. Any settlement or judgment will be paid by the federal government, not by the individual employee who may have been negligent. In private industry, both the employer and the employee can be held liable for the consequences of the employee's on-the-job negligence.

Federal employees enjoy a rare situation in American law in which a person does not face the risk of personal liability for his own negligence. This is a truly unique benefit of federal employment.

State and Local Government Liability

State governments also enjoy the protection of the doctrine of sovereign immunity, though most if not all have adopted state legislation similar to FTCA, waiving that protection under certain circumstances. These state laws are not uniform, and vary widely.

CHAPTER 10

Accident Notification, Reporting, and Investigation

EVERY AIRCRAFT operator should have an accident-response plan in place for guidance in the event of an aircraft accident. While using your best accident-prevention efforts to avoid an accident, it would be imprudent to operate on the belief that your operation will never experience one.

The time immediately following an accident is one of the most stressful and chaotic periods the flight crew, maintenance personnel, and company management will ever experience. Yet statements made and actions taken in the minutes, hours, and days following the accident by all of those involved will have far-reaching consequences in many areas. These may include FAA enforcement actions against the operator, pilots, and mechanics involved; civil litigation and related questions of insurance coverage; and even criminal charges, as well as damage to the reputations of the company and individuals involved.

This time of stress, grief, and chaos immediately following an aircraft accident is the worst of all possible times to have to first address the question, "What do we do now?"

This chapter lays out factors that should be considered in preparing that portion of your accident-response plan that addresses what to do after the initial focus on rescue of survivors. The purpose of this chapter is to help you develop that portion of your accident-response plan now, before the accident happens.

Controlling the Release of Information

After everything has been done to rescue survivors, focus should shift to securing and preserving the accident scene and wreckage and notifying those who must be notified in a timely manner, while assuring that any facts released are accurate. This damage containment effort is a necessary part of your overall risk-management plan.

Aircraft accidents excite people. Everyone wants to know what happened, and it may seem that everyone is asking at the same time. Everyone involved in the accident—and especially those most intimately involved, surviving flight crew—will be in some degree of shock, may feel overwhelming guilt and/or sadness, may have personal injuries, and will have the highest blood adrenaline level they've ever experienced. One effect of all this is a highly garrulous ("motor mouth") condition. It is in the nature of our training and personalities as pilots that whenever something goes wrong, we immediately start analyzing what went wrong and how we could have prevented it, and this process is certainly speeded up by the accident-induced adrenaline rush. The flight crew may have already arrived at one or more theories by the time they first encounter another person after the aircraft comes to a halt. Their theories are also more likely to be wrong, since speed generally decreases the accuracy of analysis (especially in a highly complex technical context such as an aircraft accident).

But the law bestows a special aura of truthfulness on *excited utterances* made by persons involved in the accident immediately after the accident. Anything you say at this point may be used later by the FAA, a plaintiff or prosecuting attorney with devastating effect as an *admission against your interest* (and your employer's) in an FAA enforcement action, civil litigation, and even criminal prosecutions that may arise out of the accident.

Although it is rare in the United States, prosecuting attorneys may even bring criminal charges (such as *murder* or *manslaughter*) against individual crewmembers or others whose conduct is believed to have led to the accident, seeking imprisonment. This happens more frequently in civil-law countries, which tend to treat virtually all misbehavior as criminal and which usually do not have a system of negligence law intended to compensate victims. Such prosecutorial behavior is, however, not unheard in the United States, especially if the prosecutor is seeking reelection or higher office and believes the attendant publicity may help his prospects. When improperly labeled oxygen generators shipped as air cargo started an in-flight fire that cost the lives of all passengers and crew aboard a Valujet DC-9 in the Florida Everglades, criminal charges were filed against the shipper. (This accident and the outcomes of the numerous cases—administrative, civil, and criminal—it generated is discussed in greater detail in Chapter 4.) For more on crimes relating to aviation, see also Chapter 15.

The press corps may be on the scene early and will diligently apply themselves to obtain every possible statement from crewmembers, other survivors, rescue personnel, and other witnesses. That is their job. Unfortunately, the popular press is notorious for failing to understand or accurately report the facts in aviation accidents, for lack of the most rudimentary technical knowledge. For example, if the pilot is heard to say: "the airplane stalled," this will most assuredly be erroneously translated by the press into a report that "the airplane's engine stalled."

Thus, your accident-response plan should initially focus on precluding people under your influence or control, such as employees, from making any initial statements about what happened, then assuring that only verified facts, *not speculation,* are released.

As a lawyer focusing on controlling damages to aircraft operator clients resulting from an accident, I prefer that clients not *unnecessarily* notify or give statements to anyone and that required notices and reports be given no sooner and in no greater detail than required. But as an observant person, I must also acknowledge that appearing to "stonewall" the news media by refusing to discuss the matter ("no comment")—or even worse, disseminating information that later proves false—may have a devastating effect on public confidence in the aircraft operator or manufacturer. Hopefully, your company will have the assistance of individuals trained and skilled in public relations to assist in the development of that portion of your accident-response plan addressing who is to respond to the news media, when and how, and to manage that response when the time comes. The Aircraft Owners & Pilots Association (AOPA) has an excellent resource available on line that may be helpful to your public relations representative in event of an accident. Titled *AOPA Media Guide for Reporting on Aviation Accidents,* it's now found at

http://www.aopa.org/special/newsroom/media_guide.html

One appropriate way to handle the inevitable barrage of news media inquiries without unduly offending the media is to patiently respond to each inquiry with a simple statement such as: "the accident is being investigated by the National Transportation Safety Board, who are the nation's experts in aircraft accident investigation and who will determine the cause." Refer all inquiries to the NTSB. Do not allow persistent reporters to draw you into speculating on what happened.

Notifications and Reports Required

In the event of an accident, do not file an Aviation Safety Report with NASA. As we saw in Chapter 2, NASA-report immunity benefits do not apply if an aircraft accident was involved. If NASA receives a report of an aircraft accident, the report is not held in confidentiality but immediately forwarded to the NTSB, where it becomes a matter of public record that can then be used against you in FAA enforcement and civil litigation.

Your accident-response plan should designate a specific person or office in the company to be notified first in the event of an accident and a person to whom all inquiries about that accident are to be directed. This enables the company to put its accident-response plan into effect immediately.

You are not required to report accidents or incidents to the FAA, nor are you required to notify the NTSB of *every* mishap involving an aircraft. Because a report may trigger FAA enforcement action (FAA and NTSB personnel do talk to each other) and may provide evidence that can be used against you in related FAA enforcement cases and civil litigation, the NTSB should be notified and written reports filed *only* when required by law.

The operator of an aircraft is required by law to *notify* the nearest NTSB field office *immediately and by the most expeditious means available* (usually the telephone) when there is an aircraft accident or certain other types of incidents. The operator is required to file a *written report* with the NTSB on a form provided by the board within 10 days after an *accident,* but only if requested by the board for one of the *incidents* for which notice is required.

Crewmembers are required to attach a statement setting forth the facts, conditions, and circumstances of the accident or incident at the same time if they are physically able. Crewmembers who are incapacitated at that time are required to submit such a statement as soon as they are able.

The reference determining whether an aircraft mishap requires immediate notification and reporting is NTSB Part 830, Notification and Reporting of Aircraft Accidents or Incidents and Overdue Aircraft, and Preservation of Aircraft Wreckage, Mail, Cargo and Records (found in Title 49 of the Code of Federal Regulations). Under those regulations, the aircraft operator is required to give the NTSB immediate notice of an aircraft accident or certain specific incidents.

ACCIDENTS

To determine whether notice is required, the operator, in consultation with an attorney, must first determine whether the mishap is an *aircraft accident* within NTSB definitions:

> *Aircraft accident* means an occurrence associated with the operation of an aircraft which takes place between the time any person boards the aircraft

10 : Accident Notification, Reporting, and Investigation — 183

with the intention of flight and all such persons have disembarked, and in which any person suffers death or serious injury, or in which the aircraft receives substantial damage.

Thus if an aircraft undergoing inspection slipped off a jack and killed or injured a mechanic working under it, NTSB notification would not be required. Neither would notification be required if an unoccupied aircraft was blown over in a windstorm or damaged by service vehicles (Fig. 10.1). Nor is notification required if the aircraft was in operation (or at least passengers or crew were aboard intending to fly) but no one was killed or seriously injured and the aircraft did not receive substantial damage. The latter situation, however, requires that we consult more NTSB definitions.

Fig. 10.1. This crop-spraying aircraft unquestionably suffered substantial damage, but because it was unoccupied when the tornado ripped it from its tie-down at a rural Arkansas airport and slammed it into a tree in someone's yard a few blocks away, the NTSB need not be notified.

What is *serious injury?* What is *substantial damage?*

Serious injury means any injury which: (1) Requires hospitalization for more than 48 hours commencing within 7 days from the date the injury was received; (2) results in a fracture of any bone (except simple fractures of fingers, toes, or nose); (3) causes severe hemorrhages, nerve, muscle, or tendon damage; (4) involves any internal organ; or (5) involves second- or third-degree burns, or any burns affecting more than 5 percent of the body surface.

Thus, simple cuts and bruises, broken noses, fingers, and toes not requiring hospitalization for more than 48 hours are not serious injuries.

Substantial damage means damage or failure which adversely affects the structural strength, performance, or flight characteristics of the aircraft, and which would normally require major repair or replacement of the affected component. Engine failure or damage limited to an engine if only one engine fails or is damaged, bent fairings or cowling, dented skin, small punctured holes in the skin or fabric, ground damage, damage to rotor or propeller blades, and damage to landing gear, wheels, tires, flaps, engine accessories, brakes, or wingtips are *not* (emphasis supplied) considered "substantial damage" for the purpose of this part.

This excludes many gear-up and other landing accidents that have not caused serious injury.

INCIDENTS

If the mishap was not an *accident* under the above definitions, you must next determine whether it is one of the specific *incidents* that require immediate notice to the NTSB. By NTSB definition:

Incident means an occurrence other than an accident, associated with the operation of an aircraft, which affects or could affect the safety of operations.

You are not, however, required to notify the NTSB of all incidents. You are required to notify the NTSB *only* if any of the following listed incidents occur:

(1) Flight control system malfunction or failure;
(2) Inability of any required flight crew member to perform normal flight duties as a result of injury or illness;
(3) Failure of structural components of a turbine engine excluding compressor and turbine blades and vanes;

(4) In-flight fire; or
(5) Aircraft collide in flight.
(6) Damage to property, other than the aircraft, estimated to exceed $25,000 for repair (including materials and labor) or fair market value in the event of total loss, whichever is less.
(7) For large multiengine aircraft (more than 12,500 pounds maximum certified takeoff weight);
   (i) In-flight failure of electrical systems which requires the sustained use of an emergency bus powered by a back-up source such as a battery, auxiliary power unit, or air-driven generator to retain flight control or essential instruments;
   (ii) In-flight failure of hydraulic systems that results in sustained reliance on the sole remaining hydraulic or mechanical system for movement of flight control surfaces;
   (iii) Sustained loss of the power or thrust produced by two or more engines; and
   (iv) An evacuation of an aircraft in which an emergency egress system is utilized.
(8) An aircraft is overdue and believed to have been involved in an accident.

The initial notification *to* the NTSB should contain no more information than is required. The only information that is required to be given, if available, in the initial notification is

(a) Type, nationality, and registration marks of the aircraft;
(b) Name of owner, and operator of the aircraft;
(c) Name of the pilot-in-command;
(d) Date and time of the accident;
(e) Last point of departure and point of intended landing of the aircraft;
(f) Position of the aircraft with reference to some easily defined geographical point;
(g) Number of persons aboard, number killed, and number seriously injured;
(h) Nature of the accident, the weather, and the extent of damage to the aircraft, so far as is known; and
(i) A description of any explosives, radioactive materials, or other dangerous articles carried.

If the aircraft accident or incident is one requiring immediate notice to the NTSB, shortly after you give the required notice you will receive from the board the forms for submitting any required written reports. The aircraft operator is required to file the written report within 10 days after an *accident*, but is only required to file a written report for an *incident* if the incident is one of those listed above and then only if requested by the board. Both the initial notification and the subsequent written notice should be directed to the nearest NTSB field office. NTSB field offices are listed under U.S. Government in the telephone directories in the following cities: Anchorage, Alaska; Atlanta, Georgia; Chicago, Illinois; Denver, Colorado; Ft. Worth, Texas; Kansas City, Missouri; Los Angeles, California; Miami, Florida; New York, New York; Seattle, Washington.

If the accident occurs outside the United States, notification and reporting requirements and definitions of accidents and incidents may be different. Notification of NTSB-equivalent officials of the country in which the accident or incident occurred is required under international agreements as well as local law. Airline and crew are bound to abide by the laws of the country in which they are operating. Failure to comply with foreign local law can antagonize foreign governments, aircraft accident investigators, and law enforcement officers, having an adverse effect not only on the accident investigation, but also on the legal consequences to the operator and crew and the operator's welcome to continue operating in that nation. ICAO Annex 13, International Standards and Recommended Practices of Aircraft Accident Investigation, provides the general framework for aircraft accident investigations worldwide. Some nations take exception to some particular provisions, but Annex 13 is a good frame of reference for what to expect in the conduct of aircraft accident investigations globally.

Regardless of the location of the accident, flight crew who are members of a union should immediately notify their union of the accident. Union personnel can be of tremendous assistance in diplomatically protecting crewmembers from the press and preventing uncontrolled release of rumors, speculation, potentially damaging admissions, and inaccurate statements of fact. The Air Line Pilots Association (ALPA) wallet card of immediate post-accident advice is reproduced here as Figure 10.2.

The operator's aircraft insurance policy must be consulted to determine the required time and procedure for reporting the accident to the insurer.

Some Techniques That Work

If crewmembers require hospitalization, they will probably be on some form of pain medication, which may cloud their thought processes. Upon request, most hospitals will ensure that the press and FAA and

**WORLD-WIDE
ALPA HOT LINE**

USA (202) 797-4180

CALL THIS NUMBER IMMEDIATELY
IF YOU ARE INVOLVED IN AN
ACCIDENT/SERIOUS INCIDENT
AT ANYPLACE OR ANYTIME
(COLLECT CALLS ACCEPTED)

For any other safety related problem, call the ALPA Engineering and Air Safety Department TOLL FREE at 800-424-2470.

ALPA PILOTS' SAFETY GUIDE

In the U.S. there is no legal compulsion for a pilot to give a statement to the FAA or the NTSB or any other public authority concerning an incident or accident unless he is served with a subpoena. Therefore, it is recommended that you make no statements and accomplish the following, if possible:

1. Keep the crew together.
2. Obtain rest facilities for *ALL* crewmembers away from the airport.
3. MAKE NO STATEMENTS ABOUT THE NATURE OF THE DIFFICULTY.
4. Refer to the back of the ALPA membership card for your rights of representation.

Outside the U.S. accident investigation procedures vary greatly. In the event of an accident in a foreign country, you are urged to call the Hot Line Number immediately and to follow the above steps to the extent possible.

Fig. 10.2. ALPA wallet card.

NTSB investigators are denied access to crewmembers while they're in the hospital.

Even though crewmembers may not appear to have suffered physical injuries that require hospitalization, they are certain to be in some degree of shock that may mask symptoms. Checking them into the hospital with instructions to hospital staff to restrict access can be helpful both to ensure their health and to protect them from interrogators. While the crew are obligated to cooperate in the NTSB investigation, they should not be required to do so until it has been determined that they are physically and mentally competent to answer questions in an intelligent manner. Crewmembers should not be questioned if under the influence of medication or the predictable wave of shock and guilt that inevitably washes over them immediately following the accident. Crewmembers should also refrain from making statements to medical personnel about the cause or details of the accident, as these may be recorded in medical records and later afforded the special aura of truthfulness of excited utterances, even if they're wrong.

Crewmembers should also be reminded, as discussed in Chapter 2 on FAA enforcement, that although they are required to show their certificates to FAA inspectors or other law enforcement personnel on request, they must be on their guard never to relinquish their certificates. They should be cautioned to refrain from making any statements to the FAA.

Once crewmembers are released from the hospital, if circumstances require that they remain in the area, it may be prudent to check them into a local hotel or motel as unobtrusively as possible under assumed names. If they are allowed to return home, it may be worthwhile to arrange for the telephone company to provide crewmembers with a temporary unlisted number.

If the NTSB conducts an informal inquiry during the on-site phase of the accident investigation, the crewmembers should insist that the FAA representatives agree in writing that nothing the pilots say during the inquiry will be used against them in an enforcement action. If the FAA refuses to agree, the crewmembers may request that the FAA representatives be excluded from the informal inquiry.

Most airlines paint their logo on the vertical tail of every aircraft and their name along the top of the fuselage. In the most disastrous aircraft accidents, the tail is often the only identifiable portion of the aircraft remaining. To minimize the adverse psychological effect of airline travelers seeing the company's logo thus displayed in the inevitable long-running news coverage of the accident, some airlines have been known to paint over the name and logo as soon as the NTSB investigator in charge will permit.

Aircraft accidents always expose the companies and individuals involved to the possibility of FAA enforcement actions, civil litigation, damaged reputations, and even criminal charges. Preparation and dissemination of an accident-response plan and following the plan carefully can help control these adverse consequences. An excellent example is the *Emergency Response Manual* published by the National Air Transportation Association (NATA) (www.nata-online.org).

The NTSB has recently received additional tasking from Congress to serve as the coordinator to integrate the resources of the federal government and other organizations (such as the American Red Cross) to support the efforts of state and local governments and the airline to meet the needs of airline disaster victims and their families. Family counseling, victim identification and forensic services, communicating with foreign governments, and translation services are among the federal services the NTSB can make available to help local authorities and airlines deal with a major airline disaster. In these disasters, a Joint Family Support Operations Center (JFSOC) is now routinely established under the NTSB's Federal Family Assistance Plan for Aviation Disasters to coordinate support to affected families.

PART III

Aircraft Transactions

CHAPTER 11

Buying and Selling Aircraft

IN MY EXPERIENCE, most litigation over aircraft purchases arises because (1) buyer and seller did not come to a clear agreement on all aspects of the transaction and failed to properly document the deal, particularly the aircraft's condition, and (2) the buyer failed to commission an adequate prepurchase inspection and title search before buying the aircraft.

State law largely governs the buying and selling of aircraft, with federal law only peripherally involved. Generally speaking, all sales and financing of products, including aircraft and aircraft components, are governed by state law. Fortunately, the law of all 50 states is now virtually identical in this area since all have adopted the Uniform Commercial Code (UCC) with few or no modifications. The UCC provides, however, that where a federal statute provides a system for recording documents of ownership and security interests in a specific class of products, federal law prevails. This is the case with aircraft under the Federal Aviation Act of 1958, as amended. As we saw in Chapter 1, the FAA Aircraft Registry in Oklahoma City maintains records showing the entire history of ownership and other legal interests in all aircraft of U.S. registry (that is, all aircraft having an N number).

The UCC regulates business almost as pervasively as the FARs regulate aviation safety. The UCC is usually intensely studied in college-level business law courses. Because of the pervasive effect of the UCC on all business transactions, including aviation (and because in my observation more aviation businesses fail as a result of poor business practices than from poor aviating), I recommend that all students supplement this aviation law course with a business law course.

The sale of an aircraft raises legal considerations not only for the buyer and seller but also for any lender who may be financing the purchase for the buyer and any person or business that may already hold a security interest in the aircraft.

If you are the buyer, you want to know (1) What am I really buying? (2) What are my legal rights if the aircraft turns out to be a lemon? (3) Am I getting clear title to the aircraft?

State law governs the first two questions, as the law of *warranty* is covered by the UCC. The third question, governed by the law of *security interests,* is answered partly by reference to state law under the UCC and partly by federal law under the Federal Aviation Act.

From the seller's point of view, there are also warranty law considerations in selling an aircraft. Sellers want to know the nature and extent of their legal liability if the buyer later becomes unhappy with the airplane and suffers a condition lawyers refer to as "buyer's remorse."

A lending institution (bank or finance company) financing a portion of the purchase price for the buyer will be concerned with these basic questions: (1) How can we assure that we will get paid, no matter what may happen to the aircraft in the future? (2) Will we have any exposure to being held liable if the aircraft is involved in an accident?

In this chapter, we will examine state and federal laws relating to these basic concerns of people in businesses buying, selling, and financing aircraft.

Security Interests

A security interest is a legal interest in an item of personal property that secures the payment of a debt. *A* person or business may acquire a security interest in an aircraft by loaning money to the purchaser and obtaining a written *security agreement* (Fig. 11.1) signed by the purchaser, by performing work or furnishing goods and services to the aircraft *(mechanics' and materialmen's liens),* or by providing storage for the aircraft *(warehousemen's liens).*

If the aircraft owner does not pay the debt when due, the holder of a security interest has the right to take possession of the aircraft (or to retain possession, as in the case of a repair station that has completed an inspection, repair, servicing, or modification of the aircraft but not yet received payment), even without resorting to judicial process, so long as this can be done without provoking a breach of the peace.

Thus, a security interest can be considered an exception to the tort law of conversion (discussed in Chapter 4). Indeed, the aviation industry has "repo men" who earn their livelihood by traveling around the country repossessing aircraft for unpaid holders of security interests (also referred to as *lienholders).* Like their counterparts in the automotive world, these people rely on stealth and speed to take the aircraft and spirit it away, often in the middle of the night, sometimes using bolt cutters to free locked tie-down chains or to gain entry to hangars. As long as the repossessor can get the airplane without a fistfight or shoot-out, the taking is legal in most states. It is obviously of great interest to buyers and lenders to ensure that the aircraft being purchased is not already subject to some unsatisfied security interest that might lead to the unhappy surprise of its being taken in a midnight repossession.

TITLE SEARCH

Because aircraft can so quickly travel from state to state and because Congress saw the need to enable buyers and lending institutions quickly and simply to determine who has what legal rights in an aircraft, the FAA Aircraft Registry was established at the FAA Aeronautical Center in Oklahoma City, Oklahoma. The Federal Aviation Act, which created the Aircraft Registry, requires that all documents reflecting ownership of aircraft and security interests in aircraft be filed there.

A *title search* at the FAA Aircraft Registry should reveal not only who owns an aircraft but also all *recorded* security interests outstanding against the aircraft. You can access the Aircraft Registry through the FAA website. There are also several private companies in Oklahoma City, including an office of the Aircraft Owners and Pilots Association (AOPA), that will perform a title search for you for a modest fee and quickly provide you a written report on the aircraft's ownership and outstanding recorded security interests. They typically back up their report with title insurance, protecting you against any error in their report (a benefit not available if you choose the on-line do-it-yourself approach). If you are borrowing to purchase the aircraft, the lender will require that you purchase a title search as a precondition of making the loan. But even if you are in the enviable position of being able to pay cash, it is still prudent first to purchase a title search to assure yourself that the seller is really the owner and that there are no lienholders who have not been paid and who may send the midnight repossessors to take the aircraft after you've paid for it.

One type of security interest that a title search may not reveal is the *possessory lien*. Under state law, a mechanic, FBO, repair station, or other business that has provided parts, labor, fuel, or storage for the aircraft is not required to release the aircraft to the owner without first being paid. Where such a business is holding the aircraft awaiting payment, it is said to have a possessory lien on the aircraft. Possessory liens are not required to be filed with the FAA Aircraft Registry, and under the law of most states there is no documentation of a possessory lien that one could file. Simply

DEPARTMENT OF TRANSPORTATION
FEDERAL AVIATION ADMINISTRATION
FAA AIRCRAFT REGISTRY
P.O. Box 25504
Oklahoma City, Oklahoma 73125

AIRCRAFT SECURITY AGREEMENT

NAME & ADDRESS OF DEBTOR

NAME & ADDRESS OF SECURED PARTY/ASSIGNOR

ASSIGNED/NAME & ADDRESS OF ASSIGNEE

ABOVE SPACE
FOR FAA USE ONLY

Date:_____
Complete description of collateral being mortgaged:
AIRCRAFT (FAA registration number, manufacturer, model, and serial number):

NOTICE: ENGINES LESS THAN 750 HORSEPOWER AND PROPELLERS NOT CAPABLE OF ABSORBING 750 OR MORE RATED SHAFT HORSEPOWER ARE NOT ELIGIBLE FOR RECORDING.
ENGINES (manufacturer, model, and serial number):

PROPELLERS (manufacturer, model, and serial number):

SPARE PARTS LOCATIONS (air carrier's name, city, and state):

together with all equipment and accessories attached thereto or used in connection therewith, including engines of _____ horsepower, or the equivalent, and propellers capable of absorbing _____ rated takeoff shaft horsepower, described above, all of which are included in the term aircraft as used herein.

The above described aircraft is hereby mortgaged to the secured party for the purpose of securing in the order named:

FIRST: The payment of all indebtedness evidenced by and according to the terms of that certain promissory note, hereinbelow described, and a renewals and extensions thereof.

Note bearing date of _____, 19___ executed by the debtor and payable to the order of _____ in the aggregate sum of $_____ with interest thereon at the rate of _____ per centum per annum, from date, payable in installments as follows: The principal and interest of said note is payable in _____ installments of $_____ each on the _____ day of each successive month beginning with the _____ day of _____ 19___. The last payment of $_____ is due on the _____ day of _____ 19___.

SECOND: The prompt and faithful discharge and performance of each agreement of the debtor herein contained made with or for the benefit the secured party in connection with the indebtedness to secure which this instrument is executed, and the repayment of any sums expended or a vanced by the secured party for the maintenance or preservation of the property mortgaged hereby or in enforcing his rights hereunder.

Said debtor hereby declares and hereby warrants to the said secured party that he is the absolute owner of the legal and beneficial title to the s aircraft and in possession thereof, and that the same is free and clear of all liens, encumbrances, and adverse claims whatsoever, except as follows: (If liens other than this mortgage, indicate "none".)

It is the intention of the parties to deliver this instrument in the state of _____.

AC Form 8050-98 (7-87) (0052-00-038-4001)

Fig. 11.1. FAA aircraft security agreement.

Provided, however, that if the debtor, his heirs, administrators, successors, or assigns shall pay said note and the interest thereon in accordance with the terms thereof and shall keep and perform all and singular the terms, covenants, and agreements in this security agreement, then this security agreement shall be null and void.

Time is of the essence of this security agreement. It is hereby agreed that, if default be made in the payment of any part of the principal or interest of the promissory note secured hereby at the time and in the manner therein specified, or if any breach be made of any obligation or promise of the debtor herein contained or secured hereby, or if any or all of the property covered hereby be hereafter sold, leased, transferred, mortgaged, or otherwise encumbered without the written consent of the secured party first had and obtained, or in the event of the seizure of the aircraft under execution or other legal process, or if for any other reason the secured party may deem himself insecure, then the whole principal sum unpaid upon said promissory note, with the interest accrued thereon, or advanced under the terms of this security agreement, or secured thereby, and the interest thereon, shall immediately become due and payable at the option of the secured party.

Upon default, secured party may at once proceed to foreclose this mortgage in any manner provided by law, or he may at his option, and he is hereby empowered so to do, with or without foreclosure action, enter upon the premises where the said aircraft may be and take possession thereof, and remove and sell and dispose of the same at public or private sale, and from the proceeds of such sale retain all costs and charges incurred by him in the taking or sale of said aircraft, including any reasonable attorney's fees incurred; also all sums due him on said promissory note, under any provisions thereof, or advanced under the terms of this security agreement, and interest thereon, or due or owing to the said secured party, under any provisions of this security agreement, or secured hereby, with the interest thereon, and any surplus of such proceeds remaining shall be paid to the debtor, or whoever may be lawfully entitled to receive the same. If a deficiency occurs, the debtor agrees to pay such deficiency forthwith.

Said secured party or his agent may bid and purchase at any sale made under this mortgage or herein authorized, or at any sale made upon foreclosure of this mortgage.

In witness whereof, the debtor has hereunto set _____ hand and seal on the day and year first above written.

ACKNOWLEDGMENT: NAME OF DEBTOR _____
(If required by applicable local law)
SIGNATURE(S) (IN INK)_____
(If executed for co-ownership, all must sign)

TITLE_____
(If signed for a corporation, partnership, owner, or agent)

ASSIGNMENT BY SECURED PARTY

For value received, the undersigned secured party does hereby sell, assign, and transfer all his right, title, and interest in and to the foregoing note and security agreement and the aircraft covered thereby, unto the assignee named on the face of this instrument at the address given, and hereby authorizes the said assignee to do every act and thing necessary to collect and discharge the same. The undersigned secured party warrants and agrees to defend the title of said aircraft hereby conveyed against all lawful claims and demands except the rights of the maker. The undersigned secured party warrants that he is the owner of a valid security interest in the said aircraft. (A Guaranty Clause or any other provisions which the parties are desirous of making a part of this assignment should be included in the following space.)

Dated this _____ day of _____, 19____.

ACKNOWLEDGMENT: NAME OF SECURED PARTY (ASSIGNOR)_____
(If required by applicable local law)
SIGNATURE(S) (IN INK)_____
(If executed for co-ownership, all must sign)

TITLE_____
(If signed for a corporation, partnership, owner, or agent)

THIS FORM IS ONLY INTENDED TO BE A SUGGESTED FORM OF SECURITY AGREEMENT WHICH MEETS THE RECORDING REQUIREMENTS OF THE FEDERAL AVIATION ACT OF 1958, AND THE REGULATIONS ISSUED THEREUNDER. IN ADDITION TO THESE REQUIREMENTS, THE FORM OF SECURITY AGREEMENT SHOULD BE DRAFTED IN ACCORDANCE WITH THE PERTINENT PROVISIONS OF LOCAL STATUTES AND OTHER APPLICABLE FEDERAL STATUTES. THIS FORM MAY BE REPRODUCED.

SEND, WITH APPROPRIATE FEE, TO: FAA AIRCRAFT REGISTRY
P. O. BOX 25504
Oklahoma City, Oklahoma 73125

AC Form 8050-98 (7-87) (0052-00-036-4001)

PLEASE REMOVE THIS PORTION AT PERFORATION BEFORE SUBMITTING TO FAA.
↓ ↓ ↓ ↓ ↓ ↓ ↓ ↓ ↓ ↓ ↓ ↓ ↓

retaining possession of the aircraft pending payment perfects a possessory lien. Thus, before closing the deal to purchase an aircraft, the buyer should inquire at the FBO or other facility where the aircraft is located whether there are any possessory liens against it for unpaid bills.

The prudent FBO, mechanic, or repair station will not release an aircraft after it has been worked on, stored, or fueled unless first paid by credit card, cash, or certified funds (a certified or cashier's check). However, if for some reason the business wishes (as to accommodate a long-time good customer claiming a temporary cash shortage), it may have the aircraft owner sign a promissory note for the amount due, secured by a security agreement, giving the creditor a security interest in the aircraft. Those documents should then be immediately filed with the FAA Aircraft Registry. If the aircraft is released without these, the lien is extinguished, but by following this procedure, the lien is preserved (but at a lower priority, behind other previously recorded security interests).

If the existence of an unsatisfied security interest (either recorded or possessory) is revealed by the title search or inquiry at the FBO, that does not necessarily mean that the purchaser should abandon plans to purchase the aircraft. The purchaser need only ensure that such lienholders are paid out of the proceeds of the sale and provide the new owner a *lien release,* which can then be filed with the FAA Aircraft Registry to clear that security interest off the aircraft's records.

PERFECTION AND PRIORITY

Filing the security agreement with the FAA Aircraft Registry perfects a nonpossessory security interest in an aircraft. If a lienholder who is not in possession of the aircraft fails to record a security agreement with the FAA Aircraft Registry, a buyer who is not otherwise aware of that security interest (a *good faith purchaser without notice*) takes clear title, and the lienholder's security interest is unenforceable.

Sometimes there may be several security interests in an aircraft, having a total value that may even exceed the value of the aircraft. In such a case, if the aircraft owner is unable or unwilling to pay these debts, the question of *priority* among the holders of these security interests becomes important. Any unpaid lienholder may repossess the aircraft and dispose of it in accordance with general procedures set forth in the UCC. The Code permits the sale of the aircraft in virtually any commercially reasonable manner, with notice of the sale to the aircraft's registered owner required before the sale can take place. If the proceeds of that sale are greater than the total of all possessory and recorded security interests, all lienholders receive the entire amounts they are still owed, and the surplus is then paid to the aircraft's pre-repossession owner. But if the proceeds of the sale are insufficient to satisfy all debts owed to lienholders, the following *order of priority* applies:

1. The person having *possession* of the aircraft under a possessory lien for parts, labor, materials, or services has first priority and is entitled to be paid in full from the proceeds of the sale before any other lienholder. This is an example of the old adage "possession is nine-tenths of the law."
2. As between the holders of *recorded* security interests (those who have filed documents with the FAA Aircraft Registry reflecting their security interests in the aircraft) priority runs from the date and time of *filing,* the rule being "first in time, first in right." Thus, after any possessory lienholder is paid in full, the earliest lienholder of record is entitled to be paid in full before the next, and so on down the line until the proceeds of the sale are exhausted.

Warranties

A *warranty* is a statement or representation made by the seller regarding year of manufacture, make and model, equipment, condition, and title. State law under the UCC governs warranties. The UCC provides for two categories of warranties: *express warranties* and *implied warranties.*

EXPRESS WARRANTIES

Express warranties are not required to be expressed in writing but may be created by oral representations made by the seller to the buyer during the course of negotiating the sale and need not be in any particular form. The UCC has the following to say about how an express warranty is created:

(1) Express warranties by the seller are created as follows:
  (a) Any affirmation of fact or promise made by the seller to the buyer which relates to the goods and becomes a part of the basis of the bargain creates an express warranty that the goods shall conform to the assignation or promise.
  (b) Any description of the goods which is made part of the basis of the bargain creates an express warranty that the goods shall conform to the description.
  (c) Any example or model which is made part of the basis of the bargain creates an express warranty that the whole of the goods shall conform to the sample or model.

(2) It is not necessary to the creation of an express warranty that the seller use formal words such as "warrant" or "guarantee" or that he have a specific intention to make a warranty, but an affirmation merely of the value of the goods or a statement purporting to be merely the seller's opinion or commendation of the goods does not create a warranty.

Let's consider some examples of the creation of express warranties. In negotiating the sale of a used general aviation light twin-engine aircraft, the seller shows the prospective buyer the engine logbooks, which indicate that both engines have received major overhauls only 10 hours previously. This can be seen as both an *affirmation of fact* and a *description of the goods* that creates an express warranty that the engines have so recently benefited from such an overhaul. If the buyer inquires about the oil consumption of these engines and the seller states that he just returned from a long cross-country trip in the airplane and it did not burn any oil, that may also constitute an affirmation of fact creating an express warranty as to the low oil consumption. If the seller agrees to deliver the aircraft with a currently effective FAA Airworthiness Certificate, that can be seen as a promise or description of the goods expressly warranting that all FAR-mandated inspections are current and all ADs have been complied with.

If the aircraft is purchased based upon examination of a manufacturer or dealer's demonstrator model, the seller expressly warrants that the aircraft delivered will be identical to that demonstrator model, except as otherwise agreed between the buyer and seller.

Not everything the seller says about the airplane creates an express warranty. Some laudatory hyperbole is considered by the law "mere commercial puffery" that does not create a warranty. Examples would be statements like "It's a great little airplane; you won't find a better one anywhere" or "It was owned by a little old lady who only flew it to church on Sundays" or "It's a super bargain that won't be here long at this price; another guy just left to meet with his banker and if he gets back first with the money, it's his."

Although the UCC does not require that the seller's statements be put in writing to create express warranties, this is another one of those situations where it is prudent to call upon your lawyer to put the purchase contract, clearly expressing the warranties, in writing. Then if a dispute should later arise, the document is clear proof of the agreement. Otherwise, you should not be surprised if the seller's recollection of the discussions differs from your own, and it may require the expense, exasperation, and unpredictability of a trial where a jury decides which of you is telling the truth

11 : Buying and Selling Aircraft

to resolve the controversy. Have *your* lawyer draft the agreement; Don't succumb to the temptation to save a little money by using a standard form offered by the other party to the transaction or one drafted by its lawyer. There is no such thing as a generic "fair" or "standard" aircraft purchase contract, and the contract I draft when I'm representing a seller may be very different from the one I draft if I am representing the buyer. If both sides use attorneys, then an agreement acceptable to both sides will surely be achieved (if it cannot, you may be better off not going through with the deal). Whether the other side uses a lawyer or not, you should always use yours.

IMPLIED WARRANTIES

The UCC also provides for implied warranties in certain circumstances. The two kinds of implied warranties under the UCC are an implied warranty of *merchantability* and an implied warranty of *fitness for a particular purpose*.

The UCC provides that unless specifically excluded (more on this shortly), the law implies a warranty that a product is "merchantable" *if the seller is a merchant with respect to goods of that kind* (that is, if the seller is in the business of selling aircraft, whether full-time or part-time). The law does not imply a warranty of merchantability if the sale is between private parties. To be *merchantable,* the product must be, in the language of the UCC, "fit for the ordinary purposes for which such goods are used." In other words, an aircraft must be fit for flight; it must be airworthy.

While the FARs do not define "airworthy," the NTSB and the courts have held this word to mean a great deal more than simply that the aircraft is capable of flight. To be airworthy, an aircraft must be in its original or properly altered (in accordance with the FARs) condition, as verified by the logbooks (Fig. 11.2).

The UCC implies a warranty of *fitness for a particular purpose*

> [w]here the seller at the time of contracting has reason to know any particular purpose for which the goods are selected and that the buyer is relying on the seller's skill or judgment to select or furnish suitable goods.

For example: A prospective buyer approaches someone offering a helicopter for sale (not necessarily a merchant) saying: "I don't know much about helicopters, but I own a construction company, and we need one. It must be capable of lifting a 10,000-pound ski-lift tower and hovering to place it at altitudes up to 14,000 MSL and temperatures up to 90° Fahrenheit." If the seller represents to the buyer that a particular helicop-

Fig. 11.2. The fact that it will fly does not prove that an aircraft is airworthy. To be deemed legally airworthy, an aircraft must be in its original or properly altered condition, as verified by its logbooks and maintenance records.

ter will do that job and the buyer relies on the seller's representation, the seller has impliedly warranted the helicopter's capability to perform that function under those conditions.

DISCLAIMER OF WARRANTIES

The UCC does, however, permit sellers to *disclaim* some warranties. Express warranties cannot be disclaimed, but implied warranties may. Such disclaimers are required to be in writing and conspicuous. All implied warranties can be disclaimed by the use of such approved expressions as "there are no warranties which extend beyond the description of the aircraft on the face of this agreement, including, but not limited to, any implied warranty of merchantability" or "the aircraft is delivered and accepted as is, with all faults," or other language that in common understanding calls the buyer's attention to the exclusion of warranties and makes it plain that there is no implied warranty.

When the buyer before purchasing the aircraft has examined it thoroughly (or has had the opportunity to examine it but refused to), there is no implied warranty covering defects that such an examination ought to have revealed.

BREACH OF WARRANTY

If a warranty is breached, the buyer must notify the seller and give the seller an opportunity to correct ("cure") the problem. If the seller fails or refuses to fix the problem, the buyer may sue for breach of warranty. The suit may seek *specific performance* (a court order for the seller to correct the deficiency, at its expense), *damages* (judgment for the seller to reimburse the buyer the cost of repairs), or *recision* (judgment for the seller to refund the purchase price and take back the aircraft). Such litigation can be expensive (perhaps prohibitively so for a relatively inexpensive aircraft), and its outcome is always something less than certain. If you have financed the purchase of the aircraft, you will have to continue to make your loan payments while the litigation is in progress.

Avoiding Litigation

To prevent the necessity for litigation over what warranties were or were not made or breached in the sale, it is in the interest of both buyer and seller to have a written purchase contract clearly expressing the warranties agreed to or excluded from the deal. Unless buying an aircraft known not to be airworthy for purposes of completion or rebuilding, buyers should not agree to contracts containing warranty disclaimers like "as is, with all faults."

It is much less expensive for a prospective buyer to learn all that can be learned about the condition of an aircraft before purchasing it than to pursue litigation claiming a breach of warranty later. Therefore, if you are considering purchasing an aircraft, you should hire an aircraft mechanic to perform a prepurchase inspection. The ideal person for the job would be someone you know and trust or who enjoys an excellent reputation (and has no relationship with the seller that might color the inspector's judgment). An airframe and powerplant (A&P) mechanic holding Inspection Authorization (IA) and having special experience and familiarity with the particular make and model of aircraft would be most desirable. This person should have the list of all airworthiness directives (ADs) and manufacturers' Service Bulletins (SBs) on the aircraft and its engines. There is no such thing as a "standard" prepurchase inspection. But if you really want to know what condition the airplane is in before you buy it, nothing less than an *annual inspection* will provide you that level of detail. It is worth the cost, and you may be able to persuade the seller to split the cost with you (Fig. 11.3).

Reliance on a recent annual inspection signed off by an IA unknown to you is unwise, as there are unfortunately some unscrupulous individuals in the industry who will sign off anything for a price.

Fig. 11.3. Appearances can be deceiving. Only a thorough prepurchase inspection to annual inspection standards by an independent IA familiar with the make and model can give you a reliable picture of an aircraft's condition.

Closing the Sale

If you decide to purchase the aircraft, it is a good practice to have a formal *closing* of the deal, much as you would when purchasing a home, with the buyer, seller, lending institution, and lienholders (or their representatives) present. Distant lienholders often arrange for the buyer's lending institution to serve as their escrow agent, sending lien releases to that institution to be recorded only after the funds to pay off the lien have been forwarded to the lienholder.

At the closing, the buyer should receive a signed *bill of sale* from the seller (Fig. 11.4). This is an FAA form available free through most FAA offices and on the FAA website. If the seller is a corporation, check to be certain that the bill of sale has been signed properly. (Review the three mandatory elements of a proper corporate signature in Chapter 5.) If this signature is incomplete, the FAA Aircraft Registry will reject the document and refuse to re-register the aircraft to its new owner until a proper signature is obtained. FAR 47.3(b) prohibits you from operating an aircraft that has not been registered to its owner. If the paperwork on the transaction is not perfect, this operates to ground your aircraft until the im-

UNITED STATES OF AMERICA U.S. DEPARTMENT OF TRANSPORTATION FEDERAL AVIATION ADMINISTRATION **AIRCRAFT BILL OF SALE**	FORM APPROVED OMB NO. 2120-0042

FOR AND IN CONSIDERATION OF $ THE UNDERSIGNED OWNER(S) OF THE FULL LEGAL AND BENEFICIAL TITLE OF THE AIRCRAFT DES-CRIBED AS FOLLOWS:

UNITED STATES REGISTRATION NUMBER   **N**

AIRCRAFT MANUFACTURER & MODEL

AIRCRAFT SERIAL No.

DOES THIS   DAY OF   ,
HEREBY SELL, GRANT, TRANSFER AND DELIVER ALL RIGHTS, TITLE, AND INTERESTS IN AND TO SUCH AIRCRAFT UNTO:

Do Not Write In This Block
FOR FAA USE ONLY

PURCHASER

NAME AND ADDRESS
(IF INDIVIDUAL(S), GIVE LAST NAME, FIRST NAME, AND MIDDLE INITIAL.)

DEALER CERTIFICATE NUMBER

AND TO   EXECUTORS, ADMINISTRATORS, AND ASSIGNS TO HAVE AND TO HOLD SINGULARLY THE SAID AIRCRAFT FOREVER, AND WARRANTS THE TITLE THEREOF:

IN TESTIMONY WHEREOF   HAVE SET   HAND AND SEAL THIS   DAY OF

SELLER

NAME(S) OF SELLER (TYPED OR PRINTED)	SIGNATURE(S) (IN INK) (IF EXECUTED FOR CO-OWNERSHIP, ALL MUSTSIGN.)	TITLE (TYPED OR PRINTED)

ACKNOWLEDGMENT (NOT REQUIRED FOR PURPOSES OF FAA RECORDING: HOWEVER, MAY BE REQUIRED BY LOCAL LAW FOR VALIDITY OF THE INSTRUMENT.)

ORIGINAL: TO FAA:
AC Form 8050-2 (9/92) (NSN 0052-00-629-0003) Supersedes Previous Edition

Fig. 11.4. FAA aircraft bill of sale form.

perfection is corrected. At this point, Murphy's Law often kicks in and the seller drops dead before the documentation can be corrected. This results in your aircraft sitting on the ground while you spend thousands of dollars and months, if not years, getting a court order clearing the title so you can register and operate it without the missing signature.

The buyer should also receive *lien releases* signed by all lienholders who are executing these releases in exchange for that portion of the sale proceeds covering the balance of the debt still owed them.

If the contract of sale prepared by your lawyer or negotiated by lawyers for both parties (clearly expressing the warranties and exclusions of warranties agreed to) has not been signed, it should be signed by both the buyer and the seller at the closing. (The contract of sale is not the same thing as the bill of sale.)

If you're financing the purchase of the aircraft, the lender will require you to sign a *promissory note* and a *security agreement* giving the lender a security interest in the aircraft to secure payment of the loan.

The bill of sale, lien releases, and security agreement should then be filed with the FAA Aircraft Registry (usually by mail, although this is sometimes done in person on extremely expensive aircraft), along with an FAA form Aircraft Registration Application (Fig. 11.5) signed by the new owner. In accordance with the Federal Aviation Drug Enforcement Assistance Act, the FAA will no longer accept aircraft registration applications that list a post office box or mail drop as the sole address. A street address or other physical location is required (although a P.O. box may also be included). The pink copy of the Aircraft Registration Application ("pink slip") must be kept in the aircraft as the temporary registration certificate until the FAA Aircraft Registry issues a new Aircraft Registration Certificate in the new owner's name. It is prudent to assure that all of these documents have been mailed before operating the aircraft. (Also remember to ensure that liability and hull insurance on the aircraft has been bound and is in effect before starting the engine.) The pink slip is legally adequate as a temporary registration for flights within the United States, but international agreements require that you have the permanent registration on board before crossing international borders. If you anticipate an international flight shortly after closing the transaction and notify the FAA Aircraft Registry of this and the need for expedited handling, it will provide you with a very quick turnaround on issuance and return of the new permanent registration.

An application for aircraft radio station license (Fig. 11.6) in the new owner's name must be filed with the Federal Communications Commission (FCC) in Harrisburg, Pennsylvania. Most FAA field offices also stock free copies of this form.

UNITED STATES OF AMERICA DEPARTMENT OF TRANSPORTATION FEDERAL AVIATION ADMINISTRATION-MIKE MONRONEY AERONAUTICAL CENTER AIRCRAFT REGISTRATION APPLICATION		CERT. ISSUE DATE
UNITED STATES REGISTRATION NUMBER	N	
AIRCRAFT MANUFACTURER & MODEL		
AIRCRAFT SERIAL No.		
		FOR FAA USE ONLY

TYPE OF REGISTRATION (Check one box)

☐ 1. Individual ☐ 2. Partnership ☐ 3. Corporation ☐ 4. Co-owner ☐ 5. Gov't. ☐ 8. Non-Citizen Corporation

NAME OF APPLICANT (Person(s) shown on evidence of ownership. If individual, give last name, first name, and middle initial.)

TELEPHONE NUMBER: ( )

ADDRESS (Permanent mailing address for first applicant listed.)

Number and street: _____

Rural Route: _____ P.O. Box: _____

CITY	STATE	ZIP CODE

☐ **CHECK HERE IF YOU ARE ONLY REPORTING A CHANGE OF ADDRESS**

ATTENTION! Read the following statement before signing this application. **This portion MUST be completed.**

A false or dishonest answer to any question in this application may be grounds for punishment by fine and / or imprisonment (U.S. Code, Title 18, Sec. 1001).

CERTIFICATION

I/WE CERTIFY:

(1) That the above aircraft is owned by the undersigned applicant, who is a citizen (including corporations) of the United States.

(For voting trust, give name of trustee: _____), or:

CHECK ONE AS APPROPRIATE:

a. ☐ A resident alien, with alien registration (Form 1-151 or Form 1-551) No. _____

b. ☐ A non-citizen corporation organized and doing business under the laws of (state) _____ and said aircraft is based and primarily used in the United States. Records or flight hours are available for inspection at _____

(2) That the aircraft is not registered under the laws of any foreign country; and

(3) That legal evidence of ownership is attached or has been filed with the Federal Aviation Administration.

NOTE: If executed for co-ownership all applicants must sign. Use reverse side if necessary.

TYPE OR PRINT NAME BELOW SIGNATURE

	SIGNATURE	TITLE	DATE
EACH PART OF THIS APPLICATION MUST BE SIGNED IN INK.	SIGNATURE	TITLE	DATE
	SIGNATURE	TITLE	DATE
	SIGNATURE	TITLE	DATE

NOTE Pending receipt of the Certificate of Aircraft Registration, the aircraft may be operated for a period not in excess of 90 days, during which time the PINK copy of this application must be carried in the aircraft.

AC Form 8050-1 (12/90) (0052-00-628-9007) Supersedes Previous Edition

Fig. 11.5.   FAA aircraft registration application form.

FCC Form 404	UNITED STATES OF AMERICA	Approved by OMB
March 1982	FEDERAL COMMUNICATIONS COMMISSION	3060-0040
	APPLICATION FOR AIRCRAFT RADIO STATION LICENSE	Expires 10/31/84

A. Read instructions before completing.
B. Use typewriter or print clearly in ink.
C. Sign and date application.
D. Mail this form to Federal Communications Commission, P.O. Box 1030, Gettysburg, PA. 17325.

DO NOT WRITE IN THIS BLOCK

1. FAA Registration or FCC Control Number (*If known*)
   N

2. Is application for a fleet license? If yes, give number of aircraft in fleet.
   No ☐ Yes ☐ No. of aircraft

3. Type of Applicant (*Check one*)
   ☐ (I) Individual   ☐ (P) Partnership   ☐ (A) Association   ☐ (C) Corporation
   ☐ (D) Individual with Business Name   ☐ (G) Governmental Entity

4A. Name of Individual (*Last, First, Middle Initial*)
4B. Name (*If other than individual*)
4C. Names of Partners (*Last, First, Middle Initial*) (*Answer only if you checked partnership in item 3*)

5. Mailing Address of Applicant (*Number and Street, City, State, ZIP Code*)

6. Will the applicant own the radio equipment? If no, give name of owner. Yes ☐ No ☐
   Name

7. Does the applicant own the aircraft on which the radio equipment is to be installed? If no, give name of owner. Yes ☐ No ☐
   Name

8. If not the owner of the radio equipment, is applicant a party to a lease or other agreement under which control will be exercised in the same manner as if the applicant owned the equipment? Yes ☐ No ☐

9. Frequencies requested (*Check all you will use under this license*)
A. Do not check both private aircraft and air carrier
   ☐ (A) Private Aircraft   ☐ (C) Air Carrier   ☐ (S) Public Service   ☐ 121.5 & 243 MHz only   (*For emergency locator transmitter*)
B1. Specify frequencies by rule number(s) if you check here.
   ☐ (E) Aeronautical Enroute ⟶ Rule Number(s)
B2. Answer only if you checked item 9B1, aeronautical enroute frequencies.
   Will a valid agreement with licensees of aeronautical enroute stations be in effect as required by the rules? Yes ☐ No ☐
C. You must submit additional information, if you check here. (*See instructions*)
   ☐ (A) Instructional   ☐ (T) Flight Test HF   ☐ (V) Flight Test VF   ☐ (O) Other (specify)

10. Categories of transmitters (*Check all transmitters to be used*)

A	Emergency Locator (121.5 & 243 MHz)	H	Radar (9300 to 9500 MHz)
B	VHF Communications (118 to 136 MHz)	I	Radar (15,400 to 15,700 MHz)
C	Distance Measuring Equipment (DME) (960 to 1215 MHz)	J	Doppler Radar (8750 to 8850 MHz)
D	Transponder (1090 MHz)	K	Doppler Radar (13,250 to 13,400 MHz)
E	Radio Altimeter (1600 to 1660 MHz) (*See instruction*)	L	High Frequency Communication (2–25 MHz)
F	Radio Altimeter (4200 to 4400 MHz)	M	Marine Transmitter for Public Service
G	Radar (5350 to 5470 MHz)	N	Other

11. Answer space for any required statements (*Use reverse side if more space is needed*)

READ CAREFULLY BEFORE SIGNING

Certification: 1) The applicant waives any claim to the use of any particular frequency or of the ether because of previous use of same, whether by license or otherwise. 2) The applicant accepts full responsibility for the operation and control of the requested station license in accordance with applicable law and rules of the FCC. 3) The applicant will have unlimited access to the radio equipment and will take effective measures to prevent its use by unauthorized persons. 4) Neither applicant nor any member thereof is a foreign government or representative thereof.

| WILLFUL FALSE STATEMENTS MADE ON THIS FORM OR ATTACHMENTS ARE PUNISHABLE BY FINE AND IMPRISONMENT, U.S. CODE: TITLE 18, SECTION 1001. | SIGNATURE of individual, partner, or authorized person on behalf of a governmental entity, or an officer of a corporation or association. | DATE |

Fig. 11.6. FCC form to license aircraft radio station.

If a 406 MHz emergency locator transmitter (ELT) is installed, that must be registered with the National Oceanic and Atmospheric Administration (NOAA), to facilitate search and rescue efforts in the event of activation. NOAA is working to enable aircraft owners to accomplish this registration online.

Tax and Registration Requirements

The purchaser of the aircraft will have to pay either a *sales tax* or a *use tax* on the transaction in the purchaser's state of residence. If the sale took place in that state, then the sales tax that applies to other sales of goods in the state applies. However, if the aircraft was purchased out-of-state and then brought into the state, a use tax applies instead of a sales tax. The law in most states provides that if the purchaser has paid a sales tax on the purchase in the state where the aircraft was purchased, that amount is credited against any use tax due in the aircraft's new home state. If the amount of tax paid in the state of purchase is less than the amount due in the aircraft's new home state, the purchaser must pay the home state the difference as a use tax. If a person paid a sales tax in the state of purchase equal to or greater than the use tax due in the aircraft's new home state, the purchaser typically has no use tax liability in the aircraft's new home state (but receives no refund of any excess).

In most states, the aircraft will be subject to some form of annual *personal property tax*. In many states, the procedure followed is similar to the annual registration of automobiles, with the aircraft owner paying both a *registration fee* (typically based upon the weight of the aircraft) and a *specific ownership tax* (a form of personal property tax having a prescribed rate for aircraft, often based upon the current bluebook value of the aircraft). In most states, at least a portion of these taxes is earmarked for airport development and provides a major source of funds that can be used to match federal funds to pay for airport improvements (discussed in greater detail in Chapter 13).

Under the law of most states, state revenue authorities automatically acquire a *tax lien* on aircraft for which these taxes have not been paid. Such a state law usually provides that upon request of state tax authorities, law enforcement officials (such as the county sheriff) may seize aircraft and sell them (usually at an auction called a *sheriff's sale*) to satisfy the owner's unpaid tax liability. As with the post-repossession sales previously discussed, if the sale brings more than the amount of the tax debt, the excess is paid to the aircraft owner.

In many states, failure to register and pay state taxes on aircraft is also a *misdemeanor* (a minor crime, as distinguished from *a felony,* a major crime). Punishments that can be meted out by the courts to recalcitrant tax evaders (in addition to the seizure and sale of the aircraft described above) typically include a fine or a jail sentence of up to one year.

When purchasing an aircraft, you should consult your accountant beforehand to determine which state taxes you will be liable for—as well as any federal taxes, tax credits, or accelerated depreciation benefits that may apply—so that you can plan your budget accordingly.

If you are selling an aircraft on which you have taken depreciation for tax purposes, your accountant should be consulted to determine the potential tax consequences of the sale. If the aircraft's value has not actually depreciated at the rate used on your business's books of account (as is often the case), selling the aircraft at a price higher than its depreciated value may result in a *recapture of depreciation.* That will require an amendment of previous tax returns to reflect the actual depreciation experienced rather than the projection previously relied upon. This may mean that additional federal and state income taxes will have to be paid for previous years. In some instances, an aircraft may even fetch a higher price than you originally paid, in which case you might face additional income tax liability not only for such a recapture of depreciation but also for a *capital gain.*

Carefully following the procedures described in this chapter assures the buyer clear title to the aircraft and assures that both buyer and seller are quite clear on what legally enforceable promises have been made regarding the aircraft and its condition. Coupled with the technique of naming the lender as the *loss payee* on the aircraft's hull insurance coverage and obtaining a *lienholder's interest endorsement (breach of warranty endorsement)* on that policy as discussed in Chapter 6, these procedures assure the lender of payment of any balance on the loan, even if the aircraft is later destroyed in an accident. The question of whether by virtue of being the holder of a recorded security interest in the aircraft the lender will have any exposure to liability if the aircraft is involved in an accident is directly and clearly answered in the negative by the Federal Aviation Act.

We have answered the questions of buyers, sellers, and lenders with which we began this chapter. Now we turn to legal considerations in the leasing, time-sharing, and management of aircraft.

CHAPTER 12

Aircraft Leasing and Co-Ownership

LEASING HAS BECOME an increasingly popular method for corporate operators, flight schools, charter operators, the airlines, and even individuals to obtain the use of aircraft without making the substantial capital investment required to purchase them. Indeed, the U.S. airline fleet is now composed of far more aircraft leased than owned by the airlines operating them.

As in aircraft purchases, much of the litigation arising out of aircraft leases results from inadequate diligence in negotiating and documenting the details of the lease agreement. The "leaseback," a composite of sale and lease, has generated a volume of litigation entirely out of proportion to the popularity of its use.

Fractional Ownership has become a very popular and economical alternative to outright ownership of large and turbine-powered business aircraft. This alternative is not, however, without its limitations and pitfalls.

The purposes of this chapter are

1. To instill in you an appreciation of the differences between a lease and leaseback (and the special problems inherent in leasebacks)
2. To provide you with a methodical approach to negotiating an aircraft lease
3. To equip you with a basic working knowledge of fractional ownership
4. To build further upon your appreciation of the prudence of using the professional services of legal counsel in a preventive role in drafting the final version of agreements

LEASING

Lease and Leaseback Distinguished

Some incorrect uses of lease terminology have permeated the aviation industry in recent years. It is important to use language precisely in aviation. A *lease* is an agreement, a contract that permits someone else to use an owner's aircraft. The lease portion of this deal is correctly referred to as a *leaseback* only where, as a part of the same "wraparound" business deal, the buyer purchases the aircraft from the seller and then turns around and leases it back to the seller for the seller's use. Not all leases are leasebacks; in fact, a minority are. It may help to think of a lease that is not tied to an aircraft purchase in this circular manner as a *lease forward* (Fig. 12.1).

The drafting of a lease or leaseback agreement is another area in which it is prudent to have your attorney either draft the agreement or review the agreement offered to you by the other party and suggest changes that may be advisable to protect your interests. A little preventive lawyer-

The sale and lease (forward): two separate transactions involving three parties

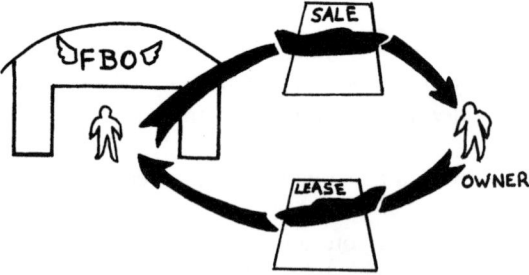

The sale and leaseback: a single circular transaction with only two parties

Fig. 12.1. Illustration distinguishing an aircraft lease from a leaseback.

ing at the drafting stage can avoid misunderstandings or disputes that might later necessitate expensive litigation having an uncertain outcome.

In any lease (forward or back), the aircraft owner is referred to in legal terms as the *lessor* and the user as the *lessee*. If you are the lessor, you should carefully check the credit rating of the prospective lessee before deciding to lease the aircraft. After all, you are entrusting the user with an extremely valuable machine. If the lessee operates or has previously operated aircraft leased from others, inquire about their experiences with the lessee, especially timely payment and aircraft care and maintenance.

Another reason to check carefully the person to whom you are considering leasing an aircraft is the potential for seizure of the aircraft by law enforcement agencies if it is used for illegal purposes such as drug smuggling. The government expects aircraft owners not only to refrain from such activities ourselves but also to exercise due diligence to ensure that others do not use our aircraft for such criminal activities. Even if the aircraft owner is not directly involved in the scheme, the aircraft may be seized and forfeited to the government if its owner fails to take reasonable measures to ensure that the aircraft is not being used for such unlawful activities. It is not enough for the aircraft owner to have seen no evil.

Once the decision is made to enter into a lease, you may save on your attorney's fees by first agreeing with the other party to as many of the details of the lease as possible before going to your attorney to draft the lease. Your attorney will need the information contained in the following checklist to draft the lease agreement. If you bring all of this information with you to the first interview, it will save you considerable time and expense.

Aircraft Lease Checklist

1. *Description of the aircraft.* Manufacturer, model, manufacturer's serial number, and aircraft registration (N) number.

2. *Name and address of registered owner.* This must be exactly as it appears on the FAA aircraft registration certificate.

3. *Name and address of lessee.* If a corporation, be sure to provide the corporation's full legal name.

4. *Maximum certificated gross takeoff weight of the aircraft.* If more than 12,500 pounds, the lease must contain the truth-in-leasing clause required by FAR 91.23.

5. *Who is the "operator" responsible for compliance with FARs governing aircraft operations?* Under the broad definition of *operate* contained in FAR 1.1, the lessor could be held responsible for FAR violations committed by the lessee. A clear statement of responsibility for compliance with operational FARs in the lease may ameliorate that risk.

6. *Exclusive or nonexclusive use.* Does the lessee have the exclusive use of the aircraft during the term of the lease, or will the owner retain some right to use the aircraft from time to time? If the owner retains any right to use the aircraft during the term of the lease, how are scheduling conflicts that may arise between the owner and the lessee to be resolved?

7. *Inspections and maintenance.* Who is responsible for scheduling required inspections? Who is responsible for paying for those inspections, and how (directly or by deduction from lease payments)? Who has the authority to order maintenance? Are maintenance expenses estimated to exceed some set amount required to be approved by the owner before work begins? Are there any requirements as to who may perform the maintenance? Who will pay for the maintenance, and how (directly or by deduction from lease payments)?

8. *Other expenses.* Where is the aircraft to be based when it is not being flown or under inspection or maintenance? Will it be tied down outside or hangared at its base when not in use? Who pays for the hangar or tie-down expenses, and how? Who pays taxes and registration fees for the aircraft, and how? Who pays for fuel, additives, oil, and other lubricants consumed by the aircraft and how? Who pays landing fees and other airport use fees, and how?

9. *Insurance.* Who provides aircraft insurance coverage for liability and hull and in what amounts? Will exclusions to that insurance be acceptable? What pilot qualifications will be required? Will a lienholder's interest endorsement (breach of warranty endorsement) be required to protect a lienholder having a security interest in the aircraft? Who will be named as insureds on the policy? To whom will the insurance company make payment (the loss payee) in the event of a loss covered by the hull insurance? What proof of insurance and notice of change or cancellation will be required to be provided, when, and to whom?

10. *Crew expenses.* Who will provide the flight crew and pay their salaries, expenses, workers compensation insurance, and unemployment compensation insurance?

11. *Lease payments.* What rent does the lessee agree to pay the lessor ($X per month, per Hobbs meter hour, etc.)? When, where, and how will this payment be made? Is some minimum monthly use or payment guaranteed by the lessee? Is there any provision to vary the amount of the lease payments to account for factors such as changes in fuel prices and/or inflation? Is either the lessor or lessee required to set aside reserve funds for engine overhaul and overhaul or replacement of other time/life limited components?

12. *Duration, renewal, and termination.* How long will the lease last?

Who can terminate the lease sooner than that, and how? Can the lease be terminated only for specific reasons (such as nonpayment of rent or destruction of the aircraft)? Does the lessee have the option to renew the lease on the same terms for an additional term? If so, how must that be done, and when?

Special Considerations in Leasebacks

In my experience, leasebacks more frequently lead to disputes and litigation than other leases. In the ordinary aircraft lease (a lease forward), the lessor's primary motive is to earn income from the aircraft and the lessee's primary motive is to obtain the use of an aircraft without having to make the capital investment required to purchase one. Once the parties' motivations have been harmonized in a lease agreement, neither the lessor nor the lessee usually has any incentive to turn around and undermine that happy working of the lease.

That is not the case with a leaseback. Aircraft leasebacks developed primarily as an aircraft sales tool, the leaseback being offered as an incentive to encourage people to purchase aircraft they might not feel they could otherwise afford. Although in a leaseback, the seller/lessee has the same motivation as a lessee in a lease forward (to obtain the use of an aircraft without having to make the capital investment to purchase one), that is generally the lessee's secondary motive in a leaseback transaction. The primary motive of the lessee in a sale and leaseback is to sell the aircraft. As we will see, the introduction of this motive may give the lessee an incentive to act later in ways that may undermine the happy working of the leaseback portion of the transaction. Additionally, the buyer/lessor may pay a substantially higher price for the aircraft when a leaseback is included in the deal than if it were not. Let's explore this in greater detail.

THE SALES PITCH

The leaseback is typically offered by an FBO to a prospective aircraft purchaser who is vacillating over whether he can afford the aircraft as a final "carrot" to close a sale. Under the leaseback, the prospective buyer is told that he will receive income from the FBO's use of the aircraft in charter, flight training, and rental to other pilots to help cover the monthly payments for the aircraft's financing, inspections, and maintenance. He is told that the arrangement will also allow the new owner to deduct as business expenses depreciation, insurance, inspection, maintenance, and storage expenses associated with ownership of the aircraft.

Aircraft are sold on commission, and the dealer may receive as much as 25% of the purchase price for selling a new aircraft. If you were purchasing an aircraft without a leaseback, you would probably find some negotiability of the price. Dealers are usually willing to reduce the price by at least a portion of their commission on the theory that a percentage of something is better than all of nothing. Some dealers are required by their dealership agreement to purchase a certain number of aircraft from a manufacturer each year (customers or no). Dealers may have to finance the purchase of those aircraft through what is referred to as *floor plan financing* of their inventory. Dealers faced with aircraft in inventory have even been known to sell aircraft below cost in order to relieve the burden of the monthly payments of principle and interest on the floor plan financing. But where the purchaser wants to lease the aircraft back to the seller, the sale price usually becomes nonnegotiable, locked in at the dealer's list price for a new aircraft or "asking price" for a used aircraft. Thus, interjecting the leaseback into the transaction may deprive the buyer of the opportunity to negotiate purchase of the aircraft at a more favorable price.

The seller will usually include in the sales pitch calculations showing the prospective buyer the income-generating potential of the aircraft based upon some hypothetical monthly use figure and inspection and maintenance costs. When the seller actually presents the proposed leaseback agreement, however, it usually states that the seller/lessee does not guarantee any minimum monthly use or payment. The form lease offered by the seller/lessee to the prospective buyer is usually either for only one year or without a fixed duration. It usually provides that either party may terminate the lease on relatively short notice (typically from 10 to 30 days) without having to show good cause for cancellation. The form leaseback agreement offered by the seller-lessee also usually provides that all maintenance will be done by the seller-lessee's maintenance shop and at the seller-lessee's discretion, but at the owner's cost. It may provide that maintenance costs can be deducted from rental payments due, and if inspection and maintenance costs exceed the amount of rental payments due to the owner in a given month, the owner has to pay the seller-lessee the difference.

TYPICAL SAD EXPERIENCES

The seller-lessee is likely to have competitors in the area who are also in the business of aircraft charter, rental, and flight training. In that competition, the FBO that has the newest aircraft available on its flight line enjoys a competitive advantage. Thus, the seller-lessee is continually faced with the competitive incentive to keep the newest and shiniest aircraft on its flight line. This puts an incentive on the seller-lessee to not keep the aircraft under leaseback for longer than two years, since an aircraft that has been in service for two years (and particularly one that has regularly been used by people who have no pride of ownership in that aircraft) is no longer a new aircraft either in actuality or appearance.

Further, the incentive of commissions on sales (one of the rare opportunities for an FBO to earn a large chunk of quick cash) remains to motivate the seller-lessee to sell similar aircraft to other prospective buyers. If by negotiating a similar leaseback (and thus adding a newer aircraft to its flight line) the dealer can close another sale and make another sizable commission, the dealer is likely to seize that advantage. That may, of course, be to the detriment of the owner of a similar aircraft already leased back, since the newer aircraft may draw customers away from the older one, which will then see less use and generate less income for its owner.

There is also an incentive for the less than perfectly scrupulous seller-lessee to defer needed maintenance when the leased aircraft is in high demand for flight operations (particularly while the warranty is still good), then to attempt to catch up on deferred maintenance to provide an income to the seller-lessee's repair facility during periods when demand for the use of the aircraft is slow (such as seasons of inclement weather). Some FBOs have even been known to perform unnecessary maintenance or falsely bill aircraft owners for maintenance not performed. This can be very difficult for the aircraft owner to prove.

Judicious use of leasebacks can assure an FBO a steady supply of new aircraft on its flight line, producing income (without requiring capital investment) and producing handsome commissions on sales. On the other hand, the purchasers of these aircraft may find that their aircraft are being abused by the nonowners who are allowed to fly them, that inspection and maintenance costs are considerably higher than forecast while income is less. They may find that as the aircraft condition and appearance deteriorate (more rapidly than an aircraft used only by its proud owners), the FBO becomes less and less interested in having the bird on its flight line.

At this point, a disillusioned owner may turn to the FBO lessee and say, "This isn't working out as I expected, and I can't handle this financial burden any more. Will you please see if you can find someone to buy the airplane?" The dealer expresses regret at the owner's disappointment but finds a buyer and takes another commission on the resale. Then, adding insult to injury, the disillusioned owner may find that due to economic factors previously discussed, the aircraft has appreciated, or at least depreciated at a lesser rate than that scheduled by the owner's accountant, so that the owner has recaptured depreciation in the sale and now must file amended income tax returns and pay additional income taxes for the years the aircraft was owned.

Careful economic analysis may reveal that the prospective aircraft purchaser would be better off not to rely on a leaseback arrangement but to buy an aircraft only if able to meet the aircraft payments and expenses independently of any income that may be generated by the aircraft. This is particularly so if the purchaser is able to justify use of the aircraft in her own business or profession. The purchaser will then be in a position to bargain down the purchase price of the aircraft considerably. Such a purchaser will also be impervious to any reversals in the anticipated tax consequences of the purchase and use of the aircraft that could otherwise be unexpectedly precipitated by unilateral action of the lessee in prematurely terminating or declining to renew the lease. If the purchaser can then find another responsible party to share the use of the aircraft and its costs of ownership through a more traditional lease (lease forward) arrangement, that might make better economic sense. Even if that opportunity did not materialize, the purchase should have no catastrophic financial consequences for the new owner.

When Is a Lease a Charter?

Some operators attempt to use leases to avoid the requirements of FAR Parts 135 and 121. The FAA very closely scrutinizes *wet leases* whereby the aircraft owner leases the aircraft *with flight crew* to another user. The basic presumption applied by the FAA is that if the aircraft and crew are both provided by the same source, the transaction is not a lease, but a charter, so the operation could not legally be conducted under the General Operating and Flight Rules of FAR Part 91, but would be subject to the far more stringent requirements of FAR Part 135 or 121, depending on the size of the aircraft.

CO-OWNERSHIP

Because aircraft ownership is so costly, individuals often go in together to buy an aircraft to share. This is not a partnership (in legal terms, a partnership is a form of business, only); it is *co-ownership*. Such owners are not partners (although this is a common misuse of the phrase, often heard around general aviation airports); they are *co-owners*. Because of the risk of vicarious liability associated with partnership (see Chapter 5), such owners would be well advised to clean up their language, introducing each other to the world as "my aircraft co-owner," not "my aircraft partner." In order to avoid later disputes, the co-ownership agreement should also be encapsulated in a legal document, signed by all of the co-owners clearly setting out responsibilities for costs, a means for resolving scheduling conflicts, and addressing the myriad other complications that can make for trouble later.

Fractional Ownership

Fractional ownership, a form that is enjoying increasing popularity across a wide range of aircraft users, is a special kind of co-ownership. It began in the business aircraft world, as corporate operators moved into turboprops, jets, and other large aircraft, but it's now becoming popular in the light piston-powered aircraft market as well.

For large and turbine-powered multiengine airplanes, FARs 91.501(c)(1) and (3) provide a very narrowly drawn exception permitting operation under Part 91 under a *joint ownership* or a *time sharing agreement*. This avoids the considerable expenses and significant limitations associated with operating under Part 135 or 121, with the limitation that only certain itemized expenses of the flight may be charged. Meticulous documentation of these charges must be maintained to show compliance with the rule. No similar exception is available to operators of small aircraft, single-engine turbine-powered aircraft, or piston-powered multiengine aircraft.

The economic and operational advantages offered by this exception to the FARs have spawned several aggressively marketed major fractional ownership programs. Some of these are offered by aircraft manufacturers such as Raytheon's Travel Air program and Bombardier's FlexJet program to boost aircraft sales (over 700 sales valued at about $13 billion are attributed to these programs, at this writing). Others are offered by aircraft fleet management services such as Executive Jet Aviation (EJA, whose program is known as NetJets) and Flight Options to promote their services. Fractional ownership is presently growing at a rate of 40–50% annually, with both corporate and wealthy individual buyers participating approximately equally. A Canada-based company, OurPLANE, is now offering fractional ownership of light general aviation aircraft in the U.S.

A fractional ownership program includes four interlocking primary agreements:

1. The *aircraft purchase agreement* (between the seller and buyers),
2. A *joint ownership agreement* (among the buyers/owners),
3. An *aircraft management agreement* (between the buyers/owners and an aircraft management company), and
4. A *master interchange agreement* (between the buyers/owners of all aircraft owned by participants in the management company's fractional ownership program).

What each owner gets is access to an appropriate aircraft (not necessarily their own), without the associated management responsibilities for scheduling, crew (not included in the light piston fractional ownership programs), hangar, insurance, inspection, and maintenance, at a cost that may be more favorable than either charter rates or full ownership (Figs. 12.2, 12.3).

Typically, the user buys that percentage of the aircraft that is expected to equal its annual use, with 50 flight hours equaling a 1/16 share. This is the smallest share offered in large and turbine-powered fixed-wing aircraft fractional ownership programs, though helicopter programs offer shares as small as 1/32. In the light piston aircraft market, expect no more than four owners per fractionally owned aircraft.

Experience has shown that for fixed-wing aircraft, fractional ownership is economical for users who will need the aircraft at least 50 hours, but less than 200 hours annually. Users requiring less than 50 flight hours per year will typically find charter services (or, for light piston personal flying, aircraft rental) more economical; those flying more than 200 hours annually will usually find outright sole ownership less costly than either charter or fractional ownership.

The four interlocking agreements establishing a fractional ownership can be quite complex (20–25 pages each is not unusual), and should be carefully reviewed by experienced legal counsel before signing.

Analysis of FAA and NTSB accident data for U.S. registered turbine-powered aircraft during the period from 1987 to 1998 shows that fractional ownership aircraft operations have been among the safest in aviation. However, safety concerns prompted the FAA to create the Fractional Ownership Aviation Rulemaking Committee (FOARC). The committee included representatives of at least nine Part 135 operators, seven fractional ownership program managers, four aircraft manufacturers, three traditional Part 91 corporate flight departments, nine traditional aircraft management companies, and five industry trade associations along with the FAA, DOT and aircraft financing and insurance companies. The Civil Aviation Authority of the U.K and Transport Canada also participated in the committee's discussions, but recused themselves from the decision-making process.

In February of 2000, the committee presented its recommendations to the FAA. FOARC reached consensus that fractional ownership program operations should continue to be regulated under FAR Part 91. However, the committee unanimously recommended FAA adoption of a new Subpart K to Part 91 to ensure adequate FAA oversight and surveillance of fractional ownership program managers equal to that experienced by Part 121 or 135 operators. Key features include

Fig. 12.2. Fractional ownership may provide the most economical access to businesses and individuals using large or turbine-powered multiengine aircraft between 50 and 200 hours per year.

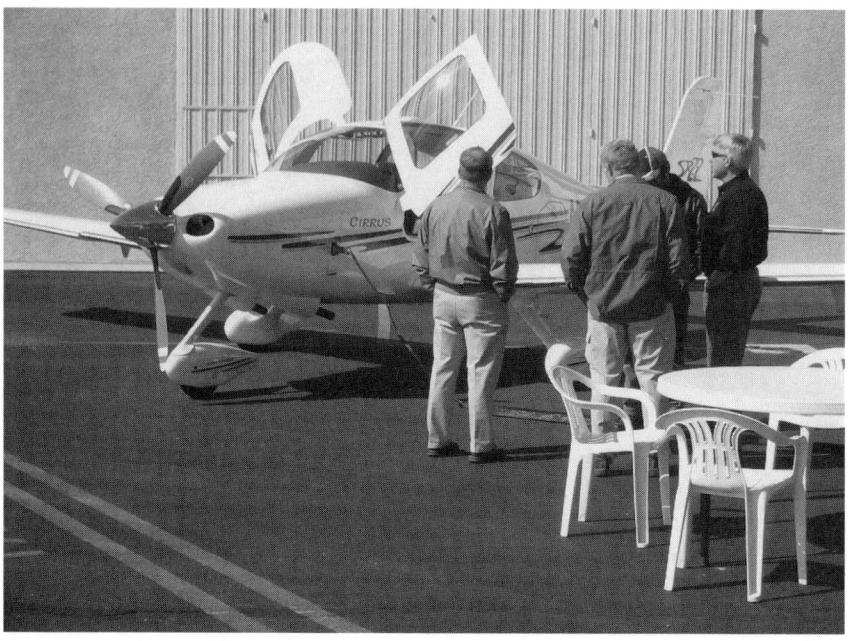

Fig. 12.3. Fractional ownership is now also gaining popularity in the new single-engine piston-powered aircraft market.

1. clarification of responsibility for operational control,
2. crew flight and duty time limitations,
3. crew training comparable to Part 135 requirements,
4. requirement for a drug and alcohol abuse recognition program for all personnel performing safety related functions,
5. aircraft equipment requirements by size, type and class of aircraft (cockpit voice recorder, flight data recorder, ground proximity warning system, thunderstorm detection equipment or airborne weather radar, TCAS),
6. establishment of minimum runway length requirements,
7. weather reporting requirements for instrument approaches, and
8. requirement for an FAA approved maintenance and inspection program.

These FOARC recommendations have recently been included in the FAR governing fractional ownership and operation of large and turbine-powered aircraft (Subpart K of Part 91). Because most of these recommendations merely reflect what were the actual current best practices that were already followed by leading existing fractional ownership program managers, it is likely that only the most marginal programs will be adversely affected to any significant degree by this new rulemaking.

PART IV

Airports, Airspace, and Aviation Security

CHAPTER 13

Airports and Terminal Airspace

SINCE DEREGULATION, airline operations have multiplied radically at airports serving major metropolitan areas, especially those selected by airlines to serve as regional hubs for hub-and-spoke route systems. This has strained airport capacity, resulting in incentives to build new airline airports and general aviation reliever airports and to expand existing airports in both categories.

The purpose of this chapter is to familiarize you with sources of power available to federal, state, and local governments to deal with the problems created by airport development and operation, particularly noise and safety issues, and to review specific techniques and examples of applications of these powers that have succeeded and others that have failed.

Most aviation litigation in the area of airports and airspace has focused on two problem areas: (1) aircraft noise and (2) keeping the airport's approaches clear of obstacles. Of these two, noise-related issues have accounted for the greater part of the litigation. In these cases, the courts struggle to weigh the rights of property owners against the public interest in safe and convenient air transportation.

Sources of Power

In the United States, all public airports that receive scheduled airline passenger service are owned and operated by state or local (city or county) governments or regional airport authorities having governmental powers. In their efforts to keep the approaches to these public airports clear of obstructions and to minimize costly aircraft noise-related lawsuits from airport neighbors, these governments have relied upon sources of power derived from both the Constitution of the United States and their inherent powers as proprietors of these airports (which are considered public utilities).

CONSTITUTIONAL POWERS

Eminent Domain. Under the power of *eminent domain*, governments have the right to take private land within their jurisdiction for public use (whether the landowner wishes to sell the land or not). The 5th Amendment to the U.S. Constitution requires, however, that when the government takes private property for public use, it must pay the landowner *just compensation*. If the landowner is unwilling to sell the property to the government or if the landowner and the government cannot agree on a fair price (just compensation), ordinarily the government files a *condemnation* lawsuit. A condemnation suit seeks a court order establishing the price to be paid and ordering transfer of title to the government upon payment of that price.

The Police Power. The *police power* is the government's right to adopt and enforce laws to protect the *public health, safety and welfare*. In the regulation of airports and airspace, this is the power that has been relied upon by state, regional and local governments as authority for adoption of *land use zoning* and *height zoning* ordinances in the vicinity of airports, as well as *noise ordinances*.

The Commerce Clause. The *commerce clause* of the Constitution, which gives the federal government the exclusive right to regulate interstate and foreign commerce, is the source of authority for all federal regulation of aviation. Judicial interpretations of the extent of this power have uniformly held that because even aircraft involved in purely local flying (such as aircraft observing and reporting on highway traffic for local news media, crop sprayers and sport flyers) operate in the same navigable airspace that may be used by aircraft traveling in interstate commerce (and could at least theoretically come into conflict with them), the FAA has the power to regulate those activities.

The Supremacy Clause. The *supremacy clause* to the Constitution has also sometimes come into play in these cases. The supremacy clause provides that where the federal government has adopted statutes or regulations governing some activity that it is authorized to regulate (such as aviation, under the commerce clause), then state, regional or local governments may not enact or enforce laws *conflicting* with federal law.

PROPRIETARY POWERS

In addition to these constitutional sources of power, the governmental entity that owns and operates the airport has a measure of authority as *proprietor* to regulate the use of that airport, much as the owner of a private airport would.

THE POWER TO TAX
All governments have the inherent power to impose taxes on persons, property, and transactions within their jurisdiction. Taxes are a major burden on every person and business, and are often a key consideration in the location or relocation of business enterprises. Increasing property taxes, in particular, are often responsible for a private airport owner's decision to sell or develop the property for some other use.

THE POWER OF THE PURSE
Proceeds of federal taxes on airline passenger tickets and aviation fuels have built up a multibillion dollar *Aviation Trust Fund*. Congress, with the FAA's advice, budgets expenditure of this money for airport planning, development and improvement through a program of grants (currently called the *Airport Improvement Program (AIP)*, although Congress seems fond of renaming the program every few years). This may include providing funds to acquire land and aviation easements for noise-abatement purposes and to soundproof existing buildings near the airport. Under that program, federal funds may be allocated to cover up to 90% of a project's costs. In this time of increased public focus on efficiency in government, grants under this program are becoming more difficult to for non-hub airports to obtain. As we will see, these grants also come with some strings attached.

Many states have similar programs, typically funded by state aircraft fuel taxes, registration fees, and specific ownership taxes, which may provide funds to cover that portion of a project not covered by federal funds. Many state grant programs also provide funding for airport projects that would not qualify for federal funding or for which it is uneconomical to go through the federal grant application process.

Additional federal funds are available under the Military Airport Program (MAP) for costs of converting closed military airfields to civilian airport use. MAP funds can be used for some projects not covered by the AIP.

Through a narrative examination of the landmark cases, we will now examine how the law governing airports and airspace has evolved to its present state, observing the interplay of the powers described above with the legal rights of property owners in the vicinity of airports.

The Power of Eminent Domain
The very first aviation case decided by the Supreme Court of the United States, *United States v. Causby,* focused on airport and airspace is-

sues. The Causby family were farmers whose principal source of income was raising chickens. Their home and chicken coops were located adjacent to a rural airport in North Carolina. That airport was not very busy, having some general aviation activity and a couple of airline DC-3 flights daily. Then World War II began. The federal government took over the airport and turned it into a heavy-bomber training base, operating around the clock with a high level of activity. A continuous stream of four-engine bombers spaced a minute or two apart roared over the Causbys' property day and night, with the landing approach bringing them as low as 30 feet over the Causbys' rooftop. The roar of the planes was deafening, and at night the landing lights illuminated the Causbys' bedroom brighter than day.

The brain of a chicken is apparently programmed to react to anything flying overhead as if it were a chicken hawk. Such a perceived threat drives chickens into a frenzy of activity. In this fashion, some 150 of the Causbys' chickens had destroyed themselves in the process of crashing around their coops in a state of panic caused by the low-flying bombers (the Causbys were probably not bearing up much better themselves). Eventually, they could take no more and hired a lawyer to sue the federal government. From this humble context would come the foundation of the law of airports and airspace in this country.

Courts are most comfortable deciding cases where a large body of legal precedent is available in the form of published decisions of other judges and appellate courts dealing with similar situations. Here, there were no such cases; this was a *case of first impression,* and the Supreme Court, having granted certiorari and recognizing the potentially far-reaching and long-lasting effect its decision would have upon the developing law of airports and airspace in this country, proceeded with great caution and deliberation.

In the quest for common-law precedent, diligent judges and lawyers would sometimes even search back to times before it became fashionable to publish judicial decisions. A primary valid source of reference to the common law as it existed in those earlier times was the writings of the Roman Glossators who, around the time of Christ, had written rather extensive treatises on the common law. Reference back to these writings in *Causby* revealed a centuries-old facet of the common law known as the *ad coelum* doctrine, which, when translated from the original Latin *(Cujus est solum, ejus est usque ad coelum)* states that a person who owns a parcel of land owns not only the surface of that land but also the airspace above it, literally "to the sky" *(ad coelum).* This ancient legal doctrine had been relied upon from time to time to resolve the kinds of airspace disputes that arose prior to the advent of flying machines—for example, to determine the ownership of apples growing on branches of a landowner's tree overhanging another's property or whether the landowner seeking maximum utilization of space might construct a building that although its foundation occupied only its owner's land, might legally have balconies or roof eaves extending over a neighbor's property.

The Supreme Court recognized, however, that application of this legal principle to the aviation situation would make flight virtually impossible; each property owner whose land was overflown could demand that aircraft keep out of that landowner's airspace or pay a toll for transiting that "property." Relying upon the commerce clause and Congress's pronouncements in the Civil Aeronautics Act of 1938 (precursor to the Federal Aviation Act of 1958), the Court held that navigable airspace is a public highway within the public domain, and that at least as it would affect the passage of aircraft, the *ad coelum* doctrine has no place in the modern world.

However, the Court went on to analogize from the constitutional law of eminent domain and terrestrial precedent, applying that law to afford the Causbys some relief for the damages they had suffered. By holding that in this situation the flights by aircraft owned and operated by the federal government were "so low and so frequent as to be a direct and immediate interference with the enjoyment and use of land," and because the value of the land was diminished as a result, these air operations constituted a *taking* of private property (in the nature of an *aviation easement)* for a *public use,* so that the Constitution required the government to pay the landowner just compensation for that taking. The Court held that the dollar amount of the just compensation would be the difference between the appraised value of the property before and after commencement of the oppressive overflights.

As previously noted, in an ordinary condemnation action, the government would have initiated the suit to take the property and determine the price. Since in this case it was the landowner who filed the suit seeking a judicial declaration that the government had *already* taken a property right and just compensation for that taking (a role reversal from the usual condemnation case), the Court characterized this lawsuit as an *inverse condemnation* case.

The next landmark case in the area, *Griggs v. Allegheny County,* would address the question of whether state, regional, and local governments would face similar liability for the impact of aircraft noise on landowners surrounding public civil airports. The Griggs's home was near the Greater Pittsburgh Airport, a county-owned and -operated airport served by several airlines. The county extended one of the runways almost to the Griggs's property line, so that airliners on approach to landing passed as low as 11 feet over the Griggs's chimney. The noise and vibration caused the plaster walls and ceilings to crack and toppled the Griggs's precious belongings from shelves and china cabinets. Griggs hired an attorney, who filed an inverse condemnation suit against the county.

The Court held that facts were sufficiently similar to those in *Causby* that the county, as operator of this public airport, had taken an aviation easement over the Griggs's property through inverse condemnation, requiring the county to pay just compensation for the taking, to be measured by the appraised fair market value of the property before and after the runway extension that led to the radical increase in noise.

This decision alarmed many public airport operators, who feared that their budgets would be depleted by similar litigation. Thus, many attorneys for state, regional, and local governments were tasked with finding a way around the *Causby* and *Griggs* decisions.

The Police Power

In the Pacific Northwest, a new regional airline airport ("Sea-Tac") was about to be built in the Seattle-Tacoma area. In an apparent effort to circumvent potential liability for suits for inverse condemnation, the legislature drafting the statute authorizing the airport included an elaborate recital to the effect that the airport was created under the police power in the interest of the public welfare. When an adjacent landowner later filed an inverse condemnation suit, however, the court held that although building a public-use airport is certainly a proper exercise of the police power, if the *effect* is to take private property rights for a public use, that exercise of the police power is also an exercise of the power of eminent domain, so that the governmental entity that owns and operates the airport must pay just compensation to property owners affected by the airport project.

This could be considered a corollary of the *duck rule:* Calling your duck an eagle doesn't make it one. The court will look not only at what a government claims it has done, but will also examine the actual effect of the government action, to decide whether there has been a taking of a private property right for a public use.

Shortly thereafter, in Riverside, California, the county was building a new general aviation airport (Ryan Field) and was concerned that the safety and utility of this public airport could be jeopardized if nearby property owners were allowed to erect structures that might block approach paths to the runway. Therefore, in the exercise of its police power, the county adopted *height zoning* restrictions that applied to property near each end of the runway to prevent landowners from building obstructions into the landing glide path. The maximum heights permitted proceeded outward and upward in a stairstep fashion, only very low structures being permitted close to the runway and progressively higher structures permitted farther away. Sneed owned a parcel of some 234 acres immediately adjacent to the runway threshold. Under the new height zoning ordinance, the tallest structure that could be built on that portion of Sneed's property farthest from the end of the runway was 24 feet, and at the end closest to the runway a mere 3 inches!

Sneed's attorney filed suit *(Sneed v. County of Riverside),* and following the rationale of the cases we have already discussed, the court found that while building and operating the airport and keeping its approaches clear was certainly a valid exercise of the county's police power, this height zoning regulation was plainly intended to keep open a public right-of-way (aviation easement) for the passage of aircraft using this public airport. Therefore, although the zoning was a valid and permissible exercise of the police power, at least in Sneed's case (when the reasonable use of the airspace above his property was so drastically restricted), the height zoning ordinance *also* constituted a taking of his private property for a public use through the power of eminent domain, requiring the county to pay him just compensation.

Meanwhile, up the coast in Santa Barbara, California, Smith owned a large parcel of land that had been zoned, platted, and approved for development as a residential subdivision, although ground had not yet been broken for the development. The county decided to build an airline airport nearby and was appropriately concerned that if development of the residential subdivision were allowed to go forward, its residents would be annoyed by noise from the aircraft coming and going from the new airport, sue the county in inverse condemnation, and win. Therefore, the county government used its police power to enact a new *land use zoning* ordinance governing the uses to which property in the vicinity of the new airport could be put, the intent being to allow only land uses that were not as sensitive to noise as homes. Under this ordinance, Smith's property was rezoned from residential to industrial use.

Smith sued the county *(Smith v. Santa Barbara County),* claiming that this rezoning constituted a taking of his property for a public use, requiring the payment of just compensation. The court found that the ordinance was a valid exercise of the county's police power, adopted for the purpose of protecting the public health and welfare by preventing residential exposure to the adverse effects of aircraft noise. The court went on to note that unlike the height zoning ordinance in *Sneed,* the Santa Barbara County land use zoning regulations did not impose height limits or evidence any intent to keep open a public right-of-way through the airspace (aviation easement). Thus, the court found that this land use zoning ordinance did not also involve any exercise of the power of eminent domain to take private property rights for a public use, so the county was not liable to pay the landowner compensation. That was probably just as well, since it turned out that industrial land in Santa Barbara County in such proximity to the city and transportation facilities was scarce and the value of the property actually increased as a result of the rezoning, so that even if an entitlement to just compensation had been found, the amount of that compensation would have been zero because the fair market value of the property had not been diminished. As a result of this decision, land use zoning is now a very popular tool used nationwide in new airport planning.

In the planning process, airport planners predict the airport's "noise footprint" as it will fall on surrounding land (Fig. 13.1). The sound level measurement method most commonly used today is *Ldn*, the average day-night sound level measure developed by the U.S. Environmental Protection Agency to permit comparison of noise levels from all types of urban sources. It measures ambient noise including aircraft noise and other noises within the same community setting and imposes a penalty for nighttime (10:00 p.m.–7:00 a.m.) operations, the duration of noise events, and aircraft noise that is above the ambient background level. It is generally accepted that noise levels of 65 Ldn or higher are incompatible with noise-sensitive land uses such as homes, schools, churches, and hospitals. Thus, industrial, commercial, and some agricultural land uses are to be preferred within the 65 Ldn noise contour. Airport industrial parks have been a particularly successful land use in these noisier areas, since a worker operating a turret lathe or other noisy machinery may be totally oblivious to the passage of a jetliner overhead, and the proximity of the airport as a transportation hub may enhance the value of the property in an industrial application. For example, at Atlanta's busy Hartsfield International Airport, aircraft on short final for landing on runway 26R pass extremely low over a major Ford Motor Company automobile assembly plant without annoying the workers inside.

An increase of 10 decibels is perceived by humans as a doubling of the noise level. Therefore, airport planners now generally agree that where aircraft noise will be 75 Ldn or greater, that land should be purchased outright and included within the airport's boundaries.

Use zoning, however, is a two-edged sword that may be used not only to protect airports from the encroachment of noise-sensitive residential communities but also to protect residential communities from the encroachment of noisy airports. In New Jersey, Garden State Farms, Inc.,

Fig. 13.1. Airport noise footprint.

Fig. 13.2. Airliners on approach to San Diego's Lindbergh Field (composite photo).

was one of the early "agribusiness" corporate farming enterprises. The corporation sought a variance to the land use zoning ordinance of the county where the corporation's headquarters was located to permit construction of a heliport outside the headquarters building so that the corporation's executives might be more efficiently transported between the corporate offices and various operating locations around the state. However, the corporate headquarters was located adjacent to a residential area, and the residents objected to the heliport. The county authorities sided with the residents and refused to permit a deviation from the zoning law to allow construction of the heliport. The corporation sued *(Garden State Farms, Inc. v. Bay),* and the court held that state and local governments may also exercise their police power to protect the public health, safety, and welfare by land use zoning to exclude aircraft landing areas.

Injunctions

Sometimes residents who are annoyed by the proximity of an airport seek to obtain an *injunction* from a court to declare the operation of the airport a *nuisance* and order it to cease operation. Nuisance is another intentional tort, but generally a continuing one rather than an isolated incident. If a court finds a particular activity to constitute a nuisance, the court has the option either to award the plaintiff money damages or to issue an injunction prohibiting continuation of the activity that constitutes the nuisance.

Much of American law, as we have seen, derives from the law of England, and at the time of the Declaration of Independence, England had two separate sets of courts, each with its own separate body of law and powers: the *courts of law* and the *courts of chancery*. In the courts of law, judges trained in the common law applied the law. In the courts of chancery, however, judges selected for Solomonic wisdom (but usually untrained in the common law) "did equity"; that is, they issued orders that just seemed fair. In this system, while the courts of law could enter judgments for money damages, orders for people to do or refrain from doing something were considered *equitable remedies* available only in the courts of chancery.

In the United States, the federal system and most state court systems now consolidate the two, with law courts having the authority to award either legal or equitable remedies. As a general rule, courts consider equitable remedies (which include injunctions) to be extraordinary remedies that should be awarded only if there is no adequate remedy at law—that is, if mere money will not suffice to compensate the plaintiff. Since injunctive relief is an equitable remedy, the court is primarily concerned with answering the question: "What is a fair result in this situation?" This may include a balancing of the interests of the public and of the parties to the lawsuit on imaginary scales of justice.

For example: The approach from either east or west to San Diego International Airport (Lindbergh Field) brings aircraft over residential areas (Fig. 13.2). When the airport opened and residents were appalled to find airliners roaring past their windows, they filed suit, seeking a judicial declaration that the operation of this municipal airport constituted a nuisance and asking for an injunction prohibiting operation of the airport *(Loma Portal Civic Club v. American Airlines).*

The court refused to hold that operation of the airport constituted a nuisance or to issue an injunction prohibiting its continued operation, finding that under *Causby* and *Griggs,* the landowners had an adequate remedy at law through suits in inverse condemnation to obtain payment of just compensation. The court held that such a suit was the only proper recourse of the landowners because the court found an "overriding public interest" in the operation of this public airport. No court has ever enjoined the operation of a publicly owned airport in the United States.

Privately owned airports, however, have not fared so well (Fig. 13.3). Some private airports have been found to constitute nuisances and have been enjoined against continuing operations. Considerations of fairness in these cases may take into account such factors as who came first, the airport or the complaining residents? If it appears that the airport was there first and the complaining residents "came to the nuisance," a judge might consider it unfair to order the airport to cease operation. In balancing the

Fig. 13.3. Private airports do not enjoy the legal protections from residential encroachment available to governments that own and operate airports, and as the area around a private airport is developed, rising property taxes may make continued operation of the airport uneconomical.

interests involved, the court may consider not only the rights and interests of the airport operator and complaining residents but also any public benefits from keeping the airport operational. If the airport is open to the public and the airport's attorneys can demonstrate that if this airport is closed, the city or county will need to build a public airport to replace it, the judge may see a public interest in allowing private enterprise to continue to fill that need. Some private airports have successfully fought off lawsuits seeking to enjoin their continued operation, while others have failed, and some have ceased operations rather than pay unaffordable damages to the surrounding residents following an adverse judgment finding the airport to constitute a nuisance.

The Power to Tax

Local governments have also effectively used their power to impose taxes on real property to force out private airports. In the typical scenario, a private property owner establishes an airport in a rural area well beyond the existing boundaries of a growing city. Property taxes in such an area (usually zoned for agricultural use, with airports being permitted) are usually quite low. But as the metropolitan area grows, residential subdivisions, businesses, and industry creep ever closer to the airport. Eventually, typically as part of a city or countywide master land use plan, the area will be rezoned to accommodate residential or business development. Although the airport will still have *grandfather rights* to continue operation as a *nonconforming use* despite this rezoning, property taxes will rise dramatically. Many such airports were financially marginal operations before the tax increase, and this sudden major increase in the cost of doing business often makes it uneconomical to continue at that location. In that circumstance, the airport owner will typically either sell out to developers or become one.

Noise Ordinances

The onset of a nationwide epidemic of aircraft noise-related litigation was triggered by the introduction into airline service of the first generation of jets (Boeing 707, Douglas DC-8, and Convair 880). These aircraft were far noisier (and smokier) than the propeller-driven aircraft that preceded them (or later generations of jet airliners). This new noise burden spurred many communities that had long been neighbors of airports to action.

The village of Cedarhurst, New York, was one such community. The village is located on Long Island, about a mile southeast of John F. Kennedy International Airport (JFK, formerly Idlewild). Several of JFK's runways point toward Cedarhurst. In response to citizen rage over the new noise level, the village government adopted a municipal ordinance that prohibited aircraft from flying over the village at less than 1,000 feet above ground level (AGL).

A suit was filed challenging the validity of the ordinance *(Allegheny Airlines v. Village of Cedarhurst)*. At trial, it was demonstrated through the use of FAA-approved instrument approach plates that many federally mandated instrument approaches to JFK required that aircraft overfly Cedarhurst at altitudes below 1,000 feet AGL. The court found a pervasive federal regulatory scheme in the FAA's establishment of JFK arrival and departure routes as part of a nationwide system plan regulating interstate and foreign air commerce. Since the village ordinance prohibited aircraft from flying over the village below 1,000 feet AGL, while the federal regulatory scheme mandated that aircraft fly over the village below 1,000 feet AGL, the village ordinance was in direct conflict with federal regulations. Therefore, the court held that the supremacy clause of the Constitution rendered the municipal ordinance unenforceable.

Nearby, citizens of the town of Hempstead were also irate over this new burden of noise from JFK. When the *Cedarhurst* decision was announced, the town council appears to have instructed the town's attorney to find a way around that decision. Soon the town adopted a municipal noise ordinance setting decibel limits on the maximum noise anyone or anything (not just aircraft) could make in the town of Hempstead. The town promptly attempted to enforce the ordinance against aircraft flying overhead, inbound to JFK.

The validity of this ordinance too was soon tested in court *(American Airlines v. Town of Hempstead)*. Expert testimony revealed that in order for a Boeing 707 overflying the town to avoid violating the town's noise limit, it would have to fly at an altitude of at least (surprise, surprise) 1,000 feet AGL. Again, numerous FAA-approved instrument approaches to the airport required the aircraft to fly over the town at altitudes below 1,000 feet AGL. Looking at this practical effect, the court found that the ordinance, *as applied against aircraft*, was in direct conflict with the federal regulatory scheme. The supremacy clause would prohibit the town from enforcing a noise ordinance against aircraft (although the town remained free to enforce the ordinance against terrestrial noise sources such as motorcycles, lawn mowers, chain saws and the like).

Not far south, in the pine barrens of New Jersey, the government of the rural township of Lakewood adopted a noise ordinance virtually identical to Hempstead's. At the time, Parachutes, Inc. was operating a commercial skydiving school at the Lakewood Municipal Airport utilizing several World War II vintage Canadian-built Noorduyn Norseman jump planes, which are surely among the noisiest single-piston engine aircraft ever conceived. These aircraft would take off from the Lakewood Municipal Airport, climb overhead in the immediate vicinity, drop their parachutists, and spiral back down to land, never straying more than a few miles from the airport.

When the township sought to enforce its noise ordinance against Parachutes, Inc., the corporation challenged the validity of the ordinance *(Parachutes, Inc. v. Township of Lakewood)*. At trial, it was shown that the federal government exercised little control over the flight patterns of these aircraft. There was no control tower at the airport, and the only contact the jump planes were required to have with ATC was to report to New York Center one minute before each jump, advising them of the altitude from which the jump would be made, then later to advise when the last jumper had landed. The aircraft were free to climb and descend in the area at the pilot's discretion and were in no way constrained by federally mandated routings. Under these facts, the court found that the enforcement of the township's ordinance against the aircraft did not conflict with any regulatory scheme, so the supremacy clause did not come into play. Therefore, the court found enforcement of this noise ordinance against these aircraft legally valid. The corporation then replaced its Lakewood fleet with a quieter fleet of Cessnas and a DC-3, which enabled them to continue operations at that airport without violating the town's noise ordinance.

Proprietary Powers: Curfews and Restrictions on Airport Use

Meanwhile, back on the West Coast, the city of Santa Monica, California, owned and operated the Santa Monica Municipal Airport (SMO). Developed before the wisdom of noise-compatible land use planning in the vicinity of airports became recognized, the airport is surrounded by residential developments (Fig. 13.4). Acting in its capacity as the *proprietor* of the airport, the city imposed a *curfew* on jet aircraft operations at the airport between the hours of 11:00 p.m. and 7:00 a.m. The validity of the curfew was challenged in court *(Stagg v. Santa Monica,* also known as *Santa Monica I* since this was only the beginning of a series of legal battles at this airport). No airlines served Santa Monica, and this case appears to have caught general aviation interests napping. The court found that the jet curfew did not conflict with any federal regulatory scheme, so that the supremacy clause was no barrier, and that it was a valid exercise of the police power since it was intended to protect the public health and welfare by affording citizens a better night's sleep.

About this time, the U.S. Supreme Court decided that the time had come for it to render another decision updating the Court's thinking in the

Fig. 13.4. Final approach over residential area to runway 21 at Santa Monica Municipal Airport (SMO). "PAPI cam" is watching.

area of airport noise law. It decided to grant certiorari to hear the case of *Lockheed Air Terminal, Inc. v. City of Burbank,* arising out of attempts by the cities of Burbank and Glendale to regulate the noise of aircraft coming and going from an airport privately owned and operated by Lockheed Aircraft Corp. Unfortunately, the case was poorly chosen; it involved the only privately owned and operated airport in the country having interstate airline service, so the Court's laborious and intricate analysis had little general relevance to other airports. (In fact, shortly after the Court's decision was issued, Lockheed sold the airport to a regional airport authority— formed by the cities of Burbank, Glendale, and Pasadena—which now operates it, so that the Court's decision no longer addresses even the facts of that previously unique airport.) As it would turn out, the most enduring contribution of *Lockheed v. Burbank* came in footnote 14 to the decision, which suggested that a governmental entity that owns and operates an airport may be legally able, *acting as proprietor,* to deny use of the airport to aircraft on the basis of noise considerations, as long as the exclusion does not discriminate against aircraft traveling in interstate or foreign commerce.

The city of Santa Monica (whose airport lay only about 15 air miles from Lockheed's) viewed that footnote as a green light from the Supreme

Court, and in its capacity as proprietor of its municipal airport adopted five more restrictions in the form of airport use regulations:

1. *Curfew.* Engine starts and takeoffs by *any* aircraft were prohibited between 11:00 p.m. and 6:00 a.m.
2. *Fixed-wing flight training.* Touch-and-go landings, stop-and-go landings, and low approaches were prohibited on weekends and holidays.
3. *Helicopter flight training.* Helicopter flight training was prohibited at all times.
4. *Noise limit.* Aircraft operations exceeding a 100-decibel single-event noise level (SENEL) were prohibited (and noise meters were installed off both runway ends).
5. *Jet prohibition.* All jets were prohibited from using the airport at all times.

The validity of these new regulations was soon challenged in court *(Santa Monica Airport Association v. Santa Monica,* also known as *Santa Monica II).* Drawing on the preceding line of cases, the court held that the constitutional validity of regulations limiting the use of a public airport adopted by a governmental entity in its capacity as proprietor of that airport depends upon a three-step test:

1. Does the regulation affect interstate commerce? If not, then the regulation is constitutionally valid. If so, the court must then consider the next question.
2. Has the governmental entity acted within its jurisdiction, and is the regulation reasonable? If not, the regulation is unenforceable. If so, the court must proceed to question 3.
3. Local interests supporting the regulation must be balanced against the burden the regulation imposes on interstate or foreign air commerce. If the regulation does not discriminate between interstate (and/or foreign) and intrastate commerce and it has only slight adverse effect on interstate (and/or foreign), it will be valid. But if the regulation discriminates against interstate (and/or foreign) commerce or if the burden on interstate (and/or foreign) commerce is clearly excessive in relation to the local benefits, the regulation is void.

Applying this line of reasoning to each of Santa Monica's five new regulations, the court found that the first four imposed an "insubstantial burden, if any, on interstate commerce" and did not discriminate against interstate commerce, that the city was within its jurisdiction, and the regulations were reasonable to minimize the impact of noise from aircraft using the city's airport on the surrounding residential community during those times of night, weekends, and holidays when the need for leisure and rest in the community was the highest. Thus, the court found those first four regulations (curfew, limitations on fixed-wing flight training, ban on helicopter flight training, and noise limits) legally valid and enforceable. As to the fifth, the jet ban, however, it was proved that some jets (such as the Cessna Citation) were actually quieter than some piston-engine aircraft regularly using the airport. The court found the jet ban to be void because it imposed an impermissible burden on interstate commerce and was unreasonable, banning some jet aircraft that were quieter than some piston aircraft that would have been allowed to continue to use the airport.

Buoyed by this decision, the city of Santa Monica almost immediately modified the single-event noise limit contained in the fourth of these regulations, reducing it from 100 decibels to 85 decibels, which virtually no powered aircraft could meet. The new regulation was also soon challenged in court *(Santa Monica III)*.

Many national aviation organizations filed *amicus curiae* ("friend of the court") briefs siding with the airport users. The FAA also finally became concerned over the potential loss of a valuable general aviation reliever airport in the Los Angeles basin. The city had received federal airport improvement funds to aid in the airport's development over the years. To obtain federal funds, the city was required to sign a contract with the federal government, known as a *grant agreement,* in which the city agreed (among other things) to keep the airport open to the general public as an airport without discriminating against any aeronautical user or class of aeronautical user. At this point, the FAA notified the city that unless it backed off to a more reasonable single-event noise limit on aircraft, the FAA would consider the city to be in breach of its grant agreements and would take legal action to compel the city to repay all federal funds it had obtained.

Motivated by that specter, the city reached a settlement agreement with the federal government and aviation interests whereby the single-event noise limit was increased to 95 decibels, and it was further agreed that the airport would remain open without any further restrictions until the year 2015.

The current state of the law in this area was most succinctly summarized in litigation arising out of the introduction of the now defunct Concorde supersonic transport (SST) into transatlantic service *(British Airways v. Port of New York Authority)*. In deciding that case, the court held that regulation of commercial aviation in the United States is a two-tiered system:

1. Exclusive control of airspace allocation and use is concentrated at the national level, and state, regional, and local governmental entities are preempted from trying to regulate planes in flight.
2. The task of protecting the local population from airport noise, however, falls on the government operating the airport, and it may achieve this goal through acquisition of property and aviation easements, zoning for compatible land uses, and the issuance of reasonable, nonarbitrary, and nondiscriminatory rules governing use of the airport that do not impermissibly burden interstate commerce.

This two-tiered system has been uniformly followed by the courts in the latest rash of litigation challenging the principle of federal preemption of the use of the navigable airspace and the regulation of airplanes in flight. In *Country Aviation, Inc. v. Tinicum Township,* the court struck down a local government's attempt to use its police power to enforce an aviation noise control ordinance against glider-towing aircraft operating at the privately owned Van Zant Airport, home to a glider club in Upper Bucks County, Pennsylvania. In *Banner Advertising, Inc. v. City of Boulder,* the Colorado Supreme Court struck down the City of Boulder's attempt to purge the city's skies of aircraft towing commercial advertising messages (usually over University of Colorado home football games) by a provision in the city's sign code (Fig. 13.5). Huntington Beach, California, adopted a similar ordinance, but rescinded it following clarification from the FAA that it was in conflict with the FAA's exclusive control of the airspace. In *Gustafson v. City of Lake Angelus,* the court struck down a southeast Michigan city's ordinance prohibiting operation by any aircraft below 500 feet over a lake owned by the city in a suit filed by a waterfront homeowner and seaplane pilot. In each of these cases, the court found the law to be long settled that except for reasonable noise control regulations adopted by airport proprietors, all state and local regulation of the noise of aircraft in flight is preempted by pervasive federal regulations governing airspace management and aviation noise control (Fig. 13.6).

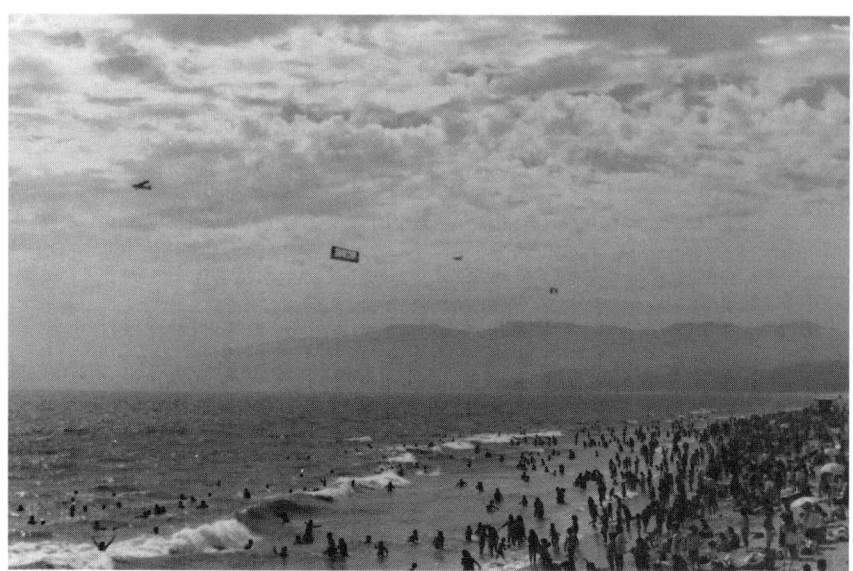

Fig. 13.5. Aircraft towing advertising banners along a Southern California beach.

Fig. 13.6. Federal preemption may protect seaplane operations on off-airport lakes and waterways as well.

The Power of the Purse, Strings Attached: Grant Agreement Constraints

Where, however, the airport proprietor has accepted federal AIP airport planning and improvement grants, the assurances to the grant agreement further limit the proprietor's latitude to regulate and restrict the use of the airport. Most significantly, the airport proprietor must agree to keep the airport open for the use and benefit of the public and "all types, kinds, and classes of aeronautical use on fair and reasonable terms without discrimination between such types, kinds, and classes unless prohibition or limitation of any given type, kind, or class of aeronautical use of the airport is necessary for the safe operation of the airport or necessary to serve the civil aviation needs of the public."

These obligations typically continue for at least 20 years from the date of the last acceptance of federal aid. Thus, by accepting federal airport planning and improvement funds, the airport proprietor forfeits the right it would otherwise have to close the airport before the expiration of that 20-year term and to exclude any particular type of aviation operation so long as it remains compatible with the safe and efficient operation of the airport.

The courts have uniformly held that only the FAA can sue to enforce these grant agreement assurances; that persons denied access to the airport do not have legal *standing to sue* as third-party beneficiaries of this contract to enforce its provisions. Thus, if an operator is denied access to a federally funded airport, the only available recourse is to file a written complaint of discrimination with the local FAA Airports District Office (ADO). The ADO is required to investigate all complaints and determine whether the airport proprietor is in compliance with the grant agreement assurances. During the investigation, the FAA usually withholds any additional grant funds that may be forthcoming. If the FAA finds that the airport proprietor is in breach of the grant agreement assurances, future aid will be denied, and the United States may initiate litigation for specific performance (a court order that the proprietor comply with the grant agreement) or to recover federal funds previously furnished.

It is entirely within the FAA's discretion to decide how to resolve each complaint of discrimination on a case-by-case basis, and the FAA has demonstrated a high degree of practicality in analyzing these complaints. For example, if you were denied access to a small, low-activity, rural, general aviation airport that had received federal funds where you proposed to operate an ultralight flight school, the FAA would likely side with you and prevail upon the airport authority to permit your proposed operation or face the consequences. On the other hand, if you complained that you were denied permission to conduct that same operation at Chicago's O'Hare International Airport, you would probably be laughed right out of the FAA office.

In recent years, the FAA has demonstrated both the will to aggressively enforce grant agreements as needed to protect recipient airports and admirable flexibility and creativity in working with airport authorities to amend the requirements of grant agreements where needed to foster and promote airport development. Denver's experience provides an excellent example. Like many airports, Denver's Stapleton International Airport had been built early in the last century, out in a country cow pasture, miles from downtown. So far out, in fact that the airport (named for then-mayor Ben Stapleton) was derisively called "Stapleton's folly." Land use planning had not yet come into vogue, and within a few decades residential subdivisions crept up to the airport fence, an experience shared by virtually all airports built during that same era. Surrounding developments limited airport expansion, limiting the airport's capacity. The runways were too close together to permit simultaneous parallel ILS approaches in instrument meteorological conditions (IMC), so that bad weather at Denver (a major hub) caused delays to ripple throughout the country. This was stifling the growth potential of the region, and hostility between the airport and its noise-sensitive neighbors was escalating.

Denver got serious about following Dallas and Fort Worth's lead to leapfrog far beyond the built-up metropolitan area to buy a vast tract of grazing land and build a new airline airport with suitable easements and land use protection. But federal grants had steadily flowed into improvements at Stapleton, presenting two obstacles to the project. The city faced a real stretch to finance the new airport, even without having to repay the federal grants expended on Stapleton over the previous 20 years. If the FAA held the city to the grant agreement, there was no way the city could afford to build the airport needed for its future. Denver also saw that by keeping Love Field open to airlines, Dallas had stunted the initial growth of DFW. Denver wanted to completely close Stapleton as an airport the day the new airport opened, forcing all airline traffic to move to the new facility, but that would also run afoul of the grant agreement.

The FAA and its parent, the DOT, wanted the new airport to happen and to succeed. They agreed with the practical need to close Stapleton contemporaneously with the opening of the new airport. To facilitate the project, the FAA agreed to waive the Stapleton grant provisions.

At 34,000 acres, the new Denver International Airport (DIA) has more land area than JFK, O'Hare, and DFW combined (Fig. 13.7). It opened during a snowstorm and immediately accepted triple simultaneous ILS ap-

13 : Airports and Terminal Airspace ——————————————— 249

Fig. 13.7. Distinctive tent-roofed Jeppesen Terminal Building and concourses at the new Denver International Airport (DIA), with control tower at top right.

proaches to IFR minimums. The airport's layout allows aircraft to taxi between any runway and the terminal without crossing any other runway (by comparison, DFW averages 147 runway crossings per hour). Stapleton closed an hour or two after DIA opened, and its land is being redeveloped for non-aviation urban uses. DIA has since added a 16,000 foot runway to accommodate takeoffs of the heaviest fully loaded jets under the highest-density altitudes occurring on the hottest summer days (and permitting quadruple simultaneous ILS approaches to minimums). There's still room left over to add six more runways to the airport, if needed.

Chicago's recent abrupt closure of downtown lakefront general aviation reliever Meigs Field (accomplished by bulldozers destroying the runway in the middle of the night, without any prior notice to either the FAA or owners of aircraft then left stranded on the field) was hotly but unsuccessfully contested by general aviation interests, and succeeded only because of a set of provisions unique to that agreement. Those provisions were included in the agreement only because the city did not own the airport property, but operated it under a long-term lease from the landowner. It was these unique contract provisions, and not any lack of will on the part of the FAA, that stymied any effort to enforce the grant agreement and compel the city to keep the airport open when the lease expired. The closure of Meigs Field, though a serious and wasteful loss, should be seen as an aberration, not a portent of things to come, since aggressive FAA enforcement of grant agreements continues at other airports.

For example, as I write this, the FAA is demanding Ocean City, Maryland, repay $13.3 million for 267 acres of land adjacent to the airport. The land was originally purchased with federal aid money for the purpose of providing a noise buffer and expansion room for the airport, but it was developed by the city instead as a golf course. The golf course (Eagle's Landing, rated one of the top 75 public courses in the U.S. by *Golf Digest*) has proved so profitable that the city decided not to go forward with two planned safety-related runway extensions that would extend into the land. The FAA has also threatened to cut off existing grants of up to a half a million dollars a year for maintenance of the airport.

Meanwhile, at Teterboro, New Jersey (TEB), long one of the busiest business jet bases on the East Coast, city officials have succeeded (at least for now and with the help of congressional legislation) in banning aircraft having a maximum gross takeoff weight of more than 100,000 lbs. Ostensibly adopted to protect pavement life, local officials and their congressional representative openly stated that the real purpose of the ban was to protect the community from the noise of the increasingly popular Boeing Business Jet derivative of the 737 (MTOW 171,000 lbs).

The Complication of Political Boundaries

A government may exercise its power of eminent domain and police power only within its geopolitical boundaries. Airport noise and required clear zones, however, frequently cross those political boundaries. For example, in the Denver metropolitan area the new Denver International Airport is almost completely surrounded by another county and three of the area's four general aviation reliever airports abut a county line, so that in all cases a substantial portion of the noise generated by aircraft using these airports falls on cities and counties other than the airport proprietor and clear zones must be maintained outside the territorial jurisdiction of the airport's proprietor.

In such a case (or when the airport is operated by a regional airport authority not possessing the police power to zone), the cooperation of surrounding county or municipal governments must be obtained and nurtured. Through an *intergovernmental agreement* (IGA), the airport proprietor may obtain the commitment of surrounding governments to use their police powers to assure noise-compatible land uses in the area impacted by the airport, to add soundproofing requirements to applicable building codes and to deny building permits to incompatible uses, to height zone as appropriate to protect the required clear zones for air traffic, and to use their powers of eminent domain to acquire necessary land and aviation easements (typically at the airport proprietor's expense, which may include federal matching funds). In exchange for this commitment, the surrounding governments may exact a price, such as seats on the airport's governing board, a say in the airport's operations, layout and preferential runway use, and a guarantee of public sector jobs at the airport for their residents.

Environmental Impact

Airport development and its funding is considered a *major federal action that may affect the quality of the environment*, bringing into play the National Environmental Policy Act of 1969 (NEPA). NEPA requires preparation of an *environmental impact statement* (EIS) for projects that could affect the environment. Some states have adopted similar requirements for state and local projects that could affect the environment. These requirements may apply to improvements to existing airports as well as the development of new airports. Opponents of airport development have achieved some success in the courts in enjoining federal funding of airport projects where the EIS did not meet NEPA requirements. Further, if the study is viewed by those who stand to be adversely affected by the project as a "railroad job" working toward a foregone conclusion with little real consideration being given to citizen concerns, the intergovernmental cooperation necessary to success of the project becomes much more difficult to achieve. It is crucial that the study leading to the EIS be thorough, objective, and legitimate and that it be completed as early as possible in the planning phase to avoid the risk of an injunction interrupting construction or financing of the project once ground has been broken.

Airports also require storage capacity for aviation fuels. Therefore, airport planners must take into account federal underground storage tank (UST) regulations promulgated under the federal Resource Conservation and Recovery Act (RCRA, pronounced "rickra"). Bringing aging fuel storage facilities into compliance has proved a major expense for many airports and has even caused some small fields to discontinue fuel service.

Other Solutions That Have Worked

Not all solutions to the twin problems of aircraft noise and keeping the airport's approaches clear of obstacles have been found in the courts. The FAA has been very actively involved in the noise problem through regulation, funding, and procedures. Progressive changes to the FARs have required new air transport aircraft to be quieter and have required the phase out of older, noisier jet transports or their silencing through engine replacement or "hush kits." The FAA has worked with local airport operators to develop noise abatement procedures appropriate to specific locations, including runway use preferences that (winds permitting) route departures over the least noise-sensitive neighboring areas and establish climb and descent profiles to reduce aircraft noise (hopefully without compromising flight safety). Federal airport development funds have also been made available for the acquisition of land and aviation easements for noise abatement and clear zone purposes and for the soundproofing of buildings affected by airport noise.

Once upon a time, a residential area of palatial homes lay between the Los Angeles International Airport (LAX) and the Pacific Ocean. With the introduction of jets into airline service, residents of that area began to file and win inverse condemnation suits against the city of Los Angeles (proprietor of LAX). The jet noise and smoke (early airline jets trailed quite a plume of black smoke and this was before mechanical clothes dryers became popular, when most people still dried their laundry outside on a clothesline) destroyed the quality of life in the area. When Congress amended the legislation governing federal funding of airport improvements to permit these federal funds (which may cover up to 90% of a project's costs) to be used to purchase land and aviation easements for noise-abatement purposes, the city of Los Angeles went on the offensive. The city targeted this noise-impacted community for maximum federal funding (which was approved), then condemned and purchased the entire residential area and removed all of the homes. The area is now a popular state beach.

In Dallas, Texas, the Love Field airport is convenient to downtown. At one time, Dallas banks became engaged in a competition to build higher and higher office towers. FAR Part 77 requires that before constructing anything that could be an obstacle to aircraft, the sponsor must notify the FAA. Upon receipt of such a notice, the FAA performs an *obstruction analysis* to determine the effects of the project on flight operations at the airport. The FAA then issues one of three determinations: (1) that it has no objection to the proposal, (2) that it has no objection to the proposal *if* certain conditions are met (such as the realignment of a traffic pattern), or

(3) that the proposal is objectionable because it would adversely affect air navigation. The FAA, however, neither permits nor prohibits the proposed construction, leaving that decision to the local government having jurisdiction over zoning and the issuance of building permits in the area.

In the case of one of Dallas's proposed skyscraper banks, the FAA found that the structure would constitute an obstruction to air navigation, requiring decommissioning of instrument approaches to the airport from the southeast. The FAA did not prohibit the construction but merely announced its finding and plans, which were well publicized in the local media. This would have greatly reduced the utility of this popular airport, and the bank apparently soon felt the brunt of considerable resentment from the local business community over the prospect of the bank's depriving them of the convenient use of this airport. The bank quickly yielded to public opinion, announcing that why, shoot, everybody knew that it was the biggest and best bank in Dallas, and it didn't have to build some silly skyscraper to prove it. The airport's approaches remained unobstructed.

Washington, D.C.'s National Airport (see Chapter 1, Fig. 1.3) has long been considered a noisy annoyance by its Virginia neighbors. In an effort to improve the situation without resorting to regulation, the airport's owner/operator (then the FAA) announced a *"voluntary jet curfew,"* requesting that corporate jets voluntarily refrain from using the airport between 11:00 p.m. and 7:00 a.m. When the voluntary program took affect, not all corporate jet users "volunteered." But then the local newspaper published the names of the major corporations whose jets, by choosing not to participate in the voluntary curfew, had awakened the airport's neighbors. The airport's neighbors wrote letters to those corporations, expressing their displeasure, often vowing not to do business with those corporations again, and sometimes highlighting the strength of their convictions by enclosing the severed remains of credit cards the corporation had issued to the writers. The corporations swiftly responded to this public reaction, and it was not long before voluntary participation in the curfew reached the 100% level.

Noise complaints are often triggered by pilots executing a lower than normal approach to an airport, "dragging it in under power." FAR 91.129(e)(3) requires that when operating in Class D airspace, an airplane approaching to land on a runway served by a visual approach slope indicator (VASI or PAPI) shall maintain an altitude at or above the glide slope until a lower altitude is necessary for a safe landing. The city of Santa Monica has installed a "PAPI-cam" at SMO, where the precision approach path indicator is set to project a 4° glide slope. It incorporates a video camera and theodolite that record and measure the descent profile of every

VFR approach to runway 21 (refer to Fig. 13.3). If a neighbor calls the airport to complain about a low approach and review of the video tape shows the aircraft to have been more than 1.5° below the glide slope when within two miles of the airport, the pilot receives a warning letter from the airport manager. A second violation by the same pilot is referred to the FAA for counseling or enforcement action. A special benefit of the system is that it is a truly unbiased observer that can also disprove neighbors' complaints by confirming that the aircraft was not below the glide slope.

Summary
PUBLICLY OWNED AIRPORTS
The *governmental entity that owns the airport* can

1. As proprietor, impose curfews and other reasonable limitations on the use of the airport as long as these limitations are not discriminatory against or unduly burdensome on interstate or foreign commerce and are reasonable.
2. Condemn and purchase land and aviation easements within their jurisdiction in the vicinity of the airport, through the power of eminent domain (and seek federal airport improvement funds to aid in financing those purchases).
3. Impose land use zoning and height zoning on land within their jurisdiction in the vicinity of the airport under the police power (but may have to pay just compensation to some landowners if height zoning diminishes their property values).
4. Add soundproofing requirements to building codes applicable to construction in areas impacted by airport noise and pay to soundproof existing structures in that area (and seek federal airport improvement funds to aid in financing that soundproofing).
5. Enter into Intergovernmental Agreements with other local governments to accomplish items 2 through 4, above, beyond the jurisdiction of the airport-owning government.
6. Close the airport (but any federal airport aid funds received may have to be repaid, unless a Denver-style deal can be struck with the FAA).

Even the airport proprietor has no control of overflights by aircraft not using the airport.

Citizens can file *Causby* suits in inverse condemnation for taking of an aviation easement over their property or suits for damages in tort (nuisance) and can recover money damages (in the amount by which the

13 : Airports and Terminal Airspace 255

value of the property was reduced by virtue of airport operations) but cannot obtain an injunction to close or restrict the airport.

Adjacent governments that do not own the airport can do nothing.

PRIVATELY OWNED AIRPORTS
The private *airport owner* can

1. Purchase adjacent lands or aviation easements over them, but only if the owners are willing to sell. (Private landowners do not have the power of eminent domain and therefore cannot condemn and take the property of other private landowners.)
2. Impose limitations on use of the airport without limit unless federal airport development funds have been accepted (which is now possible for private airports open to the public where the FAA has designated the airport as a general aviation reliever airport needed to draw general aviation traffic away from a busy airline hub airport in the area).

Citizens can bring suit against the airport owner for nuisance and obtain a judgment for money damages or an injunction compelling the airport to cease operations.

The *local government having jurisdiction over the property* can preclude construction of an airport by land use zoning or render the continued operation of an established private airport uneconomical by raising property taxes.

Adjacent governments not having jurisdiction over the property can do nothing.

CHAPTER 14

En Route Airspace

THROUGH THE Federal Aviation Act of 1958, Congress empowered the FAA Administrator to regulate the use of the navigable airspace, as she in the exercise of her discretion deems necessary, in order to assure the safety of aircraft and the efficient utilization of such airspace.

The FAA accomplishes this primarily through rulemaking published in FAR Part 71, which establishes

Class A Airspace. Positively controlled airspace above Flight Level (FL) 180, where the turbines cruise under IFR.
Class B Airspace. "Upside-down wedding cake" configurations of positively controlled airspace to protect aircraft arriving and departing from airports serving a high volume of airline traffic.
Class C Airspace. Protecting aircraft using medium-sized commercial airline airports.
Class D Airspace. Protecting traffic at smaller airports having air traffic control towers.
Class E Airspace. For en route air navigation below FL 180 and for instrument operations at airports not having an air traffic control tower.
Special Use Airspace. Airspace over which FAA has ceded control to another agency. Examples include
   —*Restricted Areas* where activities incompatible with the safe flight of civil aircraft (such as artillery or missile firing, aerial gunnery and bombardment) are conducted (R-2601 at Ft. Carson, Colorado, is an example).

—*Prohibited Areas* established for national security reasons (P-56, encompassing the White House and Capitol buildings in Washington, D.C., for example).
—*Warning Areas* to alert pilots to hazardous activities in international airspace (the FAA term "warning area" is synonymous with the ICAO term "danger area"). W-72, located 3–12 miles off the Virginia coast, is an example.
—*Military Operations Areas (MOA)* to notify pilots of areas where the armed forces regularly conduct such operations as air combat maneuvering ("dogfighting"), intercepts, aerobatics, and low-level tactics. Civilian pilots operating under VFR may choose as a matter of prudence to avoid flight through MOAs during military operations, since the military pilots may not be able to devote much of their attention to scanning for nonparticipating traffic during this type of flying. LaVeta MOA in Southern Colorado, where jet fighters engage in simulated air combat, is an example.
—*Alert Areas* to inform pilots of areas where a high volume of pilot training or an unusual type of aeronautical activity is regularly conducted. A-260 at the U.S. Air Force Academy in Colorado, which has an extraordinarily high level of flight training in powered airplanes and gliders as well as parachuting packed into a small area, is an example.
—*Controlled Firing Areas* are established instead of restricted areas where the gunnery or rocketry activities are of short duration and can be immediately suspended on notice of an intruding aircraft.
—*Military Training Routes* alert pilots of civil aircraft to routes along which the FAA allows high-speed flight below 10,000 feet MSL by military aircraft.
—*Air Defense Identification Zones (ADIZ)* and *National Security Areas* established around U.S. borders and, since the terrorist attacks of 9/11, Washington, D.C. for national security impose special requirements for penetration by civil aircraft and subject aircraft to interception by military aircraft for visual identification.

The FAA may also impose *temporary flight restrictions* (TFRs) by Notice to Airmen (NOTAM). These typically cover areas to be visited by the president, vice president, and other security-sensitive public figures as well as space flight operational areas (such as Cape Canaveral, Vandenburg, and Edwards Air Force Bases). Temporary flight restrictions are also designated in areas where sightseeing aircraft might interfere with disaster relief, law enforcement or fire fighting aircraft operations. They are also imposed where an unsafe congestion of sightseeing and other aircraft might otherwise occur above an event (such as the Super Bowl).

Temporary flight restrictions are also sometimes announced by NOTAM pending establishment and charting of restricted airspace. An example occurred in August of 1993, when the U.S. Customs Service installed an aerostat (balloon) bearing a radar system, tethered near Glencoe, California, by a 15,000-foot unlighted cable to detect low-flying drug smugglers.

Since 9/11/01, implementation of TFRs has been a major tool used by the FAA in coordination with the DHS, TSA, and Secret Service to help address domestic security concerns. TFRs have been established to help protect such potential terrorist targets as nuclear plants and chemical facilities as well as events gathering large open-air assemblies of people (including, for example, major sporting events such as NASCAR races, college football bowl games, and a variety of professional games).

What remains is *Class G Airspace* (formerly known as *uncontrolled airspace*), an endangered species.

Security Control of Air Traffic and Air Navigation Aids (SCATANA)

On September 9, 1950, Congress directed the FAA's forerunner, the CAA, to develop and implement plans for security control of air traffic whenever U.S. security is endangered. At that time, Cold War tensions between the U.S. and the Communist bloc were escalating, and the Russians were building a potentially formidable long-range bomber force. The concern was that enemy bombers might penetrate U.S. air defenses by hiding in the radar shadow of civilian airliners and home in on their targets navigating by reference to U.S. radio aids to navigation, such as VORTACs, and that the presence of civilian aircraft in the battlespace could confuse or interfere with air defense efforts.

The plan, called *SCATANA*, short for *Security Control of Air Traffic and Air Navigation Aids*, was developed in cooperation with the Department of Defense (DOD), and updated over the years. It was never actually implemented, however, until the surprise terrorist air attacks on the U.S. on Tuesday, September 11, 2001, presented a national security scenario no one had foreseen or planned for.

Immediately following those attacks, the President and Congress in essence declared the entire U.S. national airspace system a National

Security Area and the FAA implemented SCATANA. All civilian traffic in contact with ATC was diverted to the nearest suitable airport, preferably an airport some distance outside any major metropolitan area or likely target complex. Then all civilian aircraft were grounded. Some who didn't get the word were met and escorted to a nearby airfield by interceptors. The Civil Air Patrol, operating as the official civilian auxiliary of the U.S. Air Force, was allowed back into the air almost immediately, transporting relief supplies and equipment for the search, rescue, and recovery efforts and taking digital aerial photos to aid in that effort. CAP aircrews reported the eerie sensation of landing at JFK International Airport in a Cessna 182 laden with special equipment requested by the searchers and having the gigantic airport all to themselves. It would be days before airline and other civilian IFR operations were permitted to resume, and civilian VFR operations were gradually phased back in over a period of weeks, by which time many new TFRs and a new ADIZ around Washington, D.C. were in place. Since then new TFRs have been appearing and disappearing like bubbles in boiling water, often faster than notice of their existence or demise can be communicated to pilots. The problem has been exacerbated by the practice of establishing a TFR having a radius of 3–30 miles at each location to be visited by the president, vice president, and opposition candidate during the presidential election campaign, and that's an enormous number of locations. At this writing, the FAA has gotten better at providing timely notice, but errant pilots have illegally intruded into special-use airspace thousands of times since the attacks. Some have been intercepted by fighters (Fig. 14.1) and escorted to a ground reception by FAA, law enforcement, and/or Secret Service agents, and some have faced criminal (see Chapter 15) or FAA certificate action. At least none has been mistaken for a terrorist and shot down yet, as I write this sentence.

Considering the scope of the attack, although pilots and passengers were inconvenienced and aviation businesses lost a great deal of money, the adverse effect on civil aviation could have been much worse.

Implemented in response to a national security emergency other than the one for which it was designed, SCATANA worked remarkably well.

Competition for Airspace

FAA airspace allocation regulations, like all other FARs, are subject to requirements of the federal *Administrative Procedure Act (APA),* requiring (except in an emergency) publication first as a *Notice of Proposed Rulemaking (NPRM)* in the *Federal Register*, with reasonable opportunity for public comment before adoption. Where the FAA considers a potential rule likely to be particularly controversial or expects that its development

Fig. 14.1. Attention no civilian pilot wants: Intrude into an ADIZ, restricted, prohibited, or TFR airspace without authorization, and you may get a fighter escort to a welcoming committee of law enforcement or Secret Service officers. *U.S. Air Force photo.*

might benefit more than usual from outside input, it may first issue an *Advance Notice of Proposed Rulemaking (ANPRM)* to help focus the issues.

The APA also allows citizens to petition the FAA (and other federal agencies) to change existing regulations.

Like real estate, airspace is a finite resource. Many different interest groups within the aviation community assert demands for use of a share of this resource for their activities. Earthbound interests, such as the broadcasting industry, which has a need to erect tall signal transmission towers rising into the navigable airspace, also compete for the right or privilege to use a share of this resource.

Tall structures and activities on the surface, such as gunnery, may conflict with aviation activities. Various aviation activities may be incompatible in the same airspace: Military high-altitude dogfight training, unless carefully coordinated and controlled, may conflict with airliners cruising en route, and low-level, high-speed military flying may pose a hazard to general aviation fliers.

Low-flying aircraft may interfere with the solitude sought by back-country hikers and campers, spiritualists, and residents of rural areas and may disturb wildlife, hunters, and domestic animals.

The APA rulemaking procedures make it possible for all views to be voiced and considered in each instance.

AOPA (the Aircraft Owners and Pilots Association) frequently weighs in to object to proposals to erect tall transmission towers into the navigable airspace, especially near major metropolitan areas, and to proposals to set aside for military use airspace needed for general aviation's peregrinations. The FAA often provides for public hearings in addition to the required opportunity for written comment where proposals are particularly controversial.

Wilderness Airspace

All aircraft are *requested* to maintain an altitude no lower than 2,000 feet above the surface of National Parks, National Monuments, National Seashores, National Recreation Areas, and Scenic Rivers administered by the National Park Service. National Wildlife Refuges, Big Game Refuges, Game Ranges, and Wildlife Ranges administered by the U.S. Fish and Wildlife Service benefit from identical requests. So do Wilderness and Primitive Areas administered by the U.S. Forest Service. Boundaries of these areas are depicted on VFR aeronautical charts, and the vast majority of general aviation pilots honor the request (Fig. 14.2).

Fig. 14.2. Monument Valley in the Navajo Tribal Park in Utah, on descent for landing at the airstrip at Goulding's Lodge.

However, many visitors on the ground in Grand Canyon National Park complained that aircraft noise was diminishing the quality of the national park experience and traumatizing wildlife. These complaints prompted Congress in 1987 to mandate an FAA and Department of the Interior study of the problem and led to *Special Flight Rules* (SFAR) in the vicinity, imposing *"flight free zones"* (not to be confused with the diametrically opposite concept of free flight) over large areas of the park, prohibiting overflight below 10,500 feet MSL except in emergencies. Park overflights were confined to narrow corridors within which minimum flight altitudes ranging from 5,000 feet MSL to as high as 14,500 feet were mandated. Since implementation of this SFAR, visitor complaints about aircraft noise in the Grand Canyon dropped by 80% (Fig. 14.3). Some complaints continue to be received, however, and the FAA and Department of Interior continue to adjust airspace use requirements over the park.

Fig. 14.3. Grand Canyon from the air, before imposition of "flight free zones."

Over 40 aviation businesses from Arizona, California, Nevada, Utah, and New Mexico provide aerial tours of Grand Canyon National Park to almost a million tourists annually, about a fifth of the park's visitors. During peak summer vacation months, air tours exceed 10,000 flights a month over the park. The industry accounts for approximately 300 pilot jobs and generates over $250 million in economic impact. Air tour operators, who in response to increasing restrictions organized into an association, note that experience under the SFAR eliminated the impact of aircraft noise on more than 99% of the park's ground visitors. They also point out that air tours relieve congestion at the canyon's rim, contribute nothing to the erosion of trails, and provide equal access to visitors with disabilities. They note further that some 60% of the aerial tourists are foreigners on vacation and that commercial air tours provide an opportunity for visitors to enjoy park vistas when time or physical constraints might otherwise preclude them. Others have expressed concern that high-density altitude conditions typical of the area's hot summers, resulting in reduced performance, make it impossible for some aircraft (particularly helicopters) to climb to required or proposed minimum overflight altitudes, necessitating lengthy circumnavigation of the park's meandering boundaries.

Since the FAA issued the Grand Canyon SFAR, visitors to other National Parks, such as Rocky Mountain National Park in northern Colorado, as well as the entire multi-island state of Hawaii, successfully brought pressure to bear on the FAA and Department of Interior to restrict overflights (particularly commercial air tours) (Fig. 14.4).

The FAA and National Park Service (NPS) are now developing Grand Canyon-style regulations to restrict at least commercial air tour operations over thousands of square miles of as many as 345 national parks.

Only successful aviation lobbying efforts in Congress recently stopped agency plans to close and abandon the entire network of wilderness airstrips on federal lands in Idaho and Utah, cherished by many for emergency and recreational use.

NASA's new focus on technological solutions to aircraft noise reduction (see Chapter 1) are important and timely not only to airports but in the wild as well, for unless great strides are made in quiet aircraft propulsion, increasing restrictions to overflight of these areas of protected wilderness must be expected. Environmental interests can be expected to continue to mount an organized, methodical, and aggressive campaign to pursue expansion of such restrictions. Aviation interests must be prepared to take full advantage of the opportunities offered by the APA rulemaking and legislative processes to respond in kind.

14 : En Route Airspace   265

Fig. 14.4. Looking north from Corona Pass into Rocky Mountain National Park, Colorado, with the over 14,000-foot Long's Peak beneath the author's wingtip.

Dispute Resolution

Resort to the courts is rarely useful in these controversies. If the FAA and other agencies involved fail to follow procedures required by the APA, a court may set aside the agency's decision and remand the matter to the agency for reconsideration in accordance with proper procedure. This is typically an empty ritual. Having once made up its mind on a subject, an agency is likely to reach the same decision after complying with a judicial mandate to start over at square one and jump through the correct sequence of procedural hoops.

Once the agency has reached its decision through the prescribed process, the courts are unlikely to reverse the decision. In such a case, the court cannot substitute its judgment for that of the agency, but must defer to agency judgment and expertise. The court can review the agency's decision only to determine whether it is an arbitrary and capricious abuse of the agency's discretion. So long as the record shows some rational basis for the agency's decision, the court must affirm it, even if it disagrees.

Thus, presenting the most logical and persuasive argument to the agency at every opportunity is crucial. Once the agency announces its final decision, the courts are unlikely to overturn it. Petitioning Congress to change the law may then be the only potential recourse.

Effectiveness in the administrative and legislative arenas frequently depends heavily upon not only advocacy (legal and otherwise), but also diplomacy and consensus building skills. Reason may still prevail in either forum where claim of legal rights fails. A couple of successful examples from my personal experience may be illustrative.

When the FAA published (as an advance notice of proposed rulemaking under the APA) its *"straw man"* initial proposal for the configuration of the Terminal Control Area (TCA, now Class B airspace) for the new Denver International Airport (DIA) then under construction, an extremely diverse group of representatives of users of the area's airspace came together to form an ad hoc user group. The FAA cooperated by providing ATC and airspace specialists on request, to help the group understand the regulatory and procedural constraints and considerations that were required to be respected in the airspace design, but otherwise kept hands off and did not attempt to influence the group's deliberations. As could be expected, there was initially considerable distrust and disrespect among representatives of aviation interests as diverse as the airlines, military, area airport operators, general aviation pilots, and a variety of air sports, all jockeying to protect "their" airspace needs. But as they worked together over a period of months, listening to each other's concerns and capabilities, mutual respect developed and consensus was reached on an optimal airspace configuration. The group presented its written (and diagrammed) recommended configuration (far different from the initial FAA "straw man" proposal) to the FAA, with detailed explanations and justifications for each recommended change. The FAA then scheduled several public hearings, where the initial FAA proposal and the group's counterproposal were briefed, questions taken and answered, and comments received. In the end, the airspace design implemented by the FAA was almost identical to the design developed by the user group.

When the Colorado Air National Guard transitioned to F-16s at the same time many U.S. military bases were being phased out but the combat load on the armed forces was increasing, the need was recognized to reconfigure the entire web of military special use airspace in the state to accommodate the expanding and changing demand for realistic air combat and surface attack training. The National Guard Bureau's design effort came to be known as the Colorado Airspace Initiative. A coalition of interested parties formed an ad hoc working group, including a variety of interested parties who might be affected by the air operations: general aviation (represented by the Colorado Pilots Association), farmers and

Fig. 14.5. Located in Colorado's San Luis Valley along a proposed low-level training route for F-16s, the family-run ranch at the bottom of this photo is dwarfed by the soaring Sangre de Cristo mountains.

ranchers, back-country hikers and environmentalists, real estate developers, rural residents, and even monks from a monastery located along a proposed low-level route (Fig. 14.5). This group, too, met weekly for several months, with technical support as requested from the National Guard Bureau and FAA, came to understand each other's concerns, and reached consensus on a recommended tailoring of the initial design of the complex airspace to minimize the adverse effects of the operations on the people and creatures living below. Although this group's recommendations were not all adopted into the final airspace design, enough were that all participants agreed that their time was well spent in the effort.

CHAPTER 15

Crimes and Aviation Security

ALTHOUGH TERRORISM, particularly since the attacks within the United States on September 11, 2001, has brought greater public attention to the subject, civil aviation has been the target or arena for a variety of criminal activity almost since its inception. As mentioned in Chapter 1, the first reported crime against aviation occurred in France in 1784, when an early gas balloonist was accosted by a sword-wielding young man who forced his way into the basket of the balloon and demanded the aeronaut take him aloft.

In the United States today, a variety of federal criminal laws are specifically directed at protecting aircrews, passengers, aircraft, ATC and air navigation facilities, airports, and the general public against terrorism and other criminal behavior. The federalization of air carrier airport security and new focus on general aviation security has given rise to rapid growth in jobs in aviation security, in both the public and private sectors. New laws that restrict civil liberties in the interest of national security are being challenged in the courts—though at this writing, no such case has climbed far enough up the judicial ladder to establish published precedent.

The purpose of this chapter is to introduce you to those federal laws specifically directed toward civil aviation and some constitutional considerations in criminal law enforcement in aviation. Some states have also adopted criminal laws specific to aviation. Under the principle of federal preemption discussed in Chapter 13, where these do not conflict with federal law, they are generally also enforceable. General criminal laws, both federal and state, sometimes also apply in an aviation scenario. For example, the federal law that makes it a crime to make a false statement applies not only to FAA applications for pilot and medical certificates, pilot logbook entries that could show currency or qualification, and inspection and maintenance entries in aircraft logbooks (discussed in Chapters 2 and 3) but to a host of documents and records required by or submitted to any of the myriad federal agencies. As another example, a state law making reckless endangerment of others a crime can be enforced against aviators operating aircraft so as to create a hazard to persons on the ground.

Jurisdiction

Jurisdictional issues can be especially complex in the case of crimes committed aboard aircraft in flight. Because aircraft can quickly cross state and national borders and because it may be difficult to determine exactly where the aircraft was positioned at the moment a crime was committed aboard (indeed, the offense itself could span several states or nations and cross the high seas), it could be difficult to establish that a particular state or nation actually had jurisdiction to prosecute the offense.

Citations below are to the U.S. Code (USC), the compilation of all laws enacted by Congress that are currently in effect. For example, Title 18 of the U.S. Code, section 37 is cited as 18 USC 37. The code can be accessed on line through the Government Printing Office website *www.gpo.gov* or several other sources easily located with any of the Internet search engines in common use. The two titles of the code most relevant to this chapter are Title 18, Crimes and Criminal Procedure, and Title 49, Transportation.

Special Aircraft Jurisdiction of the United States. To simplify jurisdictional issues, Congress enacted legislation providing for the *special aircraft jurisdiction* of the United States. This special aircraft jurisdiction extends to crimes committed aboard (1) any civil aircraft of U.S. registry (that is, having an N-number), (2) U.S. military aircraft, (3) any other aircraft *within* the U.S., and any aircraft outside the U.S. that has either its next scheduled destination or last point of departure in the U.S. Where the crime is committed while the aircraft is on the ground, state government may have concurrent jurisdiction over the offense under state law. In such a situation, state and federal prosecutors will typically confer to agree which will prosecute. The prosecution of in-flight crimes, however, falls exclusively within federal jurisdiction.

Violence at International Airports. Congress has also provided, at 18 USC 37, for jurisdiction enabling the United States to prosecute individuals for certain crimes of violence occurring at international airports, even under some circumstances where the international airport is on foreign soil (Fig. 15.1). Here is the actual text:

15 : Crimes and Aviation Security 271

Fig. 15.1. U.S. courts have jurisdiction over crimes committed at international airports even, under certain circumstances, where the airport where the crime was committed is in another nation.

(a) Offense.—A person who unlawfully and intentionally, using any device, substance, or weapon
  (1) performs an act of violence against a person at an airport serving international civil aviation that causes or is likely to cause serious bodily injury (as defined in section 1365 of this title) or death; or
  (2) destroys or seriously damages the facilities of an airport serving international civil aviation or a civil aircraft not in service located thereon or disrupts the services of the airport, if such an act endangers or is likely to endanger safety at that airport, or attempts or conspires to do such an act, shall be fined under this title, imprisoned not more than 20 years, or both; and if the death of any person results from conduct prohibited by this subsection, shall be punished by death or imprisoned for any term of years or for life.
(b) Jurisdiction.—There is jurisdiction over the prohibited activity in subsection (a) if—
  (1) the prohibited activity takes place in the United States; or
  (2) the prohibited activity takes place outside the United States and

(A) the offender is later found in the United States; or
(B) an offender or a victim is a national of the United States (as defined in section 101(a)(22) of the Immigration and Nationality Act (8 U.S.C. 1101 (a)(22))).
(c) Bar to Prosecution.—It is a bar to Federal prosecution under subsection (a) for conduct that occurred within the United States that the conduct involved was during or in relation to a labor dispute, and such conduct is prohibited as a felony under the law of the State in which it was committed. For purposes of this section, the term "labor dispute" has the meaning set forth in section 2(c) of the Norris-LaGuardia Act, as amended (29 U.S.C. 113 (c)), and the term "State" means a State of the United States, the District of Columbia, and any commonwealth, territory, or possession of the United States.

The bar that appears in subparagraph (c) above is important, for as we shall see in Chapters 16 and 17 emotions frequently run high in labor disputes and can provoke ordinarily calm and thoughtful people (including aviation and aerospace professionals) to intemperate acts. While these acts may violate state criminal statutes, they are not subject to federal prosecution under this provision.

Some of the laws discussed below, proscribing specific aviation-related crimes also address special jurisdictional issues that may arise in their enforcement.

Aviation-Specific Federal Crimes
SECURITY-RELATED CRIMES

Violation of national defense airspace (49 USC 46307). It is not only an FAR violation, but also a federal crime to knowingly or willfully violate national defense airspace. This could include not only an ADIZ or National Security Area, but also certain Prohibited Areas and TFR airspace established for national security reasons. (See Chapter 14.) Violators are subject to fines, imprisonment of up to one year, or both.

Destruction of aircraft or aircraft facilities (18 USC 32). This law makes criminal a broad range of deliberate acts against aircraft (Fig. 15.2), air navigation facilities, airport facilities, and people. These may include not only acts of terrorism and sabotage, but also violence sometimes committed by drunken and/or angry passengers or damage done by vandals. Because the law is so pervasive as to preclude thorough and accurate summarization or paraphrasing, here is the complete text:

Fig. 15.2. Warning posted on airport fence about federal felony of disabling aircraft.

(a) Whoever willfully—
  (1) sets fire to, damages, destroys, disables, or wrecks any aircraft in the special aircraft jurisdiction of the United States or any civil aircraft used, operated, or employed in interstate, overseas, or foreign air commerce;
  (2) places or causes to be placed a destructive device or substance in, upon, or in proximity to, or otherwise makes or causes to be made unworkable or unusable or hazardous to work or use, any such aircraft, or any part or other materials used or intended to be used in connection with the operation of such aircraft, if such placing or causing to be placed or such making or causing to be made is likely to endanger the safety of any such aircraft;
  (3) sets fire to, damages, destroys, or disables any air navigation facility, or interferes by force or violence with the operation of such facility, if such fire, damaging, destroying, disabling, or interfering is likely to endanger the safety of any such aircraft in flight;

(4) with the intent to damage, destroy, or disable any such aircraft, sets fire to, damages, destroys, or disables or places a destructive device or substance in, upon, or in proximity to, any appliance or structure, ramp, landing area, property, machine, or apparatus, or any facility or other material used, or intended to be used, in connection with the operation, maintenance, loading, unloading or storage of any such aircraft or any cargo carried or intended to be carried on any such aircraft;

(5) performs an act of violence against or incapacitates any individual on any such aircraft, if such act of violence or incapacitation is likely to endanger the safety of such aircraft;

(6) communicates information, knowing the information to be false and under circumstances in which such information may reasonably be believed, thereby endangering the safety of any such aircraft in flight; or

(7) attempts or conspires to do anything prohibited under paragraphs (1) through (6) of this subsection; shall be fined under this title or imprisoned not more than twenty years or both.

(b) Whoever willfully—

(1) performs an act of violence against any individual on board any civil aircraft registered in a country other than the United States while such aircraft is in flight, if such act is likely to endanger the safety of that aircraft;

(2) destroys a civil aircraft registered in a country other than the United States while such aircraft is in service or causes damage to such an aircraft which renders that aircraft incapable of flight or which is likely to endanger that aircraft's safety in flight;

(3) places or causes to be placed on a civil aircraft registered in a country other than the United States while such aircraft is in service, a device or substance which is likely to destroy that aircraft, or to cause damage to that aircraft which renders that aircraft incapable of flight or which is likely to endanger that aircraft's safety in flight; or

(4) attempts or conspires to commit an offense described in paragraphs (1) through (3) of this subsection; shall be fined under this title or imprisoned not more than twenty years, or both. There is jurisdiction over an offense under this subsection if a national of the United States was on board, or would have been on board, the aircraft; an offender is a national of the United States; or an offender is afterwards found in the

United States. For purposes of this subsection, the term "national of the United States" has the meaning prescribed in section 101(a)(22) of the Immigration and Nationality Act.
(c) Whoever willfully imparts or conveys any threat to do an act which would violate any of paragraphs (1) through (5) of subsection (a) or any of paragraphs (1) through (3) of subsection (b) of this section, with an apparent determination and will to carry the threat into execution shall be fined under this title or imprisoned not more than five years, or both.

Aircraft Piracy (49 USC 46502). Congress enacted this law to criminalize what is commonly called *hijacking* but is formally referred to in both U.S. and international law as *aircraft piracy*. In this statute, Congress defines the offense as follows:

> "aircraft piracy" means seizing or exercising control of an aircraft in the special aircraft jurisdiction of the United States by force, violence, threat of force or violence, or any form of intimidation, and with wrongful intent.

The statute goes on to make a failed attempt at aircraft piracy also a crime, even if the attempt was made when the aircraft was not in flight. The punishment for either committing or attempting aircraft piracy is *at least* 20 years imprisonment or, if the death of someone other than the hijacker results, death or life imprisonment. The statute extends the special aircraft jurisdiction of the U.S. to any hijacking in which either (1) a national of the United States was aboard the aircraft, (2) an offender is a U.S. national, or (3) an offender is afterwards found in the U.S.

Interference with cabin or flight crew (49 USC 46504). Flight attendants and flight deck crewmembers are increasingly called upon to deal with unruly passengers, so much so that a new phrase has been coined to describe the phenomenon: *air rage*. Such abusive passenger behavior can be a federal felony under this law:

> An individual on an aircraft in the special aircraft jurisdiction of the United States who, by assaulting or intimidating a flight crew member or flight attendant of the aircraft, interferes with the performance of the duties of the member or attendant or lessens the ability of the member or attendant to perform those duties, or attempts or conspires to do such an act, shall be fined under title 18, imprisoned for not more than 20 years, or both. However, if a dangerous weapon is used in assaulting or intimidating the member or attendant, the individual shall be imprisoned for any term of years or for life.

Carrying a weapon or explosive on an aircraft (49 USC 46505). This statute makes it a federal felony for a person to either (1) board or attempt to board an airliner with a dangerous weapon concealed on their person or in a carry-on item, (2) place, attempt to place, or attempt to have someone else place a loaded firearm, explosive, or incendiary device aboard an airliner. Starter pistols, used in sporting events to fire a blank cartridge to signal the start of a race, are specifically included in the category of dangerous weapons, so traveling sports officials sometimes run afoul of this law. In this era of heightened and well-publicized airport security, it is truly amazing how many seemingly ordinary airline passengers continue to enter airport security screening with a prohibited weapon (usually a handgun—I'm not talking about nail clippers) on their person or in carry-on luggage. Often, the lame excuse is that the passenger usually travels by ground and simply forgot he had a gun in his bag. Unbelievable! Where the violation was deliberate, the offender can be fined or imprisoned for not more than 15 years. Most nondeliberate (read: *stupid*) violations are compromised to a civil fine of $10,000 or less, so long as authorities believe the passenger's story and are satisfied that he has learned his lesson. But if the passenger cops an attitude and chooses instead to try to defend the charge by asserting his (and virtually all of these offenders are male) Second Amendment constitutional right to keep and bear arms, both prosecution and conviction are inevitable. The statute makes exceptions for law enforcement officers and others authorized to carry arms in an official capacity as well as others authorized by FAR. The law does not apply to *unloaded* firearms in hold (checked) baggage inaccessible to passengers, so long as the passenger first notified the airline of the presence of the weapon.

False information (49 USC 46302). Making a false report of an impending attempt to commit aircraft piracy (hijacking), interfere with flight crew or attendants, or carry weapons or explosives aboard an aircraft is also punishable under federal law by a civil penalty (fine) of up to $10,000.

This statute applies not only to deliberate hoaxes, but also to ill-considered attempts at dark humor by passengers. Law enforcement and the judiciary have zero tolerance for such humor, and the courts have uniformly held that the First Amendment guarantee of freedom of speech does not apply to this situation, analogizing it to shouting a false warning of fire in a crowded theater. Joke, wisecrack, or otherwise smart off to security personnel or others at the airport about hijacking, weapons, or explosives, and you are guaranteed prosecution under this section.

Entering aircraft or airport area in violation of security requirements (49 USC 46314). This statute makes it a federal crime for a person to deliberately enter an aircraft or air carrier airport area in violation of security requirements (including, but not limited to passenger and baggage screening requirements). Punishment includes a fine or imprisonment up to one year, or both, except that if it is proved that the violator also intended to commit a felony under federal or state law imprisonment can be for as long as 10 years.

SAFETY AND DRUG-RELATED CRIMES
Pilots operating in air transportation without an airman's certificate (49 USC 46317). Formerly, the only punishment the federal government could impose upon an unlicensed person piloting an aircraft was a civil penalty (fine). When this proved insufficient to deter some persons (particularly pilots whose certificates had been revoked for smuggling drugs by air) from flying, Congress enacted this law:

(a) General Criminal Penalty.—An individual shall be fined under title 18 or imprisoned for not more than 3 years, or both, if that individual—
   (1) knowingly and willfully serves or attempts to serve in any capacity as an airman operating an aircraft in air transportation without an airman's certificate authorizing the individual to serve in that capacity; or
   (2) knowingly and willfully employs for service or uses in any capacity as an airman to operate an aircraft in air transportation an individual who does not have an airman's certificate authorizing the individual to serve in that capacity.
(b) Controlled Substance Criminal Penalty.—
   (1) Controlled substances defined.—In this subsection, the term "controlled substance" has the meaning given that term in section 102 of the Comprehensive Drug Abuse Prevention and Control Act of 1970 (21 U.S.C. 802).
   (2) Criminal penalty.—An individual violating subsection (a) shall be fined under title 18 or imprisoned for not more than 5 years, or both, if the violation is related to transporting a controlled substance by aircraft or aiding or facilitating a controlled substance violation and that transporting, aiding, or facilitating—
      (A) is punishable by death or imprisonment of more than 1 year under a Federal or State law; or

(B) is related to an act punishable by death or imprisonment for more than 1 year under a Federal or State law related to a controlled substance (except a law related to simple possession (as that term is used in section 46306(c)) of a controlled substance).
(3) Terms of imprisonment.—A term of imprisonment imposed under paragraph (2) shall be served in addition to, and not concurrently with, any other term of imprisonment imposed on the individual subject to the imprisonment.

Lighting violations involving transporting controlled substances by aircraft not providing air transportation (49 USC 46315). When drug runners began to endanger other aircraft by turning off their running lights (in violation of the FARs) in an attempt to avoid detection when flying at night, Congress made that action also a serious crime:

(a) Application.—This section applies only to aircraft not used to provide air transportation.
(b) Criminal Penalty.—A person shall be fined under title 18, imprisoned for not more than 5 years, or both, if—
  (1) the person knowingly and willfully operates an aircraft in violation of a regulation or requirement of the Administrator of the Federal Aviation Administration related to the display of navigation or anticollision lights;
  (2) the person is knowingly transporting a controlled substance by aircraft or aiding or facilitating a controlled substance offense; and
  (3) the transporting, aiding, or facilitating—
    (A) is punishable by death or imprisonment for more than one year under a law of the United States or a State; or
    (B) is provided in connection with an act punishable by death or imprisonment for more than one year under a law of the United States or a State related to a controlled substance (except a law related to simple possession of a controlled substance).

Interference with air navigation (49 USC 46308). Speaking of lighting, Congress also made it a federal felony for a person to attempt to mislead aircraft by displaying a false air navigation facility light or signal or interfering with the operations of a true air navigation facility light or signal (which could include radio aids to navigation and ATC voice commands). Violators are subject to fine or imprisonment for up to five years, or both.

Aircraft registration violations (49 USC 46306). Smugglers have been known to also violate FARs regulating registration of aircraft, trying to conceal their activities by changing registration numbers and supporting documents and enabling nonstop long-range flights by installing illegal fuel tanks (water bed mattresses are one popular field expedient). When the FARs alone proved insufficient to deter these practices, Congress made them federal felonies, as well, providing not only for imprisonment of offenders but also for seizure and forfeiture of the aircraft. Because this is another particularly extensive and intricate law not amenable to accurate summarization, its full text is reproduced here:

(a) Application.—This section applies only to aircraft not used to provide air transportation.
(b) General Criminal Penalty.—Except as provided by subsection (c) of this section, a person shall be fined under title 18, imprisoned for not more than 3 years, or both, if the person—
   (1) knowingly and willfully forges or alters a certificate authorized to be issued under this part;
   (2) knowingly sells, uses, attempts to use, or possesses with the intent to use, such a certificate;
   (3) knowingly and willfully displays or causes to be displayed on an aircraft a mark that is false or misleading about the nationality or registration of the aircraft;
   (4) obtains a certificate authorized to be issued under this part by knowingly and willfully falsifying or concealing a material fact, making a false, fictitious, or fraudulent statement, or making or using a false document knowing it contains a false, fictitious, or fraudulent statement or entry;
   (5) owns an aircraft eligible for registration under section 44102 of this title and knowingly and willfully operates, attempts to operate, or allows another person to operate the aircraft when—
      (A) the aircraft is not registered under section 44103 of this title or the certificate of registration is suspended or revoked; or
      (B) the owner knows or has reason to know that the other person does not have proper authorization to operate or navigate the aircraft without registration for a period of time after transfer of ownership;

(6) knowingly and willfully operates or attempts to operate an aircraft eligible for registration under section 44102 of this title knowing that—
  (A) the aircraft is not registered under section 44103 of this title;
  (B) the certificate of registration is suspended or revoked; or
  (C) the person does not have proper authorization to operate or navigate the aircraft without registration for a period of time after transfer of ownership;
(7) knowingly and willfully serves or attempts to serve in any capacity as an airman without an airman's certificate authorizing the individual to serve in that capacity;
(8) knowingly and willfully employs for service or uses in any capacity as an airman an individual who does not have an airman's certificate authorizing the individual to serve in that capacity; or
(9) operates an aircraft with a fuel tank or fuel system that has been installed or modified knowing that the tank, system, installation, or modification does not comply with regulations and requirements of the Administrator of the Federal Aviation Administration.

(c) Controlled Substance Criminal Penalty.—
  (1) In this subsection, "controlled substance" has the same meaning given that term in section 102 of the Comprehensive Drug Abuse Prevention and Control Act of 1970 (21 U.S.C. 802).
  (2) A person violating subsection (b) of this section shall be fined under title 18, imprisoned for not more than 5 years, or both, if the violation is related to transporting a controlled substance by aircraft or aiding or facilitating a controlled substance violation and the transporting, aiding, or facilitating—
    (A) is punishable by death or imprisonment of more than one year under a law of the United States or a State; or
    (B) that is provided is related to an act punishable by death or imprisonment for more than one year under a law of the United States or a State related to a controlled substance (except a law related to simple possession of a controlled substance).
  (3) A term of imprisonment imposed under paragraph (2) of this subsection shall be served in addition to, and not concurrently with, any other term of imprisonment imposed on the individual.

(d) Seizure and Forfeiture.—
  (1) The Administrator of Drug Enforcement or the Commissioner of Customs may seize and forfeit under the customs laws an aircraft whose use is related to a violation of subsection (b) of this section, or to aid or facilitate a violation, regardless of whether a person is charged with the violation.
  (2) An aircraft's use is presumed to have been related to a violation of, or to aid or facilitate a violation of—
    (A) subsection (b)(1) of this section if the aircraft certificate of registration has been forged or altered;
    (B) subsection (b)(3) of this section if there is an external display of false or misleading registration numbers or country of registration;
    (C) subsection (b)(4) of this section if—
      (i) the aircraft is registered to a false or fictitious person; or
      (ii) the application form used to obtain the aircraft certificate of registration contains a material false statement;
    (D) subsection (b)(5) of this section if the aircraft was operated when it was not registered under section 44103 of this title; or
    (E) subsection (b)(9) of this section if the aircraft has a fuel tank or fuel system that was installed or altered—
      (i) in violation of a regulation or requirement of the Administrator of the Federal Aviation Administration; or
      (ii) if a certificate required to be issued for the installation or alteration is not carried on the aircraft.
  (3) The Administrator of the Federal Aviation Administration, the Administrator of Drug Enforcement, and the Commissioner shall agree to a memorandum of understanding to establish procedures to carry out this subsection.
(e) Relationship to State Laws.—This part does not prevent a State from establishing a criminal penalty, including providing for forfeiture and seizure of aircraft, for a person that—
  (1) knowingly and willfully forges or alters an aircraft certificate of registration;
  (2) knowingly sells, uses, attempts to use, or possesses with the intent to use, a fraudulent aircraft certificate of registration;

(3) knowingly and willfully displays or causes to be displayed on an aircraft a mark that is false or misleading about the nationality or registration of the aircraft; or
(4) obtains an aircraft certificate of registration from the Administrator of the Federal Aviation Administration by—
   (A) knowingly and willfully falsifying or concealing a material fact;
   (B) making a false, fictitious, or fraudulent statement; or
   (C) making or using a false document knowing it contains a false, fictitious, or fraudulent statement or entry.

Transporting hazardous material (49 USC 46312). Intended to prevent accidents such as the ValuJet accident discussed in Chapter 4, this criminal statute puts real teeth into enforcement of the regulations governing transportation of hazardous materials ("hazmat") by air. It is curious that although it is a fundamental principle of law enforcement that every person is presumed to know the law, Congress specifically provided in this provision that ignorance of this law is no excuse for violating it:

(a) In General.—A person shall be fined under title 18, imprisoned for not more than 5 years, or both, if the person, in violation of a regulation or requirement related to the transportation of hazardous material prescribed by the Secretary of Transportation under this part—
   (1) willfully delivers, or causes to be delivered, property containing hazardous material to an air carrier or to an operator of a civil aircraft for transportation in air commerce; or
   (2) recklessly causes the transportation in air commerce of the property.
(b) Knowledge of Regulations.—For purposes of subsection (a), knowledge by the person of the existence of a regulation or requirement related to the transportation of hazardous material prescribed by the Secretary under this part is not an element of an offense under this section but shall be considered in mitigation of the penalty.

Fraud involving aircraft or space vehicle parts in interstate or foreign commerce (18 USC 38). This law was enacted by Congress at the urging of then DOT Inspector General Mary Schiavo to deal with a growing problem of so-called "bogus parts" finding their way into certified aircraft and presenting a serious safety problem. Some of these parts were manufactured to look like actual certified aircraft parts, although they did not meet certification standards, while others were actually certified parts that had been removed from service because they had reached time/life cycle limits. In either case, the part was passed off as a useable (yellow tagged) part, when in fact it was not. In use, however, these parts failed and accidents resulted. Here is the actual language of this rather complicated law:

(a) Offenses.—Whoever, in or affecting interstate or foreign commerce, knowingly and with the intent to defraud—
  (1)
   (A) falsifies or conceals a material fact concerning any aircraft or space vehicle part;
   (B) makes any materially fraudulent representation concerning any aircraft or space vehicle part; or
   (C) makes or uses any materially false writing, entry, certification, document, record, data plate, label, or electronic communication concerning any aircraft or space vehicle part;
  (2) exports from or imports or introduces into the United States, sells, trades, installs on or in any aircraft or space vehicle any aircraft or space vehicle part using or by means of a fraudulent representation, document, record, certification, depiction, data plate, label, or electronic communication; or
  (3) attempts or conspires to commit an offense described in paragraph (1) or (2), shall be punished as provided in subsection (b).
(b) Penalties.—The punishment for an offense under subsection (a) is as follows:
  (1) Aviation quality.—If the offense relates to the aviation quality of a part and the part is installed in an aircraft or space vehicle, a fine of not more than $500,000, imprisonment for not more than 15 years, or both.
  (2) Failure to operate as represented.—If, by reason of the failure of the part to operate as represented, the part to which the offense is related is the proximate cause of a malfunction or failure that results in serious bodily injury (as defined in section 1365), a fine of not more than $1,000,000, imprisonment for not more than 20 years, or both.
  (3) Failure resulting in death.—If, by reason of the failure of the part to operate as represented, the part to which the offense

is related is the proximate cause of a malfunction or failure that results in the death of any person, a fine of not more than $1,000,000, imprisonment for any term of years or life, or both.
- (4) Other circumstances.—In the case of an offense under subsection (a) not described in paragraph (1), (2), or (3) of this subsection, a fine under this title, imprisonment for not more than 10 years, or both.
- (5) Organizations.—If the offense is committed by an organization, a fine of not more than—
  - (A) $10,000,000 in the case of an offense described in paragraph (1) or (4); and
  - (B) $20,000,000 in the case of an offense described in paragraph (2) or (3).
- (c) Civil Remedies.—
  - (1) In general.—The district courts of the United States shall have jurisdiction to prevent and restrain violations of this section by issuing appropriate orders, including—
    - (A) ordering a person (convicted of an offense under this section) to divest any interest, direct or indirect, in any enterprise used to commit or facilitate the commission of the offense, or to destroy, or to mutilate and sell as scrap, aircraft material or part inventories or stocks;
    - (B) imposing reasonable restrictions on the future activities or investments of any such person, including prohibiting engagement in the same type of endeavor as used to commit the offense; and
    - (C) ordering the dissolution or reorganization of any enterprise knowingly used to commit or facilitate the commission of an offense under this section making due provisions for the rights and interests of innocent persons.
  - (2) Restraining orders and prohibition.—Pending final determination of a proceeding brought under this section, the court may enter such restraining orders or prohibitions, or take such other actions (including the acceptance of satisfactory performance bonds) as the court deems proper.
  - (3) Estoppel.—A final judgment rendered in favor of the United States in any criminal proceeding brought under this section shall stop the defendant from denying the essential allegations of the criminal offense in any subsequent civil proceeding brought by the United States.

(d) Criminal Forfeiture.—
  (1) In general.—The court, in imposing sentence on any person convicted of an offense under this section, shall order, in addition to any other sentence and irrespective of any provision of State law, that the person forfeit to the United States—
    (A) any property constituting, or derived from, any proceeds that the person obtained, directly or indirectly, as a result of the offense; and
    (B) any property used, or intended to be used in any manner, to commit or facilitate the commission of the offense, if the court in its discretion so determines, taking into consideration the nature, scope, and proportionality of the use of the property on the offense.
  (2) Application of other law.—The forfeiture of property under this section, including any seizure and disposition of the property, and any proceedings relating to the property, shall be governed by section 413 of the Comprehensive Drug Abuse and Prevention Act of 1970 (21 U.S.C. 853) (not including subsection (d) of that section).
(e) Construction With Other Law.—This section does not preempt or displace any other remedy, civil or criminal, provided by Federal or State law for the fraudulent importation, sale, trade, installation, or introduction into commerce of an aircraft or space vehicle part.
(f) Territorial Scope.—This section also applies to conduct occurring outside the United States if—
  (1) the offender is a natural person who is a citizen or permanent resident alien of the United States, or an organization organized under the laws of the United States or political subdivision thereof;
  (2) the aircraft or spacecraft part as to which the violation relates was installed in an aircraft or space vehicle owned or operated at the time of the offense by a citizen or permanent resident alien of the United States, or by an organization thereof; or
  (3) an act in furtherance of the offense was committed in the United States.

Search of Airline Passengers
PRE-BOARDING SCREENING

In the U.S., airline passenger screening was first mandated by federal law in 1973 in response to a rash of hijackings to Cuba. Most published cases to date dealing with application of the criminal law in the aviation context arose out of encounters between passengers and security personnel in the vicinity of the passenger screening magnetometer at airline airports. These cases have typically involved the discovery of either a prohibited weapon or contraband during the screening process.

The courts have consistently held that the screening of airline passengers and their baggage by magnetometers and other devices constitutes a "search" within the meaning of the 4th Amendment to the Constitution of the United States. That amendment provides

> The right of the people to be secure in their persons, houses, papers, and effects, against *unreasonable* searches and seizures, shall not be violated, and no Warrants shall issue, but upon probable cause, supported by Oath or affirmation, and particularly describing the place to be searched, and the persons or things to be seized. *(Emphasis supplied.)*

The U.S. Supreme Court has read this amendment broadly, inferring from it a general (if limited) *right to privacy*. These protections are not limited to our homes, but travel with us wherever we go (including the airport). So how can TSA personnel legally search us without a warrant every time we go to board an airliner? Because the courts have recognized certain classes of warrantless searches as reasonable, including but not limited to (1) searches carried out with the *consent* of the person being searched and (2) *emergency administrative searches*. The courts have held these two exceptions applicable to the pre-boarding airline passenger-screening program. In this era of international terrorism, when terrorists so frequently choose civil airliners as targets for destruction or to seize for the taking of hostages or use as weapons, the passenger pre-boarding screening program is considered an emergency administrative search, and passengers who present themselves at the airport's security checkpoint for pre-boarding screening are deemed to consent to that search. (A passenger who does not consent to the search must be free to turn around and depart the area without adverse consequences.)

Thus, where such a lawful search of a passenger or baggage detects a prohibited weapon, the search will pass subsequent judicial scrutiny, the weapon deemed legally seized, and the passenger can be convicted of the crime of carrying a weapon aboard an aircraft.

Sometimes, though, the pre-boarding screening search will turn up not a prohibited weapon, but contraband such as illegal drugs. In these cases, the courts must consider the specific facts of the situation to determine whether the scope of the search was reasonable. The purpose of the passenger-screening program is to prevent passengers from carrying weapons or explosives aboard airliners. If the item of contraband found was of sufficient size and texture that it might have been or contained a weapon or explosive device, the courts have generally refused to suppress that evidence in a subsequent criminal trial. For example, where a small amount of marijuana was found inside a sealed letter-size envelope in a passenger's carry-on bag, the court found that the action of security personnel in opening the envelope constituted an unreasonable search, since it was too small to contain a weapon or explosive device. Where, however, a metal foil wrapped "brick" of hashish was found, the court found it reasonable for security personnel to unwrap the hard package to assure that it did not contain, for example, plastic explosive. In the latter case, the evidence was found admissible to prosecute the passenger for felony possession of narcotics or a controlled substance.

The same is true if the passenger sets off the magnetometer alarm and submits to further search by hand-held (wand) magnetometer, pat down, or other physical search that reveals contraband other than a weapon or explosive device.

However, given the increasing miniaturization of weapons (the 9/11 terrorists succeeded in gaining control of the aircraft using simple box cutters), explosive devices (about a pound of Czech-manufactured Semtex plastic explosive, a favorite of terrorists, concealed in a portable "boom box" tape deck inside a checked bag is believed to have destroyed Pan Am flight 103 in flight over Lockerbie, Scotland, in 1985), and chemical or biological agents (such as the envelopes of anthrax powder sent through the mail to members of Congress shortly after the 9/11 attacks), I fully expect this distinction to wane.

Meanwhile, a variety of promising (if expensive) new technologies are being developed and introduced to more rapidly, efficiently, and thoroughly identify, scan, and track airline passengers, bags, and cargo. It is reasonable to expect that the courts will also consider use of these devices to constitute a search, but will find the search reasonable unless it goes too far. An example of unreasonableness might be a backscatter X-ray imaging device recently demonstrated to the TSA by the manufacturer. Designed to detect even nonmetallic items concealed under passengers' clothing, the version demonstrated was so sensitive that the passenger's body image displayed to the operator was as clear and anatomically detailed as a full strip search. This clearly went too far and raised what should have been an entirely predictable and understandable public uproar over passengers' constitutional right to privacy. At this writing, the manufacturer is working on a modification to the equipment to digitally place an electronic "fig leaf" of pixels on key areas of the image in hope of gaining passenger acceptance without compromising detection capabilities. Meanwhile, use of baggage "sniffers" such as thermal neutron analysis (TNA) devices that detect chemical traces of explosives and lower-tech search dogs with similar capabilities to screen bags appear reasonable.

It is certainly tempting as a knee-jerk reaction to recent terrorist activity to single out persons of Middle Eastern origin and Muslims for special suspicion and scrutiny in the airline screening process *("profiling")*. After all, every recent hijacker of a U.S. aircraft was of Middle Eastern origin and a follower of a version (some would say perversion) of Islam. But in fact the overwhelming majority of Middle Easterners, Muslims included, are peaceful and law-abiding citizens fully worthy of the protections against racial and religious stereotyping and discrimination that are so central to our most basic American concepts of fairness and justice. The American Civil Liberties Union (ACLU) and others have shown profiling to be ineffective and counterproductive, typically failing to catch the guilty while antagonizing the innocent. In 1996, President Clinton signed into law an Act mandating creation of the Computer Assisted Passenger Screening System (CAPS), since widely used by the airlines. Although the factors the system considers to flag certain passengers for heightened scrutiny are classified, the Department of Justice has given public assurances that CAPS does not record or consider a passenger's race, color, national origin, religion, or gender. Assuming that to be true (and I have no reason to suspect that it is not), there do not appear to be any constitutional or other legal impediments to use of this system. Likely CAPS indicators are behavior-focused, and may include such things as a pattern of frequent travel to destinations known to harbor terrorists or buying a one-way ticket with cash. The federal government has also given the airlines secure access to its list of individuals suspected of having terrorist connections *("terrorist watch list")*, to aid in airline efforts to identify passengers who may merit increased scrutiny. This, too, is likely constitutionally sound.

Airlines have implemented *baggage resolution* programs to assure that no checked bag is carried aboard an airliner unless the passenger who checked it has also boarded. (Although many of the current generation of terrorists have shown no reluctance to die in the commission of a terrorist act, and some appear to welcome such an opportunity for instant martyrdom, in the past explosive-laden bags have been checked by passengers who then failed to board the flight or disembarked short of their ticketed destination.) These programs, which match every bag to a passenger, without regard to any characteristic of the passenger, also appear legally sound.

At airports (as elsewhere in modern society), arrays of video cameras

Fig. 15.3. Video surveillance is becoming pervasive worldwide, and is an integral part of airport security. It does not constitute a search, and used discretely does not violate reasonable expectations of privacy.

monitored by security personnel are commonplace (Fig. 15.3). Such observation is not considered by the courts to be a search, but could raise right-to-privacy issues if used in areas where people of normal sensibility would reasonably expect privacy, such as restrooms.

AIRPORT ENTRY SECURITY CHECKPOINTS

At certain alert levels, airport authorities implement checkpoints to control vehicular access to the terminal's parking structures and curbside passenger pickup and dropoff areas. Although no case arising out of such a security stop and vehicle check has yet reached publication, one would expect the same principles governing passenger pre-boarding screening discussed above to apply; that is to say that the stop and security check would be deemed an administrative search, and that so long as adequate signage alerted the driver of the necessity to consent to search in order to proceed (and afforded the driver the opportunity to go elsewhere if he preferred not to submit to a search of his vehicle), the search would be found lawful. If the search is also conducted in a reasonable manner, any contraband seized would be admissible in evidence.

SEARCHES ON SUSPICION

At the airport, even away from the magnetometer screening area, law enforcement personnel sometimes submit individuals whose behavior appears suspicious to a frisk search for weapons, and sometimes that search reveals contraband other than a weapon or explosive device. Again, in such a case the court must determine whether the search was reasonable under the circumstances. Where the search appears to have been motivated by *profiling*—that is, by the passenger's apparent race, religion, or national origin—the court is likely to find it unreasonable and suppress the evidence found (preclude its use to obtain a criminal conviction). If, however, the individual was behaving in a suspicious manner—such as furtively looking around, appearing nervous, perspiring, turning and hastening away from law enforcement officers, or appearing to attempt to conceal bulky items under his clothing—the court would likely find it reasonable for the officers to stop and question the individual and frisk search him for weapons. If the contraband revealed by the search was of a size and rigidity that it could have been or contained a weapon, the court will likely find the search and seizure legally valid. As in the case of searches in the magnetometer area, opening sealed flexible envelopes that proved to contain illegal drugs has often been held to be an unreasonable search, though given the increasing miniaturization of weapons of terror previously discussed, I expect the courts to greatly expand the scope of airport searches they will find reasonable.

GENERAL AVIATION SECURITY AND PASSENGER SCREENING

At this writing, there is no published case law on general aviation security or the screening of general aviation passengers, although the subject is currently under intense scrutiny by the TSA. At the request of the TSA, general aviation associations including Aircraft Owners and Pilots Association (AOPA), the Airport Consultants Council (ACC), American Association of Airport Executives (AAAE), Experimental Aircraft Association (EAA), General Aviation Manufacturers Association (GAMA), Helicopter Association International (HAI), National Air Transport Association (NATA), National Association of State Aviation Officials (NASAO), National Business Aviation Association (NBAA), and U.S. Parachute Association (USPA), banded together as the General Aviation Airport Security Working Group to provide industry input to the TSA's Aviation Security Advisory Committee (ASAC).

This diverse group, broadly representing a wide variety of general aviation interests, reached consensus on a thorough and extensive set of recommended guidelines or best practices for security enhancements at the nation's privately and publicly owned and operated general aviation landing facilities. They include recommended security procedures for charter operations, flight schools, airports, and airspace. These recommendations were delivered in October of 2003, and as this edition was going to press were largely adopted by the TSA as nonregulatory Security Guidelines for General Aviation Airports, available free on the TSA Web page. The TSA had previously implemented a national toll-free hotline that the general aviation community can use to report any "out-of-the-ordinary" event or activity at general aviation airports. The hotline, reached by dialing 866-GA-SECURE, is operated by the National Response Center. The center serves as a centralized reporting point and relays reports to the appropriate local, state, and federal agencies. The TSA has also adopted a rule imposing enhanced security measures on the half-dozen air-taxi operators providing private charters using aircraft weighing 95,000 pounds or more.

Meanwhile, in the absence of any federal mandate, general aviation industry, aircraft, and airport operators took a pro-active, cooperative approach to the problem, proceeding with development, dissemination, and voluntary implementation of security recommendations, programs, and practices—many of which are now incorporated into the new TSA guidelines as "best practices." The AOPA developed a nationwide Airport Watch system that includes airport warning signs (Fig 15.4), feeds reports to the National Response Center, and provides educational literature and a training videotape to educate pilots and airport employees on improving aircraft and airport security. Knowing that money laundering enables terrorist operations, GAMA, in conjunction with the Treasury Department and in consultation with manufacturers, aircraft finance companies, used aircraft brokers, and fractional ownership companies, developed and published Guidelines for Establishing Anti-Money Laundering Procedures and Practices Related to the Purchase of General Aviation Aircraft. The National Agricultural Aircraft Association (NAAA) produced an educational program called the Professional Aerial Applicators Support System (PASS) specifically addressing security of aerial application operations. (In addition, NAAA members have undergone several industrywide FBI background investigations since 9/11/01.) The National Association of

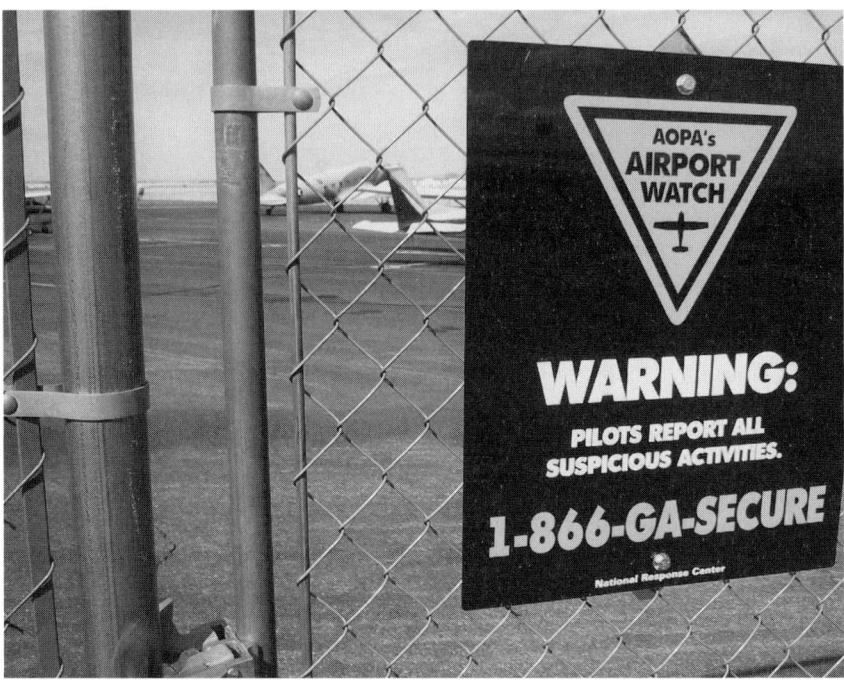

Fig. 15.4. Airport watch programs, such as this AOPA-sponsored example based on successful neighborhood watch programs, do not raise legal issues so long as suspicions are reported to law enforcement authorities for investigation, rather than being dealt with vigilante style by watchful participants.

Flight Instructors (NAFI) developed a series of security recommendations and best practices for flight schools and flight instructors. USPA disseminated detailed security recommendations to its 219 skydiving clubs and centers across the U.S., most of them based on general aviation airports, aimed at enhancing the airport watch program and ensuring the security of jump aircraft. At least to the extent that these measures are voluntarily implemented, and any observed security concerns are referred to sworn law enforcement officers (LEOs) for investigation rather than triggering any vigilante-style response, they do not appear to raise significant legal issues, though only time will tell.

PART V

Labor and Employment Law

CHAPTER 16

Labor and Employment Law, Generally

EMPLOYMENT LAW is the fastest growing area of litigation in America, today. At this writing, a web search on the subject yields 3.5 million hits. That figure could well have doubled by the time you read these words. Every business of significant size has its own personnel department, staffed with human resource professionals versed in the complexities and pitfalls of this body of law. Among aviation businesses, managers are now facing employment law problems as frequently as FAR compliance problems, if not more often.

Unionized work forces are characteristic of the giant companies in the aerospace industry today, such as major airframe and engine manufacturers. There is now a rising tide of union organizing. As the competition for skilled employees grows, employees of smaller aviation enterprises are seeking the advantages offered by collective bargaining to better their pay and working conditions.

The purpose of this chapter is to provide you a working knowledge of fundamental principles of labor and employment law, to prepare you to avoid common but costly mistakes made by employers uneducated on the subject.

Employment law principles discussed in this chapter apply to all American businesses, not only aviation enterprises. Labor law principles under the National Labor Relations Act (NLRA) discussed here apply to all American businesses, including aviation and aerospace businesses, *except* for the railroads and airlines, which are governed by the Railway Labor Act of 1926 (RLA), discussed in the chapter that follows. Where the RLA is silent on a subject, judges often turn to the NLRA and cases decided under it even in airline cases (Fig. 16.1).

Fig. 16.1. Preparing this airliner for departure, contract catering and fuel service employees are working under the NLRA, while airline employee baggage handlers, passenger service agents, dispatchers, and flight deck and cabin crews are working under the RLA. Each employee specialty group is probably represented by a different labor union.

Employment Law
EMPLOYMENT AT WILL

As a general rule, unless a collective bargaining agreement (contract) between the employer and employees' union is in force, employers have the right to terminate (fire) employees for any reason (or for no apparent reason). Collaterally, employees have the right to quit their jobs for any reason (or for no apparent reason). This is referred to as *employment at will*.

The job insecurity inherent in the doctrine of employment at will is a major incentive for employees to unionize.

Legislatures and courts have, however, made some exceptions to this general rule. Employers have been found liable in civil suits for *wrongful discharge* where

1. the action is in violation of a law prohibiting discrimination, or
2. the action is contrary to public policy, such as when the employee has been discharged for:
   a. missing work because summoned to serve on a jury, or

b. in *retaliation* for refusing to give false testimony to a court or administrative agency, or
c. in retaliation for reporting illegal conduct of an employer to law enforcement or administrative agencies (*"whistleblower protection"*), or
d. in retaliation for engaging in union activity protected by law, or
3. the employment is deemed not really at will, because the company's personnel policy or oral or written statements promising job tenure, relied upon by the employee in good faith, are found by the court to have created an *implied contract* of long term employment.

Prudent employers having nonunionized employees require new hires to sign agreements that their employment is at will, and exercise great care in choice of words in employee handbooks, position announcements and discussions to avoid statements that might later be construed as creating an implied contract for long-term employment.

Plaintiffs who have won wrongful discharge suits against former employers have been awarded (1) reinstatement of their job, (2) back pay, (3) money for damage to their professional reputation, and even (4) money damages for mental anguish suffered as a result of the termination.

HIRING

The hiring process is fraught with peril for the employer, who must take great care to comply with the intricacies of myriad federal antidiscrimination laws, which are discussed here. Some state laws provide employees even greater protection than these federal laws.

The *Civil Rights Act of 1964,* as amended by the *Equal Employment Opportunities Act of 1972*, prohibits employers from discriminating in employment and compensation against any individual because of the person's race, color, religion, sex or national origin (*"protected classes"*). *Title VII* of the act requires both the company and the union to assure that any collective bargaining agreement provides for fair representation and equal opportunity for employees regardless of race, color, religion, sex or national origin. The Equal Employment Opportunity Commission (EEOC) is the federal administrative agency primarily responsible for enforcing compliance with these laws. Some states have enacted laws that add sexual orientation to the list of protected classes. In 1991, Congress amended the Civil Rights Act to allow victims of unlawful discrimination to recover compensatory and punitive damages up to $300,000 each, in addition to job reinstatement and back pay. Congress specified that in these cases, compensatory damages include money damages for the pain and suffering of discrimination, and that where the employer's discrimination was intentional, punitive damages are appropriate if the discrimination was with "malice or with reckless or callous indifference to the federally protected rights of others."

The *Equal Pay Act,* also administered by the EEOC, prohibits employers from paying different rates of pay for the same job, based on gender or race.

The *Age Discrimination in Employment Act (ADEA)* prohibits employment discrimination against individuals over age 40 and also prohibits employers from imposing a mandatory retirement age. The act provides exceptions for certain specified occupations. These exceptions include airline pilots, whose retirement remains mandatory at age 60.

The *Americans with Disabilities Act (ADA)* applies to public and private employers having more than 15 employees. The act prohibits employment discrimination against qualified individuals with disabilities. A person is considered disabled under the ADA only if he or she has a physical or mental impairment that substantially limits one or more *major life activities.* Major life activities include such functions as caring for one's self, performing manual tasks, walking, seeing, hearing, speaking, breathing, learning, or working. Some of the impairments the courts have found covered by the ADA include vision, hearing, and speech impairments; orthopedic impairments; cerebral palsy; epilepsy; muscular dystrophy; multiple sclerosis; cancer; heart disease; diabetes; mental retardation; emotional illness; specific learning disabilities; tuberculosis; AIDS and HIV infection; *past* drug addiction; and alcoholism.

A disabled person is protected by the ADA only if otherwise qualified for the job. A *"qualified individual"* is one who can accomplish the *essential functions* of the job, with or without *reasonable accommodation.* Essential functions of the job are generally those included in a written job description. If an individual can perform those essential functions without needing any change in the work process or work environment (accommodation), the ADA prohibits the employer from discriminating against the person because of the disability. If some accommodation is needed, the ADA requires the employer to provide it, within reason. This requires at least a good faith best effort. It does not require the employer to do the impossible or suffer an undue hardship. Factors to determine whether a proposed accommodation would impose an undue hardship on the employer include

1. Nature and cost of accommodation,
2. Size and resources of the facility affected,

3. Size and resources of employer overall (financial),
4. Type of operation, composition, and structure of work force (nonfinancial), and
5. Impact of accommodation on operation.

Changes to the workplace that could be readily accomplished with little difficulty or expense, such as a simple wheelchair ramp or a magnifying lens for a computer screen, would be considered reasonable and thus required by the ADA.

If an employer believes (and can clearly and convincingly articulate a reasonable basis for the belief) that an individual with a disability cannot perform the job without creating a *direct threat* to his own safety or the safety of others, the employer is not required to hire the person.

The *Immigration Reform and Control Act (IRCA)* shifts much of the burden of immigration law enforcement from the federal government to employers by making it illegal for an employer to hire, recruit, refer for a fee, or continue to employ an alien who the employer knows is not eligible to work in the U.S. IRCA requires employers to verify and maintain records of each new employee's identity and work eligibility. These records must be kept for three years after employment or one year after termination, whichever is longer. Thousands of U.S. companies have been fined millions of dollars for violations of this act.

Additional statutory requirements apply to employers having government contracts. Executive Order 11246 requires contractors to develop *affirmative action programs* including specific goals and timetables for recruiting, selecting, training, and promoting minorities and women, although this was recently narrowed to apply only to employers having 250 or more employees and federal contracts totaling $1 million or more. This executive order is administered by the Department of Labor's *Office of Federal Contract Compliance Programs (OFCCP)*, whose powers include termination of federal contracts and barring violators from future federal contracts. The OFCCP can also award back pay to individuals who show an actual loss due to the violation. The *Vocational Rehabilitation Act of 1973* and the *Disabilities Act of 1991* require holders of federal government contracts in excess of $2,500 to develop affirmative action programs to employ and advance individuals with disabilities. The *Vietnam Era Veteran Readjustment Assistance Act* requires employers with government contracts of $10,000 or more to take affirmative action to employ and promote qualified and disabled veterans who served during that era. The *Military Selection Act* mandates that employers reemploy veterans to the position they held before entering the armed forces, at the same seniority, status, and pay.

WAGES, HOURS, BENEFITS, AND WORKING CONDITIONS

The *Occupational Safety and Health Act (OSHA)* requires all employers to provide a safe and healthy workplace. The act created the Occupational Safety and Health Administration (also called OSHA) under the Department of Labor. OSHA has adopted and vigorously enforces an extensive body of regulations to this end. OSHA regulations impose stiff fines on employers for violations, and permit an employee to refuse to work "if a reasonable person would conclude he faced an immediate risk of death or serious injury."

The *Fair Labor Standards Act (FLSA)* outlaws employment of children under age 16, provides a federal minimum wage (which Congress periodically increases), and stipulates that certain employees (*"non-exempt employees"*) must receive overtime pay of one-and-one-half times the normal pay rate when they work over 40 hours per week. Time off (*compensatory or "comp" time*) cannot be used as a substitute for overtime pay. Other (*"exempt"*) employees do not qualify for the act's overtime pay benefit. All employees are considered non-exempt (that is, they are entitled to overtime pay) unless the employer proves the employee to be exempt.

Four basic categories of employees are recognized as exempt under certain circumstances: executive, administrative, professional, and outside salespeople. Within these categories, to qualify as exempt, an employee must receive at least a minimum salary specified by regulation and have a primary duty requiring that during more than 50% of the employee's working time she must "customarily and regularly exercise discretion and independent judgment." Additionally, less than 20% of the employee's time can be spent on routine, manual, or clerical work.

For overtime entitlement calculations, a workweek is defined as 168 consecutive hours or seven consecutive days, not necessarily a calendar week. It does not matter whether the employer asked the employee to work overtime or a supervisor merely voiced no objection when noticing a non-exempt employee putting in extra hours. If the employer knows or has reason to believe that employee was continuing to work, overtime is earned.

This is a well-camouflaged potential pitfall for employers. Without any claim for overtime being mentioned, well-meaning, loyal, non-exempt employees may come to work early, work through lunch, or work late to complete a task or project. In the culture of the company, such demonstrations of dedication may routinely draw expressions of appreciation from supervisors and even help such employees advance ahead of clock-watching peers. But the company's statutory liability for overtime pay nonetheless accrues, a financial bomb waiting to explode. If the employee later becomes disgruntled and seeks legal advice, becomes concerned about the adequacy of provisions for retirement income and seeks ways to supplement that income, or complains to labor regulators, the company may be hit with a substantial judgment for back pay, with interest, plus penalties. Multiply that by the number of non-exempt employees who worked for the company during years of inattention to FLSA overtime requirements and it should be readily apparent that the liability could be catastrophic in magnitude. A clearly written policy should be adopted and enforced by the company, specifying who has authority to approve how much overtime and under what circumstances. Supervisors must be trained to be especially watchful to observe and prevent employees from accruing unauthorized overtime, no matter how well intentioned or voluntary the act (Fig. 16.2).

For calculation of the overtime rate, all compensation must be included in the regular rate of pay (not merely the employee's regular hourly pay rate). This may include pay incentives such as attendance and productivity bonuses and commissions.

Compliance with FLSA overtime requirements is a complex but important task for corporate personnel departments. Employers are moti-

Fig. 16.2. Is this aircraft mechanic smiling because he knows that the FLSA entitles him to collect a nice nest egg of back overtime pay that his employer does not yet realize it owes?

vated by overtime costs to classify the maximum number of employees as exempt, but excessive zeal in this area has resulted in millions of dollars in back pay judgments against employers. Tight control of overtime worked and compensation paid is crucial to avoid such unwanted results.

Employers in the restaurant, agricultural, tourist, and medical industries are exempt from FLSA overtime provisions.

As we settle into this information age, many workers have the ability to accomplish much of their work anywhere there is a source of electricity and internet connectivity: office, home, hotel, or in a vehicle, cafe, or Internet coffee shop and to do that work at any time of day. A great many employees yearn for the personal freedom such working arrangements offer. Employers can benefit from such working arrangements, too, as they may enable the employer to get the work done with less overhead cost for providing office or other working space. The difficulty, if not impossibility, of assuring compliance with the overtime provisions of the FLSA (along with OSHA's position that in such cases, OSHA safety requirements extend to the home or wherever else the work is done) have thus far put such working arrangements beyond the reach of non-exempt employees.

President George W. Bush promised to untie the Gordian knot of FLSA, but at this writing legislation proposed by his administration is a subject of heated debate in Congress. Many American workers rely on overtime pay to sustain their families' standard of living, and there is widespread concern that proposed changes to FLSA would deprive them of that income. A good source for current FLSA law and implementing regulations is the Department of Labor website: *www.dol.gov*.

Additional compensation legislation applies to employers having federal contracts. The *Walsh-Healey Act* requires employers with federal contracts over $10,000 to pay overtime anytime an employer works more than eight hours in a day. The *Davis-Bacon Act* requires employers holding federal construction project contracts of $2,000 or more to pay the prevailing wage rate for that particular geographic area. (In most urban areas, this will be the union wage.)

The EEOC has declared *sexual harassment* a form of *sex discrimination* prohibited by the Civil Rights Act. The EEOC recognizes two categories of workplace behavior as prohibited sexual harassment: *quid pro quo* and *hostile work environment*. *Quid pro quo* (Latin, meaning "this for that") harassment involves demands or suggestions of sexual favors in exchange for such benefits as a job or promotion, or to avoid adverse actions such as being fired or laid off. A hostile work environment may be created by verbal abuse, sexist remarks, touching, leering, or ogling (Fig. 16.3).

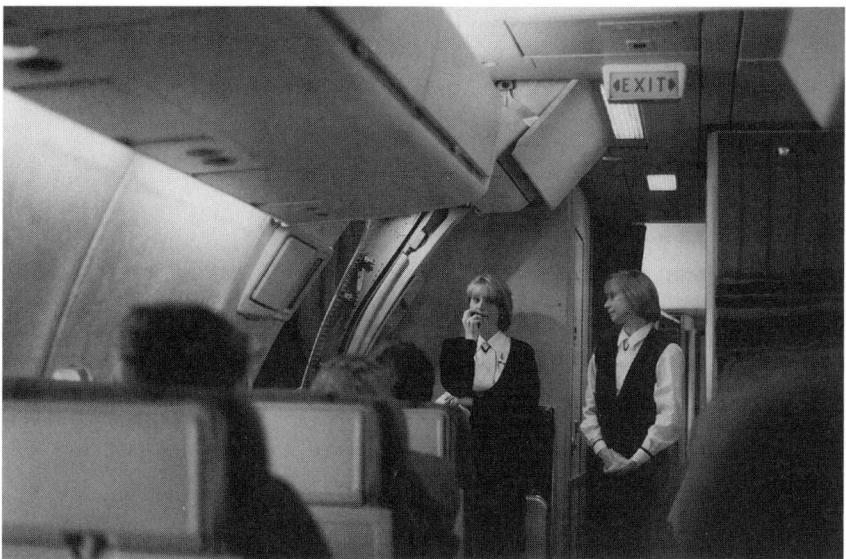

Fig. 16.3. Flight attendants are continuously exposed to risk of unwelcome sexual comments from airline travelers and coworkers. If the airline fails to take reasonable steps to protect them, this may create a hostile work environment, a form of sexual discrimination recognized by the EEOC as prohibited by the Civil Rights Act, and the airline can be held liable to the employee.

Both categories of sexual harassment are prohibited so long as the conduct (whether physical or verbal) is both *unwelcome* and *of a sexual nature*. The courts now regularly hold businesses liable for sexual harassment of their employees. This includes sexual harassment not only by co-workers in the company, but also by customers, vendors and others having work-related contact with the employee. Employer liability may accrue even if the employer was unaware of the harassment, so employers must take the initiative, encourage everyone in the company to be on the lookout for and report incidents of sexual harassment and other prohibited discrimination, thoroughly investigate each such report, and act on it in a timely and proper manner upon conclusion of the investigation.

Discipline, Suspension, and Termination. Although the doctrine of employment at will discussed earlier affords employers the general right to suspend or fire nonunionized employees for any reason or for no reason at all, there are important limits. Even employees at will cannot be subjected to adverse job actions for discriminatory reasons (within the protected classes), or in retaliation for activities protected by law. Even in employment at will states, employers should document every disciplinary action taken against an employee, including the reason for the discipline, in the worker's personnel file. Employment lawyers representing employers call this "building a *paper fortress,*" while those representing employees use the more derisive term *"papering the file."* In my experience, jurors tend to disbelieve an employer's testimony about an employee's work record and the reason an employee was fired, unless it's clearly spelled out in the personnel file. Employers (and there are still many in the small business community) who try to handle all employee problems by an off-the-record chewing-out leave their companies wide open to judgments for wrongful discharge.

Insuring Against Wrongful Discharge Claims. Because employment litigation has become so frequent, and because most general liability policies exclude coverage for these claims, employers are well advised to purchase *employment practices liability insurance.*

Layoffs and Reductions in Force. Under the *Worker Adjustment and Retraining Notification Act (WARN,* also known as the *Plant Closing Act),* enacted in 1989, most private sector employers that employ 100 or more full-time employees are required to give employees at least 60 days advance notice of impending closing of a facility or layoff of 50 or more employees in one location.

Non-Airline Labor Law

The *National Labor Relations Act (NLRA,* also known as the *Wagner Act)* applies to most private sector employers *except the railroads and airlines* (these will be discussed in the next chapter). The NLRA gave employees the right to organize without interference by the employer and to bargain collectively (through a union of their choice) with the employer. Congress' intent in enacting the NLRA was to equalize bargaining power between employers and employees and thereby minimize the disruption to interstate commerce caused by labor disputes. The NLRA created the *National Labor Relations Board (NLRB)* to adopt and enforce regulations implementing the act. Major provisions of the NLRA include the following:

1. Guarantees *employee rights* to:
    a. *organize* into unions of their own choosing,
    b. *assist* such labor unions,

c. *bargain collectively* with their employer through a union of their own choosing (which, upon election, becomes the *exclusive bargaining representative* of that group of employees, called a *"bargaining unit"*), and
d. *strike* or take other concerted action.
2. Prohibits *employers* from engaging in *unfair labor practices* made illegal by the act, including:
a. *interfering* with employee rights guaranteed by the act,
b. *discriminating* against union members or employees pursuing their rights under the act,
c. attempting to *dominate or interfere* with employee unions, and
d. *refusing to bargain in good faith* with employee representatives.
3. Provides for NLRB to:
a. determine the *appropriate bargaining unit (craft or class of employees)* (i.e.: aircraft sheet metal workers, aircraft fuelers, baggage handlers)
b. oversee union organizing efforts to prevent unfair labor practices, and
c. when at least 30% of employees in an appropriate bargaining unit authorize a union to represent them, determine who is entitled to vote (nonsupervisory employees) and conduct elections by secret ballot to select a union to represent those employees.

The *Taft-Hartley Amendments* to the NLRA, enacted to correct an imbalance in labor's favor, added the following provisions:

1. Prohibits *secondary strikes or boycotts* (aimed to force one employer to cease doing business with another employer),
2. Establishes employee *right to refrain* from any and all union activities except union shop provisions in any valid collective bargaining agreement,
3. Prohibits union unfair labor practices, including:
a. restraint or coercion of employees in exercise of their rights,
b. discrimination against an employee for not engaging in union activities, and
c. refusal to bargain in good faith with the employer.
4. Empowers states to enact *right to work laws* outlawing union shop requirements in collective bargaining agreements, to allow employees to refrain from joining the union (Fig. 16.4).

Fig. 16.4. FBO employees deicing this corporate jet for a winter departure and the aircraft's flight crew are most likely not yet unionized.

Examples of private sector employee unionization under the NLRA in the aerospace industry include virtually all nonmanagement employees of the major aircraft and component manufacturers and, most recently, flight instructors employed by Embry-Riddle Aeronautical University (ERAU). Flight instructors surely rank among the most underpaid highly skilled workers, so it will be interesting to see whether the ERAU example will be followed elsewhere in the industry.

The NLRA, as amended, narrowly circumscribes a company's options to resist employee efforts to unionize. Frequently, efforts to unionize result from long-standing employee dissatisfaction with the company's treatment of and apparent attitude toward its employees. Once union organizing efforts begin, there is little the company can legally do to resist because of the unfair labor practice prohibitions of the NLRA. Those companies that have been most successful in avoiding unionization of their work forces have been proactive in management-employee relations over the long term. Issues that, if allowed to fester, make employees receptive to union organizing efforts include not only substandard wages and benefits, but also more subjective feelings of unfairness and lack of interest in worker well being on the part of management.

Such issues lend themselves to preventive management by the company, to prevent development of worker dissatisfaction that may lead to employee efforts to unionize. Fundamental is the necessity to pay wages and provide benefits that are competitive with other employers of such employees. An FBO that wishes to keep its aircraft mechanics, and keep them unrepresented by a union, must compete in wages and benefits not only against other FBOs in the area, but also with the airlines, corporate flight departments, and even automobile dealerships and shops.

Feelings of unfairness arise where employees perceive that management is inconsistent, arbitrary, or unresponsive or shows favoritism in handling disciplinary cases. Adoption and even-handed implementation of a formal, published grievance procedure with provision for progressive discipline in most cases can go a long way toward preventing or healing employee feelings of management unfairness.

Failure to keep open effective lines of communication between management and employees can also lead to dissatisfaction. A perception (accurate or not) that management does not care about the rank-and-file employees and is disinterested in hearing their views, suggestions and concerns leaves the workforce ripe for union organizing efforts. There is no substitute for listening to the workers. Suggestion boxes, company newsletters, hotlines, and opportunities for face-to-face dialogue between workers and management can be very effective in keeping workers happy and also yield benefits in productivity. Formal and honest performance evaluations also provide an important opportunity for truthful and meaningful communication.

Training supervisors in company policies and procedures and in interpersonal skills can pay off in the company's effort to avoid feelings of unfairness and keep the lines of constructive communication open. Skilled and trusted supervisors can also keep management informed of the extent of union sentiment among workers and convey messages from management to the workers, within the extremely narrow bounds of content permitted by the NLRA and NLRB.

Companies may also legally adopt and enforce a *no solicitation/no distribution rule* placing certain restrictions on union organizing activities in the workplace. For example, such activities may be limited to nonworking time (such as breaks and mealtimes) and nonworking areas (break rooms, cafeterias, locker rooms, parking lots). Reasonable limits can be placed on where literature can be posted. Care must be taken to enforce the rule uniformly against all forms of solicitation and distribution; not merely those associated with union activities. The same rules must apply and be enforced against, for example, posting or distributing in the workplace literature promoting sales of cosmetics, homes, vehicles, and event tickets as against literature promoting union activities.

FEDERAL GOVERNMENT EMPLOYEES

Executive Orders signed by Presidents Kennedy and Nixon extended collective bargaining rights to most federal government employees. These were replaced by the *Civil Service Reform Act* enacted by Congress in 1978, which affords federal government employees rights virtually identical to private sector employees covered by the NLRA, with two important exceptions: (1) federal government employees do not have the right to strike, and (2) all collective bargaining agreements with federal employees must contain a grievance procedure providing for final resolution by binding arbitration.

The *Office of Personnel Management (OPM)* establishes the rules regulating federal civilian employment procedures and practices, the *Federal Labor Relations Authority (FLRA)* oversees the unionization and collective bargaining of federal employees, and the *Merit System Protection Board (MSPB)* hears appeals of federal employee grievances, such as those filed by terminated air traffic controllers.

Following close on the heels of enactment of the Civil Service Reform Act, the Professional Air Traffic Controllers' (PATCO) strike of 1981 was the first declared strike against the federal government. President Reagan stood fast against the unlawful strike, resulting in the FAA firing about 11,000 strikers, and the courts imposing crippling fines against union leaders and the union, and jailing some union leaders. The union was broken and dissolved, and no organization of federal employees has dared to defy this law since. FAA air traffic controllers have reorganized under a new union, the National Air Traffic Controllers Association (NATCA), an affiliate of the powerful AFL-CIO.

CHAPTER 17

Airline Labor Law

IN THE WAKE of economic deregulation of the airlines, numerous new air carriers—commuter, regional, and trunk—started business using nonunion labor and paying wages substantially below scales then paid by existing airlines (which were governed by contracts previously negotiated with elected union representatives). Competitive pressures led to "hardball" renegotiation of virtually all airline pay and benefit scales by those carriers whose workers were unionized. In nonunion airlines, discontent over persistent low pay and difficult working conditions has led to increasing interest of employees in unionizing to gain the strength of collective bargaining with management. As the industry consolidates, airline mergers and acquisitions are complicated by the necessity to merge work forces operating under different contracts. Airline pilot unions are also now in a consolidation phase, with the Air Line Pilots Association (ALPA) aggressively courting pilots presently represented by a company union.

The purpose of this chapter is to equip you with a practical working knowledge of procedures in the airline industry for unionizing employees, contract negotiations, disciplinary actions against employees, changing unions, and dealing with employee issues in mergers and acquisitions.

Railway Labor Act

Labor relations in the airline industry are governed by (of all things) the Railway Labor Act of 1926 (RLA), which Congress made applicable to the airlines in 1936. The purpose of this statute is to minimize interference in interstate commerce caused by labor disputes in the mass-transportation industries while ensuring transportation employees' right to engage in collective bargaining and collective action. General characteristics of the RLA include

1. *Union or agency shops.* If a majority of the workers in a particular craft or class (such as airlines pilots, aircraft mechanics, flight attendants, or aircraft dispatchers) vote to be represented by a union, union dues (or an equivalent service fee for those who prefer not to be listed on the union's membership roll) will be automatically withheld (by a *dues checkoff*) from the paychecks of all workers in that craft or class, and the union will become the *exclusive bargaining agent* of all of them. The RLA prohibits *"yellow dog"* contracts whereby employees agree not to join a union.
2. *Compulsory mediation and opportunity for binding arbitration.* Procedures for the resolution of major disputes between airlines and their employees' union focus on mandatory mediation and the opportunity for a resolution by binding arbitration if that fails.
3. *Postponement of right to strike.* The parties are prohibited from resorting to self-help (the employees or union from striking, the airline from unilaterally changing pay scales or other terms and conditions of employment, locking out union employees and hiring permanent replacement workers) until the major dispute-resolution process spelled out in the act has been completed.

These are mandatory and exclusive remedies, administered by the National Mediation Board (NMB). The National Labor Relations Board (NLRB) has no jurisdiction over airline labor controversies.

There are two basic types of airline labor law cases: *representation* cases and *disputes.*

Representation

In order to raise and test employee interest in unionizing, the union usually mounts an organizing campaign that may include the distribution of leaflets, informational picketing, mass meetings and speeches, even radio and television advertising. The union will then circulate authorization cards to prospective members. It is unlawful for the airline to interfere in any way with the union's efforts to organize the employees. Airline management is also prohibited from informing the workers that management prefers one union over another. If 35% of the employees eligible to vote sign authorization cards, an election is justified.

Once a union believes it has sufficient support among the workers to win, it petitions the NMB to hold an election. The NMB investigates the responsibilities and authority of various workers in the particular craft or class to determine which of them are "labor" (allowed to vote in the election) and which are "management" (prohibited from voting in the election). For example, an airline's pilots might include not only the line pilots (labor) and a chief pilot (management) but also flight instructors and company check airmen (whose authority in one company may look more like management but more like labor in another). Once the NMB has decided who can vote, an election is held under NMB supervision, and those who are qualified to vote cast ballots for or against representation by the union. If a simple majority of qualified voters cast ballots and a simple majority of those who voted cast their ballots in favor of the union, the NMB certifies that union as the official bargaining representative for that craft or class of workers.

Once a union has been so certified, it has the exclusive authority to represent all of the airline's employees in that craft or class (including those who would rather not be so represented and who voted against unionization). But correlative to that right, the union also has the *duty of fair representation* of all of the airline's employees in that craft or class (including those who voted against unionization) (Fig.17.1) in bargaining with the employer.

Upon certification, the union will enter into negotiations with airline management for an employment contract covering that craft or class of employees. At this stage, both sides have a legal duty to bargain in good faith. Many (but not all) unions' bylaws require that once union representatives and management have negotiated a new contract, the union must present the contract to the affected members for their vote to ratify or reject the agreement. In that case, if a simple majority of the affected members vote to ratify the contract, all are bound by it. If a simple majority votes to reject the contract, the union's representatives must return to the bargaining table and resume contract negotiations with the airline.

The RLA does not establish a procedure for decertifying a union in the event that the employees become disaffected with their union. Absent a statutory procedure, it has become customary in the industry in such a case to hold a new election in which an individual (rather than a union) is voted in to represent the employees instead of their previous union. The newly elected person then resigns and the goal of returning to unrepresented status is accomplished.

Disputes

After an employment contract has been agreed to, disputes may arise. Disputes between the union and the airline are divided into two categories: *minor disputes* and *major disputes*.

Fig. 17.1. United Airlines pilots, such as the one seen here performing a preflight inspection, enjoy excellent pay and benefits as a result of decades of successful bargaining by their chosen union, ALPA. An AFL-CIO affiliate, ALPA represents about 60,000 pilots at 50 U.S. and Canadian airlines.

MINOR DISPUTES

Minor disputes (also referred to as *grievances*) involve disputes over the interpretation or application of the employment contract. Most minor disputes involve company discipline of employees. For example, the pilots' contract requires pilots to report for duty one hour prior to the scheduled departure time for their flight to obtain a briefing and trip documentation from the dispatcher and perform the preflight inspection of the aircraft. A pilot arrives late, so that the airline has to call in a reserve pilot and suspends the rule breaker for 30 days without pay as punishment.

The RLA requires that the employment contract provide for the creation of a *System Board of Adjustment* to resolve minor disputes that arise under the contract, such as the foregoing example. A typical System Board in the airline industry includes two members selected by the airline and two members selected by the union. The board's procedures should also be set out in the contract. Where an employee has a legitimate claim that the airline has breached the employment agreement, the union must represent the employee in the grievance hearing of the System Board. This representative may be a union representative, rarely a lawyer. If in the tardy pilot example the employment contract specifically provided for some lesser penalty for a first offense of tardiness or (if the contract is silent regarding penalties) other employees have done the same thing but received lesser penalties from the airline, the pilot would have a valid claim.

As you might suspect, the equal balance between union and management representation on the System Board often leads to deadlock, with management representatives voting to uphold the company's action and union representatives voting to soften or reverse it. The contract should provide a way to break such deadlocks; most provide for the selection of a neutral arbitrator to decide the case. RLA provides that if a System Board is unable to resolve a minor dispute, something called the National Air Transportation Board can be convened. This has never been necessary, although there have been many thousands of minor disputes resolved by System Boards (or tie-breaking arbitrators) in the 70 years the RLA has applied to the airline industry.

Under the RLA, minor disputes cannot be brought before the courts except in the rare instance where delays or procedural irregularities in the handling of an employee's case by the System Board amount to a deprivation of the employee's right to *due process of law*. Due process of law has generally been held to include these rights: (1) to have a hearing before a fair and impartial decisionmaker, (2) to have adequate notice of the time and place of the hearing to allow one to prepare, (3) to be represented by legal counsel if one chooses, (4) to testify and present witnesses and evidence on your behalf, and (5) to cross-examine witnesses for the opposition.

Both management and coworkers may dislike a particularly obnoxious employee. In such a case, System Board members on both sides may be tempted to "railroad" the obnoxious employee by having a hearing at a time or place the employee cannot attend or by giving the employee little or no notice of the hearing. In such an extreme case, a court would hold that the employee had been denied due process of law and would send the case back to the board to afford the employee a proper hearing with reasonable notice.

MAJOR DISPUTES

Major disputes involve the negotiation of either a new employment contract or a change to the existing contract. The RLA's mandatory procedure for resolving major disputes is often referred to by attorneys and labor negotiators as the "Kabuki Theater," after the ancient Japanese style of drama that consists of ritual in the extreme, exalting form over substance.

Until this entire procedure has been completed, the RLA requires that the status quo be maintained. Both the airline and the union must continue to work together under the existing contract (or, if the employees are newly unionized and this is the first contract to be negotiated, under the company's preexisting terms and conditions of employment).

Consider this example of a major dispute: Faced with price competition from nonunionized airlines, management of a unionized airline seeks the pilots union's agreement to wage-reduction concessions, which would reduce the company's operating costs and allow the airline to compete by reducing its passenger fares. Since this would involve a change in the existing contract, it is a major dispute. The RLA requires the airline and the union to follow this procedure to resolve any major dispute:

1. The party desiring the change (in this example, the airline) must *notify* the other side (in this example, the union) of the proposed change, *in writing.* This is often referred to as a *Section 6 notice,* after the RLA section that imposes this requirement.
2. Both sides must then *confer within 30 days* and bargain in good faith in a real effort to negotiate their differences. Trade-offs and counterproposals are often brought up at this stage, which continues until at least one of the parties believes that negotiations have reached an impasse.
3. If the parties are unable to resolve the controversy by negotiation, either side can request *mediation* by the NMB. In mediation, as distinguished from arbitration, the federal mediator has no authority to enter an order deciding the case but can only serve as an intermediary between the company and the union to help them reach an agreement. The NMB can hold the parties in mediation until the mediator declares an impasse. Mediators are reluctant to declare an impasse, as it is an admission that the mediator has failed to accomplish his mission. Being held in mediation by a stubborn mediator far beyond the time all meaningful progress toward an agreement has ceased can be enormously frustrating to the parties. Nowhere is this frustration more vividly described than in Aaron Bernstein's book: *Grounded: Frank Lorenzo and the Destruction of Eastern Airlines*, listed in the bibliography.
4. If the mediator is unable to bring the parties to an agreement and declares an impasse, the NMB will *offer the opportunity for binding arbitration.* If both parties agree, a panel of three arbitrators

will be selected to hear the views of both sides and decide the result, and the parties will be bound by the decision, whether they like the result or not. If they have agreed to submit the dispute to binding arbitration, the arbitrators' decision is final and cannot be appealed. In airline labor disputes, it is extremely rare for the parties to agree to binding arbitration.
5. However, if either party rejects binding arbitration as a method of resolving the dispute, there is a mandatory *30-day "cooling off" period* during which the parties must continue to maintain the status quo.
6. Once that time is up, if the parties have still not reached an agreement, they *are free to resort to self-help.* (In this example, that would mean that the company could unilaterally reduce the employees' pay scales, the employees could strike and picket the company, and/or the company could lock the strikers out and hire permanent replacements.)

The only event that could further delay those rights would be if the president of the United States decided to convene an *Emergency Board* as a last effort to aid the parties in reaching an agreement without the transportation disruptions inherent in a strike. The president has the authority to convene an Emergency Board only if the NMB advises him that an emergency exists because a threatened work stoppage involves the transportation service of an entire region of the country (for example, if the airline was the sole regional carrier) and may cause substantial interruption of interstate commerce. It is entirely in the president's discretion to decide whether to convene an Emergency Board. If the president does convene the Emergency Board, the parties must continue to work under the previous contract or terms of employment until the board completes its investigation and hearing and reports its finding (which must be issued within 60 days). The Emergency Board's findings are not binding on the parties but may be persuasive. At this stage, each side is trying to assess how a strike will turn out. Will passengers and members of other unions honor or cross the picket lines? Will other unions join in sympathy strikes? How badly will it hurt the company to have to train and rely upon newly hired replacement pilots and any union members who may choose to not go on strike (collectively, strikebreakers or *scabs)?* In the past, the airlines had a Mutual Assistance Plan (MAP) of strike insurance under which a struck carrier would receive funds from the other participating carriers not shut down by the work stoppage. These plans were outlawed by the Airline Deregulation Act of 1978. Once the Emergency Board issues its findings, *another 30-day cooling off period* begins, during which the parties are still required to continue to work under the status quo.

The Emergency Board's findings will have been widely reported in the news media, and pollsters for both sides will sample public opinion. Discussions will be had with other unions so that each side may gain a more accurate approximation of what is likely to happen in the event of a strike. It is hoped that this new dose of reality may enable the parties to reach an agreement. If, however, at the end of this last 30-day "cooling off" period they have still not reached agreement, they are free to resort to self-help without further interruption or delay.

If the airline, the union, or employees acting independently of the union *(wildcat strikers)* refuse to follow these RLA procedures and act to change the status quo prior to exhaustion of this complete ritual sequence, the other side may file suit in court to obtain an injunction. An injunction would compel persons who made the change to return to the status quo ante until this Kabuki Theater process has been completed. In the case of a premature strike, the injunction compelling employees to return to work is usually reported in the news media as a *back-to-work order.* If the injunction is issued but not obeyed, violators (the union, union leadership, and striking members) are exposed to fines and/or imprisonment for *contempt of court.* The same would apply to the company and its managers if it were to prematurely lock out strikers and begin hiring permanent replacements.

Few things provoke we humans to a more emotional response than a threat to our job. The animosity generated in a major dispute between an airline and a union must be experienced to be believed. Seemingly unflappable silver-haired professionals may be provoked to fits of rage. Unions may orchestrate "safety campaigns" designed to raise consumer fears that the airline is unsafe. Crimes, sabotage of aircraft and threats, intimidation, and even physical violence against strikebreakers are not unheard of. The FAA puts a much closer watch on airlines involved in labor disputes to try to assure that public safety is not compromised. Even if the dispute is ultimately settled, its adverse effects may be long lasting, especially where the airline has hired permanent replacement workers who remain with the company after strikers return to work. The industry abounds with anecdotal stories of pilots who refuse to acknowledge or speak to such former "scabs," even when a member of the same crew where open cockpit communication may be essential to flight safety. There are even stories of other crewmembers playing dirty tricks on former strikebreakers, such as by deliberately entering an incorrect altitude into the altitude alerter to mislead the other pilot into an altitude deviation and FAA enforcement action. This may be understandable, given that in our society what we do for a living is not only our means of survival but also our identity. Ask people to "tell me about yourself," and the first thing they are likely to say is what they do for a living: "I'm an airline pilot and . . ." Although such extreme vehement behavior may be understandable, it is unwise and unprofessional.

If your means of survival and your identity are threatened, you may find yourself in the emotional grip of primitive base instincts that provoke such ugly behavior. Finding yourself in such a situation, I hope you will fight hard for your principles but draw the line at behavior that could jeopardize flight safety and never cross that line (Fig. 17.2).

Mergers and Acquisitions

Frequently, one of the most difficult challenges facing a merger between airlines (or acquisition of one airline by another) is that of merging

Fig. 17.2. It takes orchestrated teamwork to keep an airline moving safely and efficiently. Bitter labor disputes may jeopardize that teamwork.

the two work forces into one. Differences in employee compensation, benefits, seniority, qualifications and training must be reconciled. This task is made doubly complex where different unions represent similar employees in the two airlines. Major dispute resolution procedures continue to govern the process and employees' rights while labor and management work toward agreement over these thorny issues. Modern airline merger and acquisition agreements typically provide for a phasing-in period. Employees coming from the carrier that provided lesser pay and benefits enter the new carrier's work force on a separate scale that is programmed to catch up and merge with that of the acquiring carrier's previous employees over a period of years.

KEY AVIATION ORGANIZATIONS

AERONAUTICAL REPAIR STATION ASSOCIATION, 121 N. Henry Street, Arlington, VA 22314-2903. *(www.arsa.org)* The voice of aviation maintenance and modification facilities before the FAA, NTSB, and other federal agencies.

AEROSPACE MEDICAL ASSOCIATION, 320 South Henry Street, Alexandria, VA 223143524. *(www.asma.org)* A scientific association promoting knowledge of aviation, space, and environmental medicine. Publication: *Aviation, Space and Environmental Medicine* (monthly).

AIRCRAFT OWNERS & PILOTS ASSOCIATION, 421 Aviation Way, Frederick, MD 21701. *(www.aopa.org)* Promotes the interests of general aviation, particularly in regulatory, airspace, and airport access matters. Publication: *AOPA Pilot* (monthly).

AIR LINE PILOTS ASSOCIATION INTL., 1625 Massachusetts Avenue N.W., Washington, DC 20036. *(www.alpa.org)* The largest union of airline pilots. Publication: *Air Line Pilot* (monthly).

AIRPORTS COUNCIL INTERNATIONAL, P.O. Box 16, 1215 Geneva 15—Airport, Switzerland. *(www.airports.org)* An association of the world's airports founded to promote cooperation.

AIR TRANSPORT ASSOCIATION OF AMERICA, 1301 Pennsylvania Avenue, Washington, DC 20006-5206. *(www.air-transport.org)* Represents the interests of major airlines. Publication: *Air Transport* (annual).

AMERICAN ASSOCIATION OF AIRPORT EXECUTIVES, 601 Madison St., Alexandria, VA 22314. *(www.airportnet.org)* Promotes professionalism in civil aviation airport management. Publications: *Airport Magazine* (bimonthly), *Airport Report* (bimonthly).

AMERICAN BAR ASSOCIATION FORUM COMMITTEE ON AIR & SPACE LAW, 750 North Lake Shore Drive, Chicago, IL 60611. Members of the ABA having a special interest in air and space law. Publication: *Air & Space Lawyer* (quarterly).

AMERICAN INSTITUTE OF AERONAUTICS & ASTRONAUTICS, INC., Suite 500, 1801 Alexander Bell Dr., Reston, VA 20191-4344. *(www.aiaa.org)*

Promotes the advancement of the scientific, technical, and engineering aspects of aeronautics and astronautics. Publication: *Aerospace America.*

ASSOCIATION FOR AVIONICS EDUCATION, P.O. Box 9545, Daytona Beach, FL 32120. *(www.avionicseducation.org)*

AVIATION INSURANCE ASSOCIATION, 14 W.Third St., Kansas City, MO 64105. *(www.aiaweb.org)* An association of aviation insurance professionals. Publication: *The Binder* (quarterly).

CIVIL AVIATION MEDICAL ASSOCIATION, 775 Bank Lane, #211, Lake Forest, IL 60045. *(www.civilavmed.com)* A professional association composed primarily of FAA-designated Aviation Medical Examiners. Publication: *CAMA Bulletin* (quarterly).

EXPERIMENTAL AIRCRAFT ASSOCIATION, INC., EAA Aviation Center, Oshkosh, WI 549033086. *(www.eaa.org)* Represents the interests of sport aviation particularly. Publication: *Sport Aviation* (monthly).

FUTURE AVIATION PROFESSIONALS OF AMERICA, 4959 Massachusetts Blvd., Atlanta, GA 30337. Numerous publications to aid job-seeking pilots, flight attendants, and aircraft mechanics.

GENERAL AVIATION MANUFACTURERS ASSOCIATION, Suite 801, 1400 K Street N.W., Washington, DC 20005. *(www.generalaviation.org)* Represents the interests of manufacturers of general aviation aircraft and promotes public appreciation of general aviation's contribution to the economy. Publications: *General Aviation Statistical Data Book* (annual), *Shipment Reports* (quarterly).

INTERNATIONAL AIR TRANSPORT ASSOCIATION, 800 Place Victoria, P.O. Box 113, Montreal, Quebec H4Z 1M1, Canada. *(www.iata.org)* The organization of international airlines. Numerous publications.

INTERNATIONAL CIVIL AVIATION ORGANIZATION, Suite 327, 1000 Sherbrooke Street West, Montreal, Quebec H3A 2R2, Canada. *(www.icao.org)* An agency of the United Nations standardizing aviation technical standards and procedures and promoting safety, uniformity, and efficiency in air navigation worldwide. Numerous publications.

INTERNATIONAL COUNCIL OF AIR SHOWS, 751 Miller Dr., Suite F-4, Leesburg, VA 20175. *(www.airshows.org)* The organization of airshow producers, promoters, and performers. Publication: *ICAS News* (monthly).

INTERNATIONAL SOCIETY OF AIR SAFETY INVESTIGATORS, Park Center, 107 E. Holly Ave., Suite 11, Sterling, VA 20164. *(www.isasi.org)* Promotes professionalism in the investigation of aircraft accidents. Publication: *Forum* (quarterly).

LAWYER-PILOTS BAR ASSOCIATION, P.O. 685, Poolesville, MD 20837. *(www.lpba.org)* An organization of lawyers who are also pilots, many of whom specialize in aviation law. Publication: *LPBA Journal* (quarterly).

NATIONAL AIR TRANSPORTATION ASSOCIATION, INC., 4226 King Street, Alexandria, VA 22302. *(www.nata.aero)* "The voice of aviation Business" represents the interests of FBOs, Part 135 operators, and related suppliers and manufacturers. Numerous publications.

NATIONAL ASSOCIATION OF FLIGHT INSTRUCTORS, EAA Aviation Center, Oshkosh, WI 54903-3086. *(www.nafi.org)* Represents the interests of certified flight instructors and promotes professionalism in flight instruction. Publication: *NAFI Foundation Newsletter* (bimonthly).

NATIONAL ASSOCIATION OF STATE AVIATION OFFICIALS, Suite 505, 8401 Colesville Road, Silver Spring, MD 20910. *(www.nasao.org)* Encourages cooperation and mutual aid among local, state, and federal governments to improve air transportation. Publication: *NASAO State Aviation Newsletter* (monthly).

NATIONAL BUSINESS AIRCRAFT ASSOCIATION, INC., 1200 18th Street N.W., Suite 400, Washington, DC 20036. *(www.nbaa.org)* Represents the interests of corporate and other business users of aircraft. Numerous publications.

NATIONAL EMS PILOTS ASSOCIATION, 110 North Royal St., Suite 307, Alexandria, VA 22314. *(www.nemspa.org)* Represents the interests of pilots employed in emergency medical service aviation, promotes safety in those operations. Publication: *Air Net* (monthly).

NATIONAL TRANSPORTATION SAFETY BOARD BAR ASSOCIATION, P.O. Box 65461, Washington, DC 20036-5461. *(www.ntsbbar.org)* An organization of attorneys, in private practice and in government service, practicing before the NTSB. Several publications.

THE NINETY-NINES, INC., Box 59965, Will Rogers World Airport, Oklahoma City, OK 73159. *(www.ninety-nines.org)* The international organization of women pilots. Publication: *Ninety-nine News* (monthly).

PROFESSIONAL AVIATION MAINTENANCE ASSOCIATION, 717 Princess St., Alexandria, VA 22314. *(www.pama.org)* A professional association of aviation maintenance personnel. Publication: *PAMA News*.

SOCIETY OF AUTOMOTIVE ENGINEERS, 400 Commonwealth Drive, Warrendale, PA 15096-0001. *(www.sae.org)* A professional engineering society establishing aerospace technical standards. Numerous publications.

UNITED STATES PILOTS ASSOCIATION, Suite 10, 483 South Kirkwood Road, St. Louis, MO 63122. *(www.uspilots.org)* An organization of statewide pilots associations. Publication: *USPA Newsletter* (quarterly).

UNIVERSITY AVIATION ASSOCIATION, 3410 Skyway Drive, Opelika, AL 36801. *(www.uaa.auburn.edu)* A professional organization representing collegiate aviation education. Publication: UAA *Newsletter* (bimonthly).

WOMEN IN AVIATION INTERNATIONAL, 101 Corsair Dr., Suite 101, Daytona Beach, FL 32114. *(www.wiai.org)* A nonprofit organization dedicated to encouragement and advancement of women in all aviation fields and interests.

BIBLIOGRAPHY

Adamski, Anthony J., and Doyle, Timothy J. *Introduction to the Aviation Regulatory Process* (4th ed). Plymouth, MI: Hayden-McNeil, 1999. A thorough overview of U.S. legislation relating to civil aviation, the aviation regulatory process, and Federal Aviation Regulations.

The Aviation Quarterly. London, England: LLP Professional Publishing. A timely scholarly journal of international aviation law.

Bernstein, Aaron. *Grounded: Frank Lorenzo and the Destruction of Eastern Airlines.* New York, N.Y.: Simon & Schuster, 1990. An inside view of the most bitter airline labor dispute in U.S. history, showing workings of the "Kabuki Theater" major dispute resolution process in context.

Carrel, Michael R., and Heavrin, Christina. *Labor Relations and Collective Bargaining: Cases, Practices, and Law.* Englewood Cliffs, NJ: Prentice Hall, 1995. An excellent basic text on collective bargaining under the NLRA, with strong chapters on public employee collective bargaining and equal employment opportunity. Accompanying instructor's manual and simulation materials (available in both computerized and noncomputerized formats) facilitate an exciting, hands-on learning experience.

Cathcart, Daniel C. *Aircrash Litigation Techniques.* Charlottesville, Va.: Michie, 1985. Although written for trial lawyers, this treatise contains many interesting insights into the workings of the law in finding fault and apportioning liability in aviation accident cases.

Congress of the United States, Office of Technology Assessment. *Safe Skies for Tomorrow: Aviation Safety in a Competitive Environment.* July 1988. A thought-provoking examination of the roles of government and private industry in improving aviation safety in the wake of deregulation of airline economics.

DeHaan, Warren V. *The Optometrist's & Ophthalmologist's Guide to Pilots' Vision.* Boulder, Colo.: American Trend, 1982. Has an especially good section on obtaining FAA certification even if your uncorrected vision falls below FAA standards.

Dempsey, Paul S., and Gessell, Laurence. *Air Commerce and the Law.* Chandler, AZ: Coast Aire Publications, 2004. A *tour de force* written by two of aviation's foremost scholars. Particularly strong in air carrier economics and related regulatory theory and practice.

Dempsey, Paul S., Goetz, Andrew, and Szyliowicz, Joseph. *Denver International Airport: Lessons Learned.* New York, NY: McGraw-Hill, 1997. A detailed and thoroughly researched narrative of the development of the new Denver International Airport (DIA) by three brilliant University of Denver professors who watched it all happen.

Dempsey, Paul S., Hardaway, Robert M., and Thoms, William E. *Aviation Law and Regulation.* Austin, Tex.: Butterworth Legal Publishing, 1992. A two-volume looseleaf comprehensive overview of virtually all aspects of U.S. aviation law, written by three distinguished law professors for use as a law school text and reference for practicing attorneys. Also available as an abridged single-volume bound paperback text for student use.

Eichenberger, Jerry A. *General Aviation Law* (2d ed). New York, NY: McGraw-Hill, 1997. A very readable inexpensive paperback book of advice written by an experienced aviation lawyer, pilot, and adjunct professor at Ohio State University.

Elkins, Darrell T. *Aviation Insurance: An Introduction to General Aviation Insurance in the United States.* Porter, Tex.: J. A. Elkins Brothers, 1984. A simple introduction to general aviation insurance written by an experienced aviation insurance agent, this book provides a thoroughgoing methodology for analyzing the aircraft liability and hull policy.

Ellis, James E. *Buying and Owning Your Own Airplane.* Ames: Iowa State University Press, 1980. A good review of the many practical considerations involved in purchasing and insuring a personal airplane.

Ericsson, Lloyd B. *Aviation Insurance.* Portland: Oregon State Bar, 1983. Written primarily for lawyers, this work includes extensive citations to legal precedents interpreting many features of aviation insurance policies. The author, now deceased, was a renowned aviation lawyer and one of the underwriters at Lloyds.

Gesell, Laurence E. *Aviation and the Law* (3d ed). Chandler, Ariz.: Coast Aire, 1998. A basic text including a variety of simplified aviation case briefs written by an Arizona State University professor.

Gohmann, John W. *Air and Rail Labor Relations: A Judicial History of the Railway Labor Act.* Dubuque, Iowa: Kendall/Hunt, 1979. A review of the landmark cases in airline labor law at the dawn of deregulation.

Gohmann, John W. *Arbitration and Representation: Applications in Air and Rail Labor Relations.* Dubuque, Iowa: Kendall/Hunt, 1981. A thorough study of the law governing airline employee unionization and arbitration of airline employee grievances.

Hardaway, Robert M. *Airport Regulation, Law & Public Policy.* Westport, Conn.: Greenwood, 1991. The most complete work on airport law to date.

Hopkins, George E. *The Airline Pilots: A Study in Elite Unionization.* Cambridge, MA: Harvard Univ. Press, 1971. A fascinating and insightful historical study of the founding and development of the Air Line Pilots Association of the AFL-CIO.

International Civil Aviation Organization. *Manual of Civil Aviation Medicine.* Montreal, 1974. The international view of appropriate criteria for certification of flight crewmembers. Also contains interesting chapters on post-accident identification of victims and identification of human factors involved in the cause and survivability of accidents.

The Journal of Air Law and Commerce. Dallas, Tex.: Southern Methodist University. A wide-ranging scholarly law journal on domestic and international developments in aviation law.

The Journal of Air Transportation Worldwide. Omaha, Nebr.: University of Nebraska at Omaha. A scholarly journal for the airline industry, featuring a good variety of domestic and international issues. Available in print and online (e-mail: *journal@unomaha.edu*).

The Journal of Aviation/Aerospace Education & Research. Daytona Beach, Fla.: Embry-Riddle Aeronautical University. A scholarly publication for educators and researchers as well as for professionals in the aviation and aerospace industry, particularly oriented toward nonengineering elements.

Kaps, Robert W. *Air Transport Labor Relations.* Carbondale: Southern Illinois University Press, 1997. The most complete and current college text on airline labor relations under the RLA.

Kreindler, Lee S. *Aviation Accident Law.* New York: Matthew Bender, 1990. Written for practicing attorneys, this three-volume set is one of two tours de force minutely detailing the law governing liability for aviation accidents, especially airline accidents.

Margo, Rod D. *Aviation Insurance: The Law and Practice of Aviation Insurance, Including Hovercraft and Spacecraft Insurance* (2d ed). London: Butterworths, 1989. Although written primarily for lawyers, this extraordinarily well-annotated treatise, international in scope, contains an especially insightful chapter on the aviation insurance market.

National Transportation Safety Board. Notification and Reporting of Aircraft Accidents or Incidents and Overdue Aircraft, and Preservation of Aircraft Wreckage, Mail, Cargo and Records. 49 Code of Federal Regulations, Part 830. These are the rules governing notification and reporting of aircraft accidents and incidents.

Rayman, Russell B. *Clinical Aviation Medicine.* New York: Vantage, 1982. Written for the aviation medical examiner, a thoroughgoing overview of the relationships between various health problems and flying. Incorporates USAF standards.

Reinhart, Richard O. *FAA Medical Certification: Guidelines for Pilots* (3d ed). Ames: Iowa State University Press, 1997. An especially thoughtful FAA Aviation Medical Examiner's advice on civil aeromedical certification and health maintenance for flight crews.

Schiavo, Mary. *Flying Blind, Flying Safe.* Avon Books, 1997. A scathing indictment of FAA airline safety regulatory and enforcement efforts written by an outspoken and controversial former Inspector General for the U.S. Department of Transportation.

Speiser, Stuart M., and Krause, Charles F. *Aviation Tort Law.* Rochester, N.Y.: Lawyers Co-Operative, 1978. Written for the practicing attorney, this is the other of the two three-volume tours de force on liability for aircraft accidents.

Thoms, William E., and Dooley, Frank J. *Airline Labor Law: The Railway Labor Act and Aviation After Deregulation.* New York: Quorum Books, 1990. A good overview of the subject, well illustrated with cases.

The Transportation Law Journal. Denver, Colo.: University of Denver. A scholarly law journal touching on the full spectrum of transportation law, air, surface, and marine.

U.S. Department of Transportation, Federal Aviation Administration. *Guide for Aviation Medical Examiners.* September 2003. This is the AME's desk reference for deciding whether to issue you an aviation medical certificate. It is now available on the FAA website.

Wassenbergh, H. A. *Public International Air Transportation Law in a New Era: Economic Regulation of International Air Carrier Operations.* Netherlands: Kluwer, n.d. An essentially European view of the importance of economic regulation of international air transportation.

Wells, Alexander T. *Introduction to Aviation Insurance.* Malabar, Fla.: Robert E. Krieger, 1986. Intended as an undergraduate text in aviation insurance, about half the work consists of an appendix that reproduces sample aircraft insurance policies.

Wolfe, Harry P., and NewMyer, David A. *Aviation Industry Regulation.* Carbondale, Southern Illinois University, 1985. A good fundamental overview of federal regulation of various aspects of the aviation industry following the deregulation of airline economics.

Wright, Robert R. *The Law of Airspace.* Indianapolis: Bobbs-Merrill, 1968. Although now becoming somewhat dated, this treatise written primarily for lawyers is the foundation for any exploration of this area of the law.

Yodice, John S. *Aviation Lawyer's Manual: Representing the Pilot in FAA Enforcement Actions.* Lanham: Maryland Historical Press, 1986. Written for lawyers, this is a basic practical introduction to FAA enforcement and the NTSB appeal process. The chapter on frequently violated regulations is of general interest to all pilots.

Yules, Richard B. *The Pilot's Complete Medical Guide.* New York: Jason Aronson, 1983. Starts with a good chapter on FAA medical certification standards, then explores many other interesting areas of flight physiology as they relate to aviation safety and accident causation.

INDEX

Above ground level (AGL), 240
Accident investigation
   role of Federal Aviation
      Administration (FAA) in, 11,
      36–47, 187–88
   role of National Transportation
      Safety Board (NTSB) in, 16–17
Accident notification and reporting,
   179–89
   controlling information release,
      179–81
   notifications and reports required,
      181–82
Accident-response plan, 179–82
Act of God, war, or state, 157
ad coelum doctrine, 230–31
Administrative dispositions, 31–33
Administrative law
   under Air Transportation
      Stabilization Board (ATSB), 20
   under Civil Aeronautics Board
      (CAB), 19–20
   under Federal Aviation
      Administration (FAA), 3, 31–65
   under Immigration and Customs
      Enforcement (ICE), 21
   under International Air Transport
      Association (IATA), 29–30
   under International Civil Aviation
      Organization (ICAO), 23–29
   under National Aeronautics and
      Space Administration (NASA),
      17–19
   under National Mediation Board
      (NMB), 20
   under National Transportation Safety
      Board (NTSB), 16–17
   under President, 22
   under state agencies, 22–23
   under State Department, 22
   under Transportation Department, 22
Administrative Procedure Act (APA),
   260–61
Admission against your interest, 180
Advanced General Aviation Transport
   Experiments (AGATE), 16
Advance Notice of Proposed
   Rulemaking (ANPRM), 261
Advisory Circulars (ACs), 11, 54, 89
Aerodynamics research, 18
Aeronautical charts, production of, 10
Aeronautical Information Manual
   (AIM), 89
Affirmative action programs, 299
Age Discrimination in Employment Act
   (ADEA), 298
Agent for service of process, 105
Agreements of ownership, 218–20
Airborne collision avoidance systems,
   15
Air Carrier Reporting and Correction
   Program, 50
Air carrier risk-management tools in
   domestic operations, 151
Air carriers, foreign and regulation of,
   22

Aircraft
 buying and selling, 193–210
 carrying a weapon or explosive, 276
 crashworthiness, 16
 design of, 9
 destruction of, 272–75
 fraud, 282–85
 hijackings of, 28–29, 162, 275
 inspection of, 48
 insurance on, 121–24
  purpose of use
   business, 125–26
   commercial, 126
   commercial except instruction or rental, 126
   industrial aid, 126
   limited commercial, 126
   pleasure, 125–26
   special uses, 126–27
 leasing, 211–23
  checklist for, 213–15
 N-number for, 9
 noise, 7–8
  limitations on, 234, 263–64
 security of, 9–10
 summary seizure of, 35
 tax and registration requirements, 20
 warranties, 199–203
Aircraft accidents, 11, 179–81
 definition of, 182–83
 press reporting on, 180–81
Aircraft Condition Notice, 48
Aircraft jurisdiction, 270
Aircraft management agreement, 219
Aircraft mechanics
 and civil penalties for FAR violations, 63
 holding Inspection Authorizations (IAs), 172, 203
Aircraft Owners and Pilots Association (AOPA), 79, 181
 and performance of title search, 195
 prepaid legal service program of, 136
Aircraft piracy, 275

Aircraft purchase agreement, 219
Aircraft Radio Station License, 206, 208–9
Aircraft Registration Application, 206, 207
Aircraft registration violations, 279–82
Aircraft Safety Reporting Program (ASRP), 19
Air Defense Identification Zones (ADIZ), 21, 258
Airfoil, super critical, 17
Airframe and powerplant (A&P) mechanic holding Inspection Authorization (IA), 203
Airline accidents, probable cause, 16
Airline Deregulation Act (1978), 19, 315
Airline disaster
 counseling during, 186–89
 victims of, 20
Airline labor law, 309–18
Airline liability. *See also* Liability
 air carrier risk-management tools in domestic operations, 151
 to domestic passengers, 147–52
 to international passengers, 147, 152–56, 161
 punitive damages under, 100–1, 161–62
 Warsaw Convention, 152–56
Air Line Pilots Association (ALPA), 309
 post-accident recommendation of, 186, 187
 prepaid legal service program of, 136
Airline transport pilot (ATP) certificate, revocation of, 62
Airman, and civil penalties for FAR violations, 63
Airman record, 33
Airman Records Branch, 14
Airman's certificate, operating without, 277–78
Air navigation, interference with, 278–79

Index

Airport Improvement Program (AIP), 11, 229
Airport industrial parks, 232–33
Airports and airspaces, 227–55
  competition for, 260–62
  constitutional powers
    commercial clause, 228
    eminent domain, 228, 229–32
    police power, 228, 232–36
    purse powers, 229
    supremacy clause, 228, 241
    tax powers, 229
  en route, 257–67
  hostility to, 8, 272
  international, violence at, 270–72
  liability insurance for, 120, 134–35
    hangarkeeper's liability, 135
    premises liability, 134–35
  national, 14–15
  national sovereignty in, 25–26
  privately owned, 238–39, 255
  proprietary powers, 241–46
  publicly owned, 254–55
  purse powers of, 247–50
  restriction on access to, 21
  security checkpoints, 289–90
  security of, 9–10
  sources of power, 227–29
  violation of security requirements, 277
  wilderness, 262–64
Airport screeners, 4
Airport Watch system, 291
Air rage, 275
Air Route Traffic Control Centers (ARTCC), 12–13
Airshow waiver, 41
Air tour operators, 264
Air traffic control (ATC), 12–14
  government liability for negligent, 173–75
  as source of reports of Federal Aviation Administration (FAA) violations, 36

transferal to government corporation, 12–14
Air Traffic Control (ATC) System, 12–14
Air traffic controllers, and Federal Aviation Regulation (FAR) violations, 36
Air Traffic Controller's Handbook, 175
Air Traffic Control System Command Center, 13
Air Transport Association (ATA), 29
Air Transportation Safety and System Stabilization Act (2001), 20, 167
Air Transportation Stabilization Board (ATSB), 20
Airworthiness, 7, 48, 201
Airworthiness Certificate, 9, 177
Airworthiness certification, government liability for negligent, 176–77
Airworthiness Directives (ADs), 8, 203
Alcohol, and loss of medical certification, 69
Alcohol testing, 78
Alert areas, 258
Aliens attending flight training schools, 6
Allegheny Airlines v. Village of Cedarhurst, 239–40
Alter ego doctrine, 106
American Rule, 100
Americans with Disabilities Act (ADA), 298
amicus curiae briefs, 244
Angina pectoris, and loss of medical certification, 69
Annexes, 24
AOPA Media Guide for Reporting on Aviation Accidents, 181
Appeal
  in certificate actions, 59–60
  and Federal Aviation Administration (FAA) enforcement, 56
  in medical certification, 73

Appeal (*continued*)
  to National Transportation Safety Board (NTSB), 58, 59–60
  to U.S. Court of Appeals, 60
  to U.S. Supreme Court, 60–61
Arbitration, binding, 310, 314–15
Arrest, false, 86
Articles of incorporation, 105–6
Assault, 85
Assets, keeping personal and corporate separate, 110–11
Association of Trial Lawyers of America (ATLA), opposition to Warsaw Convention, 155
Assumption of risk, 94–95, 144
Authority to bind insurance coverage, 130
Avemco, 118
Aviation and Transportation Security Act of 2001, 4, 21
Aviation crimes, 21, 269–92
Aviation easement, 231
Aviation insurance, 117–39. *See also* Insurance; Liability; Risk management
  aircraft insurance, 121–24
  claims in, 118–19, 137–38
  coverages in, 120
  Federal Aviation Regulation (FAR) violation exclusion clause in, 129–30
  geographic coverage of, 133
  hull coverage in, 121–23
  insuring and underwriting risk in, 119
  liability coverage in, 121
  minimizing risks in, 119–20
  nonownership liability, 139
  other considerations, 129–33
  pilot qualifications, 127–29
  policy renewal, 132
  products liability, 135–36
  purpose of use in, 123–24
  and renter pilots, 138–39
  sales of, 117–18
  spreading risk in, 119
  war risk, 133–34
Aviation Investment and Reform Act for the 21st Century (AIR 21), 11
Aviation managers, 118
Aviation Medical Examiner (AME), 68, 70, 172
Aviation nonownership liability insurance, 139
Aviation safety, 10, 55–56
  Aviation Safety Reporting Program, 51–55
  regulation of, 7–8
Aviation Safety Action Program (ASAP), 55–56
Aviation Safety Reporting Program (ASRP), 51–55
Aviation security, 269–92
Aviation Trust Fund, 11, 229

Backscatter x-ray imaging device, 287
Back-to-order, 316
Baggage resolution, 288
Baggage sniffers, 288
Banner Advertising, Inc. v. City of Boulder, 245–46
Bargaining power, 142
Battery in tort law, 85
Behavioral disorder, and loss of medical certification, 69
Bill of sale, 111, 204–6
Binder and insurance coverage, 130
Bipolar disorder, and loss of medical certification, 69
Board of directors, 112
Boeing 707, 8
Boeing 747, 8
Breach
  of warranty, 203
  of warranty endorsement, 129–30, 210
British Airways v. Port of New York Authority, 245

Index

Bungee jumping and aviation insurance, 139, 142
Business
  as a corporation, 105–12
  duties to employees, 112
  forms of, 103–5
  lines of defense in risk management, 115–16
  organizing, to limit liability, 103–16
  use of aircraft for, 125–26
Buzz jobs, 37

Cabotage, 26
Capital gain, 210
Capitalization, adequacy of, 108
Cardiac pacemaker implantation, and loss of medical certification, 69
Care
  duty of, 88
  failure to use, 88–89
Carriage
  common, 148–51
  contract, 148–51
Cartography, 10
Case of first impression, 230
Central Flow Control facility, 13
Certificate
  getting back, 62
  surrendering, 61
Certificate action, 33–34, 56–62
  appeal to U.S. Court of Appeals, 60
  appeal to U.S. Supreme Court, 60–61
  current FAA enforcement priorities, 33–34
  discovery in, 58
  emergency cases in, 61–62
  getting back of certificate, 62
  hearing in, 58–59
  horror factor in, 34
  individual considerations in, 34
  informal conference in, 57
  National Transportation Safety Board (NTSB) appeal in, 58, 59–60
  notice of proposed, 56–57
  order of suspension or revocation in, 57–58, 63
  precedent, 33
  revocation, 33
  surrender of certificate, 61
  suspension of certificate, 33
Certificate of incorporation, 106
Certificate of public convenience, 19
Certification
  medical, 9, 14–15, 67–79
  role of Federal Aviation Administration (FAA) in, 8–9
Certified Design Organizations (CDOs), 172–73
Charter, consideration of lease, as, 218
Chicago Convention on International Civil Aviation (1944), 25–26
Civil Aeronautics Act (1938), 231
Civil Aeronautics Authority (CAA), 7
Civil Aeronautics Board (CAB), 19–20
Civil Air Patrol (CAP), 260
Civil Aviation Medical Institute, 14–15
Civil-law countries, 169
Civil penalties, 34–35, 62–64
Civil remedies for aviation crimes, 284
Civil Rights Act of 1964, 297
Civil Service Reform Act, 308
Claims
  9/11, 178
  administrative, 178
  in aviation insurance, 118–19, 137–38
  subrogation of, 138–39
Class A airspace, 257
Class B airspace, 257
Class C airspace, 257
Class D airspace, 257
Class E airspace, 257
Class G airspace, 259
Clearinghouse, underwriters, 118
Cold (illness) and flying, 77
Colorado Airspace Initiative, 266–67
Color vision, 71

Combatant activity, 171
Commemorative Air Force, 44
Commerce clause, 228
Commercial Space Launch
    Amendments Act of 2004, 8
Commercial use of aircraft, 126
Common carrier, 148–51
Common law, 92, 169
Communication at the workplace, 307
Comparative negligence, 95
Compensation time, 300
Compensatory damages, 99–100
Compulsory mediation, 310
Computer Assisted Passenger Screening
    System (CAPS), 288
Condemnation lawsuit, 228
Confederate Air Force (CAF), 44–45
Consciousness disturbance, and loss of
    medical certification, 69
Constitutional powers, 228
  commerce clause, 228
  eminent domain in, 228, 229–32
  police power, 228, 232–36
  supremacy clause in, 228, 241
Contempt of court, 316
Contract carriage, 148–51
Contract law, 83
Contracts, exculpatory, 99, 116, 141–45
Contributory negligence, 95–96,
    156–57
Controlled firing areas, 258
Controlled substances, transporting of,
    278, 280
Controller's bible, 175
Convair 880, 8
Convention for the Unification of
    Certain Rules for International
    Carriage by Air, 152–55, 164–67
Convention on International Civil
    Aviation, 23
Conversion in tort law, 87
Cooling off period, 315, 316
Cooperative marketing arrangements,
    27

Co-ownership, 218–19
Coronary artery disease, and loss of
    medical certification, 69
Corporate minute book, 112
Corporation, 103, 105
  capitalization for, 108
  duties to employees, 112
  forming and operating, 105–6
  keeping assets separate from
      personal, 110–11
  making and documenting, 111–12
  name of, 106–8
  shareholders for, 108
  signing for, 109–10
  talking like, 108–9
*Country Aviation, Inc. v. Tinicum
    Township,* 245
Courts of chancery, 237
Courts of law, 237
Crewmember
  hospitalization of, 186–88
  interference with, 275
Crimes
  aviation, 272–85
  and medical certification, 75
  safety and drug-related, 277–85
  security-related, 272–77
Cross-country glider flying, 86–87
Culver, Edith Dodd, 141–42
Curfew, jet, 241–45, 253
Current market value, hull coverage
    and, 121–22
Customs Service, U.S., 21

Dallas, Texas, Love Field airport, 248,
    252
Damages, 203
  exemplary, 173
  and liability, 99–101
  punitive, 100–1, 173
  under Warsaw Convention,
      161–62
Davis-Bacon Act, 302

Debt-collection methods, 87
Defective product, strict liability for, 92–93
Defenses
  act of God, war, or state, 157
  in liability for international cargo, 156–57
  lines of, in risk management, 115–16
  nature of the goods, 157
  to negligence, 93–96
  pilot or navigational error, 156–57
  shipper's contributory negligence, 157
Degree of care standard, 149, 150
Denver International Airport, 248–49
Department of Homeland Security (DHS), 5–6
Depositions in litigation, 101
Depreciation, recapture of, 210
Designated Airworthiness Representatives (DARs), 172
Designated Engineering Representatives (DERs), 172
Designated Manufacturing Representatives (DMRs), 172
Design defects, 96
Diabetes
  and loss of medical certification, 68
  and special issuance of medical certification, 71–72
Disabilities Act of 1991, 299
Disabled person, employing, 298–99
Discipline of employees, 303–4
Disclaimer of warranties, 202
Discovery
  in certificate action, 58
  in litigation, 101
Discretionary function, 171–73
Discrimination in employment, 297–98
Disputes, 311–17
Dispute settlement and consultation, 27
Documents, and displaying, 47
Domestic operations, air carrier risk-management tools, 151

Domestic passenger
  airline liability to, 147–52
  definition of, 147
Double jeopardy, 84
Dragging it in under power, 253
Drug addiction, and loss of medical certification, 69
Drug testing, 78
Duck rule, 106, 232
Due deference of Federal Aviation Regulations (FARs), 59
Due process of law, 313
Dues checkoff, 310
Duties to employees by a corporation, 112
Duty of care and negligence, 88

Education, role of Federal Aviation Administration (FAA), 11
Embry-Riddle Aeronautical University (ERAU), 22, 306
Emergency, sudden, as defense in negligence, 93–94
Emergency administrative searches, 286
Emergency Board, 315–16
Emergency cases in certificate action, 61–62
Emergency locator transmitter (ELT), 209
Emergency Response Manual, 188
Eminent domain, 228, 229–32
Employees
  classification of, 300
  determination of, 113–14
  duties of business to, 112
  liability of, 177, 178
Employers
  liability, 99
  for sexual harassment, 303
Employment at will, 296–97
Employment law, 295–308
Employment practices liability insurance, 303

Engines, fan-jet, 17
Environmental impact of aviation, 24
Environmental Protection Agency (EPA), 7
Environment impact of airports, 251
Environment impact statement (EIS), 251
Epilepsy, and loss of medical certification, 69
Equal Employment Opportunities Act of 1972, 297
Equal Employment Opportunity Commission (EEOC), 297
Equal Pay Act, 298
Equitable remedies, 237
Essential of life, 142
Event Review Committee (ERC), 56
Excess liability coverage, 120, 137
Excited utterances, 180
Exclusive bargaining agent, 310
Exculpatory contracts, 99, 141–45
Executive Order 11246, 299
Exemplary damages, 100–1, 173
Exempt employees, 300
Experimental Aircraft Association (EAA), 79
Explosive, carrying on aircraft, 276
Express warranties, 199–201

Failure to use care, 88–89
Fair and equal opportunity to compete, 27
Fair Labor Standards Act (FLSA), 300–2
Fair representation, duty of, 311
False arrest, 86
False imprisonment, 85
False information, 276
Falsification of records, 64
Fan-jet engines, 17
Federal Air Surgeon, 70, 71
Federal Aviation Act (1958), 195
Federal Aviation Administration (FAA), 12–22

Academy, 11, 14
accident inquiry, 187–88
Aeromedical Certification Branch of, 72
Aeronautical Center of, 9, 11, 14–15, 195
aircraft inspection by, 48
Aircraft Registry, 9, 14, 193, 195, 204, 206
Airman Records Branch, 14
Airport District Office (ADO), 247
Airport Improvement Program (AIP), 11, 229
airspace design, 266
Airworthiness Certificate, 9
appeal to, 38–39, 59–60
Aviation Safety Action Program (ASAP) of, 55–56
certificate actions of, 8–9, 56–62
Certification Branch, 58
Civil Aviation Medical Institute, 14–15
Civil Aviation Security, 78
and displaying documents, 47
education actions of, 11
enforcement role of, 31–65
funding actions of, 11
health standards of, 68–70
and immunity from sanction, 51–55
and international regulations, 24–29
investigatory role of, 11, 36–47
nose abatement, 252–53
Office of Commercial Space Transportation, 8
operations of
    Air Traffic Control (ATC) System, 12–14
    Flight Service Stations (FSS), 12, 13
    national airports, 14–15
    radio aids to navigation, 14
Production Type Certificate, 9
prosecution and appeal, 37–39, 56
registration actions of, 9

Index

regulatory actions of, 7–8
Safety Hotline of, 37
security actions of, 9–10
Supplemental Type Certificate, 9
talking to, 49–50
Technical Center of, 15–16
Type Certificate, 9
Wide Area Augmentation Systems (WAAS), 14
Federal Aviation Regulations (FARs), 3, 7, 32
  exclusion clause, 129–30
  investigation of violations of, 11, 36
  misinterpretation of, 39
  reports of, 36–38
  revocation for, 62
  violation of, 176
Federal Communications Commission (FCC), 206
Federal contracts and compensation, 302
Federal employees
  personal liability of, 174–75, 177, 178
  unionization of, 308
Federal Highway Administration, 6
Federal Labor Relations Authority (FLRA), 308
Federal Tort Claims Act (FTCA), 170
  liability of government under, 170–73
Federal Trade Commission, 21
Felony, 209
Ferry permit, 132
Fines, 34–35, 62–64
Fitness for a particular purpose, 201
Five Freedoms of the Air, 24–25
Fixed Base Operator (FBO), 111–12, 114–15
  offices, 42
Flight deck security, 10
Flight delays, 13
Flight free zones, 263
Flight Safety Foundation, 29
Flight Service Stations (FSS), 12, 13, 175

Flight Standards District Office (FSDO), 36
Floor plan financing, 216
Florida, State Department of Environmental Protection (DEP), 22
Flying clubs, 123
Foreign air carriers, regulation of, 22
Fractional ownership, 211, 219–23
Fractional Ownership Aviation Rulemaking Committee (FOARC), 220–23
Freedoms of the Air, 24–26
Free flight in hot-air balloons, 86–87
Free flight with navigation equipment, 13
Free market competition, 27
Funding, role of Federal Aviation Administration (FAA), 11

Garden State Farms, Inc. v. Bay, 236
General Aviation Airport Security Working Group, 289–90
General Aviation Data Improvement Team (GADIT), 16
General Aviation Revitalization Act (1994), 97–98, 135
General partnership, 103, 104
Geographic limitation to liability, 171
Glass cockpit, 18
Global Positioning System (GPS) for air navigation, 14
God, act of, 156, 157
Government contractors, 96
Government liability, 169–78. *See also* Liability
  under Federal Tort Claims Act (FTCA), 170–73
  local, 178
  negligent air traffic control, 173–75
  negligent airworthiness certification, 176–77
  personal liability of federal employees, 172–73, 174–75

Government liability (*continued*)
  state, 178
  weather-related accidents, 175–76
Grand cabotage, 26
Grand Canyon National Park and aircraft noise, 263–64
Grandfather rights, 239
Grant agreement, 244
  constraints of, 247–50
Grievances, 311–13
Griggs v. Allegheny County, 232–32
Grounded: Frank Lorenzo and the Destruction of Eastern Airlines, 314
Guidelines for Establishing Anti-Money Laundering Procedures, 291
Gustafson v. City of Lake Angelus, 245

Hail endorsement, 132
Hangarkeeper's liability, 120, 135
Hazardous materials
  dumping of, 22
  transport of, 24, 282
Health changes, and medical certification, 75
Hearing, in certificate action, 58–59
Hearing standards, 70, 71, 75
Heart attack, and loss of medical certification, 69
Heart replacement, and loss of medical certification, 69
Heart valve replacement, and loss of medical certification, 69
Height zoning, 228, 232–33
Helicopters, hull coverage for, 121–22
Highest degree of care standard, 149
Highway in the Sky program, 18
Hijacking, 28–29, 162, 275
Hindsight review, 113
Hiring, 297–99
Hoover bill, 61
Horror factor, 34
Hostile work environment, 302

Hull coverage, 121–23
Hush kits, 252
  installation of, 8

Immigration and Customs Enforcement (ICE), 21
Immigration Reform and Control Act (IRCA), 299
Implied contract, 297
Implied warranties, 201–2
Incident and reporting of, 184–85
Independent contractors, 113–15
Industrial aid, use of aircraft for, 126
In-flight hangarkeeper's liability, 135
Informal conference in certificate action, 57
Information, controlling release of, 179–81
Injunctions, 236–39, 316
Injury, and negligence, 89
Inspection Authorization (IAs), 172, 203
Instrument flight rules (IFR), and Federal Aviation Regulation (FAR) violations, 36
Instrument landing systems (ILS), 14
Insulin-treated diabetes mellitus (ITDM), and special issuance of medical certification, 71–72
Insurance. *See also* Aviation Insurance; Risk management
  employment practices liability, 303
  and leasing, 214
  liability, 142
  prepaid legal services and loss of license, 120, 136
  workers compensation, 112–13
Insurance adjuster, 118–19
Insurance agent, 118
Insurance broker, 118
Insurance companies, 118
Intelligence sharing, 5
Intentional infliction of mental distress, 85

Index

Intentional torts, 84–85, 173. *See also* Liability
   assault, 85
   battery, 85
   conversion, 87
   false arrest, 86
   false imprisonment, 85
   intentional infliction of mental distress, 85
   negligence, 88
   trespass, 86–87
Intergovernmental agreement (IGA), 251
Internal Revenue Service (IRS), 113–15
International Air Transport Association (IATA), 3–4, 29–30
International cargo, liability for, 156
International Civil Aviation Organization (ICAO), 3, 23–29
International law, 3–4, 99
International passengers, liability for, 152–56, 161
International regulations, 23–30
   under International Air Transport Association (IATA), 3–4, 29–30
   under International Civil Aviation Organization (ICAO), 23–29
Interrogatories in litigation, 101
Intrastate operations of carriers, 19–20
Inverse condemnation, 231
Investigation, role of Federal Aviation Administration (FAA) in, 11, 36–47

Jet curfew, 241–45, 253
Joint Airworthiness Resolutions (JAR), 24
Joint and several liability, 91
Joint Aviation Authority (JAA), 24
Joint Family Support Operations Center (JFSOC), 189
Joint ownership agreement, 219
Jurisdictional issues, 270, 271–72
Jury instructions, 149
Just compensation, 228
Justice, U.S. Department of, 21

Kabuki Theater, 314

Labor law, 295, 304–8
   Age Discrimination in Employment Act (ADEA), 298
   Americans with Disabilities Act (ADA), 298
   Civil Rights Act of 1964, 297
   Civil Service Reform Act, 308
   Davis-Bacon Act, 302
   Disabilities Act of 1991, 299
   Equal Employment Opportunities Act of 1972, 297
   Fair Labor Standards Act (FLSA), 300–2
   Immigration Reform and Control Act (IRCA), 299
   major disputes, 313–17
   minor disputes, 311–13
   National Labor Relations Act (NLRA), 295, 304–7
   National Mediation Board (NMB), 20
   Occupational Safety and Health Act, 300
   Railway Labor Act (RLA), 295, 309–10
   Taft-Hartley Amendments, 305
   Vietnam Era Veteran Readjustment Assistance Act, 299
   Walsh-Healey Act, 302
   Worker Adjustment and Retraining Notification Act (WARN), 304
Lakewood Municipal Airport, 240–41
Land use zoning, 228, 233–34
Last clear chance, 95–96
Layoffs of workers, 303
Ldn, daylight sound level, 234

Lease, 111, 212
  consideration of, as charter, 218
  distinguishing between leaseback and, 212–13
Leaseback, 211, 212
  distinguishing between lease and, 212–13
  special considerations for, 215
Lease forward, 212
Leasing of aircraft, 211–23
Lessee, 212
Lessor, 212
Letter of Correction, 32, 33, 50, 64
Letter of Investigation (LOI), 48–49
Liability, 83–102. *See also* Airline liability; Aviation insurance; Government liability; Intentional torts; Negligence
  for airworthiness certification, 176–77
  apportionment of, 95
  and assumption of risk, 94–95
  coverage for, in aviation insurance, 121, 137
  and damages, 99–101
  defenses to, 93–96
  for design defects, 96
  for domestic passengers, 147–52
  employers', 99
  employment practices, 303
  excess coverage, 120
  of federal employees, 177, 178
  of the government, 169–78
  hangarkeeper's, 120, 135
  insurance, 142–45
  for international cargo, 156
  for international passengers, 152–56, 161
  joint and several, 91
  lawsuits, 98
  limitations on, 151
  of local government, 178
  for negligent air traffic control, 173–75
  organizing business to limit, 103–16
  premises, 120, 134–35
  products, 120, 135–36
  for sexual harassment, 303
  of state government, 178
  strict
    for defective product, 92–93
    for ultrahazardous activities, 93
  vicarious, 99
  for weather-related accidents, 175–76
Liberal charter arrangements, 27
Lienholders, 194–95
  interest endorsement of, 129–30, 210
Lien release, 198, 206
Lighting violations, 278
Limitation
  on liability, 151
  private statutes of, 151–52
Limited commercial, use of aircraft for, 126
Limited liability companies (LLCs), 104, 105
Limited liability partnerships (LLPs), 104, 105
Limited partnership, 103, 104
Litigation
  avoiding, 203
  procedures of, 101–2
Lloyds of London, 118
Lockheed Air Terminal, Inc. v. City of Burbank, 242
Loma Portal Civic Club v. American Airlines, 237–38
Loran C network, 14
Los Angeles International Airport (LAX), 252
Loss of license insurance, 120
Loss payee, 123, 129, 210

Maintenance, deferral of, 217
Major labor disputes, 313–17
Major life activities, 298

Index 341

Manifests, crew and passenger, 21
Manufacturer production of aircraft, 9
Manufacturers' Service bulletins (SBs), 203
Maritime Administration, 6
Master interchange agreement, 219
McDonnell Douglas DC-8, 8
McDonnell Douglas DC-10, 8
Mechanics' and material men's liens, 194
Mediation, 310, 314
Medical certification, 9, 14–15, 67–79
   alcohol testing, 78
   appeal, 73
   changes in your health, 75
   drug testing, 78
   Federal Aviation Administration (FAA) health standards, 68–70
   reconsideration, 72
   requests for additional medical information, 78
   required reports, 78
   special flight tests, 70–71
   special issuance, 71–72
   suspension or revocation, 72–73
   telling truth in, 73–75
Medication, taking, and medical certification, 70, 77
Meigs Field, 249–50
Merchantability of product, 201
Mergers and acquisitions, 317–18
Merit System Protection Board (MSPB), 308
Microwave landing systems (MLS), 14
Military Airport Program (MAP), 229
Military Operation Areas (MOA), 258
Military Selection Act, 299
Military service, activities incident to, 171, 173–74
Military training routes, 258
Minor labor disputes, 311–13
Minutes, of corporate meetings, 112
Misdemeanor, 209
Montreal Agreement, 147, 155–56
Montreal Convention of 1999, 147, 164–67
Motion to produce, 101
Murphy's law, 108, 129, 132, 206
Mutual Assistance Plan (MAP), 315

National Aeronautical Charting Office (NACO), 10
National Aeronautics and Space Administration (NASA), 17–19
   Aviation Safety Reporting Program of, 51–55
   filing accident reports with, 181–82
National Aerospace Plane, 17
National Agricultural Aircraft Association (NAAA), 291
National airports, 14–15
National Air Traffic Controllers Association (NATCA), 308
National Air Transportation Board, 313
National Association of Flight Instructors (NAFI), 291–92
National Aviation Facility Experimental Center (NAFEC), 15–16
National Commission to Ensure a Strong Competitive Airline Industry, 26
National Crime Information Center (NCIC), 75
National defense airspace, violation of, 272
National Driver Registry (NDR) Database, 67, 75
National Environmental Policy Act of 1969 (NEPA), 251
National Guard Bureau, 266–67
National Highway Traffic Safety Administration, 6
National Institute of Justice, 21
National Labor Relations Act (NLRA), 20, 295, 304–7
National Labor Relations Board (NLRB), 20–21, 304–5

National Mediation Board (NMB), 20, 310–11
National Oceanic and Atmospheric Administration (NOAA), 209
National Ocean Service, 10
National Security Areas, 258
National Transportation Safety Board (NTSB)
   accident inquiry of, 11, 16–17, 186–89
   appeal to, 57–58, 61, 63, 73
   notification of following accident, 182–86
   and proximate cause, 89–90
Nature of the goods, 157
Navigation, air, interference with, 278–79
Navigational error, 156–57
Negligence, 84, 88. *See also* Liability
   of air traffic control, 173–75
   for airworthiness certification, 176–77
   comparative, 95
   contributory, 95–96
   defenses, 93
      assumption of risk, 94–95
      contributory negligence, 95–96
   doctrine of *res judicata,* 91
   duty of, 88
   exculpatory contracts, 99
   failure to use care, 88–89
   government contractors, 96
   by government employees, 174–75, 178
   injury, 89
   international law, 99
   litigation procedures, 101–2
   negligence per se, 91
   proof of, 91
   proximate cause, 89–91
   res ipsa loquitur, 91–92
   statutes of limitation, 97
   statutes of repose, 97–99
   strict liability
      for defective product, 92–93
      sudden emergency, 86–87, 93–94
      for ultrahazardous activities, 93
Negligence per se, 91
Nervous system malfunctioning, and loss of medical certification, 69
Next Generation Air Transportation System, 6–7
N-number, 9
Noise abatement procedures, 252–53
Noise footprint, 234, 235
Noise ordinances, 7–8, 228, 239–41
Nonconforming use, 239
Non-exempt employees, 300
Nontraffic stops freedom, 25–26
No solicitation/no distribution rule, 307
Notice of Proposed Certificate Action, 56–57
Notice of Proposed Rulemaking (NPRM), 260
Notice to Airmen (NOTAM), 258–59
Nuisance as intentional torts, 236–37

Obstruction analysis, 252–53
Occupational Safety and Health Act, 300
Occupational Safety and Health Administration (OSHA), 300
Off-airport landings, 86–87
Office of Federal Contract Compliance Programs (OFCCP), 299
Office of Personnel Management (OPM), 308
Open Skies Agreements, 26–27
Operations of the Federal Aviation Administration (FAA), 12–16
   Aeronautical Center, 9, 11, 14–15
   Airman Records Branch, 14
   Air Route Traffic Control Centers (ARTCC), 112–13
   Air Traffic Control (ATC) System, 12–14
   national airports, 14–15

Index

radio aids to navigation, 14
Technical Center, 15–16
Order Assessing Civil Penalty, 63
Order of priority, 198–99
Orient Express, 17
Overflight freedoms, 25–26
Overtime entitlement, 300–2
Ownership tax, 209

Pan Am Flight 103, 28
Parachute jumps, 41–42
Parachutes, Inc. v. Township of Lakewood, 240–41
Partnership, 104
Passengers
    and Federal Aviation Regulations (FARs) violations, 63
    screening of, 290–92
    search of, 285–89
Payroll taxes, withholding, 112, 113–15
Penalties for aviation crimes, 277–78, 283
Permit, foreign air carrier, 22
Personality disorder, and loss of medical certification, 69
Personal property tax, 209
Petition for Writ of Certiorari, 60, 63
Pierce the corporate veil, 106
Pilot error, 156–57
Pilot qualifications, 127–29
Plant Closing Act, 304
Pleasure, use of aircraft for, 125–26
Police power, 228, 232–36
Political boundaries, complication of, 250
Possessory lien, 195, 198
Power to tax, 239
Practices related to the purchase of general aviation aircraft, 291
Pre-boarding screening, 285–89
Precedent, Federal Aviation Administration (FAA) on, 33

Precision approach slope indicator (PAPI), 253
Premises liability, 120, 134–35
Prepaid legal services, 120
    and loss of license insurance, 136
Prepurchase inspection, 203–4
President, and regulation of foreign air carriers, 22
Press reporting on accidents, 180–81
Pricing determined by market forces, 27
Privately owned airports, 238–39, 255
Private property, taking of, 228, 231
Process of disembarking, 162
Process of embarking, 162
Production Type Certificate, 9, 177
Products and completed operations insurance, 135
Products liability, 120, 135–36
    insurance for, 120, 135–36
Professional Aerial Applicators Support System (PASS), 291
Professional Air Traffic Controllers' (PATCO) strike, 308
Profiling, racial, 288, 290
Promissory note, 110, 206
Property tax, 239
Proprietary powers, 228–29, 241–46
Prosecution, 272
    and Federal Aviation Administration (FAA) enforcement, 56
Protected classes, 297
Protecting the insurance policy, 120
Proximate cause, and negligence, 89–91
Psychosis, and loss of medical certification, 69
Public as source of reports of Federal Aviation Regulation (FAR) violations, 37–38
Publicly owned airports, 254–55
Public Utilities Commissions (PUCs), 19
Punitive damages, 100–1, 173
    under Warsaw Convention, 161–62
Purse, power of, 229, 247–50

Quality Assurance Program, and Federal Aviation Regulation violations, 36
Quick-Cert program, 72
Quid pro quo, 302

Radio aids to navigation, 14
Radio beacons, 14
Railway Labor Act (RLA) of 1926, 20, 295, 309–10
Ramp checks, 40, 48
Reasonably prudent person, 150
Recertification, 62
Recision, 203
Reconsideration of medical certification, 72
Record, clearing of, 64–65
Reexamination of pilot, 35–36
Registration, 206, 209
　role of Federal Aviation Administration (FAA) in, 9
Regulation
　international, 23–30
　role of Federal Aviation Administration (FAA) in, 3
Remedial training, 32–33
Renter pilots and aviation insurance, 138–39
Representation cases, 310–11
Res ipsa loquitur, 91–92
Res judicata, doctrine of, 91
Resource Conservation and Recovery Act (RCRA), 251
Revenue transactions between airlines, 29
Revocation of certificate, 33–34, 72–73
　order of, 62
Right to control and direct test, 113–15
Right to privacy, 286
Right to work laws, 305
Risk
　assumption of, 144, 151
　underwriting, 119

Risk management. *See also* Aviation insurance; Insurance
　exculpatory contracts in, 141–45
　lines of defense in, 115–16
Riverside, California, building airport in, 232–33
Rocky Mountain National Park and aircraft noise, 264

Sabotage, 28
SabreTech, 84–85
Safer Skies, 16
Safety
　and drug-related crimes, 277–85
　and security, 27
Safety Hotline, 37
Sale, closing of, 204–9
Sales pitch, 215–16
Sales tax, 209
San Diego International Airport, 237
Santa Barbara, California, building airport in, 233–34
Santa Monica, California, building airport in, 241–44
Santa Monica Airport Association v. Santa Monica, 243–44
Scabs, 315
Searches on suspicion, 290
Seattle-Tacoma area, building airport in, 232
Section 6 notice, 314
Security actions of airports, 9–10
Security agreement, 194, 196–97, 206
Security checkpoints in airports and airspaces, 289–90
Security Control of Air Traffic and Air Navigation Aids (SCATANA), 259–60
Security Guidelines for General Aviation Airports, 291
Security interests, 194–95, 198–99
　perfection and priority, 198–99
　title search, 195, 198

Security-related aviation crimes, 272–77
Seizure and forfeiture, 281
Senate, and regulation of foreign air carriers, 22
September 11th Victim Compensation Fund (2001), 167
Serious injury, 184
Seventh Freedom rights, 27
Sex discrimination, 302
Sexual harassment, 302–3
Shareholders in a corporation, 108
Sheriff's sale, 209
Shipper's contributory negligence, 157
Skydivers and aviation insurance, 141, 143, 144
Small Aircraft Transportation System Program (SATS), 16, 18
Smith v. Santa Barbara County, 233–34
Sneed v. County of Riverside, 233
Snitch Patch, 36
Sole proprietorship, 103–4
Sovereign immunity, doctrine of, 170
Special Drawing Rights (SDRs), 165–66
Special flight permit, 132
Special Flight Rules (SFAR), 263
Special flight tests, 70–71
Special issuance, of medical certification, 71–72
Special use airspace, 257
Special uses, use of aircraft for, 126–27
Specific performance, 203
St. Lawrence Seaway Development Corporation, 6
Stags v. Santa Monica, 241
Standards
 in civil aviation, 7
 technical, 24
Standards and Recommended Practices (SARPs), 24
State, U.S. Department of, 22
State administrative agencies, 22–23
Stated value, hull coverage in, 121–22

Statement of Demonstrated Ability (SODA), 70–71
Status of forces agreements (SOFA), 171
Statutes of limitation, 97, 151–52
Statutes of repose, 97–99
Statutory law, 92
Stock certificate, 110
Stock certificate register, 110–11
Strike, postponement of right to, 310
Stunt flying, 142
Subrogation, 138–39
Substance dependence, and loss of medical certification, 69
Substantial damage, 184
Sudden emergency doctrine, 86–87, 93–94
Summary seizure of aircraft, 35
Sumping and dumping, 22
Superseding cause, 176
Supervening cause, 176
Supplemental Type Certificate, 9, 177
Supremacy clause, 228, 240, 241
Supreme Court, appealing case to, 60
Supreme Court cases
 Allegheny Airlines v. Village of Cedarhurst, 239–40
 British Airways v. Port of New York Authority, 245
 Country Aviation, Inc. v. Tinicum Township, 245
 Garden State Farms, Inc. v. Bay, 236
 Griggs v. Allegheny County, 231–32
 Gustafson v. City of Lake Angelus, 245
 Lockheed Air Terminal, Inc. v. City of Burbank, 242
 Loma Portal Civic Club v. American Airlines, 237–38
 Parachutes, Inc. v. Township of Lakewood, 240–41
 Santa Monica Airport Association v. Santa Monica, 243–44

Supreme Court cases (*continued*)
   Smith v. Santa Barbara County,
     233–34
   Sneed v. County of Riverside, 233
   Stags v. Santa Monica, 241
   United States v. Causby, 229–30
Suspension of certificate, 33–34, 72–73
   order of, 57–58
Suspension of employees, 303–4
System Board of Adjustment, 311–12

Taft-Hartley Amendments, 305
Tailspins: A Story of Early Aviation Days, 141
Takeoff, 175–76
Tariff, 148, 151, 152
Tariff book, 151
Tax
   to fund airports, 11
   lien, 209
   ownership, 209
   personal property, 209
   power to, 229, 239
   property, 239
   and registration requirements, 209–10
   sales, 209
   use, 209
Technical Cooperation Programme, 24
Temporary flight restrictions, 36, 258–59
Termination of employees, 303–4
Terrorism, 28, 269
   attacks, 162
   and victim compensation, 20
   effect on civil aviation, 4
   and war risk insurance, 134
Terrorism Risk Insurance Act (TRIA), 2002, 134
Terrorist watch list, 288
Thermal neutron analysis (TNA) devices, 288
Time-sharing agreement, 219
Title search, 195, 198

Tort
   definition of, 83–84
   intentional, 173
   personal liability for, 105
Tort law, 83
Traffic offense and medical certification, 75
Training, remedial, 32–33
Transit Agreement, 26
Transportation, U.S. Department of (DOT), 4, 6–7
   and Federal Aviation Regulation violations, 63
   regulation of foreign air carriers, 22
Transportation Security Administration (TSA), 4, 290–92
Transportation Security Oversight Board (TSOB), 5
Transport jets and noise levels, 8
Trespass, 86–87
Type Certificate, 9, 177

Ultrahazardous activities, strict liability for, 93
Umbrella policy, 137
Uncontrolled airspace, 159
Underground storage tank, 251
Underwriters, 118
Underwriters at Lloyds, The, 118
Underwriting, 118, 119
Unemployment compensation insurance, 112
Uniform Commercial Code (UCC), 193–94
   on express warranties, 199–201
   on implied warranties, 201–2
Uninsured matters, 139
Unionization of employees, 295, 304, 306–7, 310–11
   federal, 308
United States v. Causby, 229–30
Urban Mass Transportation Association, 6

Index 347

User fees for airport services, 13
Use tax, 209

Value
  current market, 121–22
  stated, 121–22
Vehicle parts fraud, 282–85
Vicarious liability, 99
Victim compensation of terrorist attacks, 20
Victims Compensation Fund, 178
Video surveillance, 288–89
Vietnam Era Veteran Readjustment Assistance Act, 299
Violence at international airports, 270–72
Vision standards, 70–71
Visual approach slope indicator (VASI), 253
Visual flight rules (VFR), 38
Vocational Rehabilitation Act of 1973, 299

Wages and hours, 300–3
Wagner Act, 304
Waiver of subrogation endorsement, 138
Walsh-Healey Act, 302
War, act of, 156, 157
War, Hi-Jacking, and Other Perils Exclusion Clause, 133–34
Warehousemen's liens, 194
Warning areas, 258
Warning Letter, 64
Warning Notice, 32, 33
Warranties, 194, 199
  breach of, 203
  disclaimer of, 202
  express, 199–201
  of fitness for a particular purpose, 201
  implied, 201–2
  of merchantability, 201
Warranty law, 92
War risk insurance, 133–34
Warsaw Convention, 152–55, 157–61
  liabilities under, 155–56, 162–64
  punitive damages under, 161–62
Washington, D.C., Reagan National Airport, 253
Washington Metropolitan Airport Authority, 14–15
Weapon
  carrying on aircraft, 276
  prohibited, 286
  used by flight deck crewmembers, 21
Weather-related accidents, government liability for, 175–76
Wet leases, 218
Whistleblower protection, 297
Whitcomb winglet, 17
Wide Area Augmentation Systems (WAAS), 14
Wildcat strikes, 316
Wilderness airspace, 262–64
Willful misconduct, 161–62
Worker Adjustment and Retraining Notification Act (WARN), 304
Workers compensation insurance, 112–113
Workforce reductions, 303
Wrongful discharge, 296–97

Yellow dog contracts, 310

Zoning
  height, 228, 232–33
  land, 228, 233–34
  use, 234–36